"The book *Mergers, Acquisitions and International Financial Regulation: Analysing Special Purpose Acquisition Companies*, by Daniele D'Alvia, with a foreword written by my student Yochanan Shachmurove, is the first book on Special Purpose Acquisition Companies (SPACs) that uses a comparative perspective. The book provides insights to one of the re-emerging financial instruments that is currently attracting attention by financial- market practitioners and researchers. A worth-reading book"

**Professor Finn Kydland** *(Nobel Laureate), University of California, Santa Barbara, California.*

"Written with unusual clarity and insight, this is a major contribution on an important, emerging topic. Daniele D'Alvia is to be congratulated on the dual achievements of pioneering the analysis of a largely neglected topic and telling the story with a novelist's flair."

**Ross P Buckley**, *KPMG-KWM Professor of Disruptive Innovation, UNSW Sydney.*

"Daniele D'Alvia is an academic and corporate finance lawyer, and one of not many academic experts with SPAC advisory experience. The well-researched book tells the unique story of SPACs. Indeed, SPACs are financial innovations and are the disruptors of traditional M&A and IPO process. The book has chapters on SAPCs' financial regulation, its evolution and a difficult to challenge view on self-correcting market practices. Chapter 5 includes interesting thoughts on the evolving De-SPAC transactions. The book serves as a guide to sponsors, investors, listing venues, lawyers, including in-house lawyers of SPAC target companies"

**Ferdinand Mason**, *Partner at White & Case, London.*

"The book argues that SPACs are a fund-raising innovation that will stand the test of time. A richly argued resource for theoretical and up-to-date legal discussions on SPACs, a must-have for researchers and practitioners in this area"

**Iris H-Y Chiu**, *Professor of Corporate Law and Financial Regulation, University College London.*

"An insightful read from one of the few experts in SPACs at international level. The book contains some great tips to ensure your SPAC is a success. Highly practical and commercially focused, the book provides a good and provocative contribution to alternative acquisition models. Scholars, corporate finance lawyers, sponsors and investors in the field should save a place for it on their shelves"

**Luca Fabio Giacometti**, *Chairman and CEO of Galileo Acq. Corp., USA.*

"SPACs are the financial asset class poorly understood by most stakeholders and carrying undeserved label of opaqueness. This pioneer book by Daniele D'Alvia educates and explains why SPACs are viable and sustainable financing mechanism"

**Milos Vulanovic**, *Associate Professor of Finance at EDHEC Business School.*

"With torrents of money jostling for return in a zero-interest-rate-world, listed shell companies created specially to acquire growing firms (SPACs) became a popular alternative to IPOs in 2020. Daniele D'Alvia's book provides an excellent introduction to the history, operation, and rationale behind SPACs"

**Prof. David Donald**, *Attorney at Law (New York) and Professor at the Faculty of Law, The Chinese University of Hong Kong, Hong Kong SAR, China.*

"The book provides a useful and innovative contribution to the burgeoning debate on Special Purpose Acquisition Companies. It is highly informative as it discusses the origins of SPACs, and their future perspectives, across different legal systems and markets"

**Filippo Annunziata**, *Associate Professor of Financial Markets Law, Bocconi University, Milan, Italy.*

"Daniele D'Alvia has written a must-read history of SPACs…Read this book if you want to better understand the SPAC market"

**Kristi Marvin**, *Founder of SPACInsider.com.*

"The recent global rise of SPACs as an innovative way to raise finance dramatically underscore the need for academic analysis of this new phenomenon. This book provides an up-to-date analysis of the legal and economic parameters underpinning Special Purpose Acquisition Companies, how they work (or not), and what they mean for firms and investors. Presenting material in a very lucid manner, drawing on many case studies, and taking a truly global perspective, the book provides an invaluable guide for all who want to master the complex subject"

**Wolf-Georg Ringe**, *Professor of Law & Finance, University of Hamburg, Germany.*

"The sovereign debt crisis has curably changed the meaning of financial risks and systemic failures in the European Union and globally. Dr. Daniele D'Alvia's book is an indispensable companion in the post-financial crisis world of international financial transactions and laws"

**Prof. Stéphanie Laulhé Shaelou**, *Professor of European Law and Reform and Head, School of Law, University of Central Lancashire, Cyprus campus and EUI Fellow, Law Department, Villa Salviati, European University Institute, Florence, Italy.*

"Markets are full of risks. This should never worry us though, as risks can and should also be understood as profitable opportunities, especially where we can mitigate against them. But markets are also just as full of uncertainties; unknowns which cannot be quantified as risks, cannot be mitigated against, and which may offer heightened profit opportunities, but which also can spell disaster. Recalling Frank Knight's core 1921 message, but this time around with application to financial (investment) instruments, Daniele D'Alvia offers us a fascinating contemporary overview of risks, uncertainty and profit, as well as the difficult role the law plays, or sometimes doesn't play, in regulating them. This is an important book which also asks whether we can identify alternative investment risk management vehicles in our search for constant profit (Special Purpose Acquisition Companies), thus minimizing the dangers of renewed market collapse in heightened uncertainty. It is an important book also in reminding us that law too has its regulatory limits, and that we must never be complacent in our assumptions that we can simply regulate all market dangers away"

**Professor Michelle Everson**, *School of Law, Birkbeck College, University of London, United Kingdom.*

"This is a deeply researched yet very accessible book on one of the more creative and increasingly common capital markets financing techniques. For anyone thinking of issuing or investing in a SPAC, or being acquired by one, this book will help to demystify a very complex subject"

**Professor Scott Moeller**, *Founder and Director, M&A Research Centre, Bayes Business School (City, University of London).*

"Daniele D'Alvia succeeds in providing an accessible and engaging text mapping the development of SPACs and their developing financial regulation. The book is impressively researched providing significant economic and legal insight as to the use, regulation and impact of SPACs"

**Professor John K Ashton**, *Professor in Banking, Bangor University.*

"SPACs are now a mainstream way of raising capital. But there remains much confusion in practice as to the good and bad features of SPACs. This book sorts out the mechanics of SPACs and provides useful insights for academics and practitioners alike"

**Prof. Douglas Cumming**, *Distinguished Professor of Finance and Entrepreneurship, College of Business, Florida Atlantic University, Boca Raton, Florida.*

"The book provides an extensive analysis of the drivers behind the spectacular rise of SPACs and their regulation. It is an invaluable addition to the discussion regarding the benefits and perils of these transactions. A must-read for academics, students, and finance professionals"

**Alexandros Seretakis**, *Assistant Professor of Law and Director MSc in Law and Finance, Trinity College Dublin.*

"As a researcher in both corporate and financial law, I find Dr D'Alvia's book very useful, especially the chapter on international financial regulation of Special Purpose Acquisition Companies (SPACs). The book provides a unique insight into SPACs from a comparative legal perspective. Dr D'Alvia's book is a comprehensive and timely contribution to the increasingly growing literature on SPACs. I believe that this book is of interest to anyone working or researching in capital markets and financial corporations"

**Dr Alison Lui,** *Reader in Corporate and Financial Law, Associate Dean Global Engagement at Liverpool John Moores University.*

"SPACs are an alternative way to access stock markets and increasingly important. However, research on SPACs has been limited in corporate finance and related disciplines. This book offers a very detailed analysis of SPACs and regulatory frameworks. In particular, the examples discussed in Chapter 4 could be used to test the impact of regulatory changes on the use of SPACs"

**Professor Gerhard Kling,** *Chair in Finance, University of Aberdeen.*

"SPACs are gaining global popularity as an alternative to traditional IPOs. However, this area of knowledge has been largely underexplored by legal scholars. The latest book of Daniele D'Alvia is a pioneering work examining the operating mechanism of SPACs and its regulation from an international and comparative perspective. It is a must-read for researchers, practitioners and policy-makers across the world"

**Dr. Lerong Lu,** *Senior Lecturer in Law and Director of LLM Law & Technology, King's College, London UK.*

"Daniele D'Alvia's book has established himself as the expert in this niche and innovative fund raising mechanisms for the acquisition of growing firms. The book offers an insightful discussion on the history, economic rationale and systems theory on the SPACs. This is a must-read book for those practitioners, academic researchers and policy makers who have interest in the operation of the SPACs"

**Mark Hsiao,** *Associate Professor in Law, Leicester Law School, University of Leicester, UK.*

# Mergers, Acquisitions and International Financial Regulation

This is a much-needed work in the financial literature, and it is the first book ever to analyse the use of Special Purpose Acquisition Companies (SPACs) from a theoretical and practical perspective. By the end of 2020, more than 240 SPACs were listed in the US (on NASDAQ or the NYSE), raising a record $83 billion. The SPAC craze has been shaking the US for months, mainly because of its simplicity: a bunch of investors decides to buy shares at a fixed price in a company that initially has no assets. In this way, a SPAC, also known as a "blank check company", is created as an empty shell with lots of money to spend on a corporate shopping spree.

Could the trend be here to stay? Are SPACs the new legitimate path to traditional IPO? This book tackles those questions and more. The author provides a thorough analysis of SPACs including their legal framework and how they are used as a risk mitigation tool to structure transactions. The main objectives of the book are focused on finding a working definition for SPACs and theorising on their origins, definition, and evolution; identifying the objectives of financial regulation within the context of the recent financial crisis (2007–2010) and the one that is currently unfolding (Covid-19); and also describing practical examples of SPACs through a comparative study that, for the first time, outlines every major capital market on which SPACs are listed, in order to identify a possible international standard of regulation.

The book is relevant to academics as well as policymakers, international financial regulators, corporate finance lawyers as well as to the financial industry *tout court*.

**Daniele D'Alvia**, PhD, is a pioneer in SPAC's studies in law and winner of the Colin B Picker Prize. He is an Associate Research Fellow at IALS in London and a Teaching Fellow in Banking and Finance Law at Queen Mary University of London. He is the module convener in Comparative Law at Birkbeck College, University of London.

# Routledge International Studies in Money and Banking

**Monetary Policy after the Great Recession**
The Role of Interest Rates
*Arkadiusz Sieroń*

**Behavioural Public Finance**
Individuals, Society, and the State
*Edited by M. Mustafa Erdoğdu, Larissa Batrancea and Savaş Çevik*

**The Economics of Cryptocurrencies**
*Edited by J. Mark Munoz and Michael Frenkel*

**Finance and Sustainable Development**
Designing Sustainable Financial Systems
*Edited by Magdalena Ziolo*

**The Financialized Economy**
*Alexander Styhre*

**Financialization, Financial Literacy, and Social Education**
*Edited by Thomas A. Lucey*

**Moral Hazard**
A Financial, Legal, and Economic Perspective
*Edited by Juan Flores Zendejas, Norbert Gaillard and Rick Michalek*

**Mergers, Acquisitions and International Financial Regulation**
Analysing Special Purpose Acquisition Companies
*Daniele D'Alvia*

For more information about this series, please visit: www.routledge.com/Routledge-International-Studies-in-Money-and-Banking/book-series/SE0403

# Mergers, Acquisitions and International Financial Regulation

Analysing Special Purpose Acquisition Companies

Daniele D'Alvia

First published 2022
by Routledge
2 Park Square, Milton Park, Abingdon, Oxon OX14 4RN

and by Routledge
605 Third Avenue, New York, NY 10158

*Routledge is an imprint of the Taylor & Francis Group, an informa business*

© 2022 Daniele D'Alvia

The right of Daniele D'Alvia to be identified as author of this work has been asserted in accordance with sections 77 and 78 of the Copyright, Designs and Patents Act 1988.

All rights reserved. No part of this book may be reprinted or reproduced or utilised in any form or by any electronic, mechanical, or other means, now known or hereafter invented, including photocopying and recording, or in any information storage or retrieval system, without permission in writing from the publishers.

*Trademark notice*: Product or corporate names may be trademarks or registered trademarks, and are used only for identification and explanation without intent to infringe.

*British Library Cataloguing-in-Publication Data*
A catalogue record for this book is available from the British Library

*Library of Congress Cataloging-in-Publication Data*
Names: D'Alvia, Daniele, author.
Title: Mergers, acquisitions, and international financial regulation : analysing special purpose acquisition companies / Daniele D'Alvia.
Description: 1 Edition. | New York, NY : Routledge, [2022] | Series: Routledge international studies in money and banking | Includes bibliographical references and index.
Identifiers: LCCN 2021031125 (print) | LCCN 2021031126 (ebook) | ISBN 9780367609863 (hardback) | ISBN 9780367609887 (paperback) | ISBN 9781003102779 (ebook)
Subjects: LCSH: Consolidation and merger of corporations. | Financial institutions, International—Law and legislation. | Special purpose acquisition companies—Law and legislation.
Classification: LCC HD2746.5 .D35 2022 (print) | LCC HD2746.5 (ebook) | DDC 658.1/62—dc23
LC record available at https://lccn.loc.gov/2021031125
LC ebook record available at https://lccn.loc.gov/2021031126

ISBN: 978-0-367-60986-3 (hbk)
ISBN: 978-0-367-60988-7 (pbk)
ISBN: 978-1-003-10277-9 (ebk)

DOI: 10.4324/9781003102779

Typeset in Bembo
by codeMantra

"I dedicate the first book on SPACs ever to Prof. Rodrigo Olivares-Caminal: my friend, mentor, and colleague"

D.

# Contents

*Acknowledgements*   xv
*List of abbreviations*   xvii
*Foreword*   xix
*Addendum*   xxvii

**Introduction**   1

**1 Against debt: the remarkable story of SPACs**   10
   *1.1 An introduction to SPACs 10*
   *1.2 The financial crisis (2007–2010): the welfare price of under-priced private debt 12*
      1.2.1 Risk and uncertainty 17
      1.2.2 Competition and financial innovations 18
      1.2.3 The post-pandemic scenario: Covid-19 and SPACs 22
      1.2.4 SPACs: risk-free investments 25
   *1.3 SPAC: a new alternative to private equity 26*
      1.3.1 The sponsor(s), and the SPAC 32
      1.3.2 The underwriters 34
      1.3.3 The shareholders 35
      1.3.4 The exchanges and the regulators 35
      1.3.5 Mitigating risk and uncertainty in SPACs 36
   *1.4 Methodology 40*
   *1.5 Chapters overview 41*

**2 Towards a definition of SPACs: origin, limits and perspectives of SPACs in the US**   43
   *2.1 The origin of SPACs: a US innovation 43*
      2.1.1 The Rule 419 under the SEC Regulation 44
   *2.2 From blank check companies to modern SPACs 47*

    2.2.1 Modern SPACs in the US: the listing standards 49
    2.2.2 SPACs 2.0 52
    2.2.3 SPACs 3.0 and 3.5, and evolutionary trends 52
    2.2.4 Remarks on American modern SPACs 53
  2.3 *The codification of uncodified market practices in SPACs* 55
  2.4 *The international corporate features and listing standards of SPACs* 56
    2.4.1 The promote and other people's money 58
    2.4.2 Share capital and corporate structure 61
    2.4.3 Escrow account and trust 63
    2.4.4 Winding up or liquidation procedure 64
    2.4.5 Redemption right 65
    2.4.6 The tender offer procedure 66
    2.4.7 PIPE in the US 66
  2.5 *Conclusions* 67

## 3  SPACs between risk and uncertainty, and the role of the law  68

  3.1 *An introduction to the essence of risk* 68
    3.1.1 The epistemology of risk 70
    3.1.2 The ontology of risk 71
    3.1.3 The risk-taking activity vs. the risk-sharing of Shari'a 73
  3.2 *Financial risk* 77
    3.2.1 The (no)-classification of risk 79
    3.2.2 Risk and uncertainty 82
  3.3 *Financial markets and complexity* 85
    3.3.1 From risk-aversion to uncertainty-aversion 87
    3.3.2 The paradox of uncertainty in modern economies 90
    3.3.3 The human-humanity and the human-inhumanity of risk 91
  3.4 *SPACs as money creation vehicles* 92
  3.5 *SPACs, systemic failure and the law* 93
    3.5.1 Market failure and systemic risk 96
    3.5.2 The public-private divide and government failure 99
    3.5.3 Financial regulation between macroeconomic stability and microeconomic objectives 102
    3.5.4 The role of law in systemic failures and self-regulation 104
    3.5.5 SPACs and soft law 106
  3.6 *Conclusions* 107

## 4  The international financial regulation of SPACs  110

  4.1 *The regulation of SPACs at international level* 110
    4.1.1 The European regulation of SPACs 111
    4.1.2 SPACs and the London stock exchange 113
    4.1.3 SPACs and Borsa Italiana S.p.A. (Euronext Group) 119
    4.1.4 SPACs and Euronext N.V. 121
  4.2 *SPACs and the conflicts with national corporate law frameworks* 123

4.2.1 Solutions through market practices and self-regulation  128
*4.3 The multilevel SPAC definition  128*
   4.3.1 The definition of first- and second-generation SPACs  130
   4.3.2 A definition of SPACs based on market practices  131
   4.3.3 A definition of SPACs based on legal standardised regulation  131
   3.5.4 SPACs 'without law'  132
*4.4 The soft law regulation of SPACs  133*
   4.4.1 The bursa Malaysia  140
   4.4.2 The Toronto stock exchange  142
*4.5 SPACs: a 'by-law approach'  145*
   4.5.1 The Korean stock exchange  145
   4.5.2 The Borsa Istanbul exchange  147
*4.6 Conclusions  149*

**5  De-SPAC: M&As, regulatory oversight, and securities litigation**  151
   *5.1 Structuring the deal at De-SPACing: the M&A' aspects  151*
      5.1.1 Due diligence  154
      5.1.2 The sponsor(s) ownership of the target: higher the risk, higher the return  156
      5.1.3 PIPE investment and PIPE engagement letter  158
      5.1.4 Equity financing and support agreements  160
      5.1.5 Valuation of the acquisition target  161
      5.1.6 Earnout provisions  163
      5.1.7 Place of incorporation, growth capital, and high growth companies  164
   *5.2 Structuring the deal at De-SPACing in the US: the regulatory challenges  165*
      5.2.1 Form 10 information  166
      5.2.2 Form S-8  166
      5.2.3 Rule 144  167
      5.2.4 Form S-3 eligibility  168
      5.2.5 Ineligible issuers  169
   *5.3 Disclosure duties of the sponsor and underwriters in the US  169*
      5.3.1 Conflict of interests between sponsor(s) and investors  170
      5.3.2 Conflict of interests on sponsor(s) proxy statement and redemptions  171
      5.3.3 Conflict of interests between sponsor(s) and underwriters  172
   *5.4 SPAC securities litigation in the US  173*
      5.4.1 Securities litigation related to the De-SPAC transaction  175
      5.4.2 Litigation based on reports of short selling  176
      5.4.3 Breach of fiduciary duty claims  177
      5.4.3 D&O insurance  178
   *5.5 Conclusions  180*

## 6 SPACs: law, uncertainty and the market 183
*6.1 Financial markets as financial systems 183*
- 6.1.1 Self-organisation and autopoiesis of systems 186
- 6.1.2 The structures of financial systems and liquid autopoietic markets 188
- 6.1.3 The 'metamorphosis of subjects': financial markets as open systems 189
- 6.1.4 Financial systems and complexity 190

*6.2 The phenomenology of contemporary financial systems 192*
- 6.2.1 SPACs as financial innovations and observers of the markets 196

*6.3 Law and globalisation 198*
- 6.3.1 The lack of a central planner 198
- 6.3.2 SPACs as market-driven instruments 200

*6.4 SPACs as a non-legal instance 201*
- 6.4.1 SPACs and market spontaneity 202
- 6.4.2 SPACs and uncertainty 202

*6.5 Conclusions 203*

## Conclusions 205

*Bibliography* 213
*Index* 219

# Acknowledgements

Writing a book is a journey along the path of the never-ending process of research. My research on SPACs started at Queen Mary University of London in 2013, with an LLM thesis under the supervision of Prof. Alan Dignam, to whom I am grateful for the first reflections on SPACs between hard law and soft law provisions. Furthermore, I am particularly grateful to my PhD supervisor at Birkbeck University of London: Prof. Michelle Everson, to whom I owe so much, especially for the precious insights she gave me on risk and uncertainty, from both philosophical and economic perspectives. Furthermore, she introduced me for the first time in my life to critical legal studies. The experience has been one of the most significant moments of my professional and academic development and is still characterising my writing, my thinking and my life. A special thanks also goes to my personal editor who has worked hard with me over all these years of collaboration, Ms. Hilary Arundale, and to all the people who have sustained me during this project and over the years, from friends to family, the ones that see things differently, and are not fans of rules. I am also thankful to what I define the 'SPAC-disbelievers'. They have likewise been a valid source of ideas during these years. I respect their views and opinions.

During my research, I had the opportunity to visit The Hague Academy of International Law (2015) and the Sorbonne School of Law (2016), and I was appointed as a visiting researcher at the Max Planck Institute in Hamburg (2017). In 2017, I was awarded, by the American Society of Comparative Law, the Colin B. Picker Prize (honourable mention) for a paper I presented on SPACs. Between 2019 and 2021, I have led research projects on SPACs both at the Institute of Advanced Legal Studies in London, and Harris Manchester College (Commercial Law Centre), University of Oxford.

All these achievements and non-conventional ideas have been made possible by the inspiration I have received from many professors and thinkers in my life. Professors Michelle Everson, Alan Dignam, Rodrigo Olivares-Caminal, Ioannis Kokkoris, Rosa Maria Lastra, Ferdinand Mason, Robert Hockett, Milos Vulanovic, and Saule Omarova have been an important source for my ideas and for the development of the first SPACs' theory.

Finally, I thank Nobel Laureate, Professor Finn Kydland for endorsing the book and Professor Yochanan Shachmurove from the City College and The Graduate Center of the City University of New York for writing the Foreword for this research book.

In the end, ten years of work should be considered not only as work, coldly expressed in pages of black and white, but it should transmit to readers the stories behind research processes and ideas; stories created by men and women and by new encounters and discoveries. I hope to always have this drive of curiosity and to keep travelling the world in search of 'open answers' to generate further discussion, rather than looking for final answers that are relative and incomplete. Final answers and dogma are the anterooms of racism and inequality.

# Abbreviations

| | |
|---|---|
| AIFMD | Directive 2011/61/EU on the Alternative Investment Fund Manager |
| AIM | Alternative Investment Market |
| AMEX | American Stock Exchange |
| BCC/s | Blank Check Company/ies |
| De-SPAC or De-SPACing | indicates the moment where the business combination of the SPAC is performed. |
| ESMA | the European Securities and Markets Authority |
| IPO | Initial Public Offering |
| OTC | Over-the-Counter Bulletin Board |
| MIV | Market for Investment Vehicles |
| NASDAQ | the National Association of Securities Dealers Automated Quotations |
| NSYE | New York Stock Exchange |
| PIPE | private investment in public equity |
| PSM | Penny Stock Market |
| PSLRA | Private Securities Litigation Reform Act (US) 1995 |
| PSRA | Securities Enforcement Remedies and Penny Stock Reform Act (US) 1990. |
| SEA | Securities Exchange Act 1934 (US) |
| SEC | Security and Exchange Commission. |
| SPAC/s | Special Purpose Acquisition Company/s |
| UCITS | collective investment undertakings |

# Foreword

Mergers, Acquisitions, and International Financial Regulation: Analysing Special Purpose Acquisition Companies, by Daniele D'Alvia
Written by Yochanan Shachmurove, Professor
The City College and the Graduate Center of the City University of New York

In 2003, it was highly unlikely that an individual walking on the streets of New York City, Chicago, London, Zurich, Frankfurt, Singapore, Tokyo, Hong Kong or Shanghai would know what "SPAC" represents. Over time, these four letters took over Wall Street as well as other financial hubs by storm. Now, any investor can enter the world of venture capital much easier than before. Perceived as an unconventional idea and a driver for novelty, SPACs or Special Purpose Acquisition Companies have proven to be a financial force to be reckoned with.

This book, written by Dr Daniele D'Alvia, is vital for increasing our knowledge and comprehension of SPACs. The book, for the first time, puts forth a thorough, multidisciplinary theory of these unique corporations, while showcasing the significance and impacts of alternative acquisition models and other financial innovations. Furthermore, this book does not only analyse SPACs, but offers a new vision for financial markets under turbulent financial environments. D'Alvia accentuates that SPACs are alternative acquisition models to traditional Initial Public Offering (IPO). As such, D'Alvia claims, SPACs do not necessarily compete with traditional IPOs, representing an alternative path for investment.

SPACs, defined as cash-shell companies, which are an alternative form of investment vehicles, provide private companies access to public market by virtue of a reverse merger or takeover. The company, under the direction of the "SPAC sponsor", after it is established, raises capital from the IPO to then acquire a target private company, called the "de-SPAC" transaction.[1] The formation of these investment vehicles dates to 18th-century England, where blank check companies were first mentioned as "blind pools" during the South Sea Bubble (see, for example, Shachmurove and Vulanovic (2015, 2016, 2017)).

Figure 1 shows the remarkable increase in the number of SPAC IPOs in the US financial markets. It increased from 1 in 2009 to in 2021. Despite the

COVID-19 worldwide pandemic, the number of SPAC IPOs increased to 59 in 2019. In the year 2020, this measure of activities backed by SPAC was 248, an increase of 320 percent. At the time of this writing, on 17 May 2021, in less than five months, the number stands at 341 SPAC IPOs.

Figure 2 presents the gross proceeds of American SPACs in millions of US dollars (mms) from 2009 until May 2021. Again, the figure reflects the increased significance of SPACs from 36 mms in 2009 to 83,354 mms in 2019 and 106,641.7 mms in the first five months of 2021.

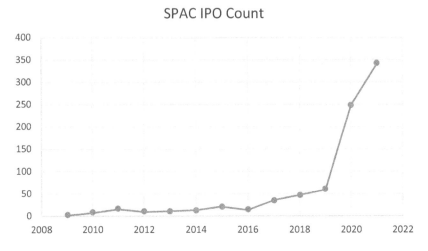

*Figure 1* SPAC IPO Count 2009–2021.

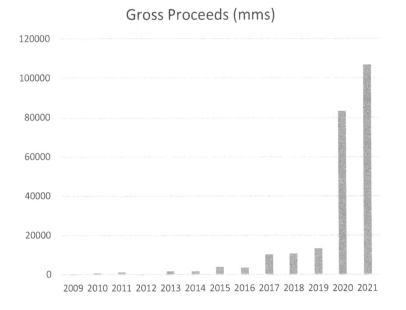

*Figure 2* Gross Proceeds by SPACs 2009–2021.

Figure 3 compares SPAC IPOs versus Total IPOs. The figure vividly shows the increased role of financing by SPACs. Figure 4 depicts American SPAC Proceeds vs Total US IPO Proceeds ($M). Again, one observes the notable increased significance or SPAC-backed financial investment.

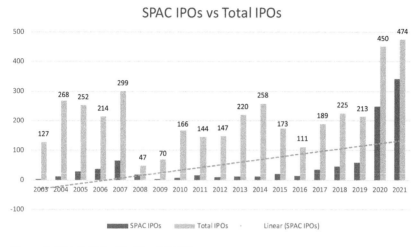

*Figure 3* SPAC IPOs Vs. Total IPOS.

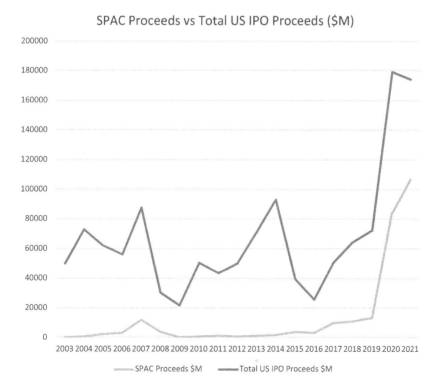

*Figure 4* SPAC Proceeds Vs. Total US Proceeds ($M).

The main question is how and why these investment vehicles are currently the centre of attention in the world of finance? This book by D'Alvia is the best source to date to answer this question.

When a company is going to "go public", historically that entails that same company will complete the transition from being private to publicly selling shares simply through the completion of an IPO. The emergence of these novel SPACs completely reinvented and redefined this traditional IPO route, seemingly reducing securities regulation compliance costs as well as almost completely removing the fees charged by underwriters. It is central why in 2020, the $88.5 billion raised from SPAC IPOs exceeded beyond the $67 billion raised in capital by traditional IPOs, why companies choose SPACs over traditional IPO, an underlying question which D'Alvia analyses by clearly and convincingly explaining in this book. Notably, when a merger agreement is formed, shareholders of the shell-company vote whether to approve the transaction and are provided with a proxy statement (Section 14(a) of the Securities Exchange Act). They are granted the option to redeem shares from their initial purchase plus the interest. This is because unlike other companies going through the traditional IPO process, the S-1 fillings that SPACs companies provide contain little information about the company since it has "no previous operations". This further showcases the novelty and evolution that these types of investment vehicles have gone through from being descendants of the controversial blank-check companies to one of the attractive investments in the financial world today.[2]

It is important to realise that SPACs hold the capability of potentially reshaping financial markets. By granting private companies, especially start-ups, an alternative, sustainable way of going public and raising funds without facing the high costs and extensive formalities, SPACs are, according to D'Alvia, revolutionising current worldwide financial institutions.

D'Alvia's book is supported by his extensive research of other contributors to the SPACs' literature. The work is supported by other studies drawn from law, economics, finance and management (see, Aydogdu, et al. (2007), Hale (2007), Riemer (2007–2008), Berger (2008), Boyer and Baigent (2008), Floros and Sapp (2011), Jenkinson and Sousa (2011), Rodrigrues and Stegemoller (2011), Howe and O'Brien (2012), Lakicevic, Shachmurove and Vulanovic (2014), Shachmurove and Vulanovic (2015, 2016, 2017))., 

The current book by D'Alvia is divided into six chapters. The book formulates a wide-ranging analysis of SPACs from a few prisms such as law, economics, finance, risk management, investment, corporate finance, industrial organisation, and behavioural finance.

There main ideas are eloquently presented and analysed by D'Alvia as follows:

- That common law jurisdiction is more "SPAC-friendly" because of the reception and codification of market practices.

- The sophisticated financial regulation framework of SPACs attracts greater investment because it grants borrowers transparency from listing procedures and the corporate governance standards.
- Considering that SPACs are cash-shell companies accompanied with a highly flexible structure, the implementation of direct soft law regulation is preferred to hard law.

SPACs are important for the future of finance because they are offering a potentially powerful vehicle for raising additional funds for investment and thus increase financial market efficiencies. Based on equity financing, rather than using debt, SPACs constitute a possible way to enhance liquidity in market exchanges, restore mergers and acquisitions and grant private companies a new, suitable way of financing.

It is undeniable though that SPACs are a financial innovation, destined to stay, as a novel but permanent feature of world's exchanges. We have seen that SPAC markets are also expanding beyond the US borders, to other international financial markets worldwide, such as Italy, Germany, France, Canada, Malaysia, South Africa, which are all embracing this new modern corporate structure and profiling of SPACs. D'Alvia, as a legal scholar and as a finance professor, has a first-hand experience in financial markets in Europe and the US, particularly, but not limited to Italy and the US.

In Chapter 1, by introducing the 2007–2010 financial crisis because of a credit bubble and an unsustainable level of debt, D'Alvia begins his approach of uncovering the origins of SPACs. He does this by clarifying that since they have never been financed by issuing debt securities, but by means of equity securities, they cannot be considered as simply a product of the 2007 financial crisis. In the same manner, D'Alvia brings about another important assumption about SPACs – they can always be understood within the theoretical framework of risk and uncertainty in terms of finance, although risks and uncertainties are increasingly associated with their structure. Thus, in the manner of presenting a more in-depth, theoretical outlook on risk and uncertainty, D'Alvia delves into the question of whether SPACs can transform uncertainty profiles into a form of risk-taking ventures, to qualify them as alternative investment vehicles. The emphasis on SPACs in relation to risk and uncertainty, employing concepts developed by Frank Knight, is important in convincing the readers, that SPACs serve as money creation, wealth-enhancing vehicles. Consequently, uncertainty underpins, rather than undermines, the money creation processes, improving efficiencies of financial markets, increasing economic welfare.

In Chapter 2, D'Alvia examines and reinforces what constitutes the SPACs "origin story". From describing them as direct descendants of the highly controversial penny stock blank-check companies of the 1980's, to their adoption of Rule 419, SPACs today have evolved by stressing the addition of corporate practices in their structure – such as the trust, the redemption right and winding up process. Because of this, a codified international standard emerged and led to the development of SPACs 3.0 and SPACs 3.5, with new advances which are further discussed in the chapter itself (fractional warrant structure and the Private Investment in Public Equity (PIPE)).

Nonetheless, the primary objective of this chapter is to investigate the historical development of SPACs and the different forms of their regulations in America in order to theorise possible definitions of these investment vehicles. SPACs function within the mantra of market practices and self-regulation, which gave rise to a unique regulatory framework that encompasses conditions such as listing standards and any applicable securities regulations that a SPAC must fulfil before listing on a stock exchange.

SPACs is currently the private companies' favoured source of financing for going public, mostly because of its market practices, which directly relate to self-regulation and advanced instruments of corporate governance. However, risk and uncertainty are two of the main structures in SPACs, due to the money creation processes of modern economies. Consequently, Chapter 3 introduces the concepts of risk and uncertainty from an epistemological point of view, in order to then explore these concepts within the framework of social theories and complex systems to be further elaborated in Chapter 6. D'Alvia explores the fundamental dichotomy in financial markets within the concept of uncertainty. Uncertainty is seen as a dangerous market feature (uncertainty-aversion) as opposed to uncertainty perceived as a necessary feature of complex systems. He introduces this as *The Paradox of Uncertainty,* where profit and the whole financial markets cannot exist without uncertainty, but also that it can never be measurable, since it brings indeterminacies in decision-making.

Then, in Chapter 4, D'Alvia shifts his focus to different approaches in global financial regulations of SPACs by examining the role of indirect and direct soft law provisions. He further investigates case studies, such as Bursa Malaysia and Korea Exchange, where a standardisation of market practices and legal regulations have developed. Furthermore, D'Alvia assesses the European legislative framework of SPACs, or in this case the lack thereof, where D'Alvia exposes the readers to the emergence of Euronext Group, as the most significant future venue for European-listed SPACs. This is put into perspective as their functions and regulatory framework is compared with both the New York Stock Exchange (NYSE) and the National Association of Securities Dealers Automated Quotations (NASDAQ), the current mecca of SPACs listings.

The emphasis is on providing a multilevel definition of these investment vehicles – which may entail labelling them as a form of financial intermediaries or investment companies depending on the nature of the transaction they pursue. Also, analysing them based on whether their "private" transactions under private law may enhance wealth creation.

Presenting the uniqueness and virtuosity in the complex lifespan of SPACs is the focal point of Chapter 5. This part of the study examines the specific disclosure duties of these companies, as they are a result of their alternating structure, under the US legal system. The US currently has the biggest number of SPAC listings on its exchange markets. Here, the De-SPAC phase is thoroughly studied, along with the transactional risks that SPACs face at this stage, highlighting their risk management.

Chapter 6 deals with defining free financial markets and the role of SPACs within them, by using the system theory developed by Luhmann (2013). D'Alvia separates his observations under three distinct stages: first and second levels of observation involve defining financial markets as closed systems. The third one defines financial markets as open systems and highlights their means to structural coupling in case of liquidation. In this light, Chapter 6 is dedicated to theorising financial markets as financial systems, where spontaneous mechanisms of adaptation of economic system inform the system itself. This is a significant issue to highlight, since SPACs are informed by self-regulation and market practices. Hence, they are part of such auto-regenerative mechanisms of economic systems.

At the time of this writing, the IPO market is set to be scorching hot this summer of 2021. Fund managers, venture capitalists, bankers and lawyers said they are busier than they have been in decades at this time of year, which is usually quieter. Some claim business is even higher than during the dot-com boom of the late 1990s (Driebusch, 2021).

Unlike any recent history, the world at large and the US economic recoveries are mainly due to firms' willingness to hire more workers and consumers' possession of trillions in extra savings. Some economists predict that businesses and employees will meet a future with far-less permanent damage, in comparison to companies in the post-recession period of 2007–2009.

In the US, workers are quitting their jobs at the highest rate in 20 years; the US household debt service burden is at its lowest since the 1980s, and the Dow Jones Industrial Average has experienced a 18% increase from its pre-pandemic rate in February. However, the high rate of this recovery process has also resulted in some drawbacks, such as, an unexpected level of shortages in goods and an unforeseeable jump in inflation (Cambon, 2021).

However, with the success of SPACs has eloquently and convincingly demonstrated by this book by D'Alvia, competition among SPACs companies to find mergers is becoming stiffer. When share-prices decline and the ticking clock to take companies public will increase the pressure and pose the challenges for the creators of special-purpose acquisition companies. The hallmarks of SPACs' success from the abundance of the deals that raised money early in 2021 may turn around as investment opportunities become scarcer. As described in this book, looming over these firms is a two-year deadline to complete a deal or hand back cash to investors. This characteristic of SPACs is a note of caution in a world where cryptocurrencies, IPOs and yes, SPACs, compete in luring investors to their investment opportunities. Only the future will tell whether those financial instruments, or others, will prevail in financial markets. This book by D'Alvia proclaims that the success of SPACs is inevitable. Whether you agree or not with D'Alvia substantiated arguments, this book opens the eyes of scholars, researchers, investors, fund managers, venture capitalists, bankers, lawyers, and policymakers to this unique old-new financial instrument.

## References

Aydogdu M, Shekhar C, *et al.*, 'Shell Companies as IPO Alternatives: An Analysis of Trading Activity around Reverse Mergers' (2007) 17 (16) Applied Financial Economics 1335

Berger C, 'SPACs: An Alternative Way to Access the Public Markets' (2008) 20 (3) Journal of Applied Corporate Finance 68

Boyer C, Baigent G, 'SPACs as Alternative Investments: An Examination of Performance and Factors that Drive Prices' (2008) 11 (3) Journal of Private Equity 8

Driebusch, Corrie (2021), "Robinhood and Didi to Kick Off a Hot IPO Summer," Wall Street Journal, June 10.

Floros I, Sapp T, 'Shell Games: On the Value of Shell Companies' (2011) 17 (4) Journal of Corporate Finance 850

Guilford, Gwynn and Cambon, Sarah Chaney, 'The Economic Recovery Is Here. It's Unlike Anything You've Seen' (2021) The Wall Street Journal, June 2.

Hale LM, 'SPAC: A Financial Tool with Something for Everyone' (2007) 18 (2) Journal of Corporate Accounting & Finance 67

Howe JS, O'Brien SW, 'SPAC Performance, Ownership and Corporate Governance' (2012) 15 Advances in Financial Economics 1

Jenkinson T, Sousa M, 'Why SPAC Investors Should Listen to the Market (Digest summary)' (2011) 21 (2) Journal of Applied Finance 38

Lakicevic M, Shachmurove Y, Vulanovic M, 'Institutional Changes of Specified Purpose Acquisition Companies (SPACs)' (2014) 28 (C) North American Journal of Economics and Finance 149

Luhmann, Niklas (2013), *Introduction to Systems Theory* (Polity Press 2013) 26

Riemer D S, 'Special Purpose Acquisition Companies: SPAC and SPAN, or Blank Check Redux?' (2007–2008) 85 (4) Washington University Law Review 931

Rodrigrues U, Stegemoller M, 'Exit, Voice, and Reputation: The Evolution of SPACs' (2011) 11–12 University of Georgia School of Law – Legal Studies Research Paper Series 2

Shachmurove Y, Vulanovic M, 'Specified Purpose Acquisition Companies in Shipping' (2015) 26 (C) Global Finance Journal 64

———, 'US SPACs with a Focus on China' (2016) 39 (C) Journal of Multinational Financial Management 1.

———, 'SPACs IPOs' in Duglas Cumming and Sofia Johan (eds.) *Oxford Handbook of IPOs* (OUP 2017)

**Yochanan Shachmurove**
**Philadelphia, USA**

# Addendum

This addendum is reporting the last SPAC's updates occurring between March 2021 and August 2021. Those months have been particularly prolific for SPACs in terms of improvement of their financial regulation, and new emerging market practices at the De-SPAC phase. This confirms that the SPAC arena is continuously evolving and transforming, and new policy reforms are expected in the US in early 2022 as well as in Europe and Asia.

## On the international financial regulation of SPACs

In Asia, the Singapore Exchange (SGX) sought on 31 March 2021 a market feedback on a proposed regulatory framework for the listing of SPACs on the SGX Mainboard. This is not the first public consultation by SGX relating to the listing of SPACs: the last was in 2010, but did not proceed further then. The proposed rules resemble in great part the US listing requirements for SPACs with a notable and unique feature concerning the minimum equity participation by sponsors and management team in the subscription value of shares or units dependent on the market capitalisation size of the SPAC at the IPO. Until now, SPAC rules have not yet come into effect. In Hong Kong, in March 2021, the Securities and Futures Commission and the Hong Kong Exchanges and Clearing Limited were asked to explore listing regimes for SPACs to further enhance Hong Kong's competitiveness as an international financial centre for SPACs while safeguarding investors' interest. The proposal for the regime in Hong Kong is yet to be released.

In Europe, the ESMA on 15 July 2021 has published a public statement seeking to promote uniform prospectus disclosure and protect investors in SPACs. This is a key document that provides greater clarity in this area, and it applies to SPAC's securities that are admitted to trading on an EU regulated market. It does not apply to UK prospectuses issued by SPACs, although the FCA might consider it. Although, in Europe there is not a consensus to provide SPACs with a uniform legal framework through a Regulation or Directive, the ESMA has encouraged regulatory consistency among European national regulators. The majority of ESMA's points are based on existing disclosure requirements under the Prospectus Regulation (Regulation

(EU) 2019/980). Specifically, the public statement is hoping that SPAC's sponsors can inform investors on future scenarios (such as possible dilution; post-acquisition governance and disclosure of the sponsor's promote; remuneration and role; future funding needs). Those disclosure at the time of the IPO can be many times unknown. Hence, it is desirable that EU regulators are pragmatic and accept that pre-IPO disclosures are possibly illustrative rather than definitive because most of those features are negotiated at the time of the De-SPAC process. In particular, the ESMA expects the SPAC prospectuses to include at least: future remuneration of the sponsors and their role after the SPAC acquires the target; information about possible changes to the SPAC's governance after it acquires a target; information about the future shareholdings of the sponsors and other related parties; details of possible scenarios that might arise if the sponsors fail to find a suitable target such as SPAC de-listing and winding up.

In the UK, after the FCA's consultation paper (CP 21/10) on 30 April 2021, a policy statement (PS21/10) has been published on 27 July 2021[3] setting out the final version of changes to the UK Listing Rules applicable to SPACs. The revised changes came into force on 10 August 2021. The FCA's aim is to provide more flexibility to larger SPACs, and setting credible standards. The rules are removing the existing presumption in the Listing Rules according to which the listing of a SPAC will be suspended when it announces a potential acquisition, provided that the SPAC raises at least £100 million from public investors, and it follows certain investor protection features in its structure as well as discloses sufficient information to the market. For example, the money raised from public investors shall be ring-fenced with an appropriate third party to ensure the money are used only to fund an approved acquisition, shareholders redemptions or repayment of capital in the event of winding up of the SPAC or granting two years for the SPAC to complete an acquisition (three years if shareholders approve a twelve-month extension) with an extension option of six months in the event a transaction is well advanced at the De-SPAC phase. Finally, a notable feature that has similarity with the ESMA public statement issued in July 2021 concerns the fact that the SPAC should provide sufficient disclosures on key terms and risks from the SPAC IPO through the announcement and conclusion of any acquisition. This relies heavily on compliance with existing disclosure requirements (e.g. Prospectus Regulation and Market Abuse Regulation). In terms of disclosures made by the sponsors at the pre-IPO phase, we should apply the same remarks we made before for the ESMA public statement, namely disclosures at this stage shall be considered as illustrative rather than definitive because they are subject to negotiation considerations of the De-SPAC momentum. Finally, the new rules prevent sponsors and strategic investors who participate in a SPAC's at-risk capital from voting on the acquisition. This is a major difference from other listing venues, and it may impact London's position as a market for SPACs compared to competing exchanges such as New York and Amsterdam. SPACs that do not meet the aforementioned requirements can still be listed, although the presumption of suspension will remain. This can be seen as a heavy penalisation that is possibly unfair and against current market practices at international level.

## On De-SPAC market practices and market trends of recent deals

Structuring the combination of a SPAC with a European business may be complex and highly transaction-specific. SPAC sponsors shall take into account the optimal tax structure for both entities in the business combination, the desired jurisdiction of incorporation of the combined business and the desired profile of the combined company as a US public company (namely, whether the combined company wish to qualify as a foreign private issuer under US securities rules and regulations). A structure of European De-SPACs might be complex. For example, it might involve placing a newly formed parent company above both the SPAC and the target, with the SPAC and the target being acquired by, or reverse-merging into subsidiaries of the new parent company. Each European jurisdiction has its own rules on business combinations and its own taxation regime. Hence, the De-SPAC structure shall be analysed for each proposed De-SPAC transaction. A significant number of SPACs targeting non-US targets are incorporated in the Cayman Islands. For instance, an important deal is the one agreed in July 2021 by the Italian luxury Group Ermenegildo Zegna that will list in New York by combining with a US investment vehicle, giving the menswear company an enterprise value of $3.2 billion and helping it expand in Asia and the US. The SPAC Investindustrial Acquisition Corp. launched by European private equity group Investindustrial and led by Sergio Ermotti was incorporated in Cayman Islands. The Zegna Group will be qualified as a foreign private issuer.

The complexity of European De-SPAC transactions can be seen in the Pershing Square Tontine Holdings Ltd (PSTH) of Bill Ackman that raised in July 2020 a record $4 billion. In a press release that came out – one year later – in 19 July 2021, Bill Ackman withdraw its offer for a 10% stake in Universal Music Group (UMG). The original deal would have valued Universal Music at $35 billion Euros including debt. This was not a direct-route reverse merger. Indeed, Ackman planned to invest in UMG through his SPAC by going through UMG's parent company Vivendi. The deal was expected to be finalised on 15 September 2021 as UMG went public independently in the Netherlands. The complex investment was supposed to maximise tax and legal benefits for Vivendi. The large size of UMG stake made difficult to bring the transaction under a more traditional SPAC deal.

The PSTH investors would have also been entitled the right to acquire a stake in a new vehicle known as a special purpose acquisition rights company, or SPARC. The deal would have shrunk the size of the SPAC allowing it to go after smaller targets. However, the deal was too complex because SPAC investors could face a potential hurdle in holding foreign securities in Europe.

The SPAC has now eighteen months to close a new deal under its current shareholder agreement. The decision came after multiple discussions with the SEC trying to address the regulator's concerns about the impossibility of PSTH to consummate the transaction. This is because the deal structure would not qualify for the New York Stock Exchange rules. The SEC stopped the deal, and Ackman communicated that public shareholders should complain to the SEC in a classic never-ending fight between market practitioners and regulators.

Finally, in the US, by the end of July 2021, the PIPE financing has started to dry up. This has forced companies to find other possible sources of funding. For instance, BuzzFeed, which has agreed in June 2021 to merge with 890 Fifth Avenue Partners to go public at $1.5 billion valuation, secured an additional $150 million through convertible bonds. In the same month, two other SPACs went this route, Boxed that raised $86 million in convertible bonds after agreeing to merge with Seven Oaks Acquisition at a $900 million valuation, and Bigbear.ai, which secured $200 million through convertible notes for its deal with GigCapital4. Convertible bonds are issued by the target company. The downside is that the interest payment that the target companies have to pay on the convertible bonds is importantly higher than average (an average of 7% against the typical yield on convertible debt that is about 1.5%). This can challenge future profitability of the De-SPAC transaction, although it provides a form of protection to the buyer through interest payments, and if the share prices go down after the merger, public investors can decide to keep the debt and be repaid the principal. This can be seen as a further route to facilitate SPAC deals and mitigate part of the concerns on the SPAC's 'promote', although the possible implementation of this market practice is unlikely to become a common practice, and it is still uncertain with only 3 SPAC deals to have adopted such structure so far according to the Financial Times.[4]

# Notes

## Foreword

1 FSC Majority Staff to Members, Committee on Financial Services, 19 May 2021, United States House of Representatives, Committee of Financial Services.
2 FSC Majority Staff to Members, Committee on Financial Services, 19 May 2021, United States House of Representatives, Committee of Financial Services.

## Addendum

3 Financial Conduct Authority, 'Investor Protection Measures for Special Purpose Acquisition Companies: Changes to the Listing Rules' (July 2021) PS21/10.
4 Ortenca Aliaj, Eric Platt, Anna Nicolaou, 'SPACs forced to fund deals with more expensive financing' (19 July 2021) *Financial Times*.

# Introduction

A smart guy owns shares worth $100 in January, sells them in May at around $500, but then buys them back in August for between $700 and $800. By September, shares are back at $100 in value. The reader might think that this is the story of modern multinational corporations today such as Apple, Facebook, Spotify, Tesla, etc. Not at all. It was Sir Isaac Newton speculating in the momentum trade of the South Sea Company. He lost the equivalent of $3 million today.

In 1720, in return for a loan of £7 million to finance the war against France, the House of Lords passed the South Sea Bill that allowed the South Sea Company a monopoly in trade with South America. At that time in England the level of debt was already unsustainable, and the country was struggling to finance its war with France. The scheme was that in exchange for exclusive trading rights, the South Sea Company would underwrite the English National Debt. The debt stood at £30 million and carried a 5% interest coupon from the government. The South Sea Company converted the government debt into its own shares. The interest from the government could be collected and then passed onto shareholders.

At that time, England saw a rampant market speculation. As soon as the South Sea Company concluded its deal with the Parliament, shares surged to more than ten times their value. The South Sea Company shares bubbled up to incredible new heights, and numerous other joint stock companies took advantage of the booming investor demand for speculative investment. Many of these companies were set up in the form of blind pools, namely companies set up to acquire or develop target companies in many different industries. Unfortunately, those blind pools were often managed by company directors, who made fraudulent claims about their business ventures for the purpose of raising capital and boosting share prices such as trading in hair, assuring of seamen's wages, insuring horses, improving the art of making soap, improving gardens, etc.[1] It was the "fear of missing out" which attracted investors into the fray without regard for the underlying risk. Once the "mania" hit

---

1 Banjamin Graham, David L. Dodd, *Security Analysis* (6th ed., McGraw-Hill 2009).

DOI: 10.4324/9781003102779-1

financial markets, then, valuation, revenue or even viable business models did not matter.

The South Sea Company shares were skyrocketing. However, the company's profitability was mediocre at best, and the abundant promises of future growth by company directors could not be kept. As the South Sea Company and other "bubble" company share prices imploded, speculators who had purchased shares on credit went bankrupt. The popping of the South Sea bubble then resulted in a contagion that spread across Europe. It was one of the first examples of interconnected financial markets, and speculation, in modern history.

It is fair to say that Sir Isaac Newton at that time initially made a profit. Indeed, after recognising the speculative mania, he liquidated his stake at a large profit. Nonetheless, after his exit, the South Sea Company had a dramatic rise in share price. The bubble kept inflating. Newton followed his emotions and went against logic by buying back shares. Unfortunately, the trend was near its peak, and afterwards it dramatically plummeted. Newton once said that he could: "calculate the motions of the heavenly bodies, but not the madness of people".[2] It is essentially such "mania" of the "fear of missing out" in financial markets that cannot be regulated, predicted or anticipated, because it finally rests with the inner deep emotions of every human being. It is what I define as the subjective feature of risk in financial markets (see Chapter 3).

After more than 300 years, today, the same story seems to be repeating, although with some crucial differences that this book, *inter alia*, would like to highlight. SPACs are not the South Sea bubble, and never will be.

From Wall Street bankers to celebrities and stars, investors from Silicon Valley, respected businessmen, famous showbiz stars and finally ordinary people, who does not love a seemingly great earning opportunity spiced with a touch of glamour and exclusivity? These are all among the cast of characters that have promoted or bought into the SPAC fever that has swept the US in the past year. SPACs are special purpose acquisition companies or, loosely translated, companies set up for the purpose of a takeover or business combination.

By the end of 2020, more than 240 SPACs were listed in the US (on NASDAQ or NYSE), raising a record $83 billion, according to SPAC research. SPACs have already surged past 2020 year's record in the first quarter of 2021, raising $98.1 billion. The general feeling is that today traditional IPOs are now under attack. For instance, take a look at Deliveroo's IPO in March 2021 in the UK. It closed down 26% on its first day of trading. The share price slump means tens of thousands of retail investors who backed Deliveroo are now sitting on heavy paper losses. This is also true of China's Ant Group's pulled IPO in 2020. SPACs are emerging as the new IPO (or IPO 2.0), all of this with fewer formal requirements and at a lower cost. And yes, when something sounds too good to be true, the number of disbelievers can only increase.

---

2 Edward Chancellor, *Devil take the Hindmost: A History of Financial Speculation* (Plume 2000).

Introduction 3

The boom that made 2020 the 'Year of the SPAC'[3] started to cool in April 2021 following warnings from the US Securities and Exchange Commission. In December 2020, the SEC explained what a SPAC is,[4] then it went on to provide new guidance on SPACs' disclosures,[5] and it issued a specific warning concerning celebrities[6] involved in SPACs. Subsequently, in March 2021, the SEC opened an inquiry into understanding how underwriters manage risks involved in SPAC transactions,[7] and *dulcis in fundo*, it raised accounting and reporting considerations for warrants issued by SPACs. The SEC suggested their inclusion as liabilities rather than equity or assets of the company.[8] Furthermore, on 24 May 2021, the US House Committee on Financial Services has received a draft legislation[9] amending the Securities Act of 1933 and the Securities Exchange Act of 1934 to specifically exclude all SPACs from the safe harbour exemption for forward-looking statements. Indeed, a critical distinction between a De-SPAC transaction and a traditional IPO is the ability to include forward-looking financial projections in a proxy or registration statement rather than historical financial results. This is a clear regulatory activism that is beneficial neither for SPACs nor their investors alike. It is an attempt to regulate uncertainty (see Chapter 3), although such progressive approach by the SEC can constitute one day the final legitimisation step for SPACs.

---

3 Brooke Masters, 'Year in a Word: SPAC' (1 January 2021) Financial Times.
4 Securities and Exchange Commission – Investor Alerts and Bulletins, 'What You Need to Know about SPACs – Investor Bulletin' (10 December 2020), available at https://www.sec.gov/oiea/investor-alerts-and-bulletins/what-you-need-know-about-spacs-investor-bulletin, accessed on 10 April 2021.
5 Securities and Exchange Commission, Division of Corporate Finance Securities and Exchange Commission, CF Disclosure Guidance: topic no. 11, 'Special Purpose Acquisition Companies' (22 December 2020), available at https://www.sec.gov/corpfin/disclosure-special-purpose-acquisition-companies, accessed on 10 April 2021.
6 Securities and Exchange Commission – Investor Alerts and Bulletins, 'Celebrity Involvement with SPACs – Investor Alert' (10 March 2021), available at https://www.sec.gov/oiea/investor-alerts-and-bulletins/celebrity-involvement-spacs-investor-alert, accessed on 10 April 2021.
7 Jody Godoy, Chris Prentice, 'Exclusive U.S. Regulator Opens Inquiry into Wall Street's Blank Check IPO Frenzy – Sources' (25 March 2021), available at https://www.reuters.com/business/exclusive-us-regulator-opens-inquiry-into-wall-streets-blank-check-ipo-frenzy-2021-03-25/, accessed on 10 April 2021.
8 Securities and Exchange Commission – Public Statement, 'Staff statement on Accounting and Reporting Considerations for Warrants Issued by Special Purpose Acquisition Companies (SPACs)' (12 April 2021), available at https://www.sec.gov/news/public-statement/accounting-reporting-warrants-issued-spacs, accessed on 20 April 2021.
9 Ran Ben-Tzur, Jay Pomerantz, 'House Releases Draft Legislation Eliminating SPAC Safe Harbor for Forward Looking Statements' (7 June 2021), available at https://corpgov.law.harvard.edu/2021/06/07/house-releases-draft-legislation-eliminating-spac-safe-harbor-for-forward-looking-statements/?utm_content=buffer848d7&utm_medium=-social&utm_source=linkedin.com&utm_campaign=buffer, accessed on 23 June 2021.

The 'SPAC craze', they call it. The new alternative acquisition models, and legitimate alternative path to traditional IPO, I define it.

The SPAC craze has been shaking the US for months, mainly for its simplicity: a bunch of investors decides to buy shares at a fixed price in a company that initially has no assets. In this way a SPAC, also known as a 'blank check company', is created as an empty shell with a lot of money to spend on a corporate shopping spree. It is a bit like a lottery ticket – the initial stake is small, but in terms of potential gains, the sky's the limit. At the same time, every SPAC is finite: if it does not find a target within a pre-set time frame (usually about a year or two), the SPAC is liquidated, and the investors get their money back, increased by a modest profit from investing in short-term US government securities (and reduced by certain expenses, commissions and fees). The asymmetrical relationship between the risk and the potential of profit leaves the impression that it is impossible to lose. SPACs are risk-free investments until the moment of the business combination. Once the SPAC finds a target company, it merges with it. Then, the business runs the same operational, financial or reputational risks as any other company.

SPACs can be sector focused or multi-sector focused. A good example of a multi-sector-focused SPAC is provided by Accor Acquisition Company (ACC) sponsored by the Group Accor, a world leading hospitality company, and listed on Euronext Paris for €300 million IPO. ACC is targeting five verticals: food and beverage, flexible working, wellness, entertainment & events, and travel technology. As it can be seen there is not a core business that ACC wanted to focus on, being the main purpose to acquire a target company that will benefit from Accor's network, scale and global presence. Furthermore, Accor is also a good example to show that SPACs are not necessarily associated with business tycoons but they can be sponsored by corporate entities. SPACs do not necessarily take private companies over but may use IPO proceeds to cash out deals. ACC may in fact bring to Accor a new client at little cost and a possible profit to the group. The same rationale has been planned in 2021 by Hong Kong's luxury Rosewood Hotel Group. This is already revealing what I define as the 'multi-level definition' of SPACs based on their functions and deal rationales (see Chapter 4). It means that in extreme cases a SPAC might be also considered as an investment company as far as the grounds to affirm this are based on proper factual and legal consideration (see Chapter 4).

In Europe and Asia at the moment little is said about this, although Singapore has opened a consultation paper in 2021 (see Addendum). Asian fintech private companies are the preferred targets of US SPACs, today. In 2020, Tokopedia (the largest e-commerce platform in Indonesia) contemplated being acquired by a SPAC that could value the company between $8 and $10 billion. Or consider the Singaporean multinational mobile App leader for deliveries, mobility and financial services in Southeast Asia: Grab holdings Inc. (Grab). The company announced on 13 April 2021 that it will use a SPAC to list on NASDAQ in what is expected to be the largest-ever US equity offering by a Southeast Asian company. India is registering the same trend, for instance, with Flipkart, that since 10 March 2021 has been exploring the possibility of being merged with a SPAC in New York. Those are just a few examples of how SPACs can represent a suitable exit strategy for fintech companies to get listed on foreign markets (mainly, NY exchanges). The SPAC represents a new stage of evolution in capitalism by virtue of providing companies with liquidity. They are flexible investment vehicles, and they allow the valuation of the acquisition target to be settled through private negotiations.

It is not by chance that the Indonesian bourse (IDX) has deepened its knowledge of SPACs by passing regulations to allow companies to go public using special purpose acquisition companies and to issue dual-class shares. Indonesia is specifically looking to allow e-commerce and fintech start-ups to be listed in the form of SPACs. This is also in line with international trends in the SPAC arena that today see exponential growth in Europe as well. Here, Euronext is leading important offerings either in Amsterdam or Paris, and the UK has modified the London Stock Exchange listing rules through the very recent Hill Report on Listing Requirements (issued in March 2021) that represents London's much-needed answer to the SPAC craze in America. The same reform spirit has been seen in 2021 in Belgium where the Financial Service Market Authority published a consultation and opinion about minimum standards for the structuring, information disclosure and trading in SPACs on Euronext Brussels. Despite Belgium being a small jurisdiction, the interest of SPACs in Brussels is based on the fact that Belgian law is a derivation of Amsterdam corporate law, and therefore, it has the same level of flexibility (see Chapter 4). In Asia, some jurisdictions have already selected SPACs as a viable alternative acquisition model, places such as South Korea, Malaysia and India, which is aiming to design new SPAC rules through its Securities and Exchange Board of India (SEBI). Hong Kong is said to be prepared to welcome its first SPAC listing by the end of 2021 (although here SPAC rules could be tighter due to the imposition of compliance with existing standards for traditional IPO and the request for the sponsor to have a track record in money management), and is evaluating a SPAC reform too (see Addendum). Therefore, the day is likely not far off in which Asia begins to SPAC-off and show the world the flexibility and attractiveness of its financial markets.

It is generally said that it is difficult to accept reality and change, but those who are against novelty cannot close their eyes to what has become one of the most prominent American inventions: the SPAC. This book provides, for the first time, a comprehensive theory of these investment vehicles, and at the same time opens the reader's eyes to recognising that alternative acquisition models and financial innovations matter. In the equity era, new ways to raise capital for private companies are key, as is growth capital through private equity investment in relatively mature companies that are looking for capital to expand or restructure operations, enter new markets or finance a significant acquisition without a change of control.

Sometimes those changes can also allow private issuers to reduce investment banks' fees, and directly place their equity securities on the market. It is not by chance that in December 2020 the SEC approved the NYSE Group Inc. plan for so-called primary direct listings or primary direct floor listings.[10] The same move was followed by NASDAQ. Indeed, originally both NYSE and NASDAQ permitted direct listings as an alternative route to going public for a limited number of companies that, instead of offering shares or raising capital on their own, sought only to register shares held by pre-existing investors, enabling them to sell their shares to the public through a resale registration statement. It means that there was a prohibition on raising new capital along with the significant valuation requirements imposed on companies seeking direct listing. Hence, only a small minority of companies could meet those requirements.

By contrast, today, in New York, a company can raise capital directly, provided that certain requirements are met. Specifically, companies need to meet higher market valuation requirements and satisfy the NYSE's existing initial listing requirements, which may be more difficult to satisfy within the context of a direct listing than a traditional IPO. For instance, initial listing requirements include that companies have at least 1.1 million publicly held shares, 400 round lot holders (on NYSE, holders of 100 shares) and a price per share of at least $4.00. Those thresholds may be challenging to meet for many private companies without the assistance of underwriters, namely investment banks that in a traditional IPO ensure these requirements are met prior to listing through the book-building process.

Nonetheless, this is a further sign of departure from traditional IPOs, in which companies rely on investment banks to sell their shares on the market. Companies can now sell shares directly on the exchange to raise capital. Since this reform, it has been argued that primary direct listings can replace the importance of SPACs, or at least constitute a challenge for them.[11] Those mechanisms are not necessarily in competition with each other. They are both financial innovations focused on raising capital on financial markets. In the case of SPACs, the role of investment banks is preserved. On the other hand, with primary direct listings, private investment bankers would see their role minimised, if not completely erased, in the future. This is one of the many reasons why SPACs would still constitute an interesting financial tool with a 'sweet' side for everyone involved in the process: investment banks, law firms, promoters and investors. Furthermore, SPACs have developed a sophisticated

---

10 Benjamin Bain, Crystal Tse, 'Silicon Valley Wins as SEC Allows New Direct Listing' (22 December 2020), Bloomberg available at https://www.bloomberg.com/news/articles/2020-12-22/silicon-valley-wins-as-sec-allows-direct-listings-to-raise-cash, accessed on 1 January 2021.
11 Simon Moore, 'New Direct Listing Rules Challenge SPACs' (28 December 2020) Forbes, available at https://www.forbes.com/sites/simonmoore/2021/12/28/new-direct-listing-rules-challenge-spacs/?sh=4b283ddf9dcb, accessed on 1 January 2021.

financial regulation framework since 2008 in the US – as we will see in this book – and on other financial markets worldwide such as Canada, France, Germany, Italy, Malaysia, South Africa, the UK, etc. Primary direct listings have not yet implemented such regulatory framework, because they are a very recent invention, whereas SPACs have been on the scene at least since 2003 with their new modern corporate structure and profiling.

We anticipated before that SPACs are entirely risk-free for their initial investors until the acquisition decision or combination materialises as investors are guaranteed full redemption of funds from the escrow account. By its structure, SPACs issue units: composite security of common shares and warrants structured in such a way that an investor eliminates any monetary risk. With absolutely no downside risk, all the funds from the IPO are deposited in an escrow account or trust, although the impossibility of finding a suitable business combination is a real risk that cannot be avoided, and external factors and circumstances can affect the SPAC's survival too. However, risk is an objective and immanent concept that cannot be eradicated *tout court*. SPACs are non-operating companies; this means that investors do not have access to a previous track record of the company or to its balance sheets, therefore the management investment decisions become the only valuable asset. This in economic terms can generate issues in terms of agency costs and information asymmetry.

Essentially, to invest in a SPAC can be seen as 'tossing a coin', as investors need to bank on the manager's expertise and diligence in finding the target/s that could provide an envisaged return. The quality of the management team is key, and public investors as well as PIPE investors are becoming more critical about the reputation of the sponsors. Furthermore, it is important to highlight that not every De-SPAC deal is further financed by a PIPE investment. This is especially true in Europe where PIPE investments are not the norm. In the US, an only cash De-SPAC is rare, meaning a SPAC that is using only the IPO proceeds held on trust as the cash consideration to the target company's equity holders. Indeed, so far only six SPACs in the US have followed this pattern. Furthermore, SPACs face other underlying transactional risks which are present in any business acquisition or M&As transaction. Indeed, there is a higher theoretical risk of not closing the acquisition deal compared to an IPO because, among other reasons, there is a significant time gap (up to two months) between signing (pricing) and closing the SPAC (shareholders' approval). However, the majority of SPACs do usually find a suitable target company within their first 18 months of operation, which in real comparative terms is a relative low risk for investors, although the price paid in market volatility can be high. For example, shares of Jeff Sagansky's fifth SPAC, Diamond Eagle Acquisition Corp., were priced initially in 2019 at $10 per share. The IPO raised $350 million on NASDAQ. Shares in the merged company (DraftKings) began trading on 24 April 2020. They opened at $20.49 and closed at $19.35 that day (down 5.6%). This is not positive news for investors who buy and sell shares on NASDAQ. However, this is no different from any shares that are publicly traded, be they SPAC shares or not. Furthermore, a 'dip' to below $20.49 of a share that was offered for $10 on the IPO is still an extraordinary gain for both IPO investors and pre-IPO SPAC investors, called SPAC sponsors. Since then, the trend has been generally higher; the shares did have another down month in October 2020 but still did not close below $35 per share. They are now worth close to $60 per share.

As the example shows, volatility can affect market price. Hence, it is clear that the SPAC is not the cause of volatility, and the price of the newly merged entity that becomes public can be affected by volatility as much as any other public listed company. The same trend can be observed in Michael Klein's SPAC Churchill Capital Corp. IV. At one point before merging with Lucid Motors (the electric vehicles company) worth more than $50 per share, and then after completion of the business combination, the price of stock crashed below $30.

It is undeniable that SPACs' disbelievers love to attack SPACs on these possible 'perverse' mechanisms.[12] They are possibly misled. The SPAC's lifespan is divided into two main life cycles: the SPAC IPO, where shares are fixedly traded at the conventional price of $10 per share, and the De-SPAC phase that is the business combination itself, and the subsequent listing of the merged entity on the market. From a legal perspective at least we are speaking of two different companies. On the one hand, the SPAC that is the investment vehicle (i.e. the cash-shell vehicle) that goes on the market with a promise: "guys (the public investors), I owe you to find a target company operating in X industrial sector or in X, Y, Z industrial sectors". On the other hand, we have the newly merged entity that is destined to become the new public listed company. From that moment, it is a normal public listed company like any other. It can sound like: "guys, we made it! Now we're a public listed company, and this was always our main desire and objective. Thanks, guys, for making it possible, we couldn't have done it without you (the SPAC)".

Those who dislike or oppose unconventional ideas, such as the SPAC, mainly argue that SPACs are dangerous investment tools, and that they represent hazards against common wisdom. These people see the traditional IPO as the sole legitimate process for providing a company with full compliance and disclosure to access capital markets;[13] or they claim value destruction mechanisms and indirect costs for SPACs' investors with a 'sober look',[14] and promise to identify SPACs as the next dotcom bubble[15] or solely as the

---

12 Lora Dimitrova, 'Special Incentives of Special Purpose Acquisition Companies, the 'Poor Man's Equity Funds'' (2017) 63 (1) Journal of Accounting & Economics 99.
13 Dimitrova (n 11).
14 Michael Kalusner, Michael Ohlrogge, Emily Ruan, 'A Sober Look at SPACs' (19 November 2020) Harvard Law School Forum on Corporate Governance, available at https://corpgov.law.harvard.edu/2020/11/19/a-sober-look-at-spacs/, accessed on 10 March 2021.
15 David Erickson, The Wharton School, University of Pennsylvania, 'Will 2020 Be Seen as the Year of the SPAC Bubble?' (21 January 2021), available at https://knowledge.wharton.upenn.edu/article/will-2020-seen-year-spac-bubble/, accessed on 20 March 2021.

next bubble to burst.[16] I believe, a 'proper look' at SPACs should be taken. In reality, those who argue against SPACs seem to confuse or at least to associate two different phases in the lifespan of the SPAC. The SPAC was born not to become a public listed company, but rather to facilitate those private companies outside to become one. SPACs are the reverse of the normal IPO procedure. Instead of an operating company seeking investors, investors seek an operating company. This is clearly irresistible, and more appealing than passivity.

For these reasons, any remark that concerns the shares' value at the moment of the De-SPAC and post-IPO shall be referred to the new merged entity that is a public company, and not the SPAC itself. Conversely, any remarks that are referred to the SPAC shall be referred to the business combination that is the main purpose of existence of every SPAC. Beyond finding a suitable acquisition target, SPACs are useless. They are just cash-shell investment vehicles with no downside risks for initial investors until the moment of the business combination. This statement recognises the limits that many are facing when trying to resist the SPAC revolution. However, as with any major historical event in the world such as the French Revolution, once you start the process, it is difficult to stop it or at least to avoid the acknowledgement of the many changes it carries. It is true. Sometimes revolutions have been made possible at any cost, whatever it takes. Revolutions have never followed an easy path, and probably the SPAC revolution will be no different and will follow the same pattern. This book is trying to explain for the first time the origins of this revolution, whether it can be made possible, and to evaluate and assess the future perspectives and pointers for SPAC sponsors and investors to look for. SPACs have definitively contributed to a possible reshaping of financial markets *tout court* with their self-regulation and market practices. Everything else is secondary.

---

16 Ivana Naumovska, 'The SPAC Bubble is About to Burst' (18 February 2021) Harvard Business Review, available at https://hbr.org/2021/02/the-spac-bubble-is-about-to-burst, accessed on 10 March 2021.

# 1 Against debt

The remarkable story of SPACs

## 1.1 An introduction to SPACs

The sun is shining brightly in Kuala Lumpur in Malaysia in 2014. Mr Jeff Lobao is chief executive officer at Matrix Capacity Petroleum Bhd, a company seeking to acquire energy assets. The potential deal has been predicted to be one of the biggest IPOs in terms of SPACs fund raising. The eyes of the world are upon this historical listing on Bursa Malaysia. Nonetheless, at the end of August 2014, the Securities Commission of Malaysia rejects the IPO application of Matrix Capacity Petroleum Bhd, despite its excellent fund-raising IPO with investors, who have been tempted by the potential profit connected to equity securities and to the uncertainty of the business combination. One could be surprised when reading the decision to delist, which has been taken specifically after consideration of the management's lack of experience in the oil exploration and production business, following the application of tighter Malaysian Equity Guidelines for SPACs' IPOs. Indeed, common-sense thinking brings us to consider uncertainty, and, in particular, the uncertainty of the business combination, as the main reason for delisting because of the impossibility of projecting or anticipating future management decisions.

This lack of experience has prevented the management from successfully directing a SPAC. On one level, it appears it is not the uncertainty of completing a business combination but the uncertainty of the board of directors' decisions that is seen as a 'bad' product of SPACs. For this reason, uncertainty itself is not seen as a negative element of financial systems, but it underpins what I will identify later as a core process of money creation.

First, SPACs are investment vehicles that pursue value maximisation by acquiring high growth target companies with high potential revenues. This translates in economic and philosophical terms into a reflection on risk and uncertainty in modern economies. Indeed, money creation and income generation processes are the main features of our capitalist system. Without risk-taking activities, the progress and wealth of the economy are destined to be irremediably hindered. In other words, risk is considered as an opportunity that has to be taken.¹ In the same fashion, managers of SPACs are taking risks when they propose acquisitions in order to generate profits for their stakeholders. Furthermore, any income generation process is always understood as a form of uncertainty rather than risk. Indeed, according to Knight,² while risk is a measurable entity, uncertainty itself is not capable of being measured, because it is a mysterious element connected to an 'entrepreneurial' instinct that can be understood only through a subjective reading of risk. This work will explore how those concepts of risk and uncertainty relate to modern economies, in order to present SPACs as financial products or financial innovations that are part of the discourse on risk and uncertainty in the contemporary paradigm of financial markets. SPACs give rise to their own features of risk and uncertainty that can also pose systemic risks for financial markets. For this reason, this work aims to discover whether the uncertainty profiles can be turned into manageable forms of risk-taking in order for SPACs to qualify as alternative investment vehicles. To achieve this objective, it is necessary to reflect on the role of law in financial markets in terms of financial regulation.³

The main question is centred on whether or not law, as an emanation of the state, should govern financial markets, and therefore money creation processes, which are informed by uncertainty. SPACs are investment vehicles that are not currently regulated on the markets, except for a few exemptions that will be examined in this work, and can be defined in general terms as 'SPACs without law'.⁴ For instance, the Malaysian regulation of SPACs is dynamic, and it is influenced by Islamic law, which presents a different conception of risk and uncertainty in the markets, based on the evolving and dynamic concept of *Gharar*.⁵ Furthermore, the Securities Commission of Malaysia (i.e. the regulator) has implemented a possible sustainable regulation of uncertainty in relation to SPACs by virtue of 'quasi-legal frameworks' enacted through the adoption of soft law guidelines.⁶ Therefore, strictly speaking, Malaysia does not over-regulate SPACs because any regulation is commonly understood as the product of a state regulation, or at least of governmental agencies inspired by paternalistic imposition and supervision. By contrast, SPACs in Malaysia are regulated by Equity Guidelines that are a form of soft law regulation enacted directly by a regulator, and not by the state. Therefore, it can be argued that the Malaysian regulation of SPACs is entirely centred on a self-regulation approach which has been developed by

---

1 See further Chapter 3.
2 Frank Knight, *Risk, Uncertainty and Profit* (first published 1921, Martino Publishing 2014).
3 See Chapter 4.
4 See Chapters 2 and 4.
5 Daniele D'Alvia, 'Risk, Uncertainty and the Market: A Rethinking of Islamic and Western Finance' (2020) International Journal of Law in Context 1; Daniele D'Alvia, '(Legal) Uncertainty: Takaful between English Common Law and Shari'a Law' (2017) 10 (1) International Review of Law 1, 4. See also further Chapter 3 for the study of risk and uncertainty under Islamic Finance.
6 See Chapter 4.

the market itself as a form of market discipline, and then registered through the reception, or better, codification of such market practices into a soft law instrument, namely the Equity Guidelines. This is what I define as the codification of uncodified market practices.[7]

Indeed, this reading of the Malaysian regulation provides an understanding of SPACs as a financial innovation characterised either by a standardisation of market practices or a legal standardised regulation. Currently no legal standardised regulation exists except – as we shall see – for South Korea and Turkey.[8] Therefore, it can be anticipated that the role of law in relation to financial regulation, and specifically in relation to SPACs, has evolved through fostering a market approach in which the law stays behind the scenes. This last sentence can also open a broader discussion as to whether law has ever succeeded in regulating financial instruments.

For these reasons, the next sections introduce the 2007–2010 financial crisis with a specific focus on the main features of risk and uncertainty in the markets that is further explained in respect of the upcoming new crisis determined by the external factor of the pandemic known as Covid-19. This is because in financial markets it is important to evaluate whether uncertainty can be regulated or controlled. Indeed, SPACs are mainly seen as risk-taking operators in financial markets. Their appetite for risk is high because SPACs are risk-takers. Nonetheless, it is also important to recognise that a risk-taking activity alone is never capable of generating profits. Indeed, as is explained below through a reading of Knight, uncertainty is the distinguishing feature of financial markets today; it is essentially the only element that can underpin money creation processes and profit.

The financial crisis is an important example for introducing those concepts of risk and uncertainty as well as evaluating whether risk management can constitute an efficient tool to avoid future crisis. SPACs, as is seen in the sections below, are vehicles through which risk and uncertainty is conveyed. For this reason, the financial crisis is seen as a macroexample of profit-making and failures, whereas SPACs represent a micro-instance of such economic mechanisms. Furthermore, this illustration serves as a theoretical background for further consideration of the role of financial regulation, and specifically the role of SPACs in a post-pandemic regulation environment.

## 1.2 The financial crisis (2007–2010): the welfare price of under-priced private debt

The financial crisis (2007–2010) has been defined as 'the biggest crisis since the Great Depression'.[9] It started pre-eminently as a mortgage-lending crisis

---

7 See Chapter 4.
8 See Chapter 4.
9 Ioannis Kokkoris, Rodrigo Olivares-Caminal, *Antitrust Law Amidst Financial Crises* (1st ed., CUP 2010) 90. Although crises are seen as a recurrent feature of financial history (see

in the US,[10] although the diffusion of speculative derivative contracts traded on over-the-counter markets is identified as one of several causes.[11]

Specifically, the lack of financial regulation and monitoring as well as of correct pricing of financial risk led to a fuelled credit bubble whose first fatal effects were seen in the collapse of the market for subprime mortgages in the US. A subprime mortgage consists of a residential loan or mortgage issued to high-risk borrowers who face bankruptcy or have a late payment history (i.e. they are subprime borrowers). Therefore, the rate of interest charged to those borrowers was higher than a prime mortgage. Nonetheless, lenders such as banks sold – through a system of securitisation[12] – their credit to investors who in turn became holders of asset-backed securities. In light of this, premiums paid on collaterals (i.e. mortgages/loans) were attractive on returns for asset-backed holders due to the higher interest rate, but the effective repayment of the principal of the mortgage would have been convenient for high-risk borrowers only in the case of an increase in house prices.

Furthermore, this form of speculation became even more aggressive when holders of asset-backed securities started to enter into derivative contracts in order to bet on the loan performance to receive additional premiums in case of an increase in housing prices. This circumstance led to a speculation spiral when, between 2004 and 2006, house prices started to drop but debt itself was not downgraded.[13] As a result, defaults on subprime mortgages began to rise and triggered devaluation of housing-related securities, causing losses to financial intermediaries, raising prices on insurance for default and reducing inter-bank lending.[14]

---

Charles Kindleberger, *Manias, Panics and Crashes. A History of Financial Crises* (3rd ed., John Wiley & Dons 1996).

10 Indeed, there are multiple causes of the current economic crisis (see Glen Arnold, *Modern Financial Markets and Institutions – A Practical Perspective* (Pearson Education 2012) 660).

11 Lynn A. Stout, 'Derivatives and the Legal Origin of the 2008 Credit Crisis' (2011) 1 Harvard Business Law Review 1, 7.

12 Yuliya Demyanyk, Otto Van Hemert, 'Understanding the Subprime Mortgage Crisis' (2011) 24 (6) The Review of Financial Studies 1848. For definition of terms see also 'Definition of Subprime', Financial Times Lexicon, available at http://lexicon.ft.com/Term?term=subprime, accessed on 10 February 2015. The sub-prime mortgages were usually packed either into Mortgage Backed Securities (MBS) or Collateralised Mortgage Obligations (CMO), namely two different forms of asset-backed security that use a mortgage or a pool of mortgages as collateral (see the definition of mortgage-backed securities MBS), *Financial Times Lexicon*, available at http://lexicon.ft.com/Term?term=mortgage_backed_securities--MBS, accessed on 10 February 2015) and were sold to investors as a form of synthetic instrument having high-risk return prospects. In other words, if the value of houses had continued to increase, the reimbursement of the original loan that constituted the underlying asset of the MBS or the CMO would have been likely to occur.

13 Niamh Moloney, 'EU Financial Market Regulation after the Global Financial Crisis: "More Europe" or More Risks?' (2010) 47 (5) Common Market Law Review 1317, 1319.

14 This circumstance is also often defined as credit crunch (see Jorgen Elmeskov, 'The General Economic Background of the Crisis' (OCDE 2009), available at http://www.oecd.org/eco/42843570.pdf, accessed on 10 February 2015).

14  *Against debt: the remarkable story of SPACs*

Indeed, before the crisis, inter-bank lending and lending activities generally represented the main instrument for financing the investment activities of private equity funds. Private equity firms are a mixture of venture capital and management buyouts. Specifically, the European Private Equity and Venture Capital Association has highlighted that in 2008, private equity investments fell dramatically, due to difficulties in obtaining bank loans to finance new deals.[15] Indeed, the economic crisis (2007–2010) was mainly perceived as a debt securities crisis and contributed to a decline in private equity operations, especially those with a high level of leverage. In other words, the possibility of obtaining new funds at low interest rates (where the interest rate has to be understood as the price for the risky activities undertaken by virtue of lending) enhanced the opportunity for aggressive speculation focusing on high-risk investments. In addition to this, the lack of strict regulatory requirements or direct supervision of financial intermediaries in some measure facilitated this process, especially in the European Union.[16]

When the crisis hit financial markets, the high reliance on debt securities (such as loans, bonds, etc.) diminished, and financial panic started to rise. For instance, the notorious collapse of one of the most important investment banks in 2007 (Lehman Brothers)[17] brought further deterioration to the economic conditions of the financial environment and gave rise to concerns in relation to moral hazard and the feasibility of bail-out procedures.[18] Hence, the new volatility of financial markets called into doubt whether Central Banks should have been in charge of financial stability as a whole in addition to their traditional monetary stability role,[19] although Central Banks were in a position to foresee the 2007–2010 financial crisis, due to

---

15 Stephen Valdez, Philip Molyneux, *An Introduction to Global Financial Markets* (8th ed., Palgrave Macmillan 2016) 39.
16 Moloney (n 13) 1319. Indeed, she highlights how

> additional difficulties beset the EU, arising from the mis-match between the pan-EU operations of some major banking groups and nationally-based supervision and resolution regimes (...) at the core of the EU crisis was a destructive imbalance in the regulatory and supervisory architecture. The regulatory structure facilitated the cross-border activities of the large EU groups which had supported integration of the banking market, but it did not adequately address cross-border supervision, co-ordination, crisis resolution, and deposit protection.

17 Glen Arnold, *Modern Financial Markets and Institutions – A Practical Perspective* (Pearson Education 2012) 660; Jennifer Hughes, 'The Bad Dread Team Part I – II' (2008 November) Financial Times.
18 It is the well-known argument 'too-big-to-fail'. See Rosa Lastra, 'Crisis Management' in *International Financial and Monetary Law* (2nd ed., OUP 2015) 154; Kenneth Ayotte, David Skeel, 'Bankruptcy or Bailouts?' (2010) 35 Journal of Corporation Law 35; also before the current crisis (2007–2010) some arguments for bail-out procedures and its Effect Were Taken into Account (see Gerard Caprio, Daniela Klingebiel, 'Bank Insolvency: Bad Luck, bad Policy, or Bad Banking?' (1997) *Annual World Bank Conference on Development Economics*, 79).
19 Howard Davies, David Green, *Banking on the Future: the fall and rise of Central Banking* (Princeton University Press 2010) 52.

the well-known phenomenon of high leverage and under-pricing of risk.[20] The crisis led to a rethinking of the classic role of Central Banks and the need for Central Banks to regulate banks[21] and other financial intermediaries,[22] as well as to focus attention on international financial conglomerates, due to the possible spill-over effect and systemic risk[23] that can be caused by their collapse.[24]

The crisis moved to the real economy, evolving into a recession and affecting households, businesses and jobs.[25] Indeed, it has been noted that price fluctuation is likely to impact on the real economy because the housing market is also part of a 'credit-fuelled asset price bubble'[26] where prices can drop, but private debt loads simply cannot. For this reason, private debt has been identified as the main cause in triggering failure cascades and detrimental spill-over effects.

Certainly, the world economy has been reshaped by the global nature of the 2007–2010 crisis,[27] which has manifested negative widespread effects on

---

20 Charles Goodhart, *The Regulatory Response to the Financial Crisis* (Edward Elgar 2009) 9. Goodhart highlights that it was clearly perceivable from Financial Stability Reviews published by Central Banks that 'differentials between risky assets and safe assets (…) declined to historically low levels. Volatility was unusually low. Leverage was high, as financial institutions sought to add to yield, in the face of very low interest rates'.
21 Charles Goodhart, *The Evolution of Central Banks* (1988 MIT Press) 85.
22 Valdez, Molyneux, (n 15) 27. One of the main concerns of the current financial crisis is focused on the phenomenon referred to as the shadow banking system, namely institutions that are not properly banks, but that carry out all the activities commonly referred to a bank or clearing house.
23 In the aftermath of the crisis financial regulation has highlighted the need to regulate and identify systematically important financial institutions (SIFIs). See Valdez, Molyneux (n 15) 128.
24 Rosa Lastra, Rodrigo Olivares-Caminal, 'Cross-border Insolvency: The Case of Financial Conglomerates' in John Raymond Labrosse et al. (eds.) *Financial Crisis Management and Bank Resolution* (Informa 2009) 269; additionally, it should be highlighted that the collapse of an international financial conglomerate or complex financial groups, as well as the global dimension of financial markets manifests the need for resolution and re-thinking of cross-border bank insolvency, see Rosa Lastra, 'International Law Principles Applicable to Cross-border Bank Insolvency' in Rosa Lastra (ed.) *Cross-Border Bank Insolvency* (OUP 2011) 161.
25 Stephen Figlewski, 'Viewing the Financial Crisis from 20,000 Feet Up' (2009) 16 Journal of Derivatives 53, 56.
26 Richard W. Vague, Robert C. Hockett, 'Debt, Deflation, and Debacle: Of Private Debt Write-Down and Public Recovery' (2013), available at http://works.bepress.com/robert_hockett/48/, accessed on 17 October 2016, accessed on 5 January 2021.
27 Arnold (n 22) 659; although some Authors have been argued the opposite view see Suzanne Konzelmann, Marc Fovargue-Davies, Olivier Butzbach, 'The 'Not So Global' Crisis' in Suzanne Knozelmann, Marc Fovargue-Davies (eds.) *Banking Systems in the Crisis – The Faces of Liberal Capitalism* (Routledge 2013) 1; on the global crisis argument see also Alan Rechtschaffen, Jean-Claude Trichet, *Capital Markets, Derivatives and the Law: Evolution after the Crisis* (OUP 2014) 3–4.

the whole economy (i.e. systemic risk and contagion)[28] due to the internationalisation of financial markets.[29]

In particular, unlike previous crises, which were seen as a successful test for the economy and were confined to certain sectors of financial markets, the 2007–2010 economic crisis stands apart due to its 'super-bubble nature', involving every sector of the financial markets.[30] As a result, financial markets still register a lack of confidence and efficiency. The economic effects of the financial crisis are experienced, on the side of investors, in terms of confidence due to information asymmetry and agency costs issues, whereas on the side of managers and financial intermediaries, they are seen in terms of systemic risk and contagion due to moral hazard concerns. Establishing a new legal and economic order, namely a new 'paradigm' in financial markets,[31] has become a necessity, due to scepticism and distrust in each financial operation including, and, in particular, borrowing and bank or inter-bank lending.

Summing up, it can be said that the 2007–2010 financial crisis is the welfare cost of under-priced private debt, where the social consequences in terms of unemployment and human dignity have far overwhelmed the classic concerns of macroeconomic entities such as inflationary or deflationary processes. To this end, the notion of systemic risk has become vital for a correct understanding of financial markets today, but the lack of an agreed definition of systemic risk[32] can give rise to both dogmatic and practical issues in terms of governance of financial markets and prevention of epidemic spill-over effects. For this reason, the main feature that this research aims to highlight is the understanding of systemic risk as a product of the mispricing of financial risk, through which private actors who create financial risk do not internalise its cost but spread it on to society. In other words,

---

28 Rosa Lastra, *International Financial and Monetary Law* (n 9) 179; Jean Helwege, Caiyan Zhang, 'Financial Firm Bankruptcy and Contagion' (2013) *Midwest Finance Association 2013 Annual Meeting Paper*, 1, 3.
29 Indeed, the internationalisation of capital markets started with petro-dollar recycling in the 1970s, but reached its peak in the 1990s after the economic reforms of Thatcher in England and Reagan in the US. See Arnold, (n 22) 659; Ravi Tennekoon, *The Law and Regulation of International Finance* (LexisNexis 1991).
30 George Soros, *The New Paradigm for Financial Markets – The Credit Crisis of 2008 and What It Means* (PublicAffairs 2008) 100. In the author's view the super-bubble hypothesis 'could be used to create a comprehensive financial history of the post-World War II period, culminating in the current crisis'.
31 Ibid., 12.
32 Alexander Kern, Dhumale Rahul, Eatwell John, *Global Governance of Financial Systems: The International Regulation of Systemic Risk* (OUP 2006) 24–33. The Authors mention the work of Dow (2000) according to whom the concept of systemic risk deals with the failure of payment and settlement system or with a type of financial failure that induces a macroeconomic crisis. In addition, other studies (Cranston, 1996) have identified systemic risk as an inherent feature of international banking in order to include global systemic risk, safety and solvency risks that arise from lending activities, and risk to depositors through the lack of bank insurance.

this is a new connotation of financial risk as a form of negative externality, or pollution.[33]

Furthermore, systemic risk is connected to a construction of moral hazard that can be seen as an outcome of the financial market itself, in turn characterised by an expanding and overwhelming idea of 'privatised Keynesianism'.[34] This is because the possible collapse of private actors such as investment banks is potentially prevented by bail-out procedures carried out by governments in order to sustain stable mass consumption, necessarily based on the role of private actors within financial markets. This emerged particularly after the Second World War, and specifically during the internationalisation and globalisation of markets where private actors started to take financial risks and manage those risks in cross-border activities. As a result, the macroeconomy was no longer in the domain of government, but was highly influenced, and even determined, by private actors such as depositors, clients, private equity firms, investment banks and commercial banks. Indeed, in accordance with this theory of Crouch's, one could say that even a bail-in procedure, designed to mitigate moral hazard concerns among private market participants and substitute bail-out procedures as much as possible to make them a remedy of last resort, is rather a means to spread the consequences of financial risk between private actors such as senior bondholders and depositors, to make them – at first glance – responsible for their own appetite for risk. However, a bail-in procedure does not completely mitigate the social costs which are indeed spread onto the society, because the potential failure of a private actor indirectly shifts the responsibility for what is 'unreasonable' onto irresponsible individuals who use 'black swan' events as a justification.[35]

### 1.2.1 Risk and uncertainty

Among other objectives, this work aims also to theorise financial markets under a Luhmannian paradigm of system theory,[36] where the observation of markets defines them as financial systems. However, the most challenging aspect of theorising financial markets as financial systems is to explain the structures of those systems. Four main structures can be identified in the markets, namely risk, uncertainty, competition, and financial innovations. Therefore, it is useful to provide preliminary remarks on those structures and how they operate in financial systems, both in terms of closed and open systems.

As was suggested in the previous sections, risk is an immanent feature of the world, and it can be described under a 'human-humanity' paradigm. However, we must now contextualise risk within markets in order to

---

33 Ibid., 24.
34 Colin Crouch, *The Strange Non-death of Neo-liberalism* (Polity Press 2011).
35 Nassim Nicholas Taleb, *The Black Swan: The Impact of the Highly Improbable* (Penguin 2008).
36 Niklas Luhmann, *Introduction to Systems Theory* (Polity Press 2013) 26.

discover its ontological meaning in a more specific way. In finance, risk can be explained through the constant interrelation that shapes the structure of financial markets between savers (i.e. lenders) and users (i.e. borrowers).[37] The financial market is where the different assets of interest of lenders and borrowers are matched. Specifically, lenders aim to be risk-averse, whereas borrowers are essentially risk-takers, and they are more aggressive because they aim for profit.

For this reason, Knight's book 'Risk, Uncertainty and Profit' sheds new light in the context of financial crisis.[38] The book has always been recognised for its outstanding contribution towards a distinction between risk and uncertainty, namely between objective and subjective dimensions of risk towards a theorisation of insurable forms of hazard and true uncertainties. To this end, it is important to underline that risk is always a measurable uncertainty, so it is possible to state that the ontological discourse on risk represents what is knowable in principle or *a priori* by virtue of laws of probability. It is knowledge of objective facts that derives from the observation of a previous experience. Therefore, if risk and, in particular, financial risk can be identified on the past line, the importance of correctly pricing the risk in financial markets becomes a fundamental feature. Where the risk assessment of the borrower is not accurately based on its credit history, but on the possibility of fuelling a credit bubble, then irremediable inconveniences are likely to soar. A practical evidence of this theoretical circumstance was the before mentioned subprime mortgages crisis.

Therefore, the under-pricing of risk can affect the solvency *status* of the borrowers, create moral hazard, and in the last instance produce a welfare cost in relation to consumers-investors. In other words, credit risk cannot be taken without a previous evaluation of the past qualification of risk.

### *1.2.2 Competition and financial innovations*

In economic terms, complexity is associated with uncertainty. Something complex cannot be controlled, and therefore cannot be predicted. Essentially our need to reduce complexity is expressed in modern economies in anxiety to reduce economic uncertainty (for instance, after 2016, the UK government tried to prevent Brexit-uncertainty undermining market conditions, and the possibility of a no-deal Brexit). Indeed, reducing uncertainty makes things more predictable, and from an epistemological point of view the knowledge of uncertainty is based on the conception of a 'controllable' future. Nonetheless, the opinions and beliefs of investors about circumstances that might arise in the future and affect future events have revealed a subjective element of financial risk that is relative and conditioned to personal instincts. It is the

---

37 Valdez, Molyneux, (n 15) 2.
38 Knight (n 2).

necessarily unknowable feature of financial risk, as Keynes argued, due to the tendencies of erroneous perceptions of instincts.[39] It is the reason why financial markets are a beauty contest where the second-guessing observation of investors can turn them back into speculators who trade information ahead of market movements.

For this reason, it is important to take into account the role of uncertainty from an ontological point of view. Reducing complexity does not only mean reducing profit; as per Knight, uncertainty tends to underpin rather than undermine money creation processes. To reduce uncertainty means to reduce competition – that is the one feature or structure that makes each financial system adaptable. Indeed, competition has two sides: on the one hand, it represents the dark side of modern economies in relation to financial crisis or business collapse (for instance, if enterprises are not adaptable and innovative enough they are out of the market, or alternatively too much innovation can generate new financial risks that might be unsustainable), and on the other hand it creates innovation that makes the system adapt to a new environment. Indeed, if in a complex system – such as complex financial systems – the investor second-guesses the opinions of other investors, it means that the interpretation of information is relative, but could also lead to inefficiencies in the economic process because knowledge is fragmented. Despite such limitations, entrepreneurs can effectively take advantage of such inefficiencies and turn them back into opportunities. To this end, in financial markets we identify risk opportunities as the lost chances of profit. This is because uncertainty is deeply connected to profit, and at the same time the inefficiencies created by speculation represent an opportunity for the entrepreneur who can turn profit into an uncertainty absorption tool.

Therefore, complexity is a process, and competition leads on a free market's complexity in terms of identifying the right risk opportunity, profit from them and innovate the system. A practical instance of such a theoretical conclusion can be found directly in the protection of competition under Art. 3 (3) TEU, and Protocol 27 to the Treaty on the Functioning of the European Union on the Internal Market and Competition that aims to ensure equal opportunities for all market participants. Specifically, equal opportunities must translate into equal treatment under competition law and avoid the distortions of competition that can hinder opportunities for equal profit, as well as lead to outcomes detrimental to consumers.[40]

---

39 Please refer to Chapter 3.
40 As can be seen in this practical example the European Union seems to directly acknowledge the importance of competition and its fundamental role in terms of profit opportunities. See Walter Frenz, *Handbook of EU Competition Law* (Springer 2016) 12. Furthermore, a good panoramic of the contrasting opinions on the role of competition in the EU is well expressed through the words of Valentine Korah, 'The Reform of EC Competition Law: The Challenge of an Optimal Enforcement System' in Ioannis Lianos, Ioannis Kokkoris (eds.) *The Reform of EC Competition Law* (Wolters Kluwer 2010) 23. Nonetheless, EU

Competition has played a prominent role ever since the 1980s with the process of liberalising key economic sectors that were traditionally under state control, such as telecommunications, energy, transport, and postal services.[41] Such policies were also necessary to satisfy the changes that occurred in the international economic order after the collapse of the Bretton Woods system in the 1970s.[42] For this reason, the privatisation of financial risk that was allowed through investment banks in cross-border operations promoted risk opportunities through the absorption of uncertainty by virtue of profit-making processes.

It has been seen that in modern economies the income generation process is the main feature of markets in terms of uncertainty. Nonetheless, financial crisis represents clear evidence of the limits and negative outcomes that uncertainty can generate when is not managed in a responsible manner. Broadly speaking, the responsibility feature gives rise to two different questions, namely which entity should be responsible for preventing market failures and within which legal framework it should operate in terms of government regulation or self-regulating approaches.[43] Indeed, it has been seen that the lack of stringent financial regulation might have led to the 2007–2010 financial crisis,[44] although the post-crisis approach of tightening up financial regulation still fails to limit the inevitable systemic risk consequences of that same economic system, especially from the philosophical and theoretical point of view of 'privatised Keynesianism'.[45] In particular, Chapters 3 and 4 are dedicated to the study of forms of global governance[46]

---

competition law can satisfy at least three objectives, namely (a) the beneficial macroeconomic effect; (b) the beneficial microeconomic effects; (c) the 'integrationist' effects (in the sense of elimination of tariff and the creation of a customs union and common market). See Damien Geradin, Anne Layne-Farrar, Nicolas Petit, *EU Competition Law and Economics* (OUP 2012) 5. Such objectives as desirable and can create economic efficiencies see Simon Bishop, Mike Walker, *The Economic of EC Competition Law: Concepts, Application and Measurement* (Sweet & Maxwell 2010) 15.

41 Giorgio Monti, *EU Competition Law* (CUP 2007) 441.
42 Ross P. Buckley, *International Financial System: Policy and Regulation* (Kluwer Law International 2008) 3.
43 Saule T. Omarova, 'Rethinking the Future of Self-regulation in the Financial Industry' (2010) Cornell Law Faculty Publications Paper 1022.
44 Moloney (n 13) 1319.
45 Crouch (n 34).
46 The term 'governance' in modern international relationships is understood as a set of rules to address collective problems. Others define governance as 'the process and institutions, both formal and informal, that guide and restrain the collective activities of groups' (see Robert O. Keohane, Joseph S. Nye, 'Globalization: What's New? What's Not? (And so What?)' (2000) 118 Foreign Policy 104, 109). Furthermore, international relations scholars refers to the term 'international governance' as 'norms, rules, and procedures agreed to in order to regulate an issue area' (see Ernst B. Haas, 'Why Collaborate? Issue-linkage and International Regimes' (1980) 32 (3) World Politics 357, 380). These legal frameworks are studied traditionally from the point of view of state actors by focusing on the operation of rules in interstate relations. By contrast, the 'global governance' refers not only

where the role of non-state actors (such as promoters or sponsors in the case of SPACs) is capable of implementing self-regulatory regimes that are the result of the intertwining of public-sector bodies and private-sector actors. Indeed, in the post-crisis regulatory environment, and even more evidently in a post-pandemic scenario, the emergence of self-regulation enacted by private actors such as market operators and institutional organisations, and the expansion of 'regulatory networks' that are often criticised for their lack of accountability and legitimacy[47] are over-complicating the law-making process. Indeed, there is a need for a 'Global Administrative Law' capable of providing national standards traditionally governed by administrative law at the international level, thereby enhancing the democratisation of decision-making processes, protecting individual rights, promoting transparency and enforcing the accountability of 'regulatory networks' such as the Basel Committee on Banking Supervision.[48]

The main question is still whether the market and its operators can govern uncertainty and provide the economic system with reliable answers. However, as anticipated in the sections above, uncertainty, being a closed system, is one of the four structures of the financial system, and it directly relates to money-making processes. For this reason, the role of uncertainty must not be underestimated because it is a central idea for profit realisation, and it is important for the activation of a spontaneous mechanism of market re-generation (autopoiesis). However, we have seen that financial markets are also complex entities. This means that financial systems are open systems and communicate with their environment, although they are characterised by an operation closure by which structures of the environment cannot be imported inside the system.

This idea is challenging, and it gives rise to a new role for law-making where the system itself develops and enacts its own regulation. Specifically, the idea of fragmented knowledge is Ladeur's central point of assertion to recognise the end of a centralised stock of knowledge administered by the public state. As opposed to a Westphalian model of legislation (see Chapter

---

to state actors, but also to non-state operators working at different levels of the international system. This definition of global governance is opposed to the one of international governance. In this work I will deal primarily with the definition of global governance in this meaning.

47 Michael S. Barr, Goeffrey P Miller, 'Global Administrative Law: The Views from Basel' (2006) 17 (1) The European Journal of International Law 15, 16.

48 Benedict Kingsbury, Nico Krisch, Richard B. Stewart, 'The Emergence of Global Administrative Law' (2005) 68 Law and Contemporary Problems 15. The authors argue for the need of a global administrative law that refers to

> the structures, procedures, and normative standards for regulatory decision-making (...) that are applicable to formal intergovernmental regulatory bodies; to informal intergovernmental regulatory networks, to regulatory decisions of national governments where these are part of or constrained by an international intergovernmental regime; and to hybrid public-private or private transnational bodies.

4 of this work), modern society is characterised by the 'a-centric' creation of order, and no central planner is contemplated within this new globalised framework.[49] For Ladeur, this means recognising society as a 'network of networks' (a term he borrowed from Eli M. Noam).[50] In other words, society is no longer based on hierarchical forms of power, but on heterarchical relationships aimed at creating, rather than individualism, a spontaneous process of cooperation. For this reason, one side-effect of such cooperation is the establishment of a collective order which is the product of self-organisation behaviours in society; so the law becomes merely a secondary instrument of integration that is no longer characterised by its authoritative conception as a form of mediation of consensus. Furthermore, the law has a political connotation that is embedded into super-structures such as the constitution of states. In this example, the constitution represents a political instrument or declaration of rights that creates a super-structure within the legal order because the constitution represents the supreme law of the state, the source of legitimisation of every other legal provision in terms of the *Grundnorm* of Kelsen.[51]

In light of this, SPACs are financial innovations which can represent a first instance of self-regulation beyond governmental policies with the sole exception of the Korea Exchange and Turkey. To this end, first remarks are illustrated in the following sections. Nonetheless, it can be anticipated that the law must not govern the markets (i.e. uncertainty) or pretend to regulate risk, but rather construct manageable forms of market risk, capable of underpinning rather than undermining social benefits, in the name of a sustainable income generation process.

### 1.2.3 The post-pandemic scenario: Covid-19 and SPACs

A glance at the Security and Exchange Commission company filings shows a steady volume of S-1 forms in 2020. This happened in a year with an unprecedented fall in economic activity of 32.9% in the second quarter, caused primarily by Covid-19. The number of listings in the US is evidence of a recent re-emergence of these alternative investment vehicles which came into being in the early 1980s and then were almost forgotten. As of 1 November 2020, 172 SPACs transactions have raised about $63 billion in capital, with an average deal size of $367 million. Just five years ago, the corresponding number was 20 deals raising $3.9 billion, each deal averaging $195 million. By the end of 2020, SPACs raised a stunning $83 billion in capital. The moment carried over into 2021, with $115.6 billion raised via more than 400

---

49 Karl-Heinz Ladeur, 'The Financial Market Crisis – A Case of Network Failure?' in Kjaer, Teubner, Febbrajo (eds.) *The Financial Crisis in Constitutional Perspective: The Dark Side of Functional Differentiation* (Hart Publishing 2011) 78.
50 Eli M. Noam, *Interconnecting the Network of Networks* (The MIT Press 2001).
51 Hans Kelsen, *General Theory of Law and State* (The Lawbook exchange 1945).

SPACs in 2021, mainly on Wall Street where SPACs make up two thirds of all IPOs. Why are SPACs finally getting their share of attention?

SPACs are cash-shell companies set up, as their name indicates, with a special purpose: to conduct an acquisition. SPACs seek funds on the primary market through an IPO of unit securities composed of common shares and warrants. The gross proceeds net of an upfront underwriting fee, operating expenses and working capital, are put into an independent trust or escrow account until the acquisition takes place. Subsequently, once the SPAC completes the envisaged business combination or reverse takeover, funds are released. This phase is also defined in the specific SPAC jargon as "De-SPAC" or "De-SPACing", which will end with liquidation of the vehicle. Generally, the release of funds must occur within 24–36 months, depending on the exchange and the jurisdiction in which the SPAC is listed. In the case of a failure of the acquisition, the SPAC will be wound up and the funds returned to investors.

As we said, the SPACs' race started intensively from summer 2020, just a few months after the commencement of the pandemic known as Covid-19 in March. As of 31 July 2020, SPACs obtained $22.5 billion in financing. The month of July was an example of their growing importance. In fact, on 30 July 2020, Michael Klein brought his fourth SPAC, Churchill Capital Corp IV, to life on the New York Stock Exchange, raising £1.8 billion. Only a few weeks earlier, Klein's third SPAC, Churchill Capital Corp. III, which raised $1 billion in February 2020, announced a $11 billion merger deal with MultiPlan, a healthcare company. Similarly, on 30 July 2020, E. Merge Technology Acquisition Corp. announced a $500 million IPO. What was a year in the SPAC world a decade ago is now a month. For instance, in the year 2010, only seven SPACs were listed in the US. Between 2010 and 2017, the average SPAC IPO volume was about 13 (minimum 7 in 2010 and maximum 20 in 2015). Only in July 2020, there were 15 SPACs. This first set of data could intuitively suggest that SPACs are simply a financial invention that directly derives from the dryness of financial markets and the constant need for liquidity imposed by the pandemic. On the other hand, low interest rates and bonds' yields have definitively made equity investments in the form of shares and stocks more attractive to investors. Finally, once lockdown was imposed in several countries in the world and freedom of movement was restricted due to healthcare needs and emergencies, Zoom became the new tool to socialise and do business. It is not the case that what in the past took several weeks in roadshows at the pre-IPO phase could now be done simply behind a screen with a few clicks and virtual handshakes. This was a revolution in itself, and it definitively contributed to accelerate the SPAC process and increase exponentially the number of offerings.

However, these are only general remarks, and merely offer an explanation of the SPAC boom in 2020. A preliminary exhaustive answer rests in the fact that the ongoing surge in the public equity markets has been coupled with a long decline in the appetite for traditional IPOs. Public company multiples are at highs, yet the number of listed companies today is half of what it was in

1996, and IPOs are down 85% since then. This means that more companies are balking at the cost, hassle and uncertainty of the typical IPO process. SPACs and direct listings are starting to fill the void.

SPACs are a financial innovation capable of reshaping financial markets by providing especially start-up companies or unicorns (essentially, privately held start-up companies with a value of over $1 billion) with an alternative and sustainable way to be a public company without facing the high costs of investment banks' fees in a traditional IPO. Indeed, SPACs have an unusual structure in terms of underwriting discount. In a traditional IPO, underwriters typically receive a discount of 5%–7% of the gross IPO proceeds. In a SPAC IPO, the discount structure is for 2% of the gross proceeds to be paid at the closure of the IPO, with another 3.5% to be deposited into the escrow account and payable to the underwriters on closure of the De-SPAC transaction. On the other hand, in part due to the severe restrictions that a traditional IPO places on how a company may communicate its story, companies not yet producing revenues had been staying private for longer. SPACs changed this, and in the process became a way for amateur investors to be part of late-stage venture capital funding. Instead of only accredited professionals and insiders providing such funding to new companies, SPACs open them up to anyone – particularly in an era where stock-market investing has been made easier thanks to apps like Robinhood and eToro.

Those who prefer SPACs claim that these investment vehicles are a cheaper way to go public by avoiding the so called IPO "pop" (essentially, the IPO is usually under-priced on the first day of trading relative to what the market is willing to pay).[52] Furthermore, to list a SPAC is less time consuming (e.g. 8 plus weeks in the US) and a faster pathway to going public; finally, being acquired by a SPAC can quickly be transformed into an outstanding growth opportunity for start-ups. Indeed, it seems that the trend in Southeast Asia's tech, healthcare and fintech start-ups is to be reverse merged with a SPAC in 2021 or to set up one for themselves.[53] This is not only limited to start-ups; for instance, a very interesting deal was announced by Perella Weinberg Partners in January 2021. The boutique investment bank agreed to be acquired by a SPAC (FinTech Acquisition Corp. IV) in a $975 million deal, and listed on NASDAQ under the symbol 'PWP' in the first of half of 2021.[54]

---

52 Aliaj Ortenca et al., 'Can SPACs Shake Off their Bad Reputation?' (13 August 2020) Financial Times. Here it is noted that '[b]y using SPACs, [companies] can skip over the expensive and time-consuming IPO process'.

53 George Russell, 'SPACs set to surge in Asia-Pacific as tech unicorns prepare for IPOs' (22 December 2020), The Asia Time Financial, available at https://www.asiatimesfinancial.com/spacs-set-to-surge-in-asia-pacific-as-tech-unicorns-prepare-for-ipos, accessed on 5 January 2021.

54 Thornton McEnery, 'Investment Bank Perella Weinberg Going Public via SPAC' (30 December 2020), New York Post, available at https://nypost.com/2020/12/30/investment-bank-perella-weinberg-going-public-via-spac/, accessed on 5 January 2021.

Those first reflections can clearly show that SPACs are competitive financial tools that potentially put traditional IPOs at risk. One day they could replace the common IPO, entirely. SPACs represent a revolution from the bottom up that has allowed many companies to raise funds in a short time and without complex formalities, especially between 2019 and 2021 in the US. Surely, as we said, Covid-19 and low interest rates have made debt less attractive and have helped SPACs to soar to this end. The 'race to liquidity' has been grounded, but even more, SPACs' rationale as well as their sophisticated regulation in the US are a sign of their growing importance in financial markets. Covid-19 being only an external circumstance that has affected markets as opposed to an endemic factor of the financial system, it should be erroneous to simply associate SPACs with the pandemic. SPACs are not a product of crisis or the post-pandemic environment, and in this fashion I shall argue, they are not even a market trend. They are destined to stay, and they are a permanent feature of American exchanges (NYSE and NASDAQ) and new emerging listing venues such as the UK and Europe.

### 1.2.4 SPACs: risk-free investments

SPACs are risk-free investments, but the benefits may be high. First, the acquisition must be approved by a certain percentage of shareholders whose money may otherwise be returned at a possible expense to the SPAC sponsors.

Furthermore, if the management cannot find a possible business combination within the settled timeframe, then the SPAC must be liquidated and funds returned to investors. For example, in 2008, H.D. Partners Acquisition Corp. was dissolved after shareholders did not approve an acquisition, and in 2009, the board of directors of Highlands Acquisition Corp. approved a liquidation plan after the impossibility of finding a profitable business combination. The same risks are still present today. For example, L.F. Capital Acquisition Corp. extended its liquidation until the first half of January 2021, under a proxy solicitation that has been costly for the issuer, although it then ended successfully on 7 January 2021 when L.F. Capital Acquisition Corp. announced its business combination with L Andsea homes Inc. In theory the extension request can be made indefinitely; in practice, it is unrealistic to think that shareholders are always ready to back up the promoters' intentions under an infinite series of deadlines, unless a higher solicitation payment is made each time by the issuer.

Historically, the threshold to stop an acquisition was 20%. Today this percentage has been increased up to 95%. For example, K Road Acquisition Corp. had a 40% threshold, or Trian Acquisition I Corp. capped the amount of stock an investor could convert into cash after voting against the acquisition. Similarly, the management as founding shareholders can step in and buy the shares of investors in a tender offer to complete the acquisition.[55]

---

55 Please see Chapter 2.

Nonetheless, this can be costly for the sponsors or underwriters who may incur expenses such as offering fees or proxy solicitation. However, this can also show how terms have become more investor-friendly and less favourable to sponsors. In this evolution lies a part of the SPACs' success.

Finally, as we have anticipated in the previous sections, risk is an objective and immanent concept of the financial system that cannot be eradicated *tout court*. SPACs are non-operating companies; this means that investors do not have access to previous balance sheets, and the management's investment decision becomes the only valuable asset. This in economic terms is understood as agency cost and information asymmetry.

To find the target/s that could provide an envisaged return involves other underlying transactional risks which are present in any business acquisition. Indeed, compared to an IPO there is a higher theoretical risk of not closing, and conversely a higher risk of acquiring a low performance target due to time limit constraints on the side of a management which is compelled to complete a business combination within 24 months.[56]

## 1.3 SPAC: a new alternative to private equity

The main subject matter of this research fits into the economic turmoil of 2007–2010, where private debt and credit risk were the main catalysts of the crisis. In particular, the income generation process in modern economies has been tightened up with uncertainty by virtue of an 'entrepreneurial' instinct.[57] However, uncertainty cannot be regulated by financial law. The economic crisis of 2007–2010 and the post-crisis regulation is a self-evident example of such a conclusion. The SPAC is a form of investment vehicle that is financed not mainly by debt,[58] but by means of equity securities, namely units of common shares and warrants. Hence, for the avoidance of doubt, SPACs are not a product of the 2007 financial crisis, although they are a form of financial innovation that is one of the main structures of financial markets as financial systems. As we have seen above, SPACs are not a product of the Covid-19 crisis, but they are an alternative legitimate path to a traditional IPO.

For these reasons, it is briefly explained below how SPACs were developed through a self-regulation approach not centred on the notion of regulation *tout court*. SPACs are not currently regulated; they are an instance of investment vehicles born outside regulation and still operating beyond legislative borders. SPACs are – as I define them – financial products 'without law', but not 'outside the law'. Indeed, it will be seen in this work how corporate features governed by corporate law provisions still play an important role in

---

56 Please see Chapter 5.
57 Knight (n 7).
58 Johannes Kolb, Tereza Tykvová, 'Going Public via Special Purpose Acquisition Companies: Frogs Do Not Turn into Princes' (2016) 40 Journal of Corporate Finance 80, 84. Indeed, as authors point out debt is not the major feature of IPOs.

implementing the agreed international listing standards that constitute the only means to regulate SPACs, although they relate to national law provisions. Nonetheless, it will be explained how the implementation of corporate law provisions can diverge from the complete fulfilment of the agreed international listing standards. This can potentially affect the success of SPACs that are still dependent on the flexibility of national law provisions.

Furthermore SPACs, in terms of their financial innovation, are a part of those financial markets that are dominated by risk and uncertainty. For this reason, it is important to introduce the reader to the specific features of risk and uncertainty in relation to SPACs, and how they could be understood as manageable forms of risk-taking, where the income generation process that is based on uncertainty can be turned into risk. Traditional scholarship argues that SPACs are value destroying because of their potential failure to conclude a business combination. The economic literature is still searching for the exact role and description of SPACs, as well as very frequently questioning the merit of their existence. For example, Jog and Sun call them a home-run for management,[59] stating that SPACs provide outstanding returns for managers, but losses for everyone else. While Lewellen terms SPACs as a new asset class,[60] Mitchell and Pulvino[61] explain how and why they crashed during the financial crisis. Similarly, Jenkinson and Sousa[62] argue that SPAC investors should listen to the market, and Kolb and Tykvova label SPACs as "Frogs, not turning into Princes".[63] This is confirmed by Dimitrova, arguing that SPACs actually create perverse incentives.[64] All these scholars of economics are arguing that SPACs are value destroying, and they are usually seen as perverse incentives for the management, who pursue egoistic interests rather than maximising stakeholders' value. Hence, there is a compelling need to examine in the next sections some of the features of risk and uncertainty, as well as incentive for promoters, investment banks, shareholders, exchanges, and regulators.

The SPAC is not legally defined by statutes, decisions or capital market regulations, with the exception of Bursa Malaysia's current soft law regulation[65];

---

59 Vijay Jog, Chengye Sun, 'Blank Check IPOS: A Home Run for Management' (2007), available at SSRN http://ssrn.com/abstract=1018242, accessed on 18 April 2019.
60 Stefan Lewellen, 'SPACs as an Asset Class' (2008), available at SSRN https://papers.ssrn.com/sol3/papers.cfm?abstract_id=1284999, accessed on 10 April 2021.
61 Mark Mitchell, Todd Pilvino, 'Arbitrage Crashes and the Sped of Capital' (2012) 104 (3) Journal of Financial Economics 469.
62 Tim Jenkinson, Miguel Sousa, 'Why SPAC Investors Should Listen to the Market' (Digest summary) (2011) 21 (2) Journal of Applied Finance 38.
63 Johannes Kolb, Tereza Tykvova, 'Going Public via Special Purpose Acquisition Companies: Frogs Do Not Turn into Prices' (2016) 40 Journal of Corporate Finance 80.
64 Lora Dimitrova, 'Special Incentives of Special Purpose Acquisition Companies, the 'Poor Man's Equity Funds' (2017) 63 (1) Journal of Accounting & Economics 99.
65 According to the equity guidelines of Bursa Malaysia, a SPAC 'means a corporation which has no operations or income generating business at the point of initial public offering and

Section 6 (4) 15 of the Enforcement Decree of the Financial Investment Services and Capital Markets[66] of the Korea Exchange; and Section 4 (1) (b) of the Communiqué No. II-23.2 on Mergers and Demergers of Turkey, which provides a detailed definition of SPAC.[67]

The lack of definition is mainly connected to the SPAC's historical development and evolutionary nature. Historically, SPACs were developed in the US during the 1980s. SPACs were the direct descendants of the notorious blank check companies, which in that period dominated the securities markets. Blank check companies were investment vehicles listed on the Penny Stock Exchange and usually perpetrated frauds against retail investors. Blank check companies' main purpose was to attract the attention of investors by virtue of an IPO in order to raise funds and complete a business combination. The acquisition could take different forms such as a merger, a share and purchase agreement, or a reverse merger. From a legal nature perspective, blank check companies did not possess records of a previous financial history, assets or any operating business: they could be generally defined as cash-shell companies. Hence, investors were not provided with balance sheets or other forms of financial data in order to evaluate the investment risk (i.e. the information asymmetry issue). If a business combination was not carried out or the acquired company did not have a consistent turnover, investors would lose their investment. Such a result could lead to economic issues that could negatively affect capital markets' efficiency and investor confidence. Problematic issues included information asymmetry, moral hazard and agency costs. For example, managers were the only individuals who knew about potential target companies to be acquired. The information asymmetry between insiders and outsiders of the firm (i.e. managers and investors, respectively) generated two issues. First, agency costs.[68] Second, the consequent possibility of moral hazards, as the management was not under any form of control. It was likely that managers could act for their own best interests rather than inventors' interests.

---

has yet to complete a qualifying acquisition with the proceeds of such offering'. For further provisions in relation to SPACs in Malaysia, please refer to www.sc.com.my/legislation-guidelines/equity, accessed on 18 October 2016.

66 Section 6 (4) 15 of the Enforcement Decree reads that: '[A SPAC is] a corporation, the sole business objective of which is to merge the corporation with another corporation and issue the stock certificates through a public offering'.

67 Communiqué No. II-23.2 on Mergers and Demergers Article 4 (1) (b) published in the Turkish Official Gazette (28 December 2013 n 28865): '[A SPAC] is a corporation which is set up to find a suitable private target in order to make it public by virtue of a reverse merger' (translation kindly provided by Prof. Gul Okutan Nilsson from Istanbul Bilgi University).

68 Michael Jensen, 'The Agency Cost of Free Cash Flow, Corporate Finance, and Takeovers' (1986) 76 (2) American Economic Review 323; Michael Jensen, William H Meckling, 'Theory of the Firm: Managerial Behaviour, Agency Costs and Ownership Structure' (1976) 3 (4) Journal of Financial Economics 305.

Thus, the US Congress enacted the Securities Enforcement Remedies and Penny Stock Reform Act (US) on 20 July 1990 (PSRA 1990 (US)). The PSRA 1990 (US) was passed to protect investors, and definitively regulate the PSM. Specifically, the PSRA 1990 (US) amended, *inter alia*, Section 7 of the Securities Act 1933 (US) entitling the SEC to enact different rules in order to impose restrictions and disclosure duties on the blank check companies. The SEC adopted Rule 419, which compelled blank check companies to, *inter alia*, fulfil three main obligations. First, all the securities and proceeds raised during the IPO must have been deposited in an escrow account or held on trust, and the interests or dividends earned on the deposited funds could not be distributed until an acquisition had been carried out within 18 months, and the funds held on trust should have been released – in the measure of at least 80 % – in the case of completion of a business combination, otherwise the funds should have been returned to investors. Third, the shareholders should have expressed their consent to the proposed acquisition, providing that those who dissented had the right to rescind from their shareholders' position and redeemed their investment. Rule 419 was a first attempt to mitigate the economic issues at stake in relation to blank check companies. However, as a result, in the late 1990s the blank check companies slowly disappeared due to the onerous conditions imposed by the SEC.

Following the PSRA 1990 (US) and the sharp fall in blank check offerings, a new phoenix arose from the ashes: SPACs started to list their equity securities on other markets where the definition of penny stock did not apply, and therefore were exempted from the application of the onerous conditions of Rule 419.

At this stage, the illustration of the evolution of SPACs can point out at least two important concerns. First, the economic issues that characterised the blank check companies are still present today in the modern conception of SPACs. Second, the categorisation of the SPAC as a form of cash-shell company does not automatically assimilate these investment vehicles to private equity funds, although they are a *species*.[69] This is because during the time of the blank check companies, SPACs were financed solely by virtue of

---

69 Steven M. Davidoff, 'Black Market Capital' (2008) Columbia Business Law Review 175, 225. According to the Author:

> SPACs are a species of private equity: these are capital pools organized to acquire individual businesses. But because the general requirement that the initial acquisition comprise eighty percent of its assets, SPACs typically only acquire a single privately-held business. Despite these important distinctions, SPACs otherwise attempt to mimic private equity returns by employing comparable structures and practices. For example, SPACs utilize similar leverage to increase the size and potential returns of their acquisitions. The managers of SPACs are also typically provided twenty percent of the initial share offering at nominal amounts; ownership they are required to maintain until and after consummation of an acquisition. This ostensibly provides them with a similar incentive compensation scheme as private equity advisers.

equity securities and this trend, with partial exceptions, continues today.[70] Furthermore, from a legal perspective, it means that the applicable regulation of private equity funds does not apply to SPACs *sic et simpliciter*.

Therefore, at first glance SPACs are a new alternative to private equity.[71] SPACs are also a medium of engagement in late-stage venture capital initiatives for retail investors. Indeed, the traditional way to invest in innovation has been so far through private equity and venture capital. Late-stage venture capital (Series C, D, E, and pre-IPO financing rounds) provide a solid source of risk-adjusted returns when investing in innovation. Today, SPACs, can, *inter alia*, provide investors with access to companies during or equivalent to late-stage venture capital investment phase. Late-stage venture capital opportunities were historically available only to accredited or sophisticated investors. This means that innovation can be seen as a market segment in which investors want to invest, like bonds, commodities or stocks.

It is important to point out that there is currently no uniform European legislation nor any European secondary legislation that takes SPACS into account. This is the case not only in Europe but in every other legal system except Korea's and Turkey's. Therefore, currently SPACs lack a uniform and harmonised legal discipline. Indeed, since the publication of guidelines[72] relating to Directive 2011/61/EU on Alternative Investment Fund Managers (AIFMD),[73] the European Securities and Markets Authority (ESMA) has not provided any clarification in this regard until the public statement on SPACs made on 15 July 2021. Here, we do not find a definition of SPAC, but rather forward-looking pointers that European national regulators should follow

---

70 One exception is the Korea Exchange where the issuance of warrants is not approved by Korean securities law. In light of this, managers of SPACs are willing to buy convertible bonds rather than warrants. Nonetheless, convertible bonds are not purely debt securities, but hybrid securities and warrants. Furthermore, some SPACs financed the acquisition with facility agreements, but in this circumstance too, the level of debt has never been identified as a pure situation of leverage such as in private equity funds (see Stefan M Lewellen, 'SPACs as an Asset Class' (2009) working paper, Yale University 1, 5, http://ssrn.com/abstract=1284999, accessed 23 October 2016).
71 Steven M. Davidoff, n 28, 227.
72 ESMA, *Guidelines on Key Concepts of the AIFMD*, 13 August 2013, n 611.
73 Indeed, the Directive 2011/61/EU on the Alternative Investment Fund Managers (AIFMD) does not take into account SPACs as a form of Alternative Investment Fund. The AIFMD is broad in scope and covers managers of all varieties of collective investment undertakings other than Collective Investment in Transferable Securities (UCITS), ranging from securities funds to funds investing in illiquid assets (real estate, private equity, infrastructure or goods like wine or art). It covers all possible investment strategies and disregards the legal form or structure of the collective investment undertaking, whether open-ended or closed-ended, or whether formed under contract or statute. For this reason, the ESMA has raised the issue in relation to the application of this directive to SPACs (see ESMA, *Consultation Paper – Guidelines on Key Concepts of the AIFMD*, 19 December 2012, n 845, 33). Nonetheless, the market operators' responses have not resolved the issue and today there is still no agreed legal framework on SPACs at either a European or national level.

in evaluating SPACs' offerings (namely, this concerns specific disclosure duties to avoid conflict of interests on the side of the sponsors and to protect investors). Hence, the difficulty in categorising SPACs as investment firms under the AIFMD derives from their nature as cash-shell companies, namely their corporate structure, that implies their recognition as non-operating companies. For this reason, it would be limitative and indeed incorrect to simply define SPACs as financial intermediaries or pure investment companies, because they would be assimilated into hedge funds or qualify for the application of a bank-like regulation.[74]

Nonetheless, as suggested in Chapter 4, SPACs are a possible form of collective investment undertaking because they mainly resemble those market operators in terms of aims, fund raising and management control. Specifically, I shall argue that SPACs must be studied under a 'multilevel' definition.[75] It means that they can even be identified as financial intermediaries or investment companies, depending on the functions and aims they pursue. Indeed, SPACs can be used to finance the acquisition of vessels,[76] or to acquire private companies with the aim of listing them on the market, or to restore and save insolvent companies, etc. This is mainly a 'private' meaning of SPACs connected to their 'private' activities in terms of 'private' transactions mainly governed by private law. However, SPACs may still be studied in terms of their 'public' purposes, meaning that SPACs could promote welfare effects in society by virtue of buying credits against, for instance, governments or public institutions. This is a completely new application for SPACs, and it has not yet occurred, but it is not legally impossible, especially if SPACs are seen as 'social' vehicles for distributing wealth. However, in this work we will deal solely with a 'private' meaning for SPACs.

Having said that, a more appropriate definition for SPACs may be that of collective investment undertakings. SPACs are in fact cash-shell companies. Furthermore, they can be wound up, in the case of non-completion of a business combination within the settled time frame; they can be dissolved, in the case of a reverse merger with the target company; and they can be used solely as a financing tool and, therefore, serve as a means to increase the capital of the target company. The word 'investment' reflects the main aim of SPACs, which is to complete a business combination and provide investors with returns deriving from the completion of the acquisition. Therefore, although the risk associated with equity securities is theoretically higher from a winding up perspective[77] (i.e. shareholders are usually the last to be paid back in a winding up distribution procedure), practically this is avoided by means of the issuance of equity securities. SPACs are not financed by

---

74 Valdez, Molyneux (n 15) 242–253.
75 See Chapter 4.
76 Shachmurove, Vulanovic, Specified purpose acquisition companies in shipping (n 34) 64, 70.
77 Roy Goode, *Principles of Corporate Insolvency Law* (4th ed., Sweet&Maxwell 2011) 4.

debt securities in the same way as private equity funds that rely on heavy leverage. Hence, the possible distribution procedure under a winding up scheme can entitle the same shareholders to a full reimbursement of their original investment, although corporate law and insolvency law provisions in the country of the SPAC's incorporation can effectively reduce this possibility. The remarkable story of SPACs confirms their tendency to keep acting against debt. In this light, SPACs are alternative to private equity. It is this feature, based on equity securities issuance, that should be appreciated, rather than the risk associated with the acquisition of the target company. At the same time, private equity firms are looking at SPACs as alternative ways of investing (SPAC sponsorship) and disinvesting (exit strategies). Indeed, private equity firms and hedge funds have sponsored SPACs, and raised around $20 billion in 2020. The Gores Group and TPG have separately raised a total of $4.82 billion through 11 SPACs. Apollo raised $1.45 billion with three SPACs over the six months ending in January 2021. Private equity firms have been also active sellers to SPACs. For example, one of the 2020's biggest transactions involved Blackstone and CVC took Paysafe public in a SPAC deal worth $9 billion.

To this end, the idea that SPACs are dangerous investment vehicles derives from an erroneous identification of risk and uncertainty in their transactional activity. SPACs are borrowers, and SPAC investors are lenders, but the uncertainty usually associated with borrowers can be turned into manageable forms of risk, as is illustrated in the next sections, and therefore it becomes a possible measurable entity. For this reason, SPACs are alternative investment vehicles which could provide financial markets with new liquidity, as they did in the US between 2020 and 2021.

### *1.3.1 The sponsor(s), and the SPAC*

SPACs are on everyone's mind. Think about Bill Ackman and the record $4 billion Pershing Square Tontine Holdings SPAC, of industries such as healthcare (DFP Healthcare Acquisition Corp.), IT infrastructure (ACE Convergence Acquisition Corp.), energy (East Resources Acquisition Corp.), real estate (Property Solutions Acquisition Corp.), sports (RedBall Acquisition Corp.), FinTech (FinServ Acquisition Corp., and the SoftBank SPAC) and electric vehicles (VectoIQ Acquisition Corp., Spartan Energy Acquisition Corp.), and the list could continue indefinitely because SPACs are dynamic investment vehicles that can operate on a various range of industries.

As we already said, SPACs are companies that can be identified in financial markets under the category of borrowers in general terms.[78] Indeed, SPACs seek new funds on the markets in order to complete a business combination. Therefore, SPAC sponsors are immediately categorised under the paradigm

---

78 Valdez, Molyneux, (n 15) 2.

of uncertainty, as speculators, or simply as entrepreneurs, in the understanding of Knight. They are perceived as 'aggressive' because SPACs are trying to find investment opportunities through risk-taking activities and are part of the money creation process through the instance of uncertainty.

Once the SPAC issues units composed of common shares and warrants, in the US, SPAC managers or sponsors usually acquire 25% of the capital raised for a nominal value (often $25,000 which equals approximately to $0.0035 or $0.00435 per share as well as a reserved offer of founder shares for a symbolic par value per share, such as $0.0001). Usually, all warrants in a SPAC are tradeable and detachable until the moment of the business combination to make this appealing to investors, and especially, as some would like to claim, to hedge funds.[79]

The mechanism is simple: SPACs aim to make a private company public by virtue of a reverse merger or takeover. For this reason, some identify SPACs as 'backdoor listings'.[80] At merger time, the SPAC shares maintain their $10 nominal value. However, the real value drops due to dilution when the merger occurs. For all shareholders, dilution arises from paying the sponsor's fee in shares (called the promote, often about 20% of the equity of the new merged entity).[81]

Summing up, SPAC sponsors receive a promote which typically grants them equity in the SPAC equal to 25% of the capital raised or 20% of the fully diluted SPAC shares. This has been defined as sponsor compensation or sometimes, in a critical way, as the SPAC bonanza.[82] For example, Michael Klein made more than $60 million from a $25,000 investment in his founders shares in June 2020 (the merger between Churchill Capital Corp IV and Clarivate Analytics PLC). It means that the initial investment of $25,000 converts into a slice of equity of the newly merged entity when the SPAC finalises a business combination. The main reason to justify the promote has been its construction as compensation for the management's efforts in finding the target company and executing the merger. In other words, the promote is the 'skin in the game' of SPACs. Hence to eliminate the inclusion of the promote – as, for example, Ackman did – would create more complex financial structures that need to impose terms on investors, such as the lock limit on the detachability of the vast majority of warrants. This mechanism locks-in investors. Restrictions and impositions are not SPACs' friends.

---

79 Antoine Gara & Eliza Haverstock, 'How SPACs became Wall Street's Money Tree' (19 November 2020) Forbes, available at https://www.forbes.com/sites/antoinegara/2020/11/19/the-looming-spac-meltdown/?sh=7a6a529770d7, accessed on 20 March 2021.
80 Naumovska (n 15).
81 For example, Third Point sponsored in 2018 the SPAC Fair Point Acquisition Corp., which raised $500 million at $10 per share. Third Point received 20% founder shares for a nominal value of $25.000 meaning that if a deal close, Third Point receives $100 million of its shareholders' investment regardless whether the investment is successful or not.
82 Ortenca Alija et al., 'The SPAC Sponsor Bonanza' (13 November 2020) Financial Times.

Furthermore, this is not sustainable for most sponsors and it is not in line with a SPAC culture and established market practices where the risk distribution between issuers and investors is construed by virtue of risk management techniques. It is also fair to highlight that sponsors often invest further cash into the SPAC at the De-SPACing phase (for example, Mr Palihapitiya had to invest $100 million in Virgin Galactic at a cost of $10 a share when it went public). Sometimes sponsors decide to align themselves with the target shareholders by giving up a portion of their promote and only letting some of their shares vest at higher stock prices in the new merged entity.

To this end, a virtuous promote scheme necessarily must focus on concessions on the side of SPACs' sponsors to target shareholders in terms of performance. For example, Morgan Stanley has developed a new promote structure called a Stakeholder Aligned Initial Listing (SAIL) vehicle.[83] Instead of the SPAC sponsor receiving 20% of the equity of the vehicle irrespective of post transaction share price performance, the SAIL promote is entirely performance based. This system is able to connect the sponsor compensation directly to performance, much like a management incentive programme does, and can reduce the economic concerns of moral hazard and opportunistic behaviours on the side of management.

Finally, another example of virtuous promote scheme is the SPAC promoted by the British investor, Mr Ian Osborne. In May 2021, he has planned to launch Europe's largest tech-focused SPAC on Euronext (€400 million) to target European tech "unicorn".[84] The promote structure of this SPAC is unique. The sponsor initially purchases the 10 % of founder shares. Then an additional 5 % if stocks rise from an initial price of €10 to €20, €25 and €30 on a sustained trading basis. This is what it is meant to have a promote aligned to SPAC investors' expectations. Those are possibly the future market practices that shall be implemented by SPACs.

### 1.3.2 The underwriters

Special purpose acquisition companies have grown from being a niche part of the equity market to a popular alternative route to public markets. The investment banks pulled in over $3.4bn advising SPACs in 2020.[85]

SPACs are listed on the primary market, and an investment bank will assist SPACs in pricing securities, selling them and underwriting any security

---

83 Morgan Stanley, 'SPACs, an IPO Alternative, Explained' (6 January 2021), available at https://www.morganstanley.com/ideas/spacs-IPO-alternative, accessed on 30 March 2021.
84 Daniel Thomas and Miles Kruppa, 'British SPAC King Plans First European Blank Cheque Listing' (11 May 2021) Financial Times.
85 Paul Clarke, 'Banks rake in record $3.4bn in fees as Spac frenzy lures Shaqille O'Neal, Playboy' (9 December 2020) Financial News London, available at https://www.fnlondon.com/articles/banks-rake-in-record-3-4bn-in-fees-as-spac-frenzy-lures-shaquille-oneal-playboy, accessed on 4 January 2021.

that the investors cannot be persuaded to buy. Therefore, investment banks act as financial intermediaries to mitigate, or rather absorb, risk by advising investors with relevant information about SPACs. To this end, investors alone have limited knowledge of when a business combination occurs, and cannot predetermine whether that event can be characterised in terms of risk or uncertainty. In other words, due to the absence of previous balance sheets, the investors, who are the lenders, and therefore seek to stay risk-averse, do not possess any data or information to be classified into a group of instances where the laws of probability can measure the real risk in objective terms. We already said that SPACs have an unusual structure of underwriter discount under Section 1.2.3 above.

### 1.3.3 The shareholders

Time is not a friend of SPACs. The management has a limited time frame to find a suitable target company and the value that is created is dependent on the transactional aspects of the business combination.

Due to the cash-shell nature of the SPAC, investors can only bank on the managements' expertise rather than evaluating balance sheets. However, it is useful to remember that investors have access to a detailed description of risk factors described in offer documents and prospectuses (i.e. the S-1 Forms in the US). This also signals management expertise and the potential risks of not completing a business combination by taking into account market volatility, industry related risks, country-specific issues, business acquisition criticalities and the SPAC's blank check-company nature. Hence, several risks are disclosed to investors and they are susceptible of being assessed by them. Furthermore, as we said SPACs are risk-free investments until the moment of the business combination. shareholders' money are kept on trust or deposited in an escrow account at the moment of the business combination. This means that the uncertainty of not completing a business combination is counterbalanced by the possibility of redemption of the SPAC's shares for a pro rata amount of the escrow account.

Finally, the transactional risk is further mitigated at the De-SPAC phase too by PIPE investments. PIPE investors are frequently taken early on transactions, and they mitigate the risk of not closing a SPAC IPO. If the PIPE is already secured at the SPAC IPO, this can be disclosed in S-1 forms too in order to show a specific commitment not only on the side of the sponsors, but also especially from qualified institutional investors that already believe in the solidity of the business plan of the SPAC.

### 1.3.4 The exchanges and the regulators

Exchanges can also play a significant role in mitigating risk in SPACs. Indeed, where exchanges have put in place a sophisticated level of regulation by virtue of codifying SPAC market practices such as on the NYSE or NASDAQ, the SPAC market has soared. Exchanges work closely with the regulators, and in the US they have been able to develop with the SEC an important legislative framework for SPACs (please see Chapter 2).

European exchanges and regulators have not developed a similar legislative framework, although this is currently a work in progress on the Old Continent (see Chapter 4). In Europe, at the moment SPACs are less popular, and the main jurisdictions with the highest numbers in terms of SPACs are the UK with the London Stock Exchange and Italy with *Borsa Italiana* S.p.A., which is now part of Euronext Group. Indeed, Euronext is destined to become one of Europe's most important venues for SPACs (see Chapter 4). Those markets have seen a surge in SPACs in recent years, but nothing in comparison with the American equity markets in New York. This is due to a lack of specific regulation combined with a difficulty in modulating a reasonable redemption right for both the promoters and the investors (see Chapter 4).

### 1.3.5 Mitigating risk and uncertainty in SPACs

The qualification of a specified circumstance in terms of risk or uncertainty is subject to the frequency with which the event occurs, relative to the frequency of changes in the underlying causal structure. When calculating the probability of an event's occurrence, the stability of the underlying causal structure is fundamental. Indeed, if the underlying causal structure changes, it is not possible to predetermine the probabilities of occurrence of an event. In this case, estimating the occurrence of an event is based on estimating the change in the underlying causal structure. It is, in Knight's words, an 'estimate of an estimate' or 'judgement of a judgement'. This is the reign of uncertainty. Nonetheless, when the underlying causal structure is stable notwithstanding the time the event occurs, it is possible to collect evidence of the probabilities with considerable confidence. The estimate of an event's occurrence is only based on a fixed underlying causal structure that can be controlled. Thus, the estimate of an event is measurable, and it is a pure form of risk, as opposed to a pure form of uncertainty.

In relation to SPACs, the underlying causal structure is represented by the process of listing on financial markets and relates to the composition of the management, whereas the probability of occurrence of the event relates to the completion of the business combination.

Therefore, SPACs can be understood under the paradigm of risk because the underlying causal structure is usually stable; the way SPACs are set up follows essential corporate structure features which are usually implemented (such as the escrow account, the redemption right, the limited time period to perform the acquisition, etc.), but the probability of completion of a business combination depends on different factors.[86] At least two can be classified as

---

86 Johannes Kolb, Tereza Tykvová, (n 31) 84. The authors point out three variables in relation to SPACs' IPOs, namely market specific variables, deal specific variables and firm specific variables. The aforementioned variables are taken into account only from an economic

endogenous factors, whereas the other two are identified as exogenous factors. The real difference between those two categories is that while endogenous factors can be mitigated and potentially prevented through an effective conversion of the initial uncertainty into measurable risk, exogenous factors are usually unpredictable and their conversion into risk is much more complex, although not always impossible.

The first endogenous factor depends on management competence (i.e. the SPAC promoters). Here is the classic problem of separating decisions and accountability. At first glance, it seems managers are only in charge of making decisions on behalf of the company and take no risks, whereas investors, namely shareholders, are the ones who take the risk of those decisions, and by assuming responsibilities, they receive profit. Furthermore, theoretically, investors cannot exercise direct control over management. This separation is illusory, because managers, unless they are identified as promoters/sponsors of the SPAC, have usually been appointed by the same shareholders. Therefore, their competences are known and can be knowable *a priori*. Hence, shareholders are taking a pure form of risk instead of uncertainty, but only when appointing the board of directors. This is not the usual way SPACs come into being; SPACs are cash-shell companies, so the promoters/sponsors of SPACs are generally the same people who sit on the board before the IPO stage. For this reason, the competences of the management can be knowable only if managers are well-known in the industry; also, in this case the impossibility of being appointed by shareholders confirms a reading of SPACs under the uncertainty paradigm. Indeed, investment decisions taken by the management of the SPAC are based purely on estimates in the form of subjective, and therefore uncertain, opinions or judgements. Nonetheless, the apparent uncertainty can be prevented through market practices that enhance the credibility of the management.[87]

---

point of view. Therefore, this section aims to point out more substantive variables in relation to SPAC deals and transactions. However, in relation to market specific variables the authors sustain that

> SPAC acquisition are less vulnerable to turbulent market conditions than IPOs because SPACs already possess liquidity at the time of the acquisition. Thus, in turbulent market environments, firms may increase their chances of becoming publicly listed by looking for an appropriate SPAC instead of aiming at an IPO.

In addition, there is another variable in relation to the IPO market, namely the cost of debt. In such circumstance, SPACs, as has been highlighted, are not financed by debt. Therefore, this potential uncertainty is avoided, in the view of the authors. Second, the deal specific variable is also mitigated in the case of SPACs. Indeed, as the author illustrates, 'SPACs have cash available in the trust account, which they use to pay out the existing SPAC firm shareholders'. Therefore, as opposed to a common IPO, the IPO of SPACs can effectively represent a chance to 'cash out' some of the shares of the existing SPAC shareholders and provide them with liquidity. Finally, the authors, *inter alia*, examine firm specific variables such as the debt *ratio* and the cost of capital. The SPAC IPO is unlikely to target companies with high leverage.

87 The case of Bursa Malaysia and Korea Exchange are perfect instances of such trends that are particularly developed, respectively, as a form of standardisation of market practices

A second endogenous factor depends on the negotiation process through which the acquisition is made. This relates more on the side of investors/shareholders and on the shareholders of the target companies. Indeed, the profitability of the investment is based on the value of the acquisition of the target company. Nonetheless, the completion of the business combination is subject to opinions of the management and to the subjective approval of the shareholders. Thus, if it is true that the competences of the management are likely to be objectively evaluated, opinions related to the profitability of the future acquisition are subjective and cannot be controlled. Furthermore, the completion of a business combination especially depends on the decisions of other company's executives (namely, directors of the target company) who can act against the transaction and end the negotiation process (for instance, the signing of a letter of intent is not always followed by the signing of a share and purchase agreement, due to inconsistencies that due diligence might have discovered). This event also can be mitigated by pre-negotiations carried out before the setting up of the SPAC, although entering into an agreement, even in the form of a letter of intent, is always prohibited before the IPO process.[88]

Two exogenous factors can also affect the perception of SPACs under the uncertainty paradigm, but here their conversion into manageable forms of risk is much more complex. Indeed, the applicable law of incorporation of the SPAC can influence the underlying causal structure because it represents a further parameter with which the shareholders or future investors can evaluate the feasibility of corporate rights, such as the essential redemption right to be exercised by the shareholders at the time of, or after, the acquisition. Specifically, the moment at which the redemption right is exercised is essential to calculate the probabilities of completion of the acquisition, because when the redemption right can be exercised before the acquisition, it means that more shareholders can vote against the acquisition and therefore express a right of veto, whereas if the redemption right can be suspended at the time of the acquisition, and effectively be subject to the successful completion of the business combination, the shareholders' meeting is likely to approve the acquisition proposal without any obstacle. Furthermore, the possibility of a full redemption of the investment can also constitute an incentive for investors to exercise their redemption right in order to keep their initial investment safe, especially if external conditions have influenced the final value of the

---

and legal standardised regulation of the same. Chapter 4 of this work will be centred on the study of those different approaches in terms of international financial regulation of SPACs.

88 This feature is, for instance, expressly proscribed by the Korea Exchange. However, the signing of a pre-agreement before the IPO is also impractical because SPACs are cash-shell companies; therefore, a target company cannot consistently rely on the acquisition funds that are only raised after the completion of IPO and only if the majority of shareholders votes in favour of the proposed acquisition.

future acquisition.[89] For this reason, the event referred to as a redemption right and its applicable law can become a factor to be evaluated under the uncertainty paradigm. Indeed, in this case the underlying causal structure can change in respect to the applicable law of incorporation of the SPAC. However, the applicable law can be chosen by the promoters/sponsors of the SPAC or recommended by the same exchange (for instance, the case of the Toronto Stock Exchange). Therefore, this potential issue can also be kept under control.

Finally, external political events, the price stability of commodities and financial assets[90] as well as the business culture of the SPAC's country of incorporation[91] can effectively determine the successful completion of the acquisition process. In these circumstances exogenous events might be unpredictable (i.e. the negative effects of a political decision) or confirm the lack of remuneration deriving from the acquisition (i.e. the case of a SPAC targeting a company whose industry is experiencing a fall in prices, such as a drop in oil prices, energy costs and green energy incentives, etc.). These facts can effectively lead investors to change their views on the profitability of the investment, and consequently to refuse the acquisition proposal by rejecting it. Indeed, in such circumstances it might be more profitable to redeem the shares and conserve the original value, though with a small margin of profit. For this reason, it seems essential that investors should take a part of the risk acquisition process that cannot entirely be shifted to the management, otherwise there is no incentive in the investing activity. These exogenous factors are usually beyond the control of investors and can be prevented only if the business culture of the country of the SPAC's incorporation is consistent with the *ratio* of SPACs. For instance, an Islamic country such as Malaysia where the conception of risk (i.e. *Gharar*) is differently perceived in comparison to Western countries can effectively constitute an element to measure and pricing risk consistently under a different conception of risk-sharing.

---

89 See further for a practical example the case of Bursa Malaysia where the fluctuations of the price of crude oil have influenced the decision of the shareholders to vote against the proposed acquisition due to the loss of value of the proposed transaction.

90 Price stability is a concept that since the financial crisis (2008–2009) applies not only with respect to the price of services and goods, but also and especially to the price of financial assets. This is the new role of Central Banks to avoid negative monetary effects, but especially negative financial effects in terms of volatility of prices in financial assets. See Howard Davies, David Green, *Banking on the Future: The fall and rise of Central Banking* (Princeton University Press 2010).

91 The country of incorporation of a SPAC can be characterised by different business cultures. Think about the case of Bursa Malaysia that is an Islamic country where Islamic finance applies, whereas Western countries are based on a different conception of risk. See Daniele D'Alvia, 'Risk, Uncertainty and the Market: A Rethinking of Islamic and Western Finance' (2020) International Journal of Law in Context 1; Daniele D'Alvia, '(Legal) Uncertainty: *Takaful* between English Common Law and *Shari'a* Law' (2017) 10 International Journal of Law, College of Law, Qatar University.

40  *Against debt: the remarkable story of SPACs*

For these reasons, it is fundamentally important to convert uncertainty into risk by investing in information and risk analysis. This approach could effectively promote greater confidence in investors and shift the discourse on SPACs into risk. Indeed, although from a brief analysis it seems that the majority of features of SPACs rest on uncertainty, corporate governance mechanisms (i.e. management credibility, the issuance of warrants, etc.) can mitigate the negative effects of uncertainty and sustain a viable income generation process.

To achieve this objective and set up SPACs as effective tools to manage risk and to prevent them being under-priced, it is important to implement at least three main features which are currently being contemplated in only one instance of 'by-law' approach[92] (i.e. hard law) and quasi-regulation framework[93] (i.e. soft law). First, corporate governance mechanisms can provide investors with information; second, specific investment banks at the IPO stage can incentivise the mitigation process of transactional risks; finally, financial literacy can be promoted in relation to these investment vehicles to inform investors at the IPO stage. For instance, investors' guidelines issued by national exchanges might serve the purpose (see Malaysia and its Equity Guidelines).

## 1.4 Methodology

The work is following a dogmatic approach based on comparative law findings. Different jurisdictions are examined (US, Canada, Malaysia, Italy, UK, Korea, and Turkey) in order to discover similarities and differences[94] in the international financial regulation of SPACs. The comparative study and the selection of those jurisdictions are based on the fact that every legal system is providing SPACs with different legal frameworks that entail a distinct approach to regulation. Additionally, those countries are also taken into account based on the volume of SPAC listings, apart from Turkey which is considered only for its legal standardised regulation of SPACs similar to Korea.

The US has implemented a SPAC-friendly approach where the initial imposed features of compliance established by the SEC Rule 419 to blank check companies have been followed by a voluntary implementation of corporate standards that has subsequently been implemented in the regulations of exchanges such as the NYSE and NASDAQ. This regulatory approach has given rise to SPACs 2.0 (see Chapter 2). On the basis of the same model new regulations have been adopted, either in the form of soft law regulation (the Malaysian legal system), hard law rules in state regulation (the Korean Stock

---

92  It is the isolated case of the Korea Exchange that has passed a law to regulate SPACs.
93  It is the case of Bursa Malaysia and Toronto Stock Exchange through their Guidelines.
94  Hugh Collins, 'Methods and Aims of Comparative Contract Law' (1991) Oxford Journal of Legal Studies 396.

Exchange, and Turkey) or mixed/hybrid regulation (Canadian legal system). Hence, this comparative study shows a development of SPAC rules that transformed the 1980s blank check companies into SPACs, as well as a codification of listing requirements that after the SEC Rule 419 has contributed to the establishment of a modern conception of SPAC. Indeed, since that moment, every SPAC has been incorporated with specific corporate law features, such as the escrow account, to be set up at the moment of the IPO, a limited time frame to carry out the business combination (usually from 24 to 36 months), and the issuance of IPO units comprised of common shares and warrants.

## 1.5 Chapters overview

It has been outlined that a credit bubble was largely responsible for fuelling the 2007–2010 financial crisis. The high level of leverage and the possibility of obtaining funds at a low price (i.e. low interest rate) as well as the growth of shadow banking incentivised risky activities that were beyond the control of investors and financial regulators. Indeed, the low volatility of financial markets experienced before the financial crisis (2007–2010) represented a clear symptom of a future collapse, due to the unsustainable level of debt. In addition, the risk-taking activities of borrowers and the impossibility of effectively controlling the risk of their investments gave rise to inefficient behaviours such as moral hazard concerns and agency costs. Nonetheless, uncertainty has been and still is the main catalyst of money creation and profit maximisation, so it is not by chance that during the pandemic, uncertainty levels are higher. Consequently, despite the collapse of many companies, business opportunities have increased, and some actors have surely monetised those opportunities in SPACs.

To this end financial regulation, particularly international financial regulation, tried to limit the negative effects of a preannounced financial crisis in 2007. However, financial regulation is not the only answer, because the most important means to mitigate or prevent future crisis centres on the correct pricing of financial risk. Therefore, economics has gained an enhanced role in financial markets, and law has lost its appeal in regulating markets. The main evidence of this new trend can be seen in the post-pandemic environment where soft law rules and self-regulation are preferred to strict law mechanisms, especially in the field of insolvency law and restructuring procedures. Here, for instance, out-of-court settlement agreements with minimal supervision by the court are strongly preferred to in-court proceedings, where the debtor has to face the stigma of insolvency. Less regulation does not necessarily equate to less quality in the legislative framework. This is true for insolvency law as well as for financial law.

In this discussion, SPACs sit at the apex of two necessary assumptions: on the one hand, they have never been financed by virtue of the issuance of debt securities, but by means of equity securities, therefore, cannot be identified as a mere product of the 2007 financial crisis (namely, the history of SPACs can show enough evidence of continuously acting against debt[95]); on the other hand, SPACs can always be understood within the paradigm of risk and uncertainty in the entrepreneurial sense, although they present their own risks and uncertainties. Specifically, the underlying causal structure of SPACs, namely their corporate structure, is identified under the risk paradigm and is measurable, whereas the completion of the business combination is described under the paradigm of uncertainty due to the profit aspect of the acquisition. Nonetheless, such reflection cannot limit the possibility of transforming uncertainty into manageable forms of risk by means of corporate governance and by investing in risk analysis and financial literacy. Therefore, as opposed to private equity funds, SPACs can effectively represent a genuinely alternative form of investment vehicle and a specification of private equity. In the end, their restructuring of uncertainty through viable forms of money creation has also been mirrored in the self-regulatory approach of their quasi-legal regimes. Indeed, the fact that SPACs are 'without law' does not prevent them from taking risks and at the same creating their own market practices in order to implement a potentially sustainable money creation process.

For this reason, the work would like to study the origins of SPACs in Chapter 2 and analyse American regulation. Furthermore, the work aims at proposing a philosophical and sociological theory on risk and uncertainty in relation to financial markets by providing further discussion on Frank Knight and by theorising financial markets as forms of financial system in Chapters 3 and 6. A theoretical approach is carried out by virtue of examining the system theory of Luhmann and Ladeur (see Chapters 1 and 6). Additionally, the work illustrates examples of market failures such as Lehman Brothers or derivative markets, to provide the reader with a practical application of the consequences that can be derived from risk and uncertainty (see Chapter 4). For this reason, one of the main fields of research where risk and uncertainty can be measured in a practical way in terms of SPACs concerns the first remarks on the M&As activities of SPACs and their potential risk of litigation by reason of disclosure duties and director's conflict of interest (see Chapter 5). Final and consolidating remarks are provided in Chapter 6.

---

95 Indeed, the pricing of financial risk in SPACs does not occur through a risk assessment of the creditor in order to measure the rate of interest. To this end, no lending activity has ever been carried out by SPACs at the IPO phase, so that the application of the interest rate and its measurement is not material to our research. However, SPACs can ask for bank lending at the De-SPAC moment in order to finance part of the consideration price to complete the business combination.

# 2 Towards a definition of SPACs

Origin, limits and perspectives of SPACs in the US

## 2.1 The origin of SPACs: a US innovation

The Special Purpose Acquisition Company (SPAC) is defined by its name; it is a company which is set up for a special purpose to carry out an acquisition, or a business combination. Although the name contains a possible definition of the object of enquiry, its formulation does not fully outline the potential of this form of investment vehicle. It will be further explained in this chapter how the concept of business combination might be constructed with a broader meaning,[1] and how the special purpose could be limited by means of capital market regulations or national corporate law provisions (for instance, the articles of association of a SPAC could limit the aims of the special purpose by identifying specific industries in which the target company operates). Nonetheless, despite the impossibility of finding a comprehensive definition, it is important to remark that the primary definition of SPAC derives from its historical development and its evolutionary progress.

Historically, SPACs developed in America in the 1980s. They are the direct descendants of blank check companies,[2] which in that period dominated the securities markets. Blank check companies were investment vehicles listed on the PSM[3] and did not possess records of a previous financial history, assets or any operating business. In other words, they could be defined in general terms as cash-shell companies.[4]

---

1 Yochanan Shachmurove, Milos Vulanovic, 'Specified Purpose Acquisition Company IPOs' in Douglas Cumming and Sofia Johan (eds.) Oxford Handbook of IPOs (OUP 2017). Indeed, SPACs have registered a successful experience in the US in the shipping industry where they were mainly used as instruments to finance the expansions of shipping companies through the acquisition of new floats of vessels.
2 Daniel S. Riemer, 'Special Purpose Acquisition Companies: SPAC and SPAN, or Blank Check Redux?' (2007–2008) 85 (4) Washington University Law Review 931, 934.
3 Tim Castelli, 'Not Guilty by Association: Why the Taint of their 'Blank Check' Predecessors Should Not Stunt the Growth of Modern Special Purpose Acquisition Companies' (2009) 50 (1) Boston College Law Review 237, 244.
4 William K Sjostrom, 'The Truth about Reverse Mergers' (2008) 2 Entrepreneurial Business Law Journal 743, 756. The author clearly defines the features of a cash-shell company. Indeed, according to the Author a cash-shell company does not have an operating business,

Hence, investors were not provided with balance sheets or other forms of financial data in order to evaluate the investment risk. Such a circumstance gives rise to economic issues, namely information asymmetry, moral hazard and agency costs (the classic principal-agent theory), which have a negative impact on the general efficiency of capital markets, and specifically on the confidence of investors. Nonetheless, the principal aim of this chapter is to analyse the historical development of SPACs and the different forms of their regulation in America in order to theorise possible definition(s) of these investment vehicles.[5]

Examining the evolution of SPACs includes the benefit of outlining listing standards that specifically constitute the corporate structure of SPACs and are at the same time the subject matter of a standardisation by market practices or of legal standardised regulations.

### 2.1.1 The Rule 419 under the SEC Regulation

In the 1980s, the PSM in America was dominated by fraud and the manipulation of asset prices, which had a negative influence on trading practices in penny stocks offerings, because the primary capital market was basically not regulated, and broker firms were usually unscrupulous associations which only pursued their economic interests in the course of share trading in the secondary markets.

Blank check companies were listed on the PSM[6], which was a non-exchange venue. Hence, it did not impose pre-trade transparency or basic listing requirements on the issuers of securities. This made the market a fertile playground for the cash-shell companies' game, so the blank check companies were soon referred to as the 'most notorious method for committing penny stock fraud'.[7]

Blank check companies were cash-shell companies, namely companies without any operating business, so they did not provide investors with any financial data. The main purpose of a blank check company was to be listed on the PSM in order to raise funds, through an IPO, and complete a business combination with an unidentified target company. At the IPO stage

---

and its securities are not necessarily listed on a capital market. Furthermore, He correctly argues that cash-shell companies are a special form of investment companies, without a previous operating business, and they usually trade securities on the capital markets in order to complete acquisitions by virtue of a merger or a reverse merger.

5 In this Chapter, we are examining only the US regulation of SPACs, for an international view point please refer to Chapter 4 of this work.
6 Shachmurove, Vulanovic (n. 1). Indeed, according to the authors the first instance of SPACs is found in the 18th century in England where 'blank checks were first mentioned as blind pools during the infamous South Sea Bubble'.
7 Castelli (n 3) 246.

the management of the blank check companies did not sell their securities directly to retail investors, but to condescending brokerage firms. Subsequently, the brokers misled the investors about a possible imminent acquisition or just circulated official statements, according to which the blank check company had merged with an important operating company with profitable turnovers. This circumstance contributed to exaggerating the price of the issued securities and it attracted new retail investors. At that point, the managers of the blank check company and the brokers sold their securities and caused a collapse of the market in relation to the price of equity and to the value of the firm with high returns for their investment portfolios. In other words, they committed fraud against investors who did not possess enough information to assess their financial risk, and who just trusted the information provided by the broker firms.

At this stage, it is important to highlight two different risk factors for investors:

- the first concerns an economic issue, which is defined as information asymmetry and is related to the legal nature of these investment companies (i.e. cash-shell companies); and
- the second relates to the legal framework which did not provide investors with any protection. Indeed, in the 1980s there were neither legal instruments nor a sophisticated legal framework to protect investors from the frauds that were often perpetrated by blank check companies.

In 1988 Mary L. Shapiro, Commissioner of the United States Securities and Exchange Commission defined the PSM and its investment vehicles as a dangerous tool in the following terms:

> (…) Many penny stocks represent legitimate investment opportunities, and the market for these stocks is an honest one. However, experience has shown that many other penny stocks are used in fraudulent schemes which involve "shell" companies with no operating history, few employees, few assets, no legitimate prospects for business success, and markets that are manipulated to the benefit of the promoters of the companies and/or the market professionals involved.[8]

Another negative opinion of blank check offerings was expressed a year later by the North America Securities Administrators Association, which strongly

---

8 Mary L. Shapiro, Seeking New Sanctions: Comments on Developments in the Commission's Enforcement Program (1990), http://www.sec.gov/news/speech/1990/030990schapiro.pdf, accessed on 1 January 2021.

argued that the blank check companies were a *per se* fraudulent investment tool:

> (...) blank check blind pool offerings are inherently defective because of failure to disclose material facts concerning the offering and issuer, and such offerings have been the subject of pervasive, recurrent abusive and fraudulent practices in the sale of securities, (...) the Association declares that the sales of blank check blind pool securities *per se* constitute fraudulent business practices[9]

The US Congress therefore enacted the Securities Enforcement Remedies and Penny Stock Reform Act[10] (US) on 20 July 1990. The PSRA 1990 (US) was passed to protect investors, and definitively regulate the PSM.

The PSRA 1990 (US) read for the first time a definition for penny stocks in Section 3 (a) of the Securities Exchange Act 1934 (US), which was further implemented by virtue of Rule 3a51-1 of the SEC.[11] Specifically, a company would be entitled to issue equity securities (i.e. penny stocks) if – *inter alia* – they had an authorised share capital value not exceeding $5 million, and the company had no less than a three-year financial history with a minimum net income of $750,000. Thus, the scope of the PSRA 1990 (US) was to define the content of penny stocks, the legal nature of the companies operating on the PSM, and to fix a minimum cap in relation to the authorised share capital.

Additionally, the PSRA 1990 (US) amended, *inter alia*, Section 7 of the Securities Act 1933[12] (US) entitling the SEC to enact different rules in order to impose restrictions and disclosure duties to the blank check companies.

The SEC adopted the famous Rule 419,[13] by which blank check companies that were issuing penny stocks as defined in Rule 3a51-1 of the SEC were, *inter alia*, compelled to fulfil three main obligations:

- first, all of the securities and proceeds raised during the initial public offering should have been deposited in an escrow account or held on trust, and the interests or dividends earned on the deposited funds could not be distributed until an acquisition was completed;

---

9 The North American Securities Administrators Association, *Resolution of the North American Securities Administrators Association, Inc., Declaring Blank Check Blind Pool Offerings to be Fraudulent Practices* (Cm 7032, 1989). Nonetheless, it should be noted that the statement made by NASAA in 1989 that described the blank check companies as a fraudulent instrument *per se* can be misleading. Indeed, a company can never become a fraudulent instrument *per se* unless unscrupulous managers direct it. Therefore, this severe judgement on blank check companies is connected to a strict policy adoption and political justification, which aimed to avoid frauds and solve an urgent risk of market collapse in the Penny Stock Market.
10 Securities Enforcement Remedies and Penny Stock Reform Act of 1990, Pub. L. 101–429, Oct. 15, 1990, 104 Stat. 931.
11 Title 17, ch. II, C.F.R. § 240.3A51-1.
12 Securities Act of 1933, May 27, 1933, ch. 38, title I, 48 Stat. 74 (15 U.S.C. 77a *et seq.*).
13 57 F.R. 18043, April 28, 1992; see Title 17, ch. II, C.F.R. § 230.419.

- second, the acquisition should have been carried out within a very short period (i.e. 18 months), and the funds held on trust should have been released – in the measure of at least 80% – in the case of completion of a business combination, otherwise the funds should have been returned in full to investors;
- finally, shareholders should have expressed their consent to the proposed acquisition, providing that those who dissented had the right to rescind from their shareholder position and receive the funds, interests or dividends of a pro rata aggregate amount of the securities held on trust (i.e. conversion right).

As a result, in the late 1990s the blank check companies slowly disappeared, due to the onerous conditions imposed by the SEC in Rule 419 and on the basis that cash-shell companies without any form of financial data were definitively forbidden from listing on the PSM (indeed, the SEC required at least one or two years of net incomes of at least $750,000).

## 2.2 From blank check companies to modern SPACs

Following the PSRA 1990 (US), and the sharp fall of blank check offerings, a new phoenix arose from the ashes with the name of Special Purpose Acquisition Company.

SPACs were exempted from the application of Rule 419 because they started to issue securities through IPOs, which did not fit into the definition of penny stocks (i.e. authorised share capital less than $5 million, etc.[14]), and they started to be listed on capital markets with less strict listing requirements, such as the Over-the-Counter Bulletin Board and the American Stock Exchange. Hence, they were subject to common provisions, which generally governed the initial public offerings in the US.[15] These first IPOs have been defined as a "(…) first generation of SPACs".[16]

However, the aforementioned SPACs voluntarily complied with the conditions set forth in Rule 419 in order to prioritise the confidence of investors. Indeed, SPACs were used to deposit the securities and proceeds of the IPO in an escrow account until the acquisition was completed, and they provided investors with a conversion right (namely, the right to convert securities into

---

14 See further in the previous Section 2.1.1.
15 Currently, SPACs in the US have only to file the following statements: a registration statement (Form S-1) with the SEC at the time of the IPO, then the information relating to the IPO are recorded in the final prospectus (Form B423), subsequently immediately after the IPO the SPAC issues another statement to disclose the amount of the fund raised on the capital market (Form 10-Q), and, finally, to announce a business combination (Form 8-K and 425).
16 Riemer (n 2) 944, specifically he referred to them as of 'first generation SPACs'. Indeed, the voluntary compliance with the Rule 419 was an original invention of Mr. David Nussbaum, Chairman of GKN Securities.

cash if the shareholders voted against the proposed acquisition). This was an example of 'self-imposed SPAC restrictions'.[17]

Furthermore, new 'self-imposed' features were implemented within this 'first generation' of SPACs:

- Important and well-known managers were used to direct them.[18]
- The equity securities could be traded even before the completion of a business combination (i.e. this feature provided investors with liquidity and with a specific form of way out from the investment).
- The time frame to carry out an acquisition was extended to 24 months (i.e. usually 18 months to announce a business combination and to sign a possible letter of intent, in addition to six months for the closing).
- The articles of association pre-established the potential sectors and industries of the target companies to be acquired.[19]

Hence, the voluntary compliance with Rule 419 and the implementation of new features made SPACs an attractive investment tool. This historical event also contributes to the development of a modern conception of SPACs different from the previous ones which had been based on fraudulent practices (i.e. blank check companies). This circumstance created a 'SPAC identity' in relation to their corporate structure and listing requirements that would have been adopted with slight modifications by other US capital markets regulations.

The following table reports the principal features of this first generation of SPACs. In addition to the old requirements imposed by Rule 419, new features are highlighted in bold:

### First Generation SPACs

*Classic provisions of the Rule 419 Framework*

| | |
|---|---|
| Escrow account or trust | Funds raised at the time of IPO must be held on trust or in an escrow account |
| **Time for acquisition** | **Twenty-four months otherwise an automatic winding up procedure of the company is commenced** |
| Funds release | At least 80% of the funds are released at the time of the acquisition |
| Conversion right | Can be exercised without any limitation by the shareholders at the time of the acquisition |

---

17 Castelli (n 3) 254.
18 Because it has been stated that SPACs are cash-shell companies, in this fashion the management at the time of the IPO is the only valuable 'asset' for the potential investors. Hence, the competences and the high expertise of the management are vital and they represent a key factor for the success of the SPAC both in terms of investor protection and successful completion of the business combination.
19 Riemer (n 2) 946.

*New features of first generation of SPACs*

| | |
|---|---|
| Management | High expertise and great reputation in terms of selecting the right target companies |
| Articles of association | Determination of the main industries in which the potential target companies operate |
| Investment way out | Shareholders could sell their shares even before the completion of a business combination |

### 2.2.1 Modern SPACs in the US: the listing standards

The American capital markets have evolved since the PSRA 1990 (US). SPACs have seen growth in America since 2003.[20]

In 2008, the NASDAQ[21] and NYSE[22] issued a proposal to allow the listing of SPACs on their financial markets. Until then, SPACs were not listed on those regulated capital markets, but only on the OTC Bulletin board and the AMEX,[23] namely capital markets with less strict and generic listing requirements.[24] In the end, the SEC approved the proposals and the SPACs started then to be listed on the NASDAQ[25] and the NYSE.[26]

The listing rules of the NYSE have always required listing companies to be operating businesses. By contrast, the current provision 102.6 of the Listing Company Manual entitles a SPAC, in other words a cash-shell company without a previous financial history, to be listed for the first time. However, the NYSE is still not open to the listing of every SPAC that starts an IPO. Indeed, specific minimum requirements have to be met, and the NYSE will

---

20 Milan Lakicevic, Milos Vulanovic, 'A story on SPACs' (n 1) 388; Carol Boyer, Glenn Baigent, 'SPACs as Alternative Investments: An Examination of Performance and Factors that Drive Prices' (2008) 11 (3) The Journal of Private Equity 8, 11.
21 Securities and Exchange Commission, *Self-Regulatory Organizations; The NASDAQ Stock Market LLC; Notice of Filing and Immediate Effectiveness of a Proposed Rule Change to Adopt New Regulatory Fees Payable by Certain Listed Companies and Applicants* (Cm 34–70627, 2008).
22 Securities and Exchange Commission, *Self-Regulatory Organizations; New York Stock Exchange LLC; Notice of Filing of Proposed Rule Change to Adopt New Initial and Continued Listing Standards to List Purpose Acquisition Companies* (Cm 34–57499, 2008).
23 The American Stock Exchange now is known as NYSE MKT LLC. Indeed, AMEX has been purchased by NYSE Euronext in 2008 and renamed NYSE MKT in 2012. It is a financial market mainly designed to support younger, high-growth companies, and it is currently in the U.S. the leading exchange for small-cap companies.
24 Castelli (n 3) 238.
25 Securities and Exchange Commission, *Self-Regulatory Organizations; The NASDAQ Stock Market LLC; Notice of Filing of Amendment No.1 and Order Granting Accelerated Approval to Proposed Rule Change, as modified by Amendment No. 1, to Adopt Additional Initial Listing Standards to List Securities of Special Purpose Acquisition Companies* (Cm 34–58228).
26 Securities and Exchange Commission, *Self-Regulatory Organizations; New York Stock Exchange LLC; Order Approving Proposed Rule Change to Adopt New Initial and Continued Listing Standards to List Securities of Special Purpose Acquisition Companies* (Cm 34–57785, 2008).

exercise broad discretion on a 'case-by-case' basis.[27] In accordance with provision 102.6, an 'acquisition company', namely a SPAC, must fulfil different parameters in order to be listed on the NYSE. The principal features required by this exchange are summarised in the following table.

*NYSE – Rule 102.6 Listing Company Manual*
*Acquisition Companies*

| | |
|---|---|
| Escrow account or trust | At least 90% of the proceeds must be held in an escrow account |
| Time for acquisition | 36 months otherwise an automatic winding up procedure of the company is commenced |
| Fund release | At least 80% of the proceeds held on trust at the time of the acquisition otherwise the funds are returned in full to investors |
| Conversion right | Until the completion of a business combination (namely, 36 months) a shareholder voting against a business combination is entitled to exercise a conversion right if does not hold less than 10% of the shares together with any affiliate of such shareholder or any person with whom such shareholder is acting as a 'group'. The conversion right is the right to convert common shares into a pro rata share of the aggregate amount held in the escrow account.<br>The SPAC is prevented from carrying out an acquisition in the case of exercise of a conversion right by a shareholder who holds no less than 40% of the share capital |

Almost the same rules apply with reference to the NASDAQ, which regulates the SPAC offerings under Section IM-5101-2 of the NASDAQ listing rules ('Listing of Companies Whose Business Plan is to Complete One or More Acquisitions'). It is interesting to highlight that the NASDAQ clearly points out on the NYSE model a non-operating company such as a SPAC is not considered to be a common listing feature. However, if the SPAC complies with the NASDAQ listing rules, it can seek a listing on this regulated exchange.

---

27 The NYSE in assessing the listing of a SPAC will take into account a set of conditions that are set forth in rule 102.6 of the Listing Company Manual such as:

> the experience and track record of management; the amount of time for the completion of the business combination prior to the mandatory dissolution of the acquisition company; the nature and extent of management compensation; the extent of management's equity ownership in the acquisition company and any restrictions on management's ability to sell acquisition company stock; the percentage of the contents of the trust account that must be represented by the fair market value of the business combination; the percentage of voting publicly-held shares whose votes are needed to approve the business combination; the percentage of the proceeds of sales of the acquisition company's securities that is placed in the trust account; and such other factors as the Exchange believes are consistent with the goals of investor protection and the public interest.

The only difference from NYSE rules is that the majority of shareholders and independent directors must approve the business combination. Therefore, a specific corporate governance feature is introduced in terms of independent directors' approval. Furthermore, the SPAC must also comply with the NASDAQ corporate governance requirements for listed companies (see Section IM-50101-1), and each SPAC must meet the conditions set forth in Section IM-5101-2 for each completed business combination.

The table below summarises the main features of the NASDAQ listing rules that are similar to the NYSE's rules and reports in bold the new specific features in terms of corporate governance requirements:

| NASDAQ – Rule IM-5101-2 | |
| --- | --- |
| Escrow account or trust | At least 90% of the proceeds must be held in an escrow account |
| Time for acquisition | 36 months otherwise an automatic winding up procedure of the company is commenced |
| Fund release | At least 80% of the proceeds held on trust at the time of the acquisition (excluding any deferred underwriters fees and taxes payable on the income earned on the escrow account) |
| Conversion right | Until the completion of a business combination (namely, 36 months) a shareholder voting against a business combination is entitled to exercise a conversion right if does not hold less than 10% of the shares together with any affiliate of such shareholder or any person with whom such shareholder is acting as a 'group'. The conversion right is the right to convert common shares into a pro rata share of the aggregate amount held in the escrow account |
| **Redemption right** | **Until the completion of a business combination the company has to provide all shareholders with the opportunity to redeem their shares for cash equal to their pro rata share of the aggregate amount held in the escrow account in accordance with Rule 13e-4 and Regulation 14E under the Securities and Exchange Act of 1934** |
| **Approval of the business combination** | **Any business combination has to be approved by a majority of the independent directors of the company** |

Finally in November 2010, the NYSE AMEX (known today as NYSE MKT LLC) adopted similar listing rules in relation to SPACs. The NYSE AMEX underlines that the exchange does not contemplate the possibility of listing a cash-shell company unless specific conditions set out in the NYSE AMEX Company Guide are fulfilled under Section 119 of the 'Listing of companies whose business plan is to complete one or more acquisitions'. A listing company must comply with the corporate governance requirement of part eight of the NYSE AMEX Company Guide.

Here below the main terms and conditions of listing requirements are summarised:

| NYSE AMEX (NYSE MKT LLC) – Rule 119 NYSE AMEX Company Guide | |
|---|---|
| Escrow account or trust | At least 90% of the proceeds must be held in an escrow account |
| Time for acquisition | 36 months otherwise an automatic winding up procedure of the company is commenced |
| Fund release | At least 80% of the proceeds held on trust at the time of the acquisition otherwise the funds are returned in full to investors |
| Conversion right | Until the completion of a business combination (namely, 36 months) a shareholder voting against a business combination is entitled to exercise a conversion right if does not hold less than 10% of the shares together with any affiliate of such shareholder or any person with whom such shareholder is acting as a 'group'. The conversion right is the right to convert common shares into a pro rata share of the aggregate amount held in the escrow account |
| Redemption right | Until the completion of a business combination the company has to provide all shareholders with the opportunity to redeem their shares for cash equal to their pro rata share of the aggregate amount held in the escrow account in accordance with Rule 13e-4 and Regulation 14E under the Securities and Exchange Act of 1934 |

### 2.2.2 SPACs 2.0

As we said, in the 1980s, SPACs were named 'blank check companies', and they were listed on the PSM where they performed 'pump-and-dump' schemes. Consequently, the SEC issued Rule 419 and the US Congress enacted the PSRA in 1990. Minimum regulation standards were imposed, and IPO funds had to be held on trust until the completion of the business acquisition or combination; the acquisition period was settled at 18 months; and dissenting shareholders were entitled to a redemption right. As a result, blank check companies disappeared from the PSM. They re-appeared in 2003, first on unregulated venues such as the OTC, next on AMEX and then on regulated markets such as the NYSE and NASDAQ. SPACs on those markets did not issue penny stocks, but they complied voluntarily with rules such as Rule 419, the escrow account rule, the requirement of minimum capitalisation, etc. This evolution was incorporated in 2008 into listing regulations, both at the NYSE (Rule 102.06) and the NASDAQ (Rule IM-5101-2), and in 2010 by NYSE AMEX (Section 119). This is referred to as SPAC 2.0.

### 2.2.3 SPACs 3.0 and 3.5, and evolutionary trends

Since 2015, SPACs have developed diverse evolutionary transactional trends, such as the decoupling of the right to vote from the redemption right. This practice was first introduced in early 2010 with the SPAC GSME Acquisition Partners I (GSME) by Douglas Ellenoff. When in discussion with the SEC, he succeeded in getting GSME to consent to apply the decoupling mechanism. Indeed, in connection with the De-SPAC phase, SPACs are required to offer shareholders the right to redeem their public shares for a pro rata portion of the proceeds held on trust. This was originally reserved only for shareholders who voted against a proposed business combination. Since 2015, SPACs have offered the ability to every shareholder to redeem their public shares by virtue of a mandatory redemption offer. This does not apply to warrants. It means that investors can now vote in favour of or against a business acquisition or combination, are still able to redeem their shares, and need only keep the warrant. This shift in practice can be referred to as SPAC 3.0. In fact, it is not by chance that in 2015, 19 SPACs completed IPOs, raising $ 3.6 billion in a 120% increase over the amount raised in SPAC IPOs in 2014, and seven more registered (for example, Double Eagle Acquisition Corp completed an IPO that raised $480 million, and Pace Holdings Corp completed an IPO that raised $400 million).

Between 2019 and 2020 the fractional warrant practice become more regular, despite its introduction in 2007 through the Liberty Acquisition Corp. SPAC. This means that each single whole warrant entitles the holder to purchase one common share and each unit is composed of one share and a fraction of one warrant. This is an incentive to buy more shares, thus to be entitled to one full warrant and an extra share. It is a consolidation of the share capital of the SPAC. The same trend is followed today in 2020 by Ascendant Digital Acquisition Corp., which issued half of one warrant, followed by similar structures with similar or different warrant percentages that have been adopted within the capital structure of DFP Healthcare Acquisition Corp., Go Acquisition Corp., Malacca Straits Acquisition Corp, HPX Corp., D8 Holdings Corp. and Jaws Acquisition Corp. This can be seen as SPAC 3.5.

SPAC 3.0 and SPAC 3.5 models add remarkably distinctive features to the original model that is still codified in NYSE and NASDAQ rules (SPAC 2.0). The table below summarises the evolutionary transactional trends in the SPAC spectrum:

*Evolutionary transactional trends in SPACs*

| | |
|---|---|
| SPAC 2.0 | Abide by SEC's Rule 419 (80% funds held on trust, redemption rights for shareholders, etc.) despite its non-applicability |
| SPAC 3.0 | Decoupling of the right to vote from the right to redeem shares |
| SPAC 3.5 | Fractional warrant structure |

### 2.2.4 Remarks on American modern SPACs

The US capital markets have evolved since the blank check companies phenomenon in the 1980s; indeed, the main regulated capital markets, such as NYSE, NASDAQ, and NYSE AMEX have adopted specific listing requirements in order to list SPACs as outlined in the previous sections.

The regulations of those capital markets clearly indicate that a SPAC must fulfil specific conditions before its listing. However, those specific conditions are only minimum mandatory requirements which do not prevent any exchange exercising its unlimited discretion in order to delist the SPAC, even when all the listing requirements are met, because the SPAC might constitute a threat to the public interest and the protection of investors' interests. This serves as a continuous reminder of the possible financial risks that were generated by blank check offerings, although modern SPACs have implemented more corporate safeguards for investors.[28]

On the other hand, the NYSE, the NASDAQ and the NYSE AMEX granted a conversion right to the dissenting shareholder(s) of the proposal of a business combination. The conversion right is strictly connected to the escrow account because it is the right to convert common shares into a pro rata share of the aggregate amount held in the escrow account. This feature is very important for protecting the dissenting shareholder(s), and at the same time makes the SPAC's corporate structure flexible.

In addition, American exchanges provide investors with the possibility of exercising the redemption right of the issued securities before the completion of a business combination.[29] However, it should be noted that the possibility of exercising the redemption right by any SPAC investor is an essential feature. Furthermore, the redemption right can be granted to the shareholders of the SPAC by virtue of specific provisions set forth directly in the articles of association. The articles of association also play an important role in determining the conditions to which the exercise of the redemption right is subject. This is true especially in Europe, where there is still a variegated legal discipline of redemption rights for the SPAC, this being one of the main concerns that prevented, up till today, a real SPAC wave on the Old Continent.[30]

The American regulation of SPACs is remarkable, and it constitutes the first real attempt to provide a legal framework for SPACs. First, the special regulations for SPACs in the US are an example of hard law provisions and are binding for the promoters of the SPAC. In particular, the issuers must comply with the listing requirements of different exchanges (such as NASDAQ, NYSE, etc.). On the other hand, SPACs that follow these requirements

---

28 The main difference with blank check offerings is connected to the safeguards for investors such as the redemption right, the conversion right, the issuance of units during the IPO process, the escrow account for proceeds, and the high profile and expertise of the management who direct the SPACs (see further in this work the international characteristics of SPACs).
29 Such provision has been enacted in order to solve practical inconveniences such as the possibility that although the majority of shareholders approve a business combination, it may fail due to external factors (e.g. failure of closing after the signing of a letter of intent). In this way, funds for the redeemable shares may be missed.
30 See Chapter 4.

will not automatically be guaranteed a listing. Indeed, a case-by-case assessment is always exercised by each exchange.

Second, the *ratio* of the new approach, which has been implemented in America since the Securities Act 1933 (US) and the Securities and Exchange Act 1934 (US), and has constituted a trend to be followed by the NYSE, NASDAQ and NYSE MKT LLC, is centred on the implementation of a *caveat venditor* approach. In other words, the issuer must comply with specific capital markets' regulations. Hence, it is an investor-centred approach.

This reading differentiates the modern regulation of SPACs in America from the old regulation of the PSM where a *caveat emptor* approach was taken, namely, buyer beware. In other words, the duty of care on the PSM was mainly on investors because no listing rules were featured for blank check companies at that time.

## 2.3 The codification of uncodified market practices in SPACs

SPACs operate within the mantra of market practices and self-regulation, rather than statute. Indeed, to date – as we said – no statutory definition of SPACs has been provided by any legal system or regulation, and the only specific legal parameters are provided by American exchanges, through their listing standards and any applicable securities regulation.

The graphic below shows the SPACs' growing listing numbers in terms of the US IPO volume[31]:

As can be seen, the previous record for SPACs IPOs in 2007 was 66, and this year it has nearly tripled, at 180 listings. This exponential growth could not be possible without what I define as the codification of uncodified market practices. In particular, in 2008, the NY exchanges codified the main SPAC evolutionary trends in the emergence of SPACs 2.0 through the codification in NYSE (Rule 102.06) and the NASDAQ (Rule IM-5101-2). Similar specific listing standards were then implemented in 2010 by NYSE AMEX (Section 119).

On the other hand, SPACs have implemented other market practices, defined as pure uncodified market practices that directly relate to self-regulation and evolved instruments of company law and corporate governance structures, rather than as listing standards. Indeed, as we said, in 2015 SPACs 3.0 introduced and normalised the corporate mechanisms of decoupling the right to vote and the right to redeem shares, and SPACs 3.5, which consolidated the practice of fractional warrant (see Section 2.2.3). Those market practices that relate to finding solutions to key SPAC company law issues such as redemption rights during the De-SPAC phase and the consolidation of the SPAC's share capital through fractional warrants have allowed SPACs to finally take off.

---

31 Graphic provided by SPACInsder as of 30 November 2020.

## SPAC IPO Deal Count by Year

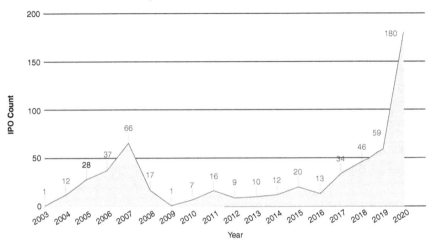

*Figure 2.1* The graphic is showing the remarkable growth of the SPAC market in the US.

In the graphic on US SPAC IPOs volume above, there is direct evidence to confirm this theory. Following the large number of liquidations witnessed in 2008, 2009 and 2010, as SPACs could not succeed in consummating a business combination, the new models of SPAC 3.0 in 2015, and subsequently SPAC 3.5, largely adopted between 2019 and 2020, show clearly that market practices are vital for SPACs. Without those market practices, SPACs cannot provide investors with safer corporate governance mechanisms to facilitate redemption rights, at the same time as consolidating their share capital by avoiding excessive dilution through the exercise of warrants and attracting hedge funds to SPACs because of their ability to sell warrant and lock-in gains.

### 2.4 The international corporate features and listing standards of SPACs

After the development of the blank check companies, SPACs started to develop as a modern conception which arises from the self-imposed adoption of Rule 419 in the US.

Since that moment SPACs started being listed in accordance with the main features that had been imposed by virtue of Rule 419 to blank check companies, and they started to implement the new features which have been explored in the sections above. This circumstance has contributed to the emergence and establishment of international features of SPACs, which can be seen as key factors for determining a 'SPAC identity' at the international level.³² These common international features have been recognised by virtue of the reception or codification of uncodified market practices as international standards to be followed to list a SPAC and preserve the interests of investors.

Thus, minimum listing requirements³³ have been agreed at the international level and they have been imposed as listing standards by virtue of hard law provisions, set forth in the regulations of capital markets such as the NYSE, the NASDAQ, and the NYSE AMEX in America. Against this trend a capital market, namely the main capital market of the Bursa Malaysia, has implemented the same features (i.e. listing requirements) with slight modifications to soft law provisions.

This means that the internationally agreed standards in relation to SPACs can be seen as either mandatory or facultative, depending on the capital market where the SPAC is going to seek its listing. Although the internationally agreed standards can be imposed by virtue of soft law provisions (i.e. the Bursa Malaysia case), this does not mean that the management or promoters of a SPAC can totally be exempted from the application of those common international standards (the exchange usually reserves the possibility to delist the SPAC if the confidence of investors is not sufficiently protected). Therefore, I argue that the regulations of capital markets might create a different environment for the listing of SPACs, depending on the degree of reception or codification of such common international standards (see Chapter 4 and the British (mis)understanding on SPACs).

It is important to highlight that it might be difficult to fully implement international standards, depending on the SPAC's country of incorporation. For instance, the corporate legal frameworks of each country differ, and this poses a question in relation to a national or domestic SPAC that sometimes cannot comply with the features developed as common standards at the international level. In other words, a tension transpires between international standards and national laws. It will be the objective of Chapter 4 to critically analyse that tension especially in Europe, but first it is important to illustrate the international financial regulation of SPACs and their international listing standards as well as their international corporate framework.

The graphic shows how modern SPACs work. The following sections are devoted to analysing each single feature that has characterised and informed

---

32 James Murray, 'Innovation, Imitation and Regulation in Finance: the evolution of Special Purpose Acquisition Corporations' (2017) 6 (2) Review of Integrative Business and Economics Research 1, 2. According to the author imitation of corporate structure can establish standardization, whereas in case of variation of such corporate standards financial innovations are implemented. It seems that the evolution of SPACs has at least initially revealed highly standardized structures. This because as the author claims SPACs mainly remain a self-regulated instrument.
33 Indeed, the main international features that have been acknowledged as international standards or market standards in relation to SPACs are the share capital, the escrow account or trust, the winding up procedure and the redemption right.

## 58  Towards a definition of SPACs

the evolution of international corporate standards and listing requirements in the SPAC arena. There are two different moments: today and tomorrow. In this chapter, we are speaking of today. In Chapter 5, we will speak of tomorrow. I shall, therefore, remind SPACs' disbelievers that their main critiques rest on the line of tomorrow. The main function of a SPAC is to get a private company listed or as we will see in Chapter 4 —with an even broader scope — to inject capital to constitute growth capital. This is why SPACs matter.

### 2.4.1 The promote and other people's money

We have already outlined, in Chapter 1, the risk and uncertainty sides of the SPAC's promote. This is one of the main international corporate features that is implemented in the US in relation to SPACs. The promote concerns the percentage that sponsors of the SPAC hold in respect to founder shares. Essentially, SPAC sponsors are committed to buy initial shares of the SPAC for an aggregate purchase price of $25,000 for a number of founder shares that equals roughly 20%–25% of the number of shares being offered in the market. Units are sold as low as $10 per unit, and the 20% founders shares are defined as the 'promote'.

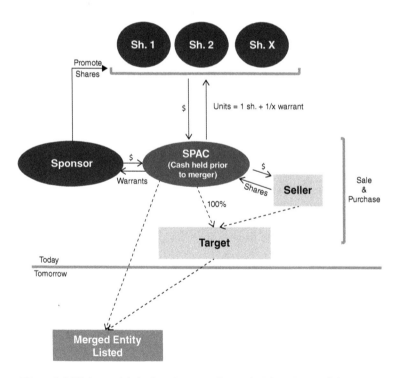

*Figure 2.2* This graphic is showing a traditional SPAC IPO and de-SPAC transaction via a reverse takeover.

It is useful to highlight that SPAC's sponsors not only buy founder shares but also founder warrants that are not redeemable, and are usually cash net settled (see Section 2.4.2 below). The common shares referred to the promote are classified under "Class B" or "Class F" common shares. The shares sold to the sponsor(s) are referred to as 'founder shares' and 'founder warrants'. Founder warrants represent the 'at-risk-capital' of the sponsor in the SPAC and are calculated as an amount equal to the upfront underwriting discount (2% of the IPO proceeds) plus $2 million of post-IPO working capital. If the SPAC does not complete a business combination within the settled timeframe, then the sponsor will lose this amount. The sponsor purchase founder warrants are usually at a price of $1.50, $1.00, $0.50 per warrant, depending on whether the units sold in the IPO include a fractional warrant structure. Units sold to the public are defined as "Class A" common shares. Those shares refer to the common shares and warrants that are offered to the public as "public shares" and "public warrants".

In many SPACs, the founder shares automatically convert into public shares at the time of the De-SPAC transaction on a one-for-one basis. Additionally, even if new shares are issued at that moment in connection with the closing of the SPAC, the exchange ratio upon which the founder shares convert to public shares is adjusted to gross the founder shares up to 20% of the total founder shares and equity-linked securities outstanding. Finally, it is also possible for sponsors in the US or institutional investors to enter into a forward purchase agreement with the SPAC, and commit to purchase equity in connection with the De-SPAC transaction to provide the business combination with additional funds in order to complete it.

Even today, the only SPAC that has not adhered to this structure is the record $4 billion Pershing Square Tontine Holdings SPAC of Bill Ackman. This has been seen as a good move, although Bill Ackman's SPAC stands on its own, and eventually its complexity has made Ackman to drop the deal to buy the 10% stake of Universal Music Group (see Addendum).

Bill Ackman has tried to redesign the terms for SPACs through his Pershing Square Tontine Holdings (Pershing Square), which so far has sponsored the largest SPAC ever raised. The structure of Pershing Square is unique:

1 Each unit is composed of one share of common stock, and one-ninth of a redeemable warrant exercisable at $23.
2 Two-ninths of a warrant exercisable at $23 provided that are not redeemed in connection with a proposed business combination.[34]

Essentially, the Pershing Square structure is based on raising $4 billion by offering 200 million units at $20 per share. This is already uncommon for a

---

34 Nicholas Jasinski, 'Bill Ackman's SPAC Splits Today. Here's What that Means' (11 September 2020) Barrons, available at https://www.barrons.com/articles/pershing-square-tontine-holdings-units-split-on-friday-heres-what-that-means-51599756914, accessed on 10 March 2021.

traditional SPAC that usually sells its units at $10 per share. The real revolution is in the second point above. This means that one-ninth of a warrant is detachable, a normal incentive for SPAC investors. However, unlike a traditional SPAC, where all warrants are detachable, here:

1. Two-thirds of the warrants issued to shareholders are not detachable, encouraging long-term investors.
2. Investors do not receive these (two-thirds of the warrants) if they choose to redeem their stock prior to the closing of the business combination. This provides the acquisition model with more certainty.
3. If investors redeem, their warrants are distributed pro rata to the shareholders who remain in the SPAC (here the name 'Tontine[35] holdings').

Finally, the compensation terms of the sponsor are new too. As we said, typically SPAC sponsors receive 20% of the shares in the SPAC for a nominal value. The founders' shares compensate the sponsor even when the value of the shares decline due to market volatility once listed. With Pershing Square, the sponsor is not taking any founders' shares. Under Pershing Square's warrant structure, the sponsor does not receive any compensation until shareholders receive a 20% return, whereas under a typical founders' shares compensation structure, the shareholders do not see any return until after the company receives a 20% return. Finally, Pershing Square paid $67.8 million for these warrants. That money will not be given back to the sponsor if a business combination is not procured and closed. Having said that, Bill Ackman's SPAC stands alone. In SPACs, it cannot be said that 'one-size fits all'. As we have highlighted before, it is unlikely that this structure will be used as a model or market practice for future SPACs due to its uniqueness in creating alternative investors' incentives (the 'tontine warrants'), while compensating the sponsor based on performance. The average SPAC cannot afford to sustain the costs of such a mechanism due to lock-up provisions in relation to the majority of warrants, a very stringent requirement on the side of investors. Freedom is key in SPAC deals.

Some criticise the classic SPAC promote structure because by the time a SPAC enters into a merger agreement, the underwriting fees and the sponsor's promote eat up more than 30% of the IPO proceeds, and because of the massively dilutive nature of founders' shares that might make it more difficult to complete a deal on attractive terms.[36] However, the SPAC's promote is a

---

35 Tontine is an investment plan for raising capital devised in the 17th century and relatively widespread in the 18th and 19th centuries. Subscribers share the risk of living a long life by combining features of a group annuity with a kind of mortality lottery. Each subscribers pays an agreed sum into the fun and thereafter receives a periodical pay-out. As members die, their pay-out entitlements devolve to the other participants, and so the value of each continuing pay-out increases. On the death of the last member, the scheme is wound up.
36 Antoine Gara, Eliza Haverstock, 'How SPACs Became Wall Street's Money Tree' (19 November 2020) Forbes, available at https://www.forbes.com/sites/antoinegara/2020/11/19/the-looming-spac-meltdown/?sh=60a2fceb70d7, accessed on 7 January 2021.

necessary feature to show 'skin in the game' on the side of sponsors who risk directly a consistent part of their potential gains in order to make an acquisition. Indeed, if the business combination is not completed, the sponsors' do not mature this incentive such as the 20% of a $300 million IPO SPAC. On the other hand, it is quite clearly understood that this type of incentive can translate into potential moral hazard behaviour on the part of the sponsors. Indeed, unscrupulous managers might still pursue an unattractive or unprofitable deal just to be sure that their high returns on equity are secured, and avoid the liquidation of the SPAC. Sponsors love to use other people's money. The same rationale applies for investment banks' or underwriters' fees that, until the business acquisition is completed, are potentially subject to litigation from investors.[37] The prospectus issued in connection with the merger can provide investors with false and misleading statements, including that the company was on the verge of profitability (see Chapter 5).

### 2.4.2 Share capital and corporate structure

After the blank check companies, SPACs evolved their capital structure in order to differentiate themselves as unique forms of cash-shell companies.[38] SPACs started to issue securities during the IPO in the form of units; nowadays a SPAC usually offers units during the IPO.[39] The possibility of issuing units is also contemplated by the NYSE listing rules.

Typically, a unit is comprised of common shares and warrants, which are neither debt nor equity securities, but a hybrid form of security.[40] Indeed, warrants constitute an option right to purchase equity common shares at a discounted pre-fixed price in the future. Both common shares and warrants can usually be traded separately one month after the IPO of the SPAC. The shareholders can exercise the call option right (i.e. warrants) 30 days after the completion of the acquisition, and the warrants are usually callable by the company at any time.[41] Hence, warrants represent a form of participation by

---

37 See Chapter 5.
38 Castelli (n 3) 268.
39 For an explanation of the concept of unit offerings please refer in a non-exhaustive way to these principal readings: Paul Schultz, 'Unit Initial Public Offerings' (1993) 34 (2) Journal of Financial Economics 199, 200; Thomas J Chemmanur, Paolo Fulghieri, 'Why Include Warrants in New Equity Issues? A Theory of Unit IPOs' (1997) 32 (1) Journal of Financial and Quantitative Analysis 1, 2; Martin Lee, Philip Lee and others, 'Unit Initial Public Offerings: Staged Equity or Signalling Mechanism?' (2000), Working Paper, Sidney University 1, 3, http://papers.ssrn.com/sol3/papers.cfm?abstract_id=238108, accessed on 12 December 2015.
40 Ellis Ferran, 'Capital Structure - Fundamental Legal Accounting, and Financing Considerations', *Principles of Corporate Finance Law* (OUP 2008) 49, 58.
41 Stefan M Lewellen, 'SPACs as an Asset Class' (2009), Working Paper, Yale University 1, 5, http://ssrn.com/abstract=1284999, accessed 30 July 2014; Lola Miranda Hale, 'SPAC: A Financing Tool with Something for Everyone' (2007) 18 (2) Journal of Corporate Accounting & Finance 67, 69.

shareholders in future capital growth.[42] We have said that a common market practice is to issue fractional warrants (see above Section 2.2.3).

The strike price of the warrants in the US is $11.50 per whole warrant with anti-dilution adjustments for splits, stock and cash dividends. The public warrants are cash settled. Hence, public investors have to pay $11.50 per warrant in cash, in exchange for a share of stock. On the other hand, the founder warrants can be net settled (i.e. cashless exercise). It means the holders are not required to deliver cash but are issued a number of shares with a fair market value equal to the difference between the trading price of the share and the warrant strike price. At the option of management, the public warrants can also be net settled. At the moment, the warrants are exercisable and the public shares trade above a fixed price that is usually $18 per share for a period of time; the public warrants become redeemable by the former SPAC for a nominal consideration. This forces the warrant-holders to take a decision: to exercise the warrants or to lose their value. The founder warrants are not redeemable. Hence, apart from the non-redeemability and the cashless exercise, the founder warrants and public warrants are identical.

These features of the share capital structure (i.e. units) represent a form of an agreed listing standard for SPACs and, therefore, they are common elements that are usually implemented by all listed modern SPACs. It is important to highlight that the *ratio* of the agreed adoption of standards is based on the necessity of building a new 'SPAC identity' to differentiate the latter from any other forms of investment vehicles or cash-shell companies (in particular, blank check companies).

Although it is highly recommendable for SPACs to issue units at the IPO stage, it is possible for a SPAC not to implement an international listing standard at national level because it is a decision that rests with the management. For instance, a SPAC might exist that issues only common shares at the IPO stage; in the US there have been SPACs that were financed only by common shares, especially in the healthcare sector. The first warrantless SPAC was Therapeutics Acquisition Corp. (Therapeutics) underwritten by Jeffries and sponsored by RA Capital, raising $118 million in July 2020. In 2020, in Therapeutics' wake, 20 more SPAC offerings were issued warrantless in the healthcare sector and another 11 in 2021. However, it is important to highlight that this is not the common trend nor is it market practice, and to afford a SPAC that is warrantless at least three conditions have to occur simultaneously: the management that runs the SPAC must be composed of top notch managers, and investors' demand must be high and mainly represented by institutional investors and funds.

The issuance of units at the IPO stage does not give rise to any legal issues at national level (namely, in the national legal framework). For this reason, there is no need for a comparison of legal systems at this point, because

---

42 Ferran (n 40) 57.

every legal system can allow a SPAC to issue units on the main capital market, with the sole exception of warrants (for instance, the Korean Stock Exchange does not allow companies to issue warrants on primary markets). Hence, the decision to issue a unit rests with the management and promoters of the SPAC.

In the Introduction to this book, we anticipated the persistent regulatory activism of the SEC from the end of 2020 and during 2021. Specifically, the SEC has issued a warning on the reporting and accounting practices of SPACs in relation to their warrants.[43] The warning on warrants does not have an implementation period, and suggests that SPAC warrants must be included as liabilities rather than equity or assets of the company. This is not a sound decision and represents an attempt to stop SPAC-frenzy. And it did, unfortunately, in April 2021. It is not grounded in economic fundamentals, as in essence before a completed merger, SPACs are convertible risk-free bonds and even the naivest investor holding SPAC securities until the merger date cannot lose even a penny on the investment sit in the balance sheet. Similarly, everyone in the SPAC game knows the nature of out of the money warrants which are worthless until the equity price of post-merger company does not hit $11.50 (the strike price) if ever. It seems that the SEC, this time, has acted well beyond its objectives as a financial regulator. On the other hand, such regulatory activism is also showing a positive aptitude of the SEC in being progressive, and in trying to legitimise the SPAC market as well as the SPAC as an investment vehicle that takes into account stakeholders' interests.

### 2.4.3 Escrow account and trust

| Operating Account | Escrow Account |
| --- | --- |
| The operating account is typically small (often ~$2M) and is meant to cover expenses over the initial SPAC lifespan of 1–2 years prior to a business combination. Expenses often include due diligence and closing costs, legal, accounting and tax services, SEC reporting costs and D&O insurance. | The large pool of funds (often hundreds of millions of dollars) raised in the public markets is held in trust with a third-party trustee appointed – often a trust company or major bank. Trust funds may only be released upon the affirmative vote of shareholders or upon liquidation of the trust to public shareholders if no operating business is acquired. |

It has been established in the previous sections that in order to protect the interests of investors the funds raised during the IPO process are either

---

43 Securities and Exchange Commission – Public Statement, 'Staff statement on Accounting and Reporting Considerations for Warrants Issued by Special Purpose Acquisition Companies (SPACs)' (12 April 2021), available at https://www.sec.gov/news/public-statement/accounting-reporting-warrants-issued-spacs, accessed on 20 April 2021.

deposited in an escrow account or held on trust, depending on the legal system where the SPAC has been set up.

The main function of the trust or escrow account is to represent a guarantee for the shareholders in the case of failure to fulfil the acquisition objectives that the management has determined at the start of the IPO. Furthermore, the funds held on trust or deposited in an escrow account might be used to refund a dissenting shareholder, who exercises the redemption right at the shareholders' meeting (namely, at the time when the management propose a business combination).

Generally, national provisions of the SPAC's country of incorporation do not give rise to any legal issue that could prevent a complete implementation of this agreed international listing standard, although a common law jurisdiction such as the UK in Europe can provide sponsors with the possibility of establishing either a trust in addition or an escrow account.

In the US, the trust account is founded with an amount that typically equals 100% of the gross IPO proceeds minus expenses and advisers' fees. Usually, 98% is funded by public investors and 2% or more funded by the sponsor. The escrow account proceeds are invested in short-term US government securities. Hence, those moneys are generating a limited amount of interest for working capital. The funds are released upon the successful completion of a business combination, the redemption of common shares due to a mandatory redemption offer or as payment of the deferred underwriting discount that is collected at the completion of the business combination.

### 2.4.4 *Winding up or liquidation procedure*

SPACs at international level have a very limited time frame to complete a business combination (i.e. usually from 24 to 36 months), providing that if they do not effect an acquisition at the expiry date of this term, they will be automatically wound up.

This feature is directly connected to the special purpose of the SPAC, namely, to complete a business combination. When the time frame is not respected, the SPAC has failed its main objective and the funds must be returned to investors. As we said at the start of this book, an extension of the duration of the SPAC can always be agreed by investors, but this can be costly for sponsors in a proxy solicitation.

Furthermore, because SPACs are cash-shell companies they do not possess any asset to distribute during the insolvency procedure. Indeed, the only asset to distribute to shareholders is the funds deposited in an escrow account or held on trust. For these reasons, the only creditors to protect during the winding up procedure of a SPAC are the shareholders who bought the securities at the time of the IPO. The sponsors would only lose the promote equivalent to the nominal $25,000 of the founder shares and the initial expenses to list the SPAC in terms of exchange fees and legal fees. In light of this, the main objectives and philosophy of corporate insolvency law[44] are not essential for SPACs, mainly because when these investment vehicles start an insolvency procedure they are not insolvent, but simply do not meet the objectives of the special purpose within the settled time frame.

However, the automatic winding up procedure might create legal issues, especially in continental European legal systems (for instance, the Italian legal system, where an automatic winding up procedure is consented to in limited and circumstantial cases).

## 2.4.5 Redemption right

According to international standards the redemption right granted to a SPAC's shareholders is a key element for assessing the level of protection of investors. In the US, up to 100% of the SPACs' shares can be redeemed by shareholders in connection with the business combination as long as the SPAC at all times has minimum net tangible assets of at least $5 million. The risk of a high number of redemptions is mitigated by the PIPE investment (see Section 2.4.7 below). However, European countries are not implementing the same American rule on redemptions. As opposed to Frankfurt where up to 100% of the SPAC's public shares can be redeemed by shareholders upon the completion of the business combination, in Amsterdam the business combination typically requires the approval of 70% of the votes cast. Effectively no more than 30% of the shares issued by the SPAC can be redeemed, as only shareholders voting against the business combination are eligible to have their share redeemed.

It is clear that the de-coupling mechanism between voting rights and redemption rights (the model SPAC 3.0) is not generally implemented at the European level. This is challenging for many sponsors that often are obliged to liquidate their vehicles (for example, the liquidations occurred in Italy in 2020, see Chapter 4).

The shareholder dissenting to the proposed business combination is entitled to withdraw from the company and redeem the investment, either in total or in part (basically, it depends on the legal system where the SPAC was initially set up). Furthermore, at international level the articles of association of a SPAC can sometimes impose a penalty for the dissenting shareholders who can redeem only part of their investment, namely a pre-established value not exceeding a certain percentage. This is usually called redemption price.

A redemption price can sound unfair to investors. In fact, it is useful to highlight that such a procedure is not common in recent SPACs that prefer to follow the model of SPAC 3.0 in order to consent an extended redemption right to every investor with the possibility of retaining the warrant. This model is still

---

44 Roy Goode, 'The Foundations of Corporate Insolvency Law', *Principles of Corporate Insolvency Law* (4th ed., Sweet & Maxwell 2011) 68.

uncodified; that it is directly related to solving a corporate law issue has surely been one of the main secrets of the success of SPACs in recent years. At least since its development in 2015. As we have seen, this feature applies mainly to American SPACs; it has not yet been implemented in continental Europe because there, redemption rights are subject to several limitations depending on the jurisdiction in which the SPAC is incorporated (see Chapter 4).

### 2.4.6 The tender offer procedure

In December 2009, SPAC market practices in the US evolved further; this was the first time a SPAC used a tender offer for the shares held by certain of its shareholders prior to completing an acquisition (57th Street General Acquisition Corp. SPAC). Since then, several new SPACs have effectively filed registration statements with a tender offer.

This uncodified market practice has since been rapidly codified. On 22 October 2010, NASDAQ filed a proposed rule change to its SPAC listing standards to allow, in lieu of a shareholder vote on an acquisition, a cash tender offer after the public announcement and before the completion of an acquisition. Shareholders who oppose the transaction may tender their shares in exchange for their pro rata shares in the SPAC's trust fund. On 12 January 2011, NYSE AMEX filed similar proposed rule changes, and on 21 January 2011, the SEC approved those proposed rules. This was followed by NYSE on 8 December 2016 and approved by the SEC on 10 March 2017. That evolution marked the first major development in listing standards for SPACs.

It is important to highlight that this practice applies to US SPACs only; the SPAC phenomenon in Europe and Worldwide is still limited and is less sophisticated. However, this is another codification of an uncodified market practice that other exchanges in the world can try to imitate as a listing standard, although the practical application of this corporate mechanism is subject to the corporate national law provisions of the SPAC's country of incorporation. Those corporate law frameworks might not allow a tender offer of public shares or they could make it more difficult to implement the US model.

### 2.4.7 PIPE in the US

After the IPO, the SPAC pursues a business acquisition. Once the target is found, the SPAC, in advance of signing an acquisition agreement, will often arrange committed debt or equity financing such as a private investment in public equity commitment, or PIPE, in order to finance a part of the consideration of the business combination and thereafter announce both the acquisition agreement and the committed financing.[45]

---

45 Ramey Layne, Brenda Lenahan, 'Special Purpose Acquisition Companies: An Introduction' (July 2018) Harvard Law School Forum on Corporate Governance available at https://corpgov.law.harvard.edu/2018/07/06/special-purpose-acquisition-companies-an-introduction/, accessed on 6 January 2021.

This is another uncodified market practice that is commonly found in SPACs and usually represents the norm in the US. However, this corporate mechanism is subject to the same comments that apply to the tender offer procedure, namely national corporate law frameworks might not consent to such committed financing, or make it subject to specific national law requirements depending on the SPAC's law of incorporation (see, for instance, the UK, where PIPE faced different regulatory issues and is still not commonly used either in the UK or Europe).

## 2.5 Conclusions

This chapter has illustrated the evolutionary story of SPACs since their origins as blank check companies on the PSM. Following the adoption of Rule 419, SPACs have evolved by registering the emergence of common corporate features such as the trust, the redemption right, the winding up process, etc. These features were recognised as an agreed form of international standard which started to be codified as listing requirements by American exchanges. This is referred to as SPACs 2.0. Pure uncodified market practices still represent the most important features of SPACs' corporate structure, such as the decoupling of the redemption right that gave rise to SPACs 3.0; the fractional warrant structure (SPACs 3.5); and the PIPE practice.

Hence, I shall argue that the "beauty" of SPACs' financial regulation is within their own market practices, or better, their uncodified market practices, that inform a more sophisticated system of SPACs' corporate governance. Such corporate evolution has placed the US as the SPAC world market leader based on its competitive regulatory environment, and on the brilliant intuition that self-regulation practices can finally be codified by exchanges rather than federal or state law.

This unique regulatory environment has shown for the first time in history that market operators may be in the right, and that they can shape the future of investment tools in far better ways than regulators can actually do alone, because market operators have more knowledge of the features of financial innovations.

However, SPACs would never have achieved success without the understanding and the recognition of these market practices by the SEC (for instance, the 2010 decoupling mechanism negotiated with the SEC by Douglas Ellenoff, the codification of the tender offer practice, etc.). In this light, the SEC was initially an essential instrument of development of SPACs' market practices.[46] This established over time a hybrid regulation model that is now opening up further discussions about establishing a principle of technical neutrality for SPACs, as well as extending this successful approach to other Wall Street financial innovations in the near future.

---

46 Between 2020 and 2021, the SEC has been more hostile to SPACs, and future policy reforms are continuously announced and in progress in the US.

# 3 SPACs between risk and uncertainty, and the role of the law

## 3.1 An introduction to the essence of risk

As has been explained in Chapter 1, risk and uncertainty are two main features of financial markets. As we said, they are also a structure of the market. This is because they characterise markets in terms of their intimate essence as venues that are capable of matching the opposing interests of lenders and borrowers and finding a perfect allocation of resources. Risk-aversion entities and risk-taker operators dominate markets, and even our own lives. It is one's approach to life that makes one a risk-taker or risk-averse. Indeed, risk characterises our own existence, and as this chapter explains, risk-takers constitute the most vibrant figure of the 'human-humanity' paradigm of risk through which human history has evolved over the centuries. In other words, to study risk and uncertainty in their essence is vital, and especially to conceptualise uncertainty in negative forms as something that cannot be controlled or governed. This chapter introduces this negative aspect of uncertainty in relation to its essence.

From a system perspective, risk and uncertainty are two of the main structures of financial systems, together with competition and financial innovations. However, in this chapter we will examine only the epistemology of risk and uncertainty, to understand why they matter in life and specifically why they are important in financial markets. Only through a deep understanding of their essence will we be able to theorise them as part of the financial system in the form of structures that work through auto-poietic or spontaneous mechanisms of regeneration. The story of risk is a remarkable one.[1] According to Bernstein it is:

---

[1] Peter L. Bernstein, *Against the Gods: The Remarkable Story of Risk* (John Wiley & Sons 1996). This Chapter does not illustrate in depth any sociological dimension of risk, but offers a pure philosophical and economic analysis of financial risk. Indeed, although policymakers are usually attentive to the social dimension of risk, this is not part of the subject matter of this work, namely to investigate further the sociological dimension and effects of risk. However, sociological approaches to risk can constitute our starting point for a possible philosophical dialogue on financial risk. In this regard, important contributions towards sociological approaches to risk can be found in Nick Pidgeon, Roger E.

DOI: 10.4324/9781003102779-4

(...) the story of a group of thinkers whose remarkable vision revealed how to put the future at the service of the present (...) [transforming] risk-taking into one of the prime catalysts that drives modern Western society. Like Prometheus, they defied the gods and probed that darkness in search of the light that converted the future from an enemy into an opportunity. The transformation in attitudes towards risk management unleashed by their achievements has channelled the human passion for games and wagering into economic growth, improved quality of life, and technological progress[2]

Risk management is a revolutionary idea whereby the future, far from being antagonist, mysterious fate or *voluntas dei*, becomes an opportunity to acquire wealth and establish favourable economic conditions. It must be understood that any reflection on the nature of risk will necessarily begin from a sociological point of view. This is because tracing a proper history of risk means reflecting on human nature in sociological terms. To this end, Giddens provides us with a brilliant introduction to this sociological dimension of risk in modern times that confirms what has been identified by Bernstein as a figurative confrontation between human beings and nature, or alternatively as a conflict with the gods, in the following terms:

> To live in the universe of high modernity is to live in an environment of chance and risk, the inevitable concomitants of a system geared to the domination of nature and the reflexive making of history. Fate and destiny have no formal part to play in such a system, which operates (as a matter of principle) via what I shall call open human control of the natural and social worlds. The universe of future events is open to be shaped by human intervention – with limits which, as far as possible, are regulated by risk assessment. Yet the notions of fate and destiny have by no means disappeared in modern societies, and an investigation into their nature is rich with implications for the analysis of modernity and self-identity. (...) Since risk, and attempts at risk assessment, are so fundamental to the colonising of the future, the study of risk can tell us much about core elements of modernity.[3]

According to Giddens, the "open human control" of nature in modern times has overwhelmed human reliance on destiny and fate, although from his sociological perspective the human beings/nature dichotomy can actually design

---

Kasperson, Paul Slovic (eds.) *The Social Amplification of Risk* (CUP 2003); Ulrich Beck, *Risk Society: Towards a New Modernity* (SAGE Publications 1992); Sheldon Krimsky, Dominic Golding (eds.) *Social Theories of Risk* (Praeger Publishers 1992); Anthony Giddens, *Modernity and Self-identity* (Stanford University Press 1991).
2 Ibid., 1.
3 Giddens (n 1) 110–114.

a new role for fate, destiny and fatalism. Giddens describes modernity as a paradigm that is composed of chance and risk. This is again a sociological approach to the subject matter of our research where specifically the term 'chance' is misleading when studied within an economic conception of risk. However, the central idea is that risk concerns the future, and human beings are agents in charge of decision-making, transforming reality with risk-taking and risk selection activities. It is, broadly speaking, the figurative conflict between men and nature, in which the former's aim is 'colonising the future'.

Although this sociological connotation of risk looks promising, I shall argue that in economic terms the architecture of the future is composed of uncertain events that are indeterminable, and can therefore pave the way to a new characterisation of risk and uncertainty. For this reason, this chapter deals with the concept from an economic point of view, specifically with a new dimension of risk and uncertainty in relation to financial risk and contemporary financial markets that will be conceptualised as a complex system. This reflection leads to different conclusions based on economic theories as well as philosophical arguments concerning political economy. According to this view, the future becomes a controllable entity only when a pure risk perspective is in place, as opposed to the uncertainty that is part of free market economies and is ungovernable and not classifiable.

Nonetheless, any examination of risk and uncertainty from any perspective, whether sociological or economic, will always start with an investigation of what risk means in ontological terms, and first of all from an epistemological point of view. Indeed, this is the main aim of this chapter, namely, to introduce the concepts of risk and uncertainty from an ontological and epistemological point of view in order to then deal in the last chapter of this work with the same concepts within the framework of social theories and complex systems.

### 3.1.1 The epistemology of risk

A philosophical dialogue on risk can be complex, especially from an epistemological point of view. If there is risk, something must be unknown or produce an unknown result. Hence, knowledge about risk is knowledge about lack of knowledge. The hendiadys of knowledge and lack of knowledge constitutes the central argument of the discourse on risk, but it explains very little about the nature of risk and the reason for its existence. Sometimes the discourse on risk and the recognition of that hendiadys can produce a tautological argument. To this end, if epistemology deals with the dissemination of knowledge in particular areas of enquiry, in relation to risk it can be said that it is the same essence of knowledge related to a lack of knowledge that itself constitutes a limit.

For this reason, the lack of knowledge that identifies the epistemology of risk points out an element of ignorance. This argument can discover a broader level of thinking in relation to the same human existence by concluding that existence itself is indeterminate and cannot be fully anticipated or controlled. As Eric Voegelin puts it:

> God and man, world and society form a primordial community of being. It is a datum of experience insofar as it is known to man by virtue of his participation in the mystery of his being. It is not a datum of experience insofar as it is not given in the manner of an object of the external world but is knowable only from the perspective of participation in it.[4]

To this end, human beings are participants, and they are conscious of this participation.[5] In particular, the study of knowledge can trace the difference between animals and humans in terms of reactions. We react to a situation before that situation is going to materialise, and the farther an organism can see the better it can adapt itself. In Knight's words 'we do not react to the past stimulus, but to the "image" of a future state of affairs',[6] so that consciousness can be identified through knowledge of the future. Knight goes on to explain that the reaction of the organism is detached from its adaptation to the system, and it is merely the product of a conscious behaviour that is expressed through action and inference procedures that involve perceptive faculties. This means that if we infer data from the present situation our perception of reality is not infallible. There is always a margin of error.

This erroneous perception is the first sign that we need to acknowledge the indeterminate nature of the world and at the same time our own impossibility of figuring out the exact features of a future event. In other words, we are not machines, and we make mistakes when we use our perceptive faculties. This is because we cannot possess a clear image of the future, in which every event or circumstance is classified, evaluated, and therefore anticipated. In other words, the future reveals uncontrollable elements of unknowns that characterise, in this first analysis, the epistemology of risk in terms of lack of knowledge.

### 3.1.2 The ontology of risk

The epistemology of risk has revealed a new aspect of knowledge and risk that relates to our ignorant or fallacious perception of the world. This is an important conclusion because it is capable of showing the finitude of human nature as well as the irremediable erroneous perception of reality. For this reason, the next question necessarily centres on the ontology of risk.

---

4 Eric Voegelin, *Order and History* (Baton Rouge: Louisiana State University Press 1956) 1–5.
5 Walter A. Weisskopf 'Reflections on Uncertainty in Economics' (1984) 9 (33) The Geneva Papers on Risk and Insurance, 335, 336.
6 Frank Knight, *Risk, Uncertainty and Profit* (first published 1921, Martino Publishing 2014) 201.

Hence, risk should be interpreted by questioning what risk is, and then by saying what the relations and features of risk are. This approach leads to the discovery of a new stage of thinking from an ontological point of view. The ontology of risk refers to its metaphysical *status* as a quality in the physical world that implies an ontological realism in order to identify which states of the world are to be conceptualised as risk.

The actor of today programmes his conduct to take action in the future, and consequently tries to be risk-averse. The agent can adapt his behaviour to a present stimulus, but his reaction or response must be based on a well-known class of instances that logically cannot be placed in the future, but only in the past. Thus, the decision-maker of today can be defined as a quasi-informed agent, because the main assumption is that we cannot avoid the presence of at least some indeterminate instances that are likely to arise – this time – in the future.[7]

From an ontological point of view the discourse on risk has manifested the objective nature of risk and has led to the illusion that risk comprises one single meaning. Essentially, risk is represented as an objective quality that is immanent and measurable by the laws of probability.[8]

From an historical point of view, such an argument has been endorsed for centuries in Western countries, from Fibonacci's *Liber Abaci* (1202), Cardano's *Liber de Ludo Aleae* (1525) and Galileo's *Sopra la Scoperta dei dadi* (1623) through the laws of probability framed, *inter alia*, by Pascal and Fermat,[9] and, in particular, the science of statistics of Graunt, Petty and Halley,[10] promoting the concept of insurance as a commercial tool in the 18th century. In other words, the story of risk was initiated by formalising its ontological meaning (a theory of being) based on an objective dimension under the laws of probability.

The discourse on risk becomes much more complex, however, when its subjective dimension is taken into account and risk is constructed as a value that varies according to the context.

Specifically, as far as the story of risk is concerned, the subjective dimension of risk was introduced in 1731 by Daniel Bernoulli[11] with the concept

---

7 This is an anticipation of one feature of uncertainty.
8 See further Section 3.2.1 when Knight draws the difference between pure probability theories and statistical approaches.
9 Bernstein (n 1) 57–72.
10 Ibid., 92.
11 Bernstein (n 1) 108. As it explained:

> Cardano, Pascal, and Fermat provided a method for figuring the risks in each throw of the dice, (...) Bernoulli introduces us to the risk-taker, the player who chooses how much to bet or whether to bet at all. While probability theory sets up the choices, Bernoulli defines the motivations of the person who does the choosing. This is an entirely new area of study and body of theory. Bernoulli laid the intellectual groundwork for much of what was to follow not just in economics, but in theories about how people make decisions and choices in every aspect of life.

of risk-taking, which linked risk with the essential figure of the risk-taker, a human being capable of facing the future and taking his chances against *voluntas dei*. In this way the concept of risk-taking came to be seen as something that related not just to objective facts but also to a subjective view concerning the desirability of the decision-making process. In other words, when a *status* of the world can be conceptualised as risk, the risk-taker is able to make a choice and decide to take that particular risk. Furthermore, his choice is determined not only by an inference decision (i.e. the perceptive faculties), but by opinions or judgements that are relative and subjective.

For this reason, in 1921 the 12 chapters of 'Risk, Uncertainty and Profit' by Frank Knight developed a philosophical argument on risk instead of a pure economic theory on profit.[12] Specifically, the subjective element of personal decisions has influenced thinkers to understand and theorise a possible methodology in order to measure risk, and distinguish it from uncertainty as a personal belief.[13] Furthermore, because risk cannot be prevented in any human activity, the conception of risk management has become a useful tool to identify risk in ontological terms, and consequently to influence the subjective decisions of the risk-taker in order – this time – to be uncertainty-averse.

### 3.1.3 The risk-taking activity vs. the risk-sharing of Shari'a

In the previous section the ontology of risk was described in terms of 'open human control', namely human beings are agents in charge of decision-making who aim to transform reality by risk-taking and risk selection activities. Risk-taking is a prominent idea in Western economies, and human beings in Western countries tend to conceptualise risk as a synonym of 'progress'.[14] Someone who takes no risk cannot evolve, so it can be said that the ontology of risk in the West contains an authentic human quality which is further explained following our discussion on risk and uncertainty in the market.[15] For now it is enough to introduce the idea that risk in its ontological dimension in the West is mainly characterised in human activities by risk-taking (and, in economic activities, by taking financial risks) rather than risk-sharing perspectives.

In contrast to the latter concept of risk-taking, *Shari'a* law has developed over the centuries a different view on risk in its ontological meaning, which focuses instead on a dimension of risk-sharing. For this reason, it is important

---

12 Knight (n. 6).
13 For the avoidance of doubt these paragraphs are not taking into any conception of legal uncertainty or legal risk in terms of uncertainties that may arise in commercial transactions or in relation to the possibility of being the subject of a claim before a court.
14 Daniele D'Alvia, 'Risk, Uncertainty, and the Market: A Re-thinking of Islamic and Western Finance' (2020) International Journal of Law in Context 1.
15 See Section 3.3.3.

74  *Risk and uncertainty and the role of the law*

to briefly explain the Islamic concept of risk-sharing, hopefully to better appreciate the nature of risk-taking activities in the West.

Muslim scholars agree that the *Qur'an* and the *Sunnah* form the primary sources of Islamic law or *Shari'a* law,[16] with its objective and purpose being the governing of all aspects of the private and public life of Muslims; itis believed to be of an all-embracing character, with its constant narrative of Islam as a religion and a civilisation.[17] *Shari'a* law refers to a set of rules, regulations, teachings and values with the category dealing with transactional matters, known as *Muamalat,* which governs individuals' interaction, including their financial and commercial affairs.[18] Two key elements distinguish *Muamalat;* first, individuals are always reminded that they need to obey God in their quest for their daily material needs,[19] and second, by acting upon the rules of *Muamalat* in daily life, a greater bond is created with God.[20]

According to Patrick Sookhdeo, Islamic finance is not so relevant to the essential practices of *Shari'a* law, and he more controversially states that *Shari'a* law in finance is neither Islamic nor efficient.[21] It has been argued to the contrary that Islamic finance is – indeed – an integral part of *Shari'a* law; although it does not address finance in its modern form, it does incorporate general principles governing the economic behaviour of Islamic society and specific instruments regulating classic commercial transactions.[22] Indeed, throughout history, Islamic banking has gone through different phases of development with time required to transfer Islamic banking principles from the theoretical to the practical domain.[23] Facilitated to a large extent by oil exports from Muslim states, Islamic finance and banking has seen huge growth in recent years.[24] Western institutions and governments have been keen to ensure they

---

16 Hans Visser, *Islamic Finance: Principles and Practice* (2nd ed., Edward Elgar Publishing 2014) 12; Wael B. Hallaq, *An Introduction to Islamic Law* (Cambridge University Press, Cambridge 2009); Bernard G. Weiss, *The Spirit of Islamic Law* (The University of Georgia Press 1998).
17 Nima Mersadi Tabari, 'Islamic Finance and the Modern World: The Legal Principles Governing Islamic Finance in International Trade' (2010) 31 (8) Company Lawyer 249.
18 Brian Kettell, *Introduction to Islamic Banking and Finance* (Wiley 2011) 15; Nuradli Ridzwan Shah Mohd Dali, *Introduction to Muamalat* (McGraw Hill 2008); Munawar Iqbal, David T. Llewellyn, *Islamic Banking and Finance: New Perspectives on Profit Sharing and Risk* (Edward Elgar 2002) 95.
19 Edwina Pio, *et al.*, 'Pipeline to the Future: Seeking Wisdom in Indigenous, Eastern, and Western Traditions' in Judi Neal (ed.) *Handbook of Faith and Spirituality in the Workplace* (Springer 2013) 207.
20 Abdul Karim Aldohni, 'The Quest for a Better Legal and Regulatory Framework for Islamic Banking' (2015) 17 (1) Ecclesiastical Law Journal 15.
21 Patrick Sookhdeo, *Understanding Shari'a Finance, The Muslim challenges to Western Economics* (Isaac Publishing 2008) 23.
22 Aldohni (n 20) 249.
23 Sookhdeo (n 21) 15.
24 Qudeer Latif, *et al.*, 29th April 2013, 'Introduction to Islamic Finance' Clifford Chance, https://www.cliffordchance.com/briefings/2013/04/introduction_to_islamicfinance.html, accessed on 15 September 2020.

are part of that economic growth, and have introduced Islamic finance and banking into their systems.[25]

This has perhaps been a contributing factor in bringing *Shari'a* law and Islamic finance to the forefront of comparative study, discussion and viable applicability. Islamic scholars found general rules governing economic activities in the *Qur'an* and within the *Sunnah*, and on that basis a doctrine of fairness in commercial dealings was established. This doctrine has four components, namely prohibition of *Riba* (usury),[26] *Gharar* (uncertainty), *Qimar* (gambling) and the encouragement of *Taa'won* (mutual cooperation).[27]

*Gharar*, literally translated, means uncertainty, hazard, chance or risk,[28] although there are several interpretations of what *Gharar* means in practice. It can refer to the lack of knowledge itself or to a contracting party's lack of

---

25 Aldohni (n 20) 7–8; Visser (n 20) 12–26.
26 Mohsin Kahn, Abbas Mirakhor, 'Islam and the Economic System' (1992) 21 (1) Review of Islamic Economics 1.
27 Sookhdeo (n 21) 249.
28 Indeed, according to the Financial Times Lexicon *Gharar* means risk, uncertainty or hazard, http://lexicon.ft.com/term?term=gharar, accessed on 16 September 2016; in particular, the Arabic word for *Gharar* is غرر that means risk in its etymology, see Salman Bin Lambak, '*Shariah* Juristical Effect of *Gharar* in Predetermining *Takaful* Contribution' (2013) 1 (2) *International Journal of Education and Research* 1. Although there is not any verse in the Holy *Qur'an* that proscribes *Gharar*, vanity is forbidden in two Islamic verses that are usually connected to the prohibition of *Gharar*. The first one is under the Holy *Qur'an*, *Surah* 2 verse 188 that in Arabic is as follows: << وَلَا تَأْكُلُوا أَمْوَالَكُم بَيْنَكُم بِالْبَاطِلِ وَتُدْلُوا بِهَا إِلَى الْحُكَّامِ لِتَأْكُلُوا فَرِيقًا مِّنْ أَمْوَالِ النَّاسِ بِالْإِثْمِ وَأَنتُمْ تَعْلَمُونَ>> it is translated by the Islamic scholar Muhammad Sarwar in the following terms: <<do not use your property among yourselves in illegal ways and then deliberately bribe the rulers with your property so that you may wrongly acquire the property of others>>. Furthermore, the other verse of the Holy *Qur'an* that concerns *Gharar* is the *Surah* 4, verse 29 that in Arabic is as follows: << يَا أَيُّهَا الَّذِينَ آمَنُوا لَا تَأْكُلُوا أَمْوَالَكُم بَيْنَكُم بِالْبَاطِلِ إِلَّا أَن تَكُونَ تِجَارَةً عَن تَرَاضٍ مِّنكُمْ وَلَا تَقْتُلُوا أَنفُسَكُمْ إِنَّ اللَّهَ كَانَ بِكُمْ رَحِيمًا>>, the verse translated by the Islamic scholar Muhammad Sarwar is reported in the following terms: <<Believers, do not exchange your property in wrongful ways unless it is in trade by mutual agreement. Do not kill one another. God is All-merciful to you>>. For an interpretation of these verses in terms of *Gharar* prohibitions see Abdul-Rahim Al-Saati, 'The Permissible *Gharar* (Risk) in Classical Islamic Jurisprudence' (2003) 16 (2) Journal of King Abdul Aziz University: Islamic Economics 7. Finally, on the possible definitions of *Gharar* also see Mohammad Al-Ameen Siddiq, Al-Dhareer, '*Al-Gharar* in Contracts and Its Effects on Contemporary Transactions' 1997 (16) IRTI, IDB, Eminent Scholars Lecture Series 10. Indeed, Al-Dhareer divides *Gharar* in jurisprudential terms in three main definitions: <<first, *Gharar* applies exclusively to cases of doubtfulness or uncertainty as in the case of not knowing whether something will take place or not. This excludes the unknown. The definition by Ibn Abidin is a case in point: "*Gharar* is uncertainty over the existence of the subject matter of sale"; second, *Gharar* applies only to the unknown, to the exclusion of the doubtful. This view is adopted by the *Zahiri* School alone. Thus, according to Ibn Hazm: "*Gharar* in sales occurs when the purchaser does not know what he has bought and the seller does not know what he has sold"; third, a combination of the two categories above; *Gharar* here covers both the unknown and the doubtful, as exemplified by the definition proposed by Al-Sarakhsy: "*Gharar* obtains where consequences are concealed". This is

knowledge.[29] However, this is a broad interpretation of the term that needs to be defined and narrowed. In particular, the concept of *Gharar* is connected to the concept of legal uncertainty as well as to uncertainty itself in economic terms.[30] It has been noted that contracts are forbidden under conditions of excessive uncertainty and unacceptable levels of risk;[31] in this first meaning, the concept of *Gharar* is linked to the concept of risk; it is, as will be further explained, a pure form of risk, in accordance with the argument to represent uncertainty as opposed to risk that is understood by Knight as a measurable uncertainty.[32] With the moral aim of ensuring that contracting parties are clear on what they are agreeing to and understand their rights and obligations, beyond legal uncertainty *Gharar* is not permissible when there is an unknown outcome in an exchange and that it is interchangeable with ignorance. It is important to state that *Shari'a* law in reference to *Gharar* usually does not go beyond the contract to ascertain what is in the minds of contracting parties.

However, the reality is that with commercial contracts there will be some element of risk and uncertainty,[33] hence some *Gharar* is, therefore, acceptable as it will not always be possible to eliminate uncertainty totally from exchange contracts.[34] In other words, the prohibition of *Gharar* and therefore, of risk-taking, lead the contracting parties to find risk-sharing solutions (for instance, the *Takaful* instrument, namely Islamic insurance) instead of risk-trading tools. To this end, the risk of a commercial transaction is admissible only if all the contracting parties share the same level of acceptable risk inside a transaction.

It is clear that *Gharar* in Islamic finance is not without issues, primarily as there is no universally agreed definition among Muslim jurists about what degree of legal uncertainty is permissible in commercial transactions, thus making *Gharar* a matter of interpretation, which in itself can cause issues.[35] In an attempt to counter such issues, learned scholars are generally relied upon to distinguish between contracts containing minor *Gharar* (ineffective) and therefore allowed, as well as for the clarification of contracts containing substantial *Gharar* and therefore void (forbidden).[36]

---

the view favoured by most jurisprudents. I have opted for this last definition because of its more exhaustive coverage of the jurisprudential elements collated under *Gharar*>>.
29 Maha-Hanaan Balala, *Islamic Finance and Law: Theory and Practice in a Globalized World* (I.B. Tauris 2010) 29.
30 Al-Saati, 'The Permissible *Gharar* (Risk) in Classic Islamic Jurisprudence' (2003) 16 (2) Journal of King Adbul Aziz University: Islamic Economics 5.
31 Aldohni (n 20) 249.
32 Knight (n 6).
33 Aldohni (n 20) 249.
34 M. Kabir Hassan, Mervyn K. Lewis, *Handbook of Islamic Finance* (Edward Elgar 2007) 241.
35 Balala (n. 29) 42. See Nehad Khanfar, 'A critical Analysis of the Concept of *Gharar* in Islamic Financial Contracts: Different Perspective' (2016) 36 (1) Journal of Economic Cooperation and Development 1.
36 Balala (n. 29) 39. In particular, she reported how the concept of *Gharar* is usually distinguished between forbidden *Gharar* and permissible *Gharar*. Only the forbidden *Gharar* can

This different conception of risk-sharing has also prevented Islamic finance from engaging in excessive risk-taking activities. Specifically, it seems that the prohibition of *Gharar* and especially of forbidden *Gharar* has for centuries indirectly prevented Muslim societies from taking excessive risks or being involved in excessively risky activities. This is because – as we have seen – risk is composed of an objective dimension that can be measured, and of a subjective dimension that cannot be measured and, therefore, cannot be accurately calculated. Hence, the opinions or subjective beliefs of human beings cannot find a place inside commercial transactions that must only be carried out in accordance with a permissible *Gharar* paradigm. This is also because philosophically *Shari'a* law is a direct derivation of the *Qur'an* which is in turn a direct expression of the word of God. For this reason, in Islam a selection of risk activities that allows excessive risks would have always been constructed as an act against God, and Bernstein is very clear on this when he states that the story of risk is a story against the gods in the Western paradigm.

This comparison with the risk-sharing dimension of *Shari'a* has been useful to highlight the importance of subjectivity of risk in the West, and the unlimited perspectives that the West has allowed in risk selection activities. This is because the West sees risk as a tool for determining the progress of society, so it acknowledges its subjective aspect that relates directly to the fragility of human beings and to their desires, hopes, and speculative visions of profit. Only in this way can progress be an outcome of the human activities that are evidence of relativity and subjectivity, leading to – sometimes – the negative outcomes experienced during financial crisis, market failures or generally in the establishment of risk societies where any human activity is the result of risk distribution.[37]

## 3.2 Financial risk

Now that the ontology of risk has been explored it is important to contextualise risk inside a financial perspective. It has already been explained how the objective and subjective meanings of risk in the West have contributed to a new vision of risk-taking as synonym of 'progress'. That vision has brought to finance the essential concepts and methods of portfolio selection, diversification, the capital asset pricing model and the prospect theory in behavioural economics.[38] In philosophical terms those economic methods and statistics are related to the laws of probability, and they have paved the way for the activities of risk-taking, transfer, and pooling (i.e. banking, investment, insurance, etc.) that constitute *per se* a source of legitimate profit in Western countries. In other words, risk management has become the new means of

---

render a contract void. That is also the distinction that Al-Baji, a Maliki scholar has made between major *Gharar* (forbidden) and minor *Gharar* (ineffective).
37 Beck (n 1).
38 Bernstein (n 1) 260–270.

identifying risk, in ontological terms, and specifically from a financial point of view.

The risk argument in finance is explained as the constant relationship that shapes the structure of financial markets between savers (i.e. lenders) and users (i.e. borrowers).[39] According to this understanding of the market, the lenders are represented by individuals, companies or governments with funds to invest in the business activities of the users, otherwise known as borrowers.[40] The financial market is the place where those opposite interests of lenders and borrowers are encountered and matched. Furthermore, those two categories of agents (lenders and borrowers) bear different types of risks and one could say they have different needs and perspectives in relation to risk.

Essentially, the main objective of any lender or better, of any investor, is to stay risk-averse, and to evaluate through risk assessment the solvability of the borrower as well as his credibility (for this reason, the interest rate becomes the price for the level of risk borne by the lender, at least from a philosophical point of view, whereas in a pragmatic view the interest rate is the cost of the supply and demand of money). On the other hand, the borrower is an aggressive agent who pursues profit maximisation through risk-taking activities (such as issuance of shares through IPO, issuance of bonds on the debt market, etc.). The risk assessment of the borrower and the interactions between those two categories of investors[41] are facilitated by financial intermediaries (essentially investment banks, hedge funds, mutual funds, etc.), which traditionally exercise the main function of absorbing and mitigating investment risk.

Therefore, definition and study of the concepts of risk assessment, investment risk and financial risk become important in order to efficiently govern financial markets. Financial risk thus becomes a *status* of the world to be controlled and governed in order to enhance the investors' confidence and allow them to become risk-averse. Risk assessment has indeed been defined in sociological terms as the most important activity for colonising the future,[42] but its proper functioning in contemporary financial markets is always limited

---

39 Stephen Valdez, Philip Molyneux, *An introduction to Global Financial Markets* (8th ed., Palgrave 2016) 2.
40 The term 'borrowers' is broad and comprises of individuals who are looking for bank loans, companies that need short-term money, governments, municipalities and public corporations.
41 Indeed, a lender can become a borrower and *vice versa*. For this reason, they can be generally both defined as investors. For instance, think of a client of a bank who deposits his/her savings into a bank account. He/she is in this example a lender, and the bank is a borrower. Nonetheless, the same bank that is a borrower is soon going to become a lender, when it will start to enter into facility agreements with other borrowers. In the same fashion, the depositor of our example can become the borrower of tomorrow if he/she enter into a facility agreement with another lender or can use a part of the deposited amount of money to invest in a company's shares, so becoming a new lender.
42 Giddens (n 1) 114.

by the acknowledgement of imperfect information and adverse selection in the market,[43] so there is – as we pointed out – always an element of indeterminateness in reality and therefore, in our specific case, in financial markets. This is what can be defined as uncertainty in the market.[44]

### 3.2.1 The (no)-classification of risk

Section 3.1.1 introduced the idea of the limits to human perceptive faculties achieving relative, but not absolute, knowledge. The tension between knowledge and risk is one that aims towards absolute knowledge, but it is irremediably destined to fail. In this section, the hendiadys of knowledge and risk is examined from an economic point of view in order to understand why the risk-taker in financial markets (the borrower, in the sense that we have explained before) is incapable of taking reasonable financial risks, and, in particular, why currently the existence of global financial markets seems to have strengthened the private forms of control and governance of private money.[45] This has irremediably changed the classification of risks; it is impossible to classify variegated and non-homogenous forms of private risk, of which SPACs are one of the main instances, as new forms of financial innovation or financial instrument.

The connection between risk and classification is indeed derived from insurance, which is the main economic model for colonising the future in sociological terms[46] and at the same time it answers the principal question as to what extent the world is intelligible. However, insurance – in pure economic terms – is the demand for protection against risks in order to hedge the positions of the agents in the market. Indeed, the main aim of insurance is to distribute risks and set prices by means of classification.[47] Nonetheless, classification is a costly activity for the insurer in traditional common insurance, and also for a central clearing counterparty of derivatives in financial markets whose aim is to diversify risks on the basis of different classes by means of risk assessment. The latter process separates similar risks into different classes, so the necessary feature of any risk classification system is the homogeneity of risk classes; the more homogeneous the risk classes, the more effectively the price of the premium is settled.

This is a model theory of traditional insurance that should be translated into global financial markets to maximise their utility and avoid, or at least

---

43 See further Sections 3.2.1, 3.2.2, 3.3.2.
44 See further Section 3.2.2.
45 Michelle Everson, 'Banking on Union: EU governance between risk and uncertainty' in Mark Dawson, Henrik Enderlein, Christian Joerges (eds.), *Beyond the Crisis: The Governance of Europe's Economic, Political and Legal Transformation* (OUP 2015).
46 Giddens (n 1) 113.
47 Kenneth S Abraham, *Distributing Risk: Insurance, Legal Theory and Public Policy* (Yale University Press 1986)

reduce, moral hazard. However, moral hazard has permeated today's banking system and the economy, due to strong dependence on 'privatised Keynesianism',[48] and it has become a collective good. Indeed, public demand in Keynesian terms, especially since the Great Depression, has been managed through the expansion of credit markets to satisfy the needs of low and middle-income people, and by virtue of derivative markets for the very wealthy. This means that private individuals rather than governments are used to take risks and service debt to stimulate economic growth. Therefore, if moral hazard becomes a collective good, governments bail out irresponsible firms in order to sustain the expansion of stable mass consumption. For this reason, moral hazard is a product of a financial system that is highly connected to private firms and private banks and to their private clients. Specifically, the futurisation of markets[49] has established a 'heterarchical' rather than a hierarchical form of governance where the Central Bank at the 'vertex controls the transactions and operations as far as the periphery'.[50] This means that decisions and information are distributed among many agents and economic operators, especially including private parties who operate on the market. For this reason, it is difficult to classify risks in a system where risks are multiplied by financial innovations and private decisions, and where risks are packed into financial instruments in order to be hedged against future risks of collapse through derivative instruments. Private actors clearly play an essential role of risk-bearing is this economic system and they influence the present as well as the future creation of money. For this reason, private risks are widespread in financial markets and they are variegated because they are created to satisfy the different needs of citizens according to their income and social status. The impossibility of classification has legitimised irresponsible and inefficient behaviours that as an indirect product of financial risk have created moral hazard. In a heterarchical system financial risk is the catalyst for systemic risk and systemic risk is the result of 'privatised Keynesianism' where mass consumption constitutes the answer for the management of public demand and moral hazard represents its practical application.

For instance, when the model theory of insurance was translated into financial terms, the notorious phenomenon of under-pricing financial risk emerged as the main catalyst for spill-over effects and systemic risk in the 2007–2010 financial crisis. This is why a correct risk assessment is vital for the efficient functioning of financial markets, and it can be achieved only through the distribution of risks and classification, albeit the main hurdle to such a result is the difficulty involved in identifying homogeneous instances in a risk class as well as anticipating all the possible 'private risks'.

---

48 Colin Crouch, *The strange non-death of neo-liberalism* (Polity Press 2011).
49 Elena Esposito, *The Future of Futures: The Time of Money in Financing and Society* (Edward Elgar 2011).
50 Ibid., 85.

Concerning the concept of homogeneity, we have to return to philosophical arguments and specifically to Knight's distinction between statistical and *a priori* judgements under the laws of probability. For now, it is sufficient to state that the *ratio* behind distribution of risks through classification is to settle fair prices and, in particular, to achieve market equilibrium where efficient behaviours can essentially be promoted. Nonetheless, our own ignorance and our awareness of the indeterminateness of the instances and variables that exist in the world remains an important obstacle, and can lead to a reduction in accuracy.[51] The resulting unknowability of the instances justifies the need for classification and distribution of risks[52] that leads to homogeneity of classes, but it is that same impossibility of predicting all the variables that reduces homogeneity. If any risk class were absolutely homogenous, there would be no probability in the results, and the idea of probability becomes meaningless.

In particular, in a statistical judgement, chances are determined empirically and instances are classified with a greater degree of accuracy because the risk classes are mainly composed of homogeneous facts and are focused on particular instances (a common example is the game of dice, where each throw of the dice is held alike in a degree), therefore the degree of accuracy for determining the possible variables is high; whereas in the case of *a priori* judgements the group of instances is absolutely homogenous, but the variables of each class are indeterminate (i.e. the chances of a building burning down on a particular day cannot be measured with a high degree of probability). Therefore, the difference between the two judgements rests on the level of accuracy in the classification of risk[53] that is technically defined as separation of risk classes. It means that in the case of *a priori* probability, the possibility of separating classes of risk is made more difficult by the indeterminateness of factors and the degree of computing chances through general assumptions and principles that are rarely objective. For this reason, a poor risk classification can generate an inefficient insurance system incapable of really hedging the financial positions of agents in the market. Furthermore, if a risk classification is incorrect, inefficient behaviours (i.e. moral hazard) on the part of the insured can be incentivised because the price of insurance will not reflect the real probability of loss. This is the paradox of probability theory, which tends to achieve objective results by risk classification, but deals with subjective connotations that are determined by the absolute ignorance and indeterminateness of instances.

Hence, if probability is applied to estimates, it is manifestly clear that risk cannot be classified; it is a case of mere judgement or subjective opinion. This last reflection paves the way to the category of uncertainty and brings us to the next section.

---

51 Abraham (n 47) 66.
52 Knight (n 6) 218–219.
53 Abraham (n 47) 69.

### 3.2.2 Risk and uncertainty

Theorising financial risk[54] in philosophical terms has never been proposed before, but it is now a matter of compelling importance.[55] I should say that the concepts of risk and uncertainty are rather unclear in ordinary language; for this reason, it is essential to be aware that they are not synonyms in economic terms, although it is interesting to note that risk in ordinary language is associated with a negative connotation of danger and harm, while uncertainty is connected to doubt.[56] However the Chinese word for risk, 'weij-ji', combines two meanings, danger and doubt, so we could say risk and uncertainty are contained in a single word.[57] On the other hand, in Germany there is a straightforward distinction between *gefahr* and *risiko*. The first means hazard and threat, whereas the second relates to risk.[58]

It might look like a word game, but it is not. Indeed, as a result of this linguistic exercise we see that uncertainty is connected to hazard, doubt and threat (*gefahr* in German), whereas risk is related more closely to harm and loss. In fact, we usually say that we take a risk to get positive results, although we might end up with a loss. It seems that we are used to seeing risk as a growth opportunity (the Chinese approach to the word risk is self-evident), but we do not take uncertainty as far as we can; we only experience uncertainty, and this is why mankind has always been worried by uncertainty about the future.[59] In other words, we cannot predict and anticipate uncertainty, we

---

54 The issue of financial risk and its mitigation is a contemporary issue that has not been perceived in the past with the same emphasis. Nonetheless, a possible extended view of Frank Knight's distinction between risk and uncertainty in financial terms was proposed by Jack Guttentag and Richard Herring in 1986 and it is further examined in this chapter. As opposed to financial risk, different theorisations of business risk have been proposed especially by Prof Irving Fisher, *Nature of Capital and Income* (Macmillan 1906). See further, for an overview of business risk Charles O. Hardy, *Risk and Risk-Bearing* (Risk Books 1923). On the other hand, the first thinker of risk in relation to economic policy and political economy is Keynes with his macroeconomic analysis focused on fiscal stimulus.
55 The negative effects of the global financial crisis of 2008–2009 and the euro sovereign debt crisis in 2010–2011 have generated reams of studies on the failure of the modern economic policy.
56 Clarence L. Barnhart, Robert K. Barnhart (eds.) *The World Book Dictionary L-Z* (World Book Inc. 1987) 1081, 2269. Risk is defined as 'chance of harm or loss; danger' and uncertainty as 'uncertain quality or condition; doubt'.
57 Brian Corby, 'On Risk and Uncertainty in Modern Society' (1994) 19 (72) The Geneva Papers on Risk and Insurance 235, 236.
58 Susanne Billes, Elisabeth Erpf, *et al.*, *Langenscheidt Handwörterbuch Englisch*, vol. 1 (2nd ed., Langenscheidt KG 2010) 962, 1278. It is also interesting to highlight how the German word *risiko* has a close meaning with the Italian word *risicare* that means to dare. Indeed, if we take a risk we take it in order to likely get a positive result, therefore we dare, we bet on the future through the laws of probabilities.
59 Luhmann, *Risk: a sociological theory* (n 81) 8. In particular, Luhmann reconstructs the possible etymology of the word 'risk' by stating that:

> (...) The etymology of the word is unknown. Some suspect it to be Arabic in origin. In Europe the word is to be found already in medieval documents, but it spread only

can only be subject to its results. Before uncertainty we have doubt and we do not know what the final outcome will be, whereas although risk can have a potentially negative outcome in terms of damage, it is still worth taking a risk if we want to progress.

Now it is time to translate this first taste of risk and uncertainty into economics.

All of us were affected by the collapse of one of the most important financial institutions, Lehman Brothers, in 2008. The qualification of risk in financial terms has become the main reason for our existence since the start of the contagion risk. Since that moment, contagion risk has been linked with financial risk. Financial risk, legal risk and contagion risk all refer to one common concept: risk, but in relation to different connotations and qualifications. To state plainly, the main question today is: what is risk and how can the consequences of financial risk be prevented?

A possible answer to this question is based on Knight's 'Risk, Uncertainty and Profit'.[60] This book is recognised for its outstanding contribution towards creating a distinction between risk and uncertainty, namely between objective and subjective dimensions of risk towards a theorisation of insurable form of hazards and true uncertainties. It has been perceived as a challenge to classical economics. However, this is only a limited interpretation of Knight's conception of risk because for the first time the philosophical discussion goes beyond a mere formal separation of objective and subjective instances of risk to discover what can be referred to as the 'past qualification' of risk. Indeed, today this is the real essence of risk, and represents the start of a new philosophical discourse in the phenomenology of contemporary financial markets. First it is important to underline that risk is always a measurable uncertainty. In Knight's words:

> (...) the practical difference between the two categories, risk and uncertainty, is that in the former the distribution of the outcome in a group of

---

with the advent of the printing press, in the initial phase apparently in Italy and Spain. There are no comprehensive studies on the etymology and conceptual history of the term (...). It finds significant application in the fields of navigation and trade. Maritime insurance is an early instance of planned risk control. (...) Risk calculation is clearly the secular counterpart to a repentance-minimization programme; in any case an attitude inconsistent in the temporal sequence of events: first this, then that. Thus, it is at all events a calculation in terms of time. And in the difference between the religious and secular perspectives lies the tension of the well-known wager proposed by Pascal: the risk of unbelief is in any case too high, for it is salvation that is at stake. The risk of belief, that we genuflect quite unnecessarily, appears by contrast insignificant.

For this reason, this brilliant introduction by Luhmann confirms our understanding of risk as a complex subject where even religious and secular visions are capable of being taken into account.

60 Knight (n 6).

instances is known (either through calculation *a priori* or from statistics of *past experience*), while in the case of uncertainty this is not true (....) the best example of uncertainty is in connection with the exercise of judgement or the formation of those opinions as to the future course of the events, which opinions (and not scientific knowledge) actually guide most of our conduct.[61]

So, it is possible to state that knowledge about risk is knowledge of a knowable situation. In other words, the ontological discourse on risk represents what is knowable in principle or *a priori* by virtue of laws of probability and the science of statistics. It is knowledge of objective facts that derives from the observance of a past experience, as Knight has outlined. For this reason, Knight's revolutionary idea is the categorisation of risk on the past line.[62]

Indeed, the recognition of risk on the past line effectively prevents the risk-taker from interpreting the future in terms of opportunity within Bernstein's remarkable story on risk. In other words, the ignorance of variables in a group of instances and the acknowledgement of the indeterminateness of facts reveal the limit of knowledge in relation to experience both empirical and *a priori*. For this reason, the only available instances that can be classified homogenously are those on the past line. Nonetheless, this is the paradox of probability theories because to simply distribute risks through classification on the past line has no real effect on probability. It is a form of perfect knowledge that does not require statistics or probabilities at all. By contrast, it is the judgement that is based on general principles in *a priori* probability and the opinion that is focused on perspective faculties of inference in statistical probability that give rise to uncertainty in subjective terms. This makes the discourse on risk theoretically and practically complex because it is not possible to measure opinions or judgements, especially if one makes reference to the inference or prediction processes that are only based on projections and opinions of the agent reacting to the stimulus. For these reasons, uncertainty represents an immeasurable risk.

---

61 Knight (n 6) 233. Italics have been used intentionally to highlight the key concepts in relation to the past qualification of risk.
62 Indeed, the semiotics of the word event has confirmed this understanding in the previous Section 3.1.2. It is now intelligible how the risk assessment that is carried out by the lender on the solvability of the borrower is based on its past performance or alternatively on its past credit experiences. Furthermore, a modification of the price of the nominal value of shares of a listed company can be predicted by examining the past performance of the company through its balance sheets or past conduct of the management in relation to strategic decisions. Here, the instances that are examined are limited and objective, and therefore the lender, who is the shareholder, can have a high probability of calculating the risk of its investment. The price of the nominal value of the shares reflects the risk assessment of the borrower, namely the company itself.

## 3.3 Financial markets and complexity

We have seen how in financial markets the borrower is identified as a risk-taker and the decisions of this agent are based on both objective and subjective connotations of risk. We have called the first risk and the second uncertainty, in Knight's terms.

In general, risk can be measured through *a priori* or statistical assumptions, but in financial markets risk has to be approached from an actuarial point of view. From a pure statistical angle, a risk exists where it is statistically measurable and when probabilities can be estimated, but from an actuarial point of view the economic consequences of these events are also important. When probability, capital and profitability are taken into account, then financial evaluation is requested.

Classical economics introduced the idea of the risk-taker in terms of *homo economicus*, namely the man who takes a rational decision to maximise its utility. The premise is based on perfect information[63] where competition does not play any significant role, and it can be philosophically defined as a mechanical approach.[64] In such a system uncertainty is not even mentioned because every agent in the system possesses the same level of information and is capable of inferring the same data from a homogenous class of instances. Hence, variables can be predicted and anticipated. Here, statistics or the *a priori* probability explained by Knight are superfluous; to reach a market equilibrium where all participants possess the same level of information there is no need to anticipate or classify instances in risk classes, because every risk class is composed of homogenous instances.

*Homo economicus* has become *homo stocasticus*, essentially the man who takes decisions in terms of probability and is especially influenced, in Bernoulli's view, by the desirability of choices. Because those choices cannot be measured, uncertainty is expressed as the unintended consequence of human action derived from ignorance and the indeterminateness of the economic system, and life, in general, is seen in terms of anxiety.[65]

---

63 Knight (n 6) 174.
64 Rene Passet, 'The Paradigms of Uncertainty' (1984) 9 (33) The Geneva Papers on Risk and Insurance 370. The mechanical approach is also defined the Newtonian paradigm that has been referred to by several economists such as

> Jevons defines economics as the mechanics of utility and of individual interest; (...) Reuff [who asserted that] dynamics is that part of the mechanics which studies motion and the way it is related to the influences which cause it...economic dynamics has recourse to the same method.

65 Weisskopf (n. 5) 337. The author mentions Kierkegaard who

> pointed to the ontological roots of this anxiety as an essential part of human being. It stems from our being thrown into an unknown world and from having to struggle continuously with the mystery, the uncertainty and the meaninglessness of our life. Our anxieties, centring around our obsession with forecasting, can ultimately be traced back to the unpredictability of the time of our death, combined with the fact

This paradigm has been influenced in physics by Heisenberg's principle, according to which:

> the influence of the observer on the position and the velocity of particles makes it impossible to ascertain both, their position and velocity, together. This leads to a different view of reality: there is no complete causal determination of the future on the basis of available knowledge of the present. It means that every measurement... creates a unique, not fully predictable situation.[66]

Translated into economic thinking, it means that uncertainty is an important feature of the economic system where competition also plays an important role, and in addition uncertainty is considered as the main catalyst of profit.[67] This is the position of neo-classical economics, as opposed to traditional economics, according to which uncertainty was reduced or eliminated through belief systems where the unknowable became knowable by means of symbols, which were also in charge of reducing human anxiety.[68] The 'invisible hand' of Adam Smith, who is a classic economist, is self-explanatory in this regard.

For this reason, the next step is to introduce the environment in which the economic agent faces risks today. This paves the way for a new phenomenology of contemporary financial markets that can be defined as a complex system[69] dominated by risk and uncertainty and especially by competition in terms of financial innovations and adaptability. As in physics the concept of the disorganisation of the universe is measured as entropy, and in the same way entropy measures the uncertainty of a system, so free markets always look disorganised, but uncertainty produces competition that is the equilibrium feature of the system itself. To continue the analogy with physics, we could say that the complexity of the systems was introduced by thermodynamics, which for the first time took into account a dissipative structure that highlights how 'a movement towards greater complexity (...) can be

---

> that the only certainty which human beings have is death itself. Certainty and uncertainty about death are equally at work to make us anxious.

66 Ibid., 351.
67 Knight (n 6). See further Chapter 5.
68 Weisskopf (n 5) 337.
69 John H. Holland, *Complexity A very Short Introduction* (OUP 2014) 4. Complex systems are not complicated systems. Indeed, the distinction between the two is centred on the concept of

> emergence (the whole is more than the sum of the parts) (...) hierarchical organization is thus closely tied to emergence. Each level of a hierarchy typically is governed by its own set of laws. (...) emergent properties at any level must be consistent with interactions specified at the lower level(s).

For further consolidating arguments please refer to Chapter 5 of this work.

created spontaneously under the impulse of energies that are sufficiently powerful to push a system away from the areas of Boltzmann's equilibrium thermodynamics'.[70]

This means that in the contemporary phenomenology of financial markets there is no central planner, and competition serves the role of decentralised planning. If this image is imposed onto the broader economy, we come to the concept of the entrepreneur, who faces risks and adapts his actions to answer in terms of financial innovations. The entrepreneur becomes manager of the plan and by taking on responsibilities and engaging in uncertain activities contributes to the money creation process.[71] In other words, it can be said that the entrepreneur explains the function of absorbing uncertainty from the system.

In the end, disorder can be neutralised through information. Indeed, in economics, risk and uncertainty are also defined as information economics or informed economics.

### 3.3.1 From risk-aversion to uncertainty-aversion

The concept of risk is vital to understanding financial markets. To this end, the subjective dimension of risk in terms of uncertainty as an estimate of an estimate in Knight's theory is particularly engaging.

Before Knight, Daniel Bernoulli introduced the subjective dimension of risk in 1731 with the concept of risk-taking, which linked risk with the essential figure of the risk-taker. The idea of risk-taking came to be seen as something that was not only related to objective facts, but to a subjective view concerning the desirability of the decision-making process.

The philosophical discourse on risk becomes more complex when the subjective meaning of risk is illustrated. In other words, it has been said that risk refers in the first place to an objective *status*: knowledge of the past circumstance, and hence, knowledge of the knowledgeable situation is not a subjective impression. It is not a personal belief. It is not the 'desire' of Bernoulli, but a simple reference to a choice that is capable of being made (namely, the decision of lending based on the risk assessment of the lender is self-explanatory in this regard). Nonetheless, the intimate question is centred on whether risk can be perceived as having value that can vary depending on context.

In light of this, theoretical economics has understood that financial markets are dominated by an objective conception of risk, but a subjective conception of risk is nevertheless still vital for their functioning. Indeed, financial speculation (from Latin '*speculum*' – mirror) as opposed to investment is based on a subjective belief in order to become profitable. Keynes, in his

---

70 Passet (n 64), 375.
71 Knight (n 6).

famous book 'The General Theory of Employment, Interest and Money' (1936) confirms this by pointing out the difference between knowable in principle and necessarily unknowable. What is knowable in principle refers to an objective conception of risk (it is an *a priori* knowledge), but the necessarily unknowable refers to this new subjective feature of financial markets.

On this point, Keynes compared the financial markets to a beauty contest. Here the judges, instead of focusing their attention on the winner, therefore on the most beautiful girl, try to second guess the opinion of other judges. Similarly, in capital markets the speculator's effort tends to focus not on the objective reality of financial assets sold or offered on the market, but on the information that other speculators will trade on in the near future. Hence, the evaluation of financial assets is not only based on an assessment of past performance of assets, but on the uncertainty of the decision that will be taken by other speculators. To state it plainly, the objective discourse on risk does not apply alone in the phenomenology of financial markets, because there will always be a subjective component in the final decision of the speculator. Indeed, this trade in information is vital to unwind positions early and it is also essential to set up the price of the financial asset.[72] In this game the value of information for a speculator depends on the uncertain behaviour of another speculator (i.e. necessarily unknowable). In addition, because the markets will always present a lack of perfect information (i.e. information asymmetry) basing the value of the financial assets on new as well as erroneous information might lead to mispriced assets. The real point is that even a speculator in good faith can affect the value of financial assets in a negative way. This is why supervision of financial markets is required, but cannot definitively solve the issue.[73]

Nonetheless, Keynes considered the subjective dimension of risk in finance mainly for policy-making reasons and concerning the influence of macroeconomic trends on political economy. The distinction between risk and uncertainty called 'Knightian uncertainty' was further developed with a view to the financial markets by Jack Guttentag and Richard Herring.[74] According to them, disaster myopia in financial markets happens when financial intermediaries underestimate the occurrence of shock probabilities, namely the possible event of default. This is because whatever model of risk evaluation has been used, potential shocks are uncertain events that cannot be measured, and therefore their intelligibility is limited due to a lack of knowledge and the limited information to which financial intermediaries or investors have access. In other words, their understanding of economic

---

72 Markus K. Brunnermeier, *Asset Pricing under Asymmetric Information: Bubbles, Crashes, Technical Analysis and Herding* (OUP 2001).
73 Charles Goodhart, *The Evolution of Central Banks* (MIT Press 1988). See further Chapter 4.
74 Jack Guttentag, Richard Herring, 'Disaster Myopia in International Banking' (1986) Essays in International Finance No. 164, Princeton University Press.

shocks is imperfect, and therefore uncertain events are not properly reflected in the value of financial assets.

Disaster myopia is the final outcome of the subjectivity of financial risk in terms of the necessarily unknowable element theorised by Keynes and introduced by Knight.

Knight and other authors have provided the reader with a theoretical background which distinguishes between risk and uncertainty and provides a dogmatic justification for the sharp devaluation of financial assets, but they have not been able to guide policymakers in preventing future crisis.[75] This is because financial risk is not only composed of its objective dimension in terms of ontological realism, but it is also especially influenced by a subjective element that leads to a more complex dialogue on its essence and that seems at first glance ungovernable. Therefore, the impossibility of measuring opinions and judgements has rendered the discourse on financial risk much more complex. Hence, disaster myopia becomes the definition of this unperceivable essence of financial risk in its subjective dimension. The next section will show that the feature of uncertainty in the market is a necessary connotation that cannot be eliminated and, one could say, does not pretend to govern or control. This because money creation processes based on profit are strictly dependent on uncertainty.

It seems that financial regulation, whether in place or not, is not capable of modifying this essential connotation of the markets, but a new role of economic, and specifically of market, self-regulatory approaches must be investigated and explained. This time it is with the hope that financial regulators will start to re-think their approaches to uncertainty-aversion, especially because the *ratio* of the new post-crisis financial regulation (2007–2010) has revealed its limits in terms of disaster myopia. Additionally, this is evidence of the understanding of the phenomenology of contemporary financial markets in a new light of complex systems and autopoiesis[76] where it has been

---

75 Stephan Valdez, Philip Molyneux, *An Introduction to Global Financial Markets* (8th ed., Palgrave Macmillan 2016) 489.
76 Indeed, it is explained in Chapter 6 of this work how according to Luhmann complex systems are autopoietic or reflexive systems. To this end, I draw on his theory of complexity and systems theory in order to describe financial systems as complex systems and particularly as autopoietic systems. Indeed, today the observer in financial systems is influenced not only by its own observation, but by the observations of other observers or financial operators. This makes the system complex and reflexive and justify uncertainty as a necessary mechanism for the functioning of the system where in financial markets uncertainty is perceived not only with reference to the future course of events, but also as uncertainty of the opinions and decisions of other operators. Indeed, in financial markets the lack of knowledge of the future is an essential source to construct new presents, and it is this second-observation level (namely, the observation of the observer of other observers) that determines financial markets as an autopoietic system. According to this view, financial markets can regenerate their self because their understanding is not simply related to a direct observation of their essence (first level observation), but it is the same second level observation that mainly characterised their nature.

suggested that a spontaneous order will be found in the market itself, rather than through reliance on a central planner (in this sense the paternalistic approach of the state to regulation).[77]

### 3.3.2 The paradox of uncertainty in modern economies

If the subjectivity of financial risk is, therefore, intelligible but not knowable due to its necessarily unknowable nature, the future, at least in the phenomenology of contemporary financial markets, is no longer perceived as an opportunity, but as something that is feared and must be controlled. Since the collapse of Lehman Brothers in 2008 and the start of the 2007–2010 global economic crisis, uncertainty-aversion has dominated the markets, but the management and correct pricing of risk in its objective dimension is still vital for governing markets.[78] Therefore, the figure of the risk-taker, namely the investor in financial markets, has shifted to the figure of the speculator who through his second-guessing influences the choices of other speculators and can contribute to a potential mispricing of the negotiated financial assets.

As a result, the figure of the risk-taker who sees the future as an opportunity has shifted to an uncertainty-aversion paradigm by means of what can be defined as the contemporary phenomenology of financial markets, where their subjectivity has superseded and overwhelmed the objective realism of their own ontology. Indeed, the figure of the speculator has contributed to the current financial crisis, while supervisors, financial regulators and financial institutions cannot be blamed for their actions insofar as they are inside the disaster myopia discourse.[79]

Nonetheless, justification for the idea of uncertainty-aversion is controversial because according to Knight's theory, profit is connected to uncertainty, and complex systems such as financial markets cannot exist without uncertainty. Without uncertainty, there is no profit. Indeed, any money creation process, rather than being undermined by uncertainty, is underpinned by it. Therefore, a new economy characterised by uncertainty-aversion such as is being proposed today by financial regulators and governments can be translated, in the worst possible scenario, into a considerable diminution, or indeed full elimination, of profit. In Knight's words:

> the only "risk" which leads to a profit is a unique uncertainty resulting from an exercise of ultimate responsibility which in its very nature cannot be insured nor capitalised nor salaried. Profit arises out of the inherent, absolute unpredictability of things, out of the sheer brute fact that the results of human activity cannot be anticipated and then only

---

77 See Section 3.3 and Chapter 4.
78 Claudio Borio, Haibin Zhu, 'Capital Regulation, Risk-taking and Monetary Policy: A Missing Link in the Transmission Mechanism?' (2008) 268 BIS Working Papers, 3.
79 Guttentag, Herring (n 74).

in so far as even a probability calculation in regard to them is impossible and meaningless. The receipt of profit in a particular case may be argued to be the result of superior judgement. But it is judgement of judgement, especially one's own judgement, and in an individual case there is no way of telling good judgement from good luck, and a succession of cases sufficient to evaluate the judgement or determine its probable value transforms the profit into a wage.[80]

This is the paradox of modern economies. On the one hand, we blame uncertainty due to the indeterminacies of the decisions of the speculator and its mysterious character that prevents us from measuring it, but on the other hand the elimination or diminution of uncertainty inside free markets can irreversibly contribute to the diminishing of progress and innovation. Without uncertainty there is no competition and without competition there is no adaptability of the system. It seems that the contemporary phenomenology of financial markets would benefit from finding a spontaneous order by allowing the functioning of a free market structure beyond financial regulation concerns.

### 3.3.3 The human-humanity and the human-inhumanity of risk

Now that the concept of risk has been explained in epistemological and ontological terms it is important to highlight the 'human' feature of risk. This is because the story of risk is interpreted as the story of the human beings who have criticised the absolute truths of God in order to colonise the future. Additionally, risk is permeated by a subjective aspect that is directly connected to the *a priori* judgements of man who, with his fragilities and false beliefs, makes risk an unmeasurable and evanescent entity. It is this subjective feature that characterises risk in terms of 'human-humanity'. It means that the main agent of any choice or decision-making is a man (human in this sense), but also that the nature of such decisions features subjective intentions, sentiments, desires and hopes. This is all the 'humanity' that can be expressed by a man and that makes such decisions subjective.

On the other hand, the 'human-humanity' of risk can also be translated into an opposite paradigm of 'human-inhumanity'. This is to highlight two different phenomena in financial markets; on the one hand the shifting of the paradigm of the *homo stocaticus* into the *homo technologicus* where the fintech era combined with the globalisation of markets seems to have superseded even the possibility of human decision-making processes, especially if one sees the blockchain developments of smart contracts and bitcoins as a form of pre-packaged decision-making. In all these instances, the main agent of decision-making is a man, but his desires or fragilities are not taken into

---

80 Knight (n 6) 310–311.

account, especially when he enters into smart contracts; on the other hand, the 'human-inhumanity' of risk is directly connected to uncertainty. As we said before, uncertainty is an immeasurable entity that cannot be controlled. It is beyond the 'open human control' of Giddens that uncertainty can be defined in terms of its 'inhumanity' in order again to highlight the intrinsic limits of human beings when dealing with something that is necessarily unknown and cannot be either discovered or accurately identified to be anticipated and prevented. Nonetheless, the impossibility faced by the man in dealing with uncertainty can be potentially superseded by the entrepreneur in Knightian terms, who can absorb the negative aspect of uncertainty as lack of knowledge in order to take immeasurable risks that will eventually lead to a profit.

## 3.4 SPACs as money creation vehicles

SPACs are companies that can be identified in financial markets under the category of 'borrowers'.[81] SPACs seek new funds on the markets in order to complete a business combination, therefore, they are categorised under the paradigm of uncertainty as speculators. Their immediate perception is 'aggressive' because SPACs try to find investment opportunities through risk-taking activities. Thus, SPACs are part of the uncertainty paradigm in Knight's terms because, as borrowers in financial markets seeking high profits, they have a positive attitude to risk. This is the main feature of modern economies, where profit is seen as a form of payment for the exercise of judgement involving risk and responsibility in terms of uncertainty. The uncertainty that informs SPACs makes them a direct instance of the money creation process. According to this view, SPACs are a form of money creation instrument that tends towards the efficiency of financial markets by offering a reasonable distribution of investment risks among stakeholders (see Chapter 1). The concept of responsibility in the face of uncertainty is indeed vital, according to Knight, and in SPACs especially, the management can never undertake irresponsible risks.

SPACs are part of financial markets. They are a direct product of competition in free markets, and they differ from a conception of 'privatised Keynesianism'[82] due to their equity being based on shares and warrants. If in modern economies macroeconomic growth is boosted by the expansion of private debt incurred by private parties rather than governments, SPACs as private actors seek economic growth based on equity instead of debt (today the Korean Stock Exchange represents the only exception to this rule, due to its reliance on convertible bonds rather than warrants[83]). They are more connected to the 'reality' of the economy because they are highly liquid

---

81 Valdez, Molyneux (n 75) 2.
82 Colin Crouch, *The Strange Non-death of Neo-liberalism* (Polity Press 2011).
83 See Chapter 4.

instruments, so their primary objective is to offer stability and allow financial markets as complex systems to reach economic equilibrium and achieve efficiencies through a direct increase in liquidity without relying on leverage instruments.

To achieve these objectives, it is vital to convert uncertainty into risk by investing in information and risk analysis. This approach will promote greater confidence in relation to investors and shift the discourse on SPACs towards risk. It will also reflect the spontaneous organisation of the free market, where information can provide an effective solution for disorganisation. In other words, the managers of SPACs become decentralised planners, and the market itself is able to generate important results for investor confidence.

It will be the task of the following sections to examine which role the law will play in free markets and specifically in terms of SPACs.

## 3.5 SPACs, systemic failure and the law

After World War II the Allied Powers met at the United Nations Monetary and Financial Conference, held in Bretton Woods, New Hampshire in July 1944, and negotiated different agreements in order to redesign the global economic order.

The main objectives were to prevent future crises after the Great Depression of 1929 and particularly to design a sustainable economic system capable of avoiding wars.[84] To this end, the Bretton Woods agreements[85] established the creation of two international organisations, namely the International Monetary Fund (IMF, or Fund) and the International Bank of Reconstruction and Development (World Bank) to address the floating exchange rates of the 1920s and the currency devaluations of the 1930s. The main instrument to achieve exchange stability was a system of fixed exchange rate parity enshrined in Article IV of the IMF Articles of Agreement. The parties that

---

84 Ross Philip Buckley, *International Financial System: Policy and Regulation* (Kluwer Law International 2008) 3–14. Specifically, the author highlights that from 1873 until World War I the economic conditions were favourable due to increasing trade agreements between states, but the decade after World War I was determined by

> isolationism between countries and declining trade and capital flows, and this lead to the Great Depression of 1929. The Depression in many ways persisted until the advent of World War II. So it was to the forefront of the minds of those who designed the post-was system.

85 Ibid., 3. In particular, the Bretton Woods' negotiations were based on proposals inspired by two important economists of the time: Keynes and White. They were intellectuals that belonged to the most influential allied powers of that time, namely the UK and the US. In the end, the proposal that largely inspired the Bretton Woods' negotiation process was modelled on White's approach that was mainly centred on the establishment of a fund to regulate exchange rate stability and a global bank for reconstruction and development. The choice of following White's proposal was based on the fact that the US was the dominant partner in the wartime alliance and strongest economic power.

were members of the Fund would undertake to maintain official par values for their currencies, expressed in gold or US dollars. The par value could be changed only in case of 'fundamental disequilibrium' in a country's balance of payments, and any divergence in excess of 10% from initial parity would require IMF approval. The members of the IMF furthermore consented under Article VIII to the implementation of a system of conversion for their currencies. As a result, the final removal of controls over currency transactions, combined with a predictable system of exchange rates, was intended to promote international trade. Rather than the World Bank, which was designed as an international organisation whose main aim was to alleviate global poverty, the IMF became by far the more important institution for the functioning of the international financial system. The main objectives of the IMF as agreed at Bretton Woods were:

a   To promote international monetary cooperation through a permanent institution, which provides the machinery for consultation and collaboration on international monetary problems.
b   To facilitate the expansion and balanced growth of international trade, and to contribute thereby to the promotion and maintenance of high levels of employment and real income and to the development of the productive resources of all members as primary objectives of economic policy.
c   To promote exchange stability, to maintain orderly exchange arrangements among members, and to avoid competitive exchange depreciation.
d   To assist in the establishment of a multilateral system of payments in respect of current transactions between members and in the elimination of foreign exchange restrictions which hamper the growth of world trade.
e   To give confidence to members by making the general resources of the Fund temporarily available to them under adequate safeguards, thus providing them with opportunities to correct maladjustments in their balance of payments without resorting to measures destructive of national or international prosperity.
f   In accordance with the above, to shorten the duration and lessen the degree of disequilibrium in the international balances of payments of members.[86]

These objectives were far too ambitious and/or difficult to apply in practice. The possibility of modifying the par value system was limited, and the system itself was rigid, especially considering most countries were reluctant to devalue their currencies as a response to external imbalances. This is because

---

86 International Monetary Fund, 'Articles of Agreement of the International Monetary Fund', available at www.imf.org/external/pubs/ft/aa/index.htm, accessed on 14 May 2017.

the devaluation process was seen as an indirect admission of economic failure that could expose those countries to currency speculation and lead to capital flight.[87] Therefore, the initial objectives of Bretton Woods in terms of promoting international trade were not fulfilled due to the formal rigidity of a system which led countries to adopt or maintain capital controls in order to manage foreign exchange risk.

For these reasons, although this first implementation of Bretton Woods partially avoided volatility in currency markets,[88] in the early 1970s US President Nixon eliminated the Bretton Woods fixed exchange rate parity with gold, and the Bretton Woods system as it was first designed was overturned. This was the start of a process of privatisation of foreign exchange risk.[89] Specifically, under the original Bretton Woods legal framework each member of the IMF was obliged to pay the Fund at least 25% of the quota in gold or US dollars and the remainder in the member's own currency. This compelled national banks of non-reserve countries to peg their currency to the dollar and to keep sufficient dollar reserves in order to intervene in their currencies by buying or selling dollars to maintain fixed exchange rates. Hence, in the aftermath of the 1970s, banks started to implement hedging strategies to diversify their investment portfolios.[90] Consequently, governments began to liberalise and deregulate their financial markets with the main objective of allowing banks to diversify their investments as well as manage financial risk more efficiently.

However, this privatisation of financial risk contributed in the long term to a process of socialisation of risks as bail-out procedures, and it made the international financial markets more permeable to systemic risk. The clearest example of the privatisation of financial risk can be identified in the conflict of interest of rating agencies that occurred during the 2007–2010 financial

---

87 Buckley (n 84) 7. According to the author, the limit of a rigid exchange rate parity was more evident with the growth of capital mobility as well as following two important political events: the Cold War that created limitations to the level of economic cooperation that could be achieved and decolonisation in the 1950s and 1960s that resulted in the creation of new nations such as Asia and Africa. These latter were highly interested in benefiting from the World bank funds, but they could not apply for those funds without first being official members of the IMF. This result in an evident limitation.
88 Alexander Kern, Dhumale Rahul, Eatwell John, *Global Governance of Financial Systems: the International Regulation of Systemic Risk* (OUP, 2006), 21. In this light, according to the authors

> the Bretton Woods framework sought to avoid the economic disaster of the interwar period when microeconomic instability spread like contagion through the financial sector and destabilized the macro economy. Those lessons were now embodied in appropriate policies and institutions. Important among these institutions were powerful regulatory structures and interventionist central banks dedicated to the reduction of systemic risk.

89 Ibid., 20.
90 Ibid., 22.

crisis. Before the crisis it was believed that market forces could effectively provide a discipline for rating agencies, but one of the main causes of the 2007 credit bubble of mortgage-backed securities was in fact created by 'private' ratings assigned to 'private' clients.[91]

Finally, in this changing environment the role of the IMF was also subverted. Now the IMF is 'no longer a stabilisation fund but has instead become a broader international financial institution focused on debtor nation crisis management, surveillance, conditional financial support and technical assistance'.[92] This is because at the global level the financial system lacks a common and uniform bankruptcy regime, a single financial regulator, and a lender of last resort.

Summing up, the process can be described as the beginning of globalisation and the internationalisation of financial markets in modern economies by the implementation of liberal policies; this phenomenon can be understood as a new paradigm entailing the definition of a new phenomenology of contemporary financial markets which can be represented as a complex system.[93]

### 3.5.1 Market failure and systemic risk

The most important feature of financial markets today is their integration and globalisation, made possible by rapid technological improvements. As Buckley suggests, the globalisation era finds

> its fullest expression in global capital flows and capital markets. The level of financial integration within, and across, the international economy is high and increasing because capital is perfectly suited to a global market – it moves around the world at the touch of a keyboard, and in response to information that comes in, principally, on a computer screen.[94]

The integration of the markets contributes to their intimate connection and interdependence, and their global nature makes them international. Capital flows are no longer restricted to national borders and financial risk is diversified through cross-border investments. In other words, in global financial markets today, space and time are irrelevant, and this revolution has been

---

91 Committee of European Securities Regulators Press Release, 'CESR Advises the European Commission to Take Steps and Offers its Proposals to Enhance the Integrity and Quality of the Rating Process' (19 May 2008), available at https://www.esma.europa.eu/document/press-release-cesr-advises-european-commission-take-steps-and-offers-its-proposal-enhance, accessed on 18 May 2017.
92 Buckley (n 84) 10.
93 The first mention to financial markets as a complex system has been illustrated in Chapter 3 of this work, but for final and consolidating remarks please refer to this Chapter and to Chapter 5.
94 Buckley (n 84) 16.

achieved mainly by liberal policies and deregulation, and the reformation of the initial Bretton Woods system.

It has been noted[95] there is no proof that the absence of domestic capital controls in terms of inflows and outflows can make one country more prosperous than another, but the most contentious question today, especially in the aftermath of the financial crisis of 2007–2010, is whether regulation or deregulation can still be considered as one of the main triggers for a financial crisis.[96]

For these reasons, if the nature of today's financial markets is global, the nature of a financial crisis is global too, and it can potentially affect every single sector of the financial markets. Consequently, the classic and rhetorical question is whether markets can achieve efficiency by themselves, or regulation is needed in order to guarantee, or at least promote, a national economic order.

It has already been said that the global financial crisis of 2007–2010 is connected to the internationalisation of financial markets, as well as to the privatisation of financial risk and the emergence of systemic risk. Indeed, in global financial markets issuers may be interested in raising funds outside their local or domestic capital market due to the process of globalisation and internationalisation of markets.[97]

There are different justifications for raising funds outside of the local market (i.e. from an investment diversification perspective to a cost funding advantage). However, it is important to bear in mind that the motivations for raising funds generally follow the classification of 'completely segmented' or 'completely integrated' capital markets that represents what Modigliani and Fabozzi[98] termed 'world capital market' as an ideal representation of markets. As opposed to 'world capital market', the 'real capital market' can face hurdles or specifications such as diversity in regulatory provisions, tax regimes, foreign exchange rates and many other variables that can effectively hinder and frustrate the possibility of raising new funds abroad in certain primary markets and lead to an identification of the 'real capital market' as 'mildly segmented' or 'mildly integrated'. In other words, the pragmatic concerns that exist in 'reality' can change the perception of how issuers approach primary capital markets for funding. This is why in global financial markets speculation can be seen potentially as the rational choice of the investor rather

---

95 Peter Nunnenkamp, 'Liberalisation and Regulation of International Capital Flows: Where the Opposite Meet' in Grote and Marauhn (eds.) *The Regulation of International Financial Markets: perspectives and reform* (CUP 2006) 262.
96 See further Sections 4.1.2 and 4.3.
97 Indeed, the internationalisation of capital markets started with the petro-dollar recycling in the 1970s, but reached its peak in the 1990s after the economic reforms of Thatcher in England and Reagan in the US. See Ravi Tennekoon, *The Law and Regulation of International Finance* (LexisNexis 1991).
98 Frank Fabozzi, Franco Modigliani, *Capital Markets: Institutions and Instruments* (2nd ed., Prentice Hall 1996) 125–157.

than as a form of exploitation of resources for the self-interested achievement of profit. In other words, today an under-regulated market can be perceived as a suitable environment for a firm to reduce costs, so that states under globalisation should protect themselves against 'imported fraud' and this can lead to regulatory competition concerns. This phenomenon has also been defined as a 'race to the bottom' or regulatory arbitrage where companies tend to transfer their investments to states that offer favourable economic conditions in order to reduce wage costs.[99]

The global nature of capital markets gives rise to two further consequences. First, the openness of financial markets today to going beyond national borders makes financial risk systemic, and second, the information asymmetry that dominates the market can constitute at least potentially a theoretical justification for an effective need of regulatory responses.[100]

Although there is no agreed definition of systemic risk[101] the main feature that this research aims to highlight –anticipated in the first Chapter – is to understand systemic risk as the product of the mispricing of financial risk, through which private actors who create financial risks do not internalise its cost, but spread it onto society. In other words, this new connotation of financial risk is seen as a form of negative externality similar to pollution.[102] In addition, in the attempt to reduce financial risk in complex financial systems, banks and corporations have started to use financial innovations to diversify risks, and have engaged in cross-border activities offering a wide range of financial services that normally incorporate insurance and securities activities as well as traditional banking facilities. This is what is defined as financial conglomerates[103] that call for supervision due to the contagion risk and the failure cascades effect that might arise in case of their collapse.[104]

For this reason, overexposure to financial risk, its privatisation and the 'socialisation' of its cost make global markets endemically destined to fail or collapse. This is a central argument for regulation, and at the same time it

---

99 Karl-Heinz Ladeur, 'Globalization and the Conversion of Democracy to Polycentriy Networks: Can Democracy Survive the End of the Nation State?' in Karl-Heinz Ladeur (ed.) *Public Governance in the Age of Globalization* (Ashgate 2004) 89.
100 Joseph E. Stiglitz, 'Government Failure vs. Market Failure: Principles of Regulation' in Balleisen and Moss (eds.) *Government and Markets toward a New Theory of Regulation* (CUP 2010) 16.
101 Kern *et al.* (n 5) 24–33.
102 Ibid., 24.
103 International Organisation of Securities Commissions, *Principles for the Supervision of Financial Conglomerates* (Cmd 1992) para 2. According to the report

> there are three different kinds of financial conglomerate where this might be the case: i) groups where securities business is the predominant activity; ii) groups where securities business is not predominant activity, although the predominant business is financial (eg banking or insurance); iii) groups where the predominant activity is commercial or industrial.

104 The Joint Forum, *Principles for the Supervision of Financial Conglomerates* (Cmd 2012) para 2.

outlines the need for an uncertainty-aversion paradigm, although the latter assumption fully reveals the paradox of modern economies that still reject uncertainty and try to govern it, though its full negation or mitigation can translate into a significant reduction in, or even elimination of, profit as well as a reduction in the creativity of market participants in relation to financial innovations, of which SPACs represent one direct instance.

### 3.5.2 The public-private divide and government failure

The endemic failure of markets shows a need for regulation and supervision. To this end, it is essential to outline what financial regulation is in modern economies and how the paternalistic role of the state has been irreversibly modified towards a new global governance paradigm in financial markets.

If internal capital controls are reduced or eliminated, then domestic firms gain more room for taking financial risks. This theoretically is not an issue as long as there is perfect competition and perfect information in the market. However, markets always register a lack of perfect information, as has been shown in Chapter 3, so that 'financial markets will (…) be affected to some degree of adverse selection, moral hazard, principal-agent problems, and herding behaviour'.[105] Furthermore, the lack of theoretical grounds for the justification that self-regulated markets can achieve market equilibrium alone has always supported the argument for top-down government interventions. To this end, the theory of Smith that markets can be efficiently self-governed by an 'invisible hand'[106] has always been contrasted to the Westphalian system,[107] a model based on a paternalistic view of the

---

105 Barry Eichengreen, Michael Mussa, *et al.*, 'Capital Account Liberalization: Theoretical and Practical Aspects' (1998) IMF Occasional Paper n. 172.
106 In particular, the idea of an 'invisible hand' has been borrowed by Smith from Shakespeare, Daniel Defoe and others. It is a thinking that reminds us how human beings as well as animals are governed by instincts. These natural instincts spur us to create order and progress in communities. Specifically, the progress becomes the natural outcome of a general instinct that is not determined by conscious motives. In the Wealth of Nations, Smith illustrates whether legal restrains on trade would harmonise private interests with public ones. Smith concludes that no restrain is desirable because business traders prefer to keep their capital at work in their domestic country. This because in Smith's view merchants know domestic laws and also they trust more people of their national system. This it means that more capitals will stay with Britain, therefore, favouring the economic growth of the country and generating a greater number of jobs and security. In Smith's words:

> (…) By preferring the support of domestic to that of foreign industry [the merchant] intends only his own security; and by directing that industry in such a manner as its produce may be of the greatest value, he intends only his own gain, and he is in this, as in many other cases, led by an invisible hand to promote an end which was no part of his intention.

(see Adam Smith, The Wealth of Nations (Harriman House, 2009) 293)
107 Marauhn (n. 97) 8. The author mentions private actors such as the IOSCO that is a private organisation, the International Association of Insurance Supervisors or the Basle

state in which regulation is imposed from the top as an expression of classic state sovereignty. According to this paternalistic view, the state is also capable of influencing the expansion of domestic markets by legal impositions and internal capital controls.

Nonetheless, one of the most relevant features of financial markets today is that markets are not exclusively based on state regulation, but especially on private actors' decisions and inter-agency forums that give rise to hybrid forms of regulation. In other words, the current dynamics of market governance are global rather than international.[108] Additionally, this trend has given rise, *inter alia*, to democratic, discriminatory and participatory concerns[109] as well as to the establishment of an ambiguous legal status for such private organisations or non-state actors.[110]

Apart from the political issues that hybrid regulation gives rise to, which are the result of the process of privatisation of financial risk, the hybrid feature of the system makes the involvement of private actors a fundamental instance of regulatory responses, as opposed to governments or governmental agencies which are part of the public sphere. Indeed, it has been noted[111] that the Westphalian model of regulation in its classic conception has failed from several angles in a post-regulatory world; in its inability to design effective legal rules for addressing complex social problems (instrument failure), its incapacity to implement rules (implementation failure), and its inability to persuade regulated entities and individuals to comply with those rules (motivational failure). In other words, nowadays it is not possible to rely exclusively on states' intervention in governing complex financial markets or complex financial systems, where it can be said that the final outcome of the regulation processes derives from a mixture of sources, especially self-regulatory responses elaborated by the private industry.[112]

In light of this, the role of government is overturned from the classical conception that it acts externally and outside of the markets, although the financial crisis of 2007–2010 has provided evidence for opposite conclusions,[113] and

---

Committee that is hosted by the Bank for International Settlements. These actors have reframed the classic public-private divide.
108 See for additional remarks Chapter 1 of this work where the concepts of international governance and global governance have been further explained.
109 Marauhn (n 97) 14.
110 Chris Brummer, 'Why Soft Law Dominates International Finance – And Not Trade' in Cottier, Jackson and Lastra (eds.) *International Law in Financial Regulation and Monetary Affairs* (OUP 2012) 95.
111 Julia Black, 'Decentring Regulation: Understanding the Role of Regulation and Self-Regulation in a "Post-Regulatory" World' (2001) 54 (1) Current Legal Problems 106.
112 Omarova, 'Rethinking the future of self-regulation in the financial industry' (2010) Cornell Law Faculty Publications Paper, 1022.
113 Stavros Gadinis, 'From Independence to Politics in Financial Regulation' (2013) 101 (2) California Law Review 322. To this end, in the aftermath of the financial crisis 2008–2009 it has been noted as the role and paradigm of independent agencies has

one could say there is a counter trend with the re-emergence and reaffirmation of a new Westphalian system that aims to reframe and disempower the traditional role of independent agencies in financial regulation. Indeed, according to other scholars,[114] although a new role for the government as an entity external to the market can be identified, there are also clear instances where the government exercises a foundational role; in other words, it is internal to markets.

For this reason, it can be misleading to illustrate the global governance of financial markets as a public-private divide *tout court,* as if the government was relegated to the public sphere and the market to the private one with society internal to the market's logics. This is only a preliminary and simplistic view of the financial system because there are instances where governments act in a 'market actor role' using private means to public ends and in so doing they act as private actors in markets.[115]

Nonetheless, although there are instances of governments acting in markets by virtue of private means,[116] one must bear in mind that governments always pursue public ends, at least to re-distribute justice and establish or influence prices. Those activities are not pertinent to private actors. This is because in some instances, private actors lack financial resources or trust in the market, and this can also prevent them from implementing government-like strategies because of competition concerns (for instance, a private market participant will never be allowed to influence or impose prices because such behaviours

---

been re-structured. Indeed, governments have started to be again in charge of banking supervision and empowered in order to impose veto rights in relation to the liquidation of financial institutions as well as restructuring plans or insolvency declarations of banks. This trend is against the traditional role of independent agencies that have always been in charge especially in financial regulation of overseeing delegated powers.

114 Robert C. Hockett, Saule T. Omarova, '"Private" Means to "Public" Ends: Government as Market Actors' (2014) 1016 Cornell Law Faculty Publications 54, 55.
115 Ibid., 56.
116 Ibid. The authors first mention the existence of private laws that exercise a foundational role of the markets such as laws establishing proprietary interests in market exchange or contract law in the case of future performance in market exchange. Furthermore, they identify for expository purposes four different forms of the 'market actor role' of governments, namely 'market-making', 'market-moving', 'market-levering' and 'market-preserving'. Governments in 'market-making' roles bear risks that private actors are 'unable or unwilling to bear' such as the risk that some products will not be sold on the market and they agree to act as a 'buyer of last resort' through a private means that is underwriting. Governments in 'market-moving' are affecting prices on certain markets instead of allowing private actors to do this, for instance, when central banks open market operations such as the purchasing or selling of treasury securities or the 'short-selling commodities whose quantitative easing-inflated prices disproportionately harm the poor'. Governments in 'market-levering' form can improve existing private markets' outcomes such as in the case of public pensions whose investments can influence the practices of other firms, and finally when they act in 'market-preserving' roles possible collapses of the market are prevented in order to avoid negative externalities, in other words it is the role of the government to act as a collective agent.

are clearly against competition concerns which aim to avoid the creation of market abuses or dominant positions). For this reason, if it is true that, on the one hand, markets are destined to experience systemic failures due to their internationalisation and privatisation, on the other hand it is not possible for private actors to rectify or even counterbalance such collapses. Furthermore, private actors operate within a 'recursive collective action problem'[117] that prevents them from achieving public ends. By contrast, they do pursue egoistic objectives based on the achievement of profit. For these reasons, private actors can be responsible for systemic failures, although markets themselves are destined to collapse.

The dynamics of financial markets are therefore very unstable, and one can say that if there is a recursive collective action problem on the side of private actors, governments are not totally exempted from what can be termed a 'recursive agent problem'. In this case governments, market actors in the sense that they are collective agents playing a market-moving role,[118] can be as unstable as their private counterparts, influencing speculative spirals (for instance, the decision by a Central Bank to employ quantitative easing policies can influence the money supply by maintaining low interest rates, and this in turn can translate into speculative activities). For this reason, the phenomenology of contemporary financial markets looks complex, and one can say that one possible way to understand it better is to make reference to network theories and the study of complex systems in markets (see Chapters 1 and 6).

### 3.5.3 Financial regulation between macroeconomic stability and microeconomic objectives

The economic crisis (2007–2010) has shown that macroeconomic elements play a more important role than microeconomic elements in the regulation of financial markets.[119] Nonetheless, I shall argue that although macroeconomic or financial stability is a virtuous objective of modern financial regulation, especially after the emergence of systemic risk, one cannot deny the remarkable role that microeconomic actors have played during and since the economic

---

117 Robert C. Hockett, 'Recursive Collective Actions Problems: The Structure of Procyclicality in Financial and Monetary Markets, Macro Economies and Formally Similar Contexts' (2015) 3 (2) Journal of Financial Perspectives 36. Robert C. Hockett, 'A Fixer-Upper for Finance' (2010) 87 (6) Washington University Law Review 1213. With the idea of recursive collection action problem Hockett would like to highlight how decisions that are taken rationally by multiple individuals can generate and result in self-defeating outcomes. The problem is recursive because the negative movement in one direction is destined to move further in the same direction ending in unsatisfactory equilibrium. For instance, the case of mortgage-backed securities in 2007 leading to the credit crunch is an evident sign of recursive collective action problem.
118 Hockett, Omarova (n 117).
119 Mathias Dewatripont, Xavier Freixas, Richard Portes (eds.) *Macroeconomic Stability and Financial Regulation: Key Issues for the G20* (Centre for Economic Policy Research 2011).

crisis (2007–2010). Indeed, as has been seen in this chapter the creation of risks and the decisions of risk-takers in financial markets mainly concern private actors and their subjective appetite for financial risk. This is also part of that feature of risk that has been defined in terms of 'human-humanity' to differentiate it from the 'human-inhumanity' paradigm of uncertainty where people's desires go far beyond 'open human control'.

Specifically, the crisis (2007–2010) – at international level – has given rise to the need for rethinking the supervisory activity and the regulatory system of financial markets. Those are macroeconomic objectives. In particular, one of the most important G20 Summits was held in September 2009 in Pittsburgh when the financial crisis reached one of its peaks. The Summit concluded that 'systematic international cooperation' is the key element needed to face the current global crisis on the grounds of systemic risk and contagion effects. Thus, the G20 promoted macroeconomic objectives such as the reshaping of the role of the IMF and the strengthening of capital standards in banking supervision[120] as well as regulatory responses for OTC derivatives, credit rating agencies and hedge funds by highlighting the importance of achieving microeconomic objectives. One year later, the Basel III Committee on Banking Supervision (2010) designed a voluntary regulatory framework with different accords on bank capital adequacy, stress testing and market liquidity risk.[121] The Basel III Committee on Banking Supervision tried to achieve two main objectives, namely to preserve the real economy from the spill-over effect and contagion risk initiated by the financial sector, and second to strengthen the forms of capital requirements and retained earnings of banks. Indeed, the specific regulation on equity instruments issued or retained by banks might reveal how equity is also not a completely risk-free security.

These approaches show how the effect of the crisis (2007–2010) can reflect on macroeconomic stability, especially since the internationalisation of financial markets, but microeconomic elements are still vital to govern financial risk due to the inalienable uncertainty feature. To this end, the next sections show how post-crisis regulatory responses as well as industry regulation have mainly aimed at preserving financial stability rather than focusing on microeconomic objectives. This comparative study also highlights the re-emergence of a Westphalian system of regulation where governments intervene as outsiders to the markets and impose evaluations and judgements that should be left to private firms.

---

120 See 'Declaration G20 Leaders Summit' (Pittsburgh 2009), available online at http://www.g20.utoronto.ca/2009/2009communique0925.html, accessed on 18 February 2017. The objectives that were fixed during the Pittsburgh Summit are important in order to completely understand the reforms that took place both in America and Europe.
121 See the revised document 'Basel III: A Global Regulatory Framework for More Resilient Banks and Banking Systems'(2011) available online at http://www.bis.org/publ/bcbs189.pdf, accessed on 18 February 2017.

### 3.5.4 The role of law in systemic failures and self-regulation

It has been seen in this chapter that financial markets are dominated by risk and uncertainty and therefore the role of derivatives has been to allow private actors to diversify risks and hedge against them.

Nonetheless, derivatives are complex financial products that can hardly be defined in law because of the uncertainty of their objects. A derivative product can be seen as a contract whose value is based on the value of underlying assets, which in turn can be a commodity or a financial product, such as interest or exchange rates. The determination of the value of the derivative can be contested because of the impossibility of determining the actual financial and real value of those instruments.[122] This can translate in turn into speculation and betting behaviours that are responsible for the creation of pure risks in subjective terms.[123] Although derivatives can be criticised *per se* for their functioning and their value-assessment, it has been noted[124] that one of the real causes of the financial crisis (2007–2010) was not the inability of the system to keep up with the pace of financial innovations, but the possibility, guaranteed under the law, of trading derivatives on non-regulated and private venues. To this end, it is worth noting that a 'law' consented to the trading of derivatives on a non-regulated venue, namely the OTC market. This created the assumption that a lack of regulation can be responsible for an increase in opportunistic behaviours and inefficient market dynamics. In particular, the lack of regulation in those venues led to a rise in financial speculation, and in addition, the emergence of a credit default swaps market was critical in the determination of negative outcomes such as the subprime mortgage and securitisation schemes.

However, regulation itself can be seen and is often perceived as a limit to a free market economy where the symbol of the 'invisible hand' is preferred to restrictions and controls. Despite the instincts of human society towards progress and wealth, we have also previously outlined that the absence of perfect competition and perfect information leads to a 'need' for regulatory responses.[125] Among those regulatory instances the Westphalian model of

---

122 Donatella Alessandrini, 'Regulating Financial Derivatives? Risks, Contested Values and Uncertainty Features' (2011) Social & Legal Studies 1, 2.
123 See Section 3.3.
124 Lynn A. Stout, 'Derivatives and the Legal Origin of the 2008 Credit Crisis' (2011) 1 Harvard Business Law Review 1, 3. The author outlines how the law passed by the Congress in 2000 called the Commodities Futures Modernization Act was mainly responsible for the financial crisis (2007–2010) because it allowed the trading of derivatives on OTC venues. Therefore, according to this view changes in the law have been responsible for the collapse of the system rather than the absence of regulatory guidelines.
125 Charles Goodhart, Philipp Hartmann, *et al.*, *Financial Regulation: Why, How and Where Now?* (Routledge 1998) 2. Indeed, famous economists are supporters of free banking such as Dowd, Benston and Kaufman, who theorise how regulation plays a negative role in financial crisis. Before them one can think of Adam Smith's invisible hand that represents a symbol of free markets.

regulation seems to be gaining ground today due to a trend for reinforcement of regulatory controls by public centralised authorities or institutions. Llewellyn has pointed out several of the downsides or negative outcomes[126] to which regulation can lead. Although his critique can be perceived as a statement against regulation itself and the possible negative effects of over-regulation, it should be considered as a pure critique of an 'external' approach to regulation, namely top-down models or Westphalian approaches. Indeed, in contrast to top-down approaches of regulation, one can find bottom-up instances that are market-oriented and directly represent the output of market operators and the financial industry.

This is identified as self-regulation, and as has been anticipated in Chapters 1 and 2, it constitutes one of the most important elements of the modern global governance of financial systems that are today governed by a mixture of self-regulation and paternalistic approaches. Therefore, the role of the law is modified towards hybrid models of regulation.

Indeed, as Coase argues,[127] the efficiency of free markets is reliant on considerable internal infrastructure and self-regulation with minimal transaction costs. Although parties can enter into private agreements in order to set interests, the sanctioning of those agreements or their practical enforcement must always be carried out by public laws such as contract law and commercial law. Therefore, looking at free markets through Coase seems to reduce the role of private actors, who in the end must rely on the state, or rather on laws enacted by the state, to enforce their private rules and agreements.

The absence of a serious approach to self-regulation in the modern financial architecture is justified, according to Omarova, by the unpopularity of the concept, due to casino capitalism and the negative image of financial markets and Wall Street. However, a new paradigm of self-regulation will be advocated in the form of 'embedded self-regulation'.[128] It has been seen that state regulation can be evaded by financial arbitrage,[129] therefore it seems crucial to take into account the opinions of private actors in regulatory processes, and sometimes even to allow private actors to become rule makers. According to Omarova, self-regulation is vital for achieving two main objectives: 'timely

---

126 David T Llewellyn, 'Re-engineering the Regulator' (1996) 1 (3) The Financial Regulator 21, 23–24. According to the author highly prescriptive regimes of regulation can lead, *inter alia*, to the following downsides: (a) the industry can perceive such regime as excessive and redundant; (b) risks are usually so complex that cannot be covered by mere rules; (c) prevent financial innovation; (d) can cause rules escalation by which new provisions are added into the system, but the old norms are not withdrawn; (e) information loss; (f) over-regulation s not responsive to market conditions.
127 Ronald Harry Coase, *The Firm, The Market and the Law* (University of Chicago Press 1988).
128 Saule T. Omarova, 'Wall Street as Community of Fate: Toward Financial Industry Self-regulation' (2011) 159 (2) University of Pennsylvania Law Review 412.
129 Victor Fleisher, 'Regulatory Arbitrage' (2010) University of Colorado Law Legal Studies Research Paper No. 10–11, 1–67.

access to market information, on the one hand, and the need to monitor and manage risk across jurisdictional borders, on the other'.[130] Self-regulation must take into account public ends, especially financial stability and social values (this is the 'embedded' conception of self-regulation), but through private enforcement. This new role of self-regulation is, therefore, delicate and requires the imposition of collective self-restraint in order to avoid or limit the unscrupulous profit-oriented activities of private members. This is what Omarova terms 'community of fate'; community belief in achieving a common future through self-restriction.

Nonetheless, a macroeconomic approach is more popular today, where no space is left for self-regulation in the financial industry. The financial industry, in contrast to other industries, is permeated by systemic risk and public safety nets, such as bail-outs and deposits schemes, that prevent private and public actors from being seriously interested in the implementation or enforcement of self-regulation approaches within their industry. Today it seems that there is a lack of practical examples of self-regulation in financial systems; SPACs represent an exception and can therefore be identified as a practical instance of self-regulatory responses. Indeed, SPACs can be theorised in Omarova's terms as embedded self-regulation instruments, because they aim towards public objectives such as the protection of investors and market stability through the private enforcement that is carried out by the SPAC management.

### 3.5.5 SPACs and soft law

Soft law is sometimes defined as a form of self-regulation.[131] I shall argue that this is the case, especially if one looks at soft law as an instance of bottom-up regulation. Indeed, according to Lastra[132] 'top-down' soft law differs from the 'bottom-up' soft law approach, which entails self-regulation. Specifically, in the case of 'bottom-up' soft law, it is possible to identify instances of regulation coming from private actors in order to regulate their community as 'community of fate' in Omarova's view. The advantage of having a soft

---

130 Omarova, Wall Street as Community (n 131) 418.
131 Omarova, Wall Street as Community (n 131) 424. Indeed, according to the author there are
> many forms of self-regulation in practice, as well as many definitions of what it is – or should be – in the academic and policy debate. "Self-regulation" is often used interchangeably with other, similar terms, such as "self-governance", "co-regulation", "voluntarism", "private regulation", "soft law", "quasi-regulation", "communitarian regulation", and so on. Each of these terms tends to emphasize a particular characteristic that arguably distinguishes "self-regulation" from regulation – the purely voluntary nature of regulation, the nongovernment actors as the sole rulemaking authority, or the nonbinding or non-legal nature of the rules.

132 Rosa Lastra, *Legal Foundations of International Monetary Stability* (OUP 2006) 462.

law approach in financial markets reflects the dynamicity of financial innovations, and specifically provides flexibility in order to enforce quasi-legal regimes for complex financial products.[133]

For instance, in relation to SPACs, soft law plays an essential role due to the complexity of these investment vehicles. Indeed, the 'bottom-up' regulation approach has been identified in the first generation of SPACs (namely, the SPACs that came into existence after the disappearance of the blank check companies on the PSM). As opposed to SPACs of the first generation, the second generation were provided with a 'top-down' soft law regulation (namely, through the guidelines issued by the Securities Commission of Bursa Malaysia).[134] In this latter case SPACs received a specific kind of discipline through an institutionalised private actor, although in the form of soft law provisions. The guidelines recognises the international standards of SPACs in relation to their corporate features and provide a possible answer to economic concerns.

This codification is the result of the reception of international or market standards that in turn were developed by a 'bottom-up' self-regulation approach. It is the industry and the SPAC promoters that contributed to the formation of corporate standards to imitate. For this reason, I shall argue that without a self-regulation approach that starts with a community of financial operators (in the case of SPACs the promoters or managers), it is harder for institutionalised private actors to impose (such as in the case of exchanges) or to discipline (such as in the case of the Securities Commission in Malaysia) financial innovations. This is why SPACs represent a practical instance of self-regulation in the financial industry that can inspire the enforcement of new private regulations and quasi-legal regimes for new financial products.

## 3.6 Conclusions

SPACs are cash-shell companies that cannot be assimilated to private equity funds, although they are a form of alternative investment vehicle to access public markets. SPACs sit in the apex of free market dynamics because they are a product of competition in financial innovations, and at the same time they constitute an expression of uncertainty due to the money creation processes of modern economies.

Uncertainty is perceived as a dangerous feature of the markets, so there is a tendency to try to eliminate or reduce it, especially in the period of post-crisis financial regulation (2007–2010). The same is true for the external shock known as Covid-19 where governments' main policy objective is to reduce market uncertainty and anxiety of market participants. This trend has been defined in this chapter as uncertainty-aversion, as opposed to the

---

133 Chris Brummer, 'Why Soft Law dominates International Finance – And Not Trade' (2010) 13 (3) *Journal of International Economic Law*, 623. Ibid, *Soft Law and the Global Financial System: Rule Making in the 21st century* (CUP 2012).
134 See Chapter 4.

risk-aversion that was the common approach of *homo stocasticus*. This is because the uncertainty that is currently perceived in the market is responsible for information asymmetry, agency costs and moral hazard, especially when the classification and distribution of risks cannot be fully achieved because of the system's ineradicable features of ignorance and indeterminateness, which are linked to uncertainty. Nonetheless, investing in information is an efficient answer to the disorder of the system that can find a spontaneous economic equilibrium (see Chapter 6).

On the other hand, uncertainty is a necessary feature of the system. Without uncertainty, the money creation process is reduced or even eliminated altogether. Furthermore, any legislation or attempt to suppress uncertainty is responsible for eliminating competition and progress as well as financial innovation. For instance, SPACs as a form of financial innovation are a direct expression of the competition processes that are sustained by information asymmetry. Uncertainty is the cost that free markets impose on market operators.

This reflection is part of a broader picture, where the phenomenology of contemporary financial markets is understood as a complex system which is determined, in particular, by its pyramidal organisation. The structure of the market at the international level is global, but the qualities of the markets at a micro- or local level are characterised by randomness. This is a typical feature of complex systems that present a global structure within a random functioning. In a system of this kind a central planner, such as the government, is absent and the market operators become its planners. Specifically, in economic terms, the entrepreneur has a responsibility to confront uncertainty, and profit becomes payment for the exercise of judgement involving risk. It is the managers who can provide the markets with financial innovation. Competition, financial innovation and decentralised planning are parts of a spontaneous *motus* through which free markets organise themselves.

It can be said that it is the entrepreneur who as a decision taker colonises the future, in the words of Giddens, but it should be added that he is also the one who possesses enough intuition to confront uncertainty and reduce anxiety by taking responsibility for the risk that necessarily accompanies uncertainty.

The main role of uncertainty has become clearer from the evolution of financial risk. From Bretton Woods until Basel the conception of financial risk has evolved, and it has been privatised. The banks and private actors or financial operators started to diversify risks in global markets where cross-border investments became the common practice, and domestic markets collapsed due to a lack of international financial controls.

This caused systemic risk, spill-over effects and failure cascades. The interconnection of the financial systems became the reason for speculation, but also an opportunity for growth. Thus, any missed opportunity was perceived as a loss, or rather as an opportunity risk faced by financial operators within a new phenomenology of financial systems.

For this reason, the central question was raised in relation to law and to its role in financial crises. Surely a free market economy rejects the idea of highly specialised regulation imposed by the state. Indeed, the Westphalian system is perceived as the external activity of the government in relation to markets. As opposed to this externality we saw the role of self-regulation in accordance with a view of global governance. This means that self-regulation as postulated by Omarova should be 'embedded' with values and should be added to governmental regulations.

It seems that one of the most significant instances of the regulatory approach can today be identified in SPACs. Indeed, SPACs of the first generation adopted a 'bottom-up' self-regulation approach through which self-restraint in relation to corporate features was imposed by managers. Soon afterwards these behaviours were translated into a codification or reception of market practices by other private actors such as exchanges or specialised commissions. For this reason, SPACs were always informed by 'bottom-up' regulatory approaches rather than 'top-down' regulation responses. This contributes to their qualification as what I term 'SPAC without law' but not 'outside of the law' (in fact, general corporate law will always be applicable to corporate features of SPACs as is contractual law or trust law in relation to the escrow agreement).

The acknowledgement of this phenomenon constitutes an intellectual challenge for financial operators and regulators and calls for a rethinking of a new role for the law in financial markets. It should start through self-regulation practices and the recognition of a new process of regulation not exclusively generated through parliaments and political debates, but from a 'bottom-up' claim and private enforcement. The next chapter and the last one are trying to convey for the first time the establishment of a new financial order where the auto-regeneration process of self-regulation can justify the same existence of the system *tout court*. It is indeed this new approach based on financial systems that tries to justify academically the idea of a new legal order where risk, uncertainty, competition and financial innovation constitute the main structures of the system.

For this reason, the next chapter examines the role of soft law and how self-regulation can play a vital role in SPAC regulations. The chapter also explores whether in general terms a soft law approach can be preferred to hard law rules for governing financial markets in a post financial crisis era, and especially today in a post-pandemic scenario.

# 4 The international financial regulation of SPACs

## 4.1 The regulation of SPACs at international level

The American financial regulation of SPACs has revealed the evolutionary process of these investment vehicles. They began being listed on the PSM, a non-regulated venue, but soon after the enactment of Regulation 419 by the SEC, they disappeared from the PSM and were reborn as SPACs, bringing with them the corporate features already discussed in Chapter 2.

For this reason, the following sections are devoted to illustrating a different story. Specifically, they outline the financial regulation of SPACs at international level. Other exchanges and regulators have recently begun to provide SPACs with specific disciplines, for instance, the Bursa Malaysia and the Toronto Stock Exchange. Those rules can be referred to as a standardisation of market practices and soft law regulations. On the other hand, a by-law approach has been implemented by the Korea Exchange and the Turkish Stock Exchange.

The chapter also examines for the first time the variegated discipline of SPACs in Europe where there is no specific SPAC regulation modelled on the American standards, with the exception of the UK that has started to implement a similar model, although with crucial differences. This is at least the current overview and perception of the financial regulation of SPACs in Europe. However, this apparent lack of regulation is not a negative feature *per se*. It is capable of generating competition between Member States and identifying the most SPAC-friendly jurisdictions, although the limit on the application of corporate frameworks related to redemption rights today still constitutes one of the main obstacles to a SPAC wave in Europe. For instance, as anticipated, the UK has recently evaluated the possibility of changing its own market rules to accommodate SPACs' needs.[1]

Finally, the chapter examines for the first time a 'multilevel SPAC definition' that relates to the adoption of a dynamic concept by which the 'special

---

1 Camilla Hodgson, 'London Explores Hopping on SPACs Bandwagon: Blank-cheque Companies are Booming in the US, but the UK is Being Left Behind' (6 October 2020) Financial Times.

purpose' justifies a broader conception of SPACs. This means that the concept of the SPAC and its definition(s) may vary from time to time and from legal system to legal system.

### 4.1.1 The European regulation of SPACs

In Europe SPACs are a recent phenomenon, and the Italian legal system has definitively attracted the most attention in terms of SPACs. Europe lacks a direct positive legal discipline for SPACs. There is no uniform and harmonised legal discipline in the form of a regulation or directive (secondary sources of law of the European Union) that provides a specific legal discipline. The same lack of a positive discipline is registered at international level. The ESMA once issued its guidelines[2] on the Dir. 2011/61/EU on the Alternative Investment Fund Manager (AIFMD) neither mentioning SPACs nor providing any clarification on whether AIFMD can be applied to them, despite their being a possible instance of collective investment undertakings (UCITS). As per the ESMA guidelines, a collective investment undertaking:

a   does not have a general commercial or industrial purpose;
b   the undertaking pools together capital raised from its investors for the purpose of investment with a view to generating a pooled return for those investors and
c   the unit holders or shareholders of the undertaking – as a collective group – have no day-to-day discretion or control.

According to this description, SPACs may be categorised as UCITS because they are cash-shell companies, hence they do not follow industrial aims, but aim to raise money in IPO processes, and are directed by managers, as opposed to unit holders that do not have a direct control or discretion on the firm. However, this is only a possible interpretation under the current European financial legal framework that has not yet received a practical application or become official either in Europe or in other legal systems. Indeed, some systems directly exclude the inclusion of SPACs into collective investments (see below the example of the Korea Stock Exchange). According to the definition above, a SPAC can be identified as a UCITS only if it is a sector-focused SPAC as opposed to multi-sector-focused SPACs, namely a specific target company shall be identified to make the UCITS discipline applicable to SPACs. Furthermore, the challenge for SPACs in all EU Member States is to argue that they are to be considered a 'holding' and benefit from the holding exemption provided for in AIFMD.

Recently, on 15 July 2021, giving the growing interest of SPACs in Europe, the ESMA has issued a public statement on SPACs, although it has

---

2   ESMA, *Guidelines on key concepts of the AIFMD*, August 2013, n. 611.

not provided a precise definition of them leaving opened the discussion of whether SPACs can be identified as UCITS or Alternative Investment Funds (see the Addendum for consolidating remarks) in Europe.

This interpretation also makes SPACs similar to private equity funds, at least because they are a specification, especially in terms of management's compensation schemes structures, although with remarkable features that distinguish them from the latter, such as the fact of relying on equity rather than debt (for instance, the well-known LBO process of private equity firms will never be seen in SPACs[3]).

For these reasons, we can state that currently, SPACs in Europe are experiencing a lack of direct regulation, and the financial law environment appears quite under-regulated, or, as I can better define, de-regulated, although for the clearance of doubts, SPACs' prospectuses in Europe are always subject to existing disclosure requirements under the Prospectus Regulation (Regulation 2017/1129). However, the Prospectus Regulation only applies to issuers on regulated markets meaning that unregulated venues or better multilateral trading facilities can benefit from exceptions and provide investors with a less stringent offer document such as on the Alternative Investment Market. This feature does not have to be seen from a negative perspective. SPACs, since their ancestors (blank check companies), have never liked regulation *tout court*, especially if we think of SEC Rule 419, and the consequent disappearance of BCCs from the PSM.

Additionally, it has been observed before that SPACs' lack of positive law or codification/reception in the form of statutes and capital markets' regulations means they can be identified as 'without law', but not 'outside of the law'. This because even if a SPAC is not regulated in a specific capital market or legal system, this does not equate to a lack of regulation *tout court*. As we said, if modern SPACs follow a self-regulation approach, they will always implement and enforce the corporate features that have been recognised as international standards in Chapter 2. Therefore, those corporate features will always be disciplined by the general corporate law frameworks that each legal system has enforced.

For this reason, we speak of SPACs 'without law' in order to identify the lack of a positive discipline where no compulsory definition of SPACs is provided except for the Bursa Malaysia and the Korea Exchange, but at the same time we assert that SPACs are not 'outside of the law'. This is because the corporate features of SPACs will find their general law in the respective corporate law system of each legal order. Despite the existence of a general law that each legal system has in relation to corporate law, sometimes SPACs will also be regulated by private actors such as the exchanges or regulators, although this is for dealing with standard listing requirements (for example,

---

3 Nonetheless, please note that the SPAC can try to rely on facility agreements and lending from banks at the time of the business combination or De-SPACing in order to pay part of the consideration needed to cover the value of the target company.

the listing requirements provided for in the market rules of the NYSE and NASDAQ). At other times the managers of SPACs will provide them with a specific regulation, such as in the case of the London Stock Exchange and *Borsa Italiana* where a specific market discipline for SPACs is absent. Indeed, when there is in place a specific or special regulation for a SPAC, it is always in addition to the general discipline of corporate law. It seems that for SPACs a simple by-law approach does not reflect the complexity of investment vehicles based closely on customary evolution. For this reason, self-regulation approaches in terms of soft law or hard law provisions of capital markets regulations seem to better illustrate the complex features of SPACs.

Finally, company law represents a legal constant in the SPAC world, but at the same time it can be the ground for a diversified discipline on shareholders' redemption rights. This is especially so in European SPACs or civil law jurisdictions where redemption rights are generally subordinated or limited to specific circumstances provided by the law, such as in Italy, France, and Germany. As a result, common law jurisdictions are seen as more SPAC-friendly in relation to the redemption right to shareholders, where greater flexibility seems more appealing to investors and consequently to the managers creating these vehicles.

However, it is desirable to imagine that as the SPAC revolution makes its way through Europe, exchanges and regulators will work together towards the establishment of a SPAC-friendly environment where capital markets regulation is modified and tailored to meet the specific needs of these investment vehicles, and investors are protected against possible frauds and egoistic behaviours on the part of the management.

### 4.1.2 SPACs and the London stock exchange

In 2017, the UK saw a resurgence of SPACs despite the notorious scandals that occurred on the AIM, such as in the case of Langbar International, formerly known as Crown Corporation, which raised £140 million on the AIM in 2003. Subsequently, Crown Corporation invested the money in construction contracts in Argentina worth £365 million and in a series of international investments. However, those investments turned out to be potential frauds perpetrated against investors' interests to pursue a sort of 'pump-and-dump' scheme. Langbar International claimed to be one of the biggest cash shells on the AIM, although it is worth pointing out that it was not a SPAC.

Nonetheless, the notoriety connected to cash shells listed on the AIM, and particularly to oil and gas companies, has surely decreased confidence on the part of investors. The AIM is still seen as a more flexible market venue which lacks strict regulation (for instance, the 'name-and-shame' system to prevent frauds is rarely implemented; AIM's regulators, known as nomads, do not carry out detailed companies' screening, etc.). All these market features encourage the possibility of weak verification and oversight, although the Financial Conduct Authority in the UK has the duty to oversee misconduct by market operators.

For these reasons, the FCA has tried to provide some insight into SPACs as a species of general definition of cash-shell companies. Under the Financial Conduct Authority Listing Rules there is no definition of SPAC or cash-shell. However, as it is underlined in the FCA technical note on SPACs, the latter are qualified as:

> 'new company[ies] incorporated to identify and acquire a suitable business opportunity or opportunities' [They] may also have been referred to as 'search fund[s]'.[4]

According to the FCA, SPACs generally seek a listing under Chapter 14 of the Listing Rule that regulates the requirements for the standard listing of shares. They are not eligible for a premium listing on the main market of the London Stock Exchange. This is because they do not possess balance sheets nor are they an independent business (under the requirement LR6) because they are cash-shell companies; therefore, they are non-operating companies. On the other hand, if a SPAC is listed under LR 14, it does not have to be an 'investment entity'. This means that SPACs in the UK can seek a quotation on either the LSEs' AIM market or the main market standard listing on the LSE under Chapter 14 of the FCA Listing Rules.

After 2015, the AIM scandals forced the LSE to modify the listing rules of this market venue, and SPACs were compelled to raise at least 6 million during the IPO. Subsequently, a SPAC must deploy its capital within 18 months of being admitted to AIM, and SPAC promoters must appoint a nomad (nominated adviser, namely an investment bank) as well as seek shareholder approval for any further listing period beyond 18 months.

These conditions have limited the application of SPACs in London. SPACs like flexibility and the period of 18 months to find a business combination might be perceived as too short for the sponsors' tastes. The same applies on the side of the target companies that can see the possibility of SPAC's liquidation as one of the main concerns. Last but not least, the AIM requires that reverse takeovers must be approved by shareholders. Hence, this is one of the main reasons why a standard segment is generally considered to be a more attractive venue in most cases.

A standard listing on the main market can guarantee more prestige to SPACs' promoters, and the listing requirements are more flexible. A SPAC listed on the main market through a standard listing procedure does not have to appoint a financial adviser, sponsor or nomad and is exempted from any corporate governance procedures. Furthermore, the SPAC must have capital reserves of at least £700,000. However, the SPAC must prepare an IPO prospectus, have at least 25% of its shares in public hands and the duration of the SPAC can be from 24 to 36 months window to deploy funds as there is no

---

4 Financial Conduct Authority. 2018. *Technical Note on Cash Shell and Special Purpose Acquisition Companies (SPACs)*, January 2018 UKLA/TN/420.2, https://www.fca.org.uk/publication/ukla/ tn-420-2.pdf, accessed on 1 January 2021.

specific requirement. Additionally, the shareholder approval for acquisition is not a requirement of the standard segment, and they do not have to approve any delisting. Nonetheless, the standard segment requires them to make annual corporate governance statements, including, *inter alia*, confirmation of the corporate governance code applied and explaining any non-compliance with its provisions.

The following table summarises the main features that SPACs need to satisfy to be listed either on the AIM or the Standard segment on the London Stock Exchange. It is important to highlight that after the UK SPAC reform in August 2021, some of those requirements have been modified, especially in terms of shareholders' approval for acquisition and minimum capital raise for IPO as explained below and in the Addendum.

|  | *AIM* | *Standard Listing* |
|---|---|---|
| Listing document | AIM admission document | FCA approved prospectus |
| Minimum capital raise for IPO | £6,000,000 | £700,000 |
| Initial term for acquisition[5] | Must release the funds in escrow within 18 months or seek further shareholder approval | Must release the funds in escrow within a 24–36-month window as there is no specific requirement |
| Shareholder approval for acquisition | Yes, and it will be a reverse takeover for AIM Rule purposes | No |
| Listing document required for re-admission of enlarged group following acquisition | Yes – AIM Admission Document | Yes – FCA approved prospectus |
| Financial adviser requirements | Nominated adviser required to be appointed by SPAC for the purposes of the IPO and on an ongoing basis thereafter | No requirement under Listing Rules, but financial adviser often appointed in practice |
| Corporate Governance | AIM companies must confirm the corporate governance code they have chosen to apply and explain how they comply with that code – the reasons for any non-compliance must also be explained | Requirements to make annual corporate governance statement, including (among other things) confirmation of the corporate governance code applied and explaining any non-compliance with its provisions |

5 The minimum capital raise for IPO is currently under review by the FCA, which in accordance with the Hill Report would like to riase – for instance – such limit on the Standard Segment as much as £50 million.

| | | |
|---|---|---|
| Free float | No minimum percentage free float requirement, but will need to be comfortable there will be sufficient liquidity post-IPO | 25% of the shares but be in public hands on admission to listing and at all times thereafter |
| Shareholder approval required for delisting | Yes | No |

The IPO of J2 Acquisition (the largest SPAC since 2011 in the UK) and Landscape Acquisition Holding, both pursuing a standard listing in the UK, were particularly successful in 2017, raising in excess of $1.75bn between them.[6] This shows that the standard listing on the main market has become the most popular choice of promoters, although the compliance costs of an IPO prospectus are higher than the admission document of the AIM.

In 2020, the LSE saw almost zero SPAC launches.[7] This is due also to the fact that as opposed to the US, UK rules are not specifically tailored for SPACs, and, in particular, once a business acquisition is announced the SPAC has to suspend the trading of shares, and investors are then barred from trading again until the deal completes – which could be three to five months.[8] This condition is not appealing for SPACs and it is increasing sponsors' costs. Hence, the decision of the LSE to think about changing market rules for SPACs in the UK.[9]

On 3 March 2021, Lord Jonathan Hill's review of the UK's listing regime[10] recommended a series of reforms to make the UK a more attractive venue for initial public offerings post-Brexit. The Hill Report represents, *inter alia*, the LSE much-needed answer to the 'SPAC craze' in the US that started in 2020. Unlike in the US, there are no specific listing requirements for SPACs either on the LSE or in other European capital markets, with the exception of *Borsa Italiana* S.p.A. that has some specific rules for escrow accounts and requirements for sponsors (such as the fact that the sponsor must have a track record in money management and public companies, etc.). However, those do not represent an organic SPAC reform based on the US model of financial regulation. Hence, the UK would like to position itself

---

6 Furthermore, Ocelot Partners and Wilmcoter Holdings are other two main SPAC listings that occurred in 2017 for a total of 15 SPACs listed.
7 Camilla Hodgson, 'London Explores Hopping on SPACs Bandwagon: Blank-Cheque Companies are Booming in the US, But the UK is Being Left Behind' (6 October 2020) Financial Times.
8 Hugh Osmond, 'Time for UK Regulators to Open Door to SPACs: London Listing Rules Badly Need Reform to Help Companies Access Capital' (17 December 2020) Financial Times.
9 Osmond, (17 December 2020) Financial Times.
10 UK Listing Rules – Hill Report (3 March 2021), available at https://assets.publishing.service.gov.uk/government/uploads/system/uploads/attachment_data/file/966133/UK_Listing_Review_3_March.pdf, accessed on 20 April 2021.

as the first, sophisticated jurisdiction for accommodating SPAC sponsors' and investors' needs.

Under the current UK legal regime – as we said – there is a presumption that a SPAC has to suspend the trading of shares once a target is acquired because of reverse takeover rules. Hence, investors are locked in, even if they do not approve a potential purchase. The Hill report calls for the removal of this presumption and introduces new safeguards, such as the right of SPAC shareholders to vote on the acquisition, and the right to redeem their initial investment prior to the completion of the business combination. Furthermore, the following recommendations, *inter alia*, must be highlighted: lowering the limit on the free float of shares in public hands to 15%. This means that SPAC sponsors need to sell fewer shares to list; and dual-class share structures even for premium listings. These allow SPAC founders to retain control through stock that carries more than one vote.

The UK government must examine those recommendations, many of which require consultation with the FCA. The consultation paper is expected to be published by the FCA by summer 2021. Indeed, on 30 April 2021, the FCA opened its consultation paper (CP21/10)[11] to prospective investors and issuers in SPACs as well as law firms, exchanges, intermediaries, etc. The consultation is open for four weeks. The FCA seems to be mainly concerned about investors' protection, and highlights the complexity of SPACs. On the other hand, it seems that the FCA does not take into account the needs of SPACs' promoters. Specifically, the consultation seeks feedback on five main points:

1   Ring-fencing proceeds: money from public investors shall be ring-fenced to either fund an acquisition or be returned to shareholders.
2   Shareholders' approval and redemption: SPAC sponsor(s) shall secure first the consent of public investors on every proposed business combination, allowing those who do not consent to exit.
3   Time limits: SPACs should find an acquisition target within two years of admission to listing with a possible 12-month extension.
4   Disclosure: establishing a system through which the SPAC sponsor(s) disclose any risk related to the IPO, announcement and conclusion of a review takeover.
5   Size thresholds: setting a minimum amount of £200 million to be raised when a SPAC's shares are initially listed.

SPAC issuers unable to meet the conditions, or those choosing not to, will continue to be subject to a presumption of suspension on reverse takeovers.

---

11   Financial Conduct Authority, 'CP21/10: Investor Protection Measures for Special Purpose Acquisition Companies: Proposed Changes to the Listing Rules' (30 April 2021), available at https://www.fca.org.uk/publication/consultation/cp21-10.pdf, accessed on 1 May 2021.

Hence, the FCA is proposing a dual system: the 'good' SPACs that follow the imposed rules (some of them are unreasonable, such as the minimum capitalisation of £200 million), and the universe of 'bad' SPACs that might decide not to follow those rules, and be penalised and subject to suspension. This seems unfair even to the most naïve person in financial markets.

Specifically, a time extension of the SPAC can be costly on the side of sponsor(s). The FCA should have opened a consultation on the de-coupling mechanism between voting and redemption rights. This could facilitate acquisition as well as providing investors with a safe way-out.

The FCA highlights that investors have to be careful when investing in SPACs, and should be informed and assess both the capital structure of each SPAC, and the potential value and return prospects of any acquisition target that is later proposed. On the other hand, the Hill Report was focused on capital markets' flexibility: this a key feature for any cash-shell company. It seems that the FCA has taken its distance from this approach. Dual-class shares have been dropped as a viable idea for UK SPACs, and the possible imposition of £200 million minimum capitalisation is a clear signal that SPACs in the UK will one day be the preserve of institutional investors and sponsors mainly composed of hedge funds and private equity funds. This is only one side of SPACs. SPACs are investment vehicles that serve many different purposes: they list pre-revenue companies, start-ups, high growth companies and they buy and invest in other people's dreams. Furthermore, the size threshold of £200 million,[12] excluding any funds the sponsors have provided either in cash or shares is possibly against a sophisticated SPAC framework. This encourages only high-level investor participation – as we said – and might cause a swift exit of sponsor(s) from London to more flexible exchanges such as *Borsa Italiana S.p.A.* in Italy (that for instance, since August 2021 requires on the AIM market only €10 million minimum threshold) or Euronext in Amsterdam.

Some additional SPAC features also merit consideration and will be further analysed, such as the percentage of IPO proceeds to be held on trust and the possibility of including the appointment of independent directors in SPACs' board of directors. The Hill Report is silent on those features, and the FCA consultation paper too. By contrast, since 2008, NASDAQ rules (Rule IM-501–2) and NYSE rules (Rule 102.06) impose rules on the escrow account proceeds. Additionally, NASDAQ expressly requires the appointment of independent directors in SPACs' board of directors.

On 27 July 2021, the FCA has issued a policy statement (PS21/10)[13] setting the final version of changes to the UK Listing Rules applicable to SPACs. The

---

12 This is not market capitalisation under LR 2.2.7R that refers to the aggregate market value. By contrast, the thresholds refer to the amount raised from public investors at the IPO.
13 FCA, "Investor protection measures for special purpose acquisition companies: changes to the Listing Rules" (July 2021) Policy Statement PS 21/10, available at: https://www.fca.org.uk/publication/policy/ps21-10.pdf, accessed on 27 August 2021.

revised changes came into force on 10 August 2021 (for additional remarks see the Addendum). The FCA has reduced the minimum threshold of capital to be raised from public investors from £200 million to £100 million. This is a more reasonable target but still high, although the FCA took the view that a minimum size of £100 million was necessary to attract significant investment by institutions, whose monitoring would in turn operate as mechanism for investor protection. In other words, larger SPACs are favoured in the UK, and this shows the need for sponsor's credibility.

Finally, the most notable feature to mention is that the UK has distanced itself from current established financial frameworks of SPACs, especially with reference to preventing sponsors and strategic investors who participate in a SPAC's at-risk capital from voting on the acquisition. This is a major difference from other listing venues, and I argue that it may impact London's ability to soar in the SPAC market. Indeed, this is not required by competing Exchanges such as NYSE, NASDAQ, and Euronext.

Apart from those potential hurdles, the overall SPAC reform in the UK seems to be consistent with the international trend of guaranteeing more pubic investor's protections in SPAC deals, and it represents the first harmonised regime on SPACs in Europe.

### 4.1.3 SPACs and Borsa Italiana S.p.A. (Euronext Group)

In Italy, there was a wave of SPACs between 2017 and 2018, with over 30 listings on the AIM and MIV segments MIV (namely, the market segment dedicated to the listing of investment vehicles), and a new wave is expected. The AIM and the MIV are segments under the umbrella of the *Mercato Telematico Azionario* (MTA) market. However, the history of SPACs in Italy is traced back in 2011, when the first Italian SPAC has been sponsored by Mr Luca Fabio Giacometti, who set up Made in Italy 1 S.p.A., which then has successfully merged with SESA S.p.A. This De-SPAC operation still remains in the World as one of the most prolific SPAC transactions ever. Indeed, SESA S.p.A. is a company active in the distribution of information technology (IT) for business sectors and end users and its stocks are traded at €138.60 per share. A unique example of how SPACs can effectively contribute to increasing national wealth and sustaining national economy. Indeed, Mr Giacometti is one of the most prolific Italian sponsors and serial SPAC investor.[14] For instance, in July 2015, he founded together with Gino Lugli, Stefano Malagoli and Silvio Marenco, Glenalta Food S.p.A., a SPAC focused on the Italian food sector that, after an IPO of €80 million performed a business combination with G.F. Group S.p.A. on 28 October 2016. The combined entity, namely Orsero S.p.A. is currently listed on the Italian AIM market.

---

14 Luca Fabio Gaicometti, Gaetano Antonio Tasca, *La SPAC tra diritto, finanza e impresa* (Giuffre 2020).

Furthermore, Giacometti in 2019 set up Galileo Acquisition Corp. and closed in October an IPO for $138 million on NYSE. Galileo completed its business combination in summer 2021 with Shapeways a 3D printing service bureau in a $410 million deal.

This eye-catching activity is directly connected to the function of SPACs as alternative investment vehicles to private equity as well as more convenient investment tools to go public by virtue of avoiding the many formalities required for a traditional IPO. For instance, in Italy a traditional IPO on the MTA within its STAR segment (a renewed market segment for blue chip companies) managed by *Borsa Italiana* S.p.A. would require high compliance costs and time-consuming roadshows and formalities. Hence, the Italian trend is to first list a SPAC on the AIM, and then once the acquisition is made to seek a further (more official) listing on the MTA – STAR. In this case, access to the segment is simplified because the company is already listed on the market, and it can access further capital in a more prestigious market venue. This is one of the old functions of SPACs, namely, to act as a backdoor listing to more prestigious venues. However, it is also useful to highlight that this is not the only function of SPACs in the US that is seen today as a reputable listing on its own, and that they constitute a valid alternative to the traditional IPO. Probably, this Italian practice can confirm that where market rules are not tailored for SPACs, sponsors can take advantage of a lack of regulation, and they might later transform their own practice into a potential regulatory arbitrage. Nonetheless, such practice is not against the law, and the Italian jurisdiction is direct evidence that in a globalised economy, market players can take advantage of the lack of stringent legislative frameworks as well as more favourable legal terms.

The possible regulatory arbitrage is confirmed by a recent Italian SPAC. Indeed, one of the last Italian SPACs to follow this path is TheSpac which was listed on the AIM in 2018, and entered into a framework agreement with Franchi Umberto Marmi S.p.A. (a leading company in the processing and marketing of Carrara marble) on 18 June 2020. TheSpac was incorporated with the purpose of being merged with a target company promoted by the sponsors Mr Marco Galateri and Mr Vitiliano Borromeo-Arese to raise 60 million Euros from Italian and foreign institutional investors. The business combination was completed on time and it has been promising. TheSpac merged by virtue of a reverse merger with Franco Umberto Marmi S.p.A. After the business combination, TheSpac filed its application to be listed on the MTA. This essentially has brought a luxury brand connected to Carrara marble into a prestigious market venue where blue chips are usually listed as well as increasing the value of the shares for the merged entity. In summer 2021, there has been a new wave of SPACs in Italy. One of the most successful listings has been Revo S.p.A., the SPAC of Minali and Costamagna which targets insurtech markets. Revo S.p.A. has been listed on the AIM market with an over-subscription from investors for €220 million. Once completed the business combination, Revo S.p.A. would like to seek a listing on the MTA that is – as we said – a more prestigious venue.

Unlike the London Stock Exchange, Italy does not impose any specific requirement on SPACs listed on the AIM and the same is true for the MIV segment, with the exception that on the MIV segment in Italy the redemption right can be subject to specific limitations imposed on public companies listed on this market (please see below Section 4.2) and very well-known sponsors with a track record in management of public companies must be the only ones qualified to apply for a SPAC filing. Furthermore, the Italian promote is quite flexible. Sponsors do not follow a fix structure in terms of the promote (founder shares). Hence, in Italy, the "at-risk-capital" is generally equal to operating budget for the life of the SPAC plus the front-end broker commission. The promote is not directly to the "at-risk-capital". By contrast, sponsors usually acquire preference/special shares, and used instead of the American founder warrants as the Italian tax codes allows the instrument. Similarly, SPACs in London have commonly subscribed for a class of founder preferred shares, entitling them to an annual dividend amount (payable in shares or cash) subject to a share value hurdle being met. The economics of these terms can be flexible.

This de-regulation aspect of the Italian and English markets can be particularly appealing for sponsors. As we said, regulation and especially strict financial regulation is not the right answer if promoters are willing to list a SPAC. In light of this, the move of the FCA in the UK to impose a £100 million minimum capital raised at the IPO phase may favour the Italian Stock Exchange (*Borsa Italiana S.p.A.*) as a preferable venue for SPACs that want to raise less capital, say €50–100 million on the AIM.

The last remark directly concerns the Exchange, namely *Borsa Italiana S.p.A.*, which has always been part of the London Stock Exchange group, and is now part of the Euronext Group. This possibility can be appealing for sponsors in Europe due to the many interconnections that Euronext will have in the near future, including Italy. For this reason, the next section is dedicated to explaining the current market conditions of Euronext in Europe.

### *4.1.4 SPACs and Euronext N.V.*

Euronext N.V. is located in Amsterdam and operates one of the most liquid exchange groups, operating markets in Amsterdam, Brussels, Dublin, Lisbon, Milan, Oslo and Paris. The Euronext N.V. exchanges in Europe, and trades equities, bonds and monetary notes and a diverse array of derivative products. In particular, Euronext N.V. operates non-regulated activities in 16 countries across the world including – as we said – 7 listing venues. It is the first stock exchange in Europe for technology companies with 670 tech companies listed as well as the first exchange in Europe for small and medium enterprises (SMEs) with over 1,400 SMEs listed. Euronext N.V. saw a recent surge in SPACs offerings, although those listings are still low both in numbers and in terms of raised capital (with the exception of the last French SPAC which was able to raise €300 million in December 2020 or the SPAC listed in May 2021 by Mr. Ian Osborne, who closed a €460 million IPO on

Euronext – Amsterdam). By the end of June 2021, 18 SPACs have raised about $5 billion between them according to Refinitiv. It is a very different picture from the US with $115.6 billion raised via more than 400 SPACs in 2021.

There most notable SPACs recently listed on the Euronext N.V. include:

- Dutch Star Companies ONE (DSC1) was listed in February 2018, and its purpose was to acquire a significant minority stake in a business with principal operations in Europe. In this case, 99% of the equity was raised in the IPO with a market capitalisation of €55.4 million priced at €10 per share. As always, the proceeds were deposited in an escrow account. However, the completion of the business combination required a qualified majority of 70% of the shareholders. This final approval eventually came in February 2020.
- Dutch Star Companies TWO was launched in November 2020. Dutch Start Companies Two is seeking to acquire a minority stake in a single mid-market company enjoying a strongly competitive position within their industry, with its principal operations in Europe, and preferably in Netherlands. Dutch Star Companies TWO is supported by the sponsors who were successful in DSC1 SPAC which combined with CM.com in 2020. This time the market capitalisation has reached €112 million always priced at €10 per share.
- In December 2020, the billionaire Xavier Niel together with Matthieu Pigasse and Moez-Alexandre Zouari sponsored a new SPAC in Euronext's regulated market in Paris: 2MX Organic. This SPAC intends to meet consumers' new expectations and to enable a growing number of Europeans to consume better, at an affordable price, safely and in sufficient quantities. It is interesting to note that 2MX Organic listed through the admission to trading and direct listing of 30,000,000 preference shares and 30,000,000 stock warrants, after the exercise of the extension clause. The SPAC has to acquire a new business within 12 or 24 months. This is the second French SPAC introduced in Paris, following the creation of Mediawan in 2016 by Xavier Niel and Matthieu Pigasse that raised €250 million from institutional investors and was listed on the professional segment (*Compartiment Professionel*) of the regulated market of Euronext Paris. Mediawan successfully completed its business combination in 2017 with *Groupe* AB. Following the business combination, *Groupe* AB has become a fully owned subsidiary of Mediawan. Since then, Mediawan has created the first successful SPAC in France.
- In February 2021, ESG Core Investment B.V. listed a SPAC on the Euronext Amsterdam at €250 million sponsored by Infestos Nederland B.V., an investment firm focused on entrepreneurial sustainable investments.
- In April 2021, Pegasus Europe successfully raises €500 million. Pegasus becomes the largest European SPAC and started to trade on Euronext – Amsterdam. Pegasus is sponsored by Tikehau Capital, the global

alternative asset management group, alongside co-sponsors Financière Agache, Jean Pierre Mustier and Diego De Giorgi. It is interesting to note the sponsor Tikehau Capital has invested €25 million from its balance sheet into the private placement and agreed on a €50 million forward purchase agreement that may be called at the time of the business combination. The SPAC will target either unique digital models or companies that benefit from tailwinds in the three verticals of investment management, insurance and diversified financials.
- In July 2021, Odyssey Acquisition S.A. (Odyssey Acquisition), a SPAC focusing on the European Healthcare and TMT (technology, media and telecom) sectors sponsored by a team of investors with experience in deal-making and know-how as well as specific industry expertise. Specifically, the SPAC is sponsored by the Zaoui brothers that have teamed up with several prominent European executives. Odyssey Acquisition has successfully raised €300 million in its private placement, and it has listed on Euronext Amsterdam.

It can be seen that the Euronext N.V. SPACs experience is growing in terms of numbers and market capitalisation. It is a first sign of the growing interest that SPACs are generating in Europe. Euronext N.V. does not have any specific market rule for SPACs and clearly the absence of a specific legal discipline is encouraging sponsors to raise capital creatively. In Amsterdam the promote (founder shares) was approximately 8–10% or 21% of the SPAC's shares outstanding. There is not a fix structure. Where the SPAC sponsors acquired additional shares through an additional cornerstone investment in the IPO, the founder shares converted into 20% of the shares outstanding, but the sponsor actually held shares equal to up to approximately 35% of the SPAC's shares outstanding at closing. Dutch law is flexible. Furthermore, under Netherlands regulatory framework the costs of the SPAC are usually borne by promoters and by 1% of the total proceeds. The structure of the financing and the units are flexible in the Euronext Amsterdam market, allowing for replicating the US SPACs' features (see Chapter 2).

Finally, it is worth noting that 2MX Organic has raised IPO proceeds from 30,000,000 preference shares. This is not a common feature of SPACs, which are usually and traditionally financed by common shares, or what are called ordinary stocks in America. Nonetheless, the solution of conferring on investors more detailed and particular rights by virtue of preference shares has resulted in market participants being offered a financial innovation which the market has apparently not disliked. SPACs are not a science, but an art.

## 4.2 SPACs and the conflicts with national corporate law frameworks

As we said in Chapter 1, SPACs are at the apex of risk and uncertainty paradigms; one of the main exogenous factors that can influence the casual structure of these investment vehicles is the applicable law. SPACs are companies, and though they act as cash-shell companies they must follow national laws at the moment of their incorporation. For these reasons, shareholders can face a diversified discipline in terms of redemption rights. Furthermore, frequently underwriters prefer the SPAC to be incorporated under the national corporate law framework of the country where the listing is supposed to happen. It means, for instance, if a sponsor wants to be listed on the AIM in Italy then the SPAC has to be incorporated as an Italian joint stock company. For jurisdictions such as Italy, this means the minimum share capital is €50,000.

One of the main corporate features of SPACs is centred on the exercise and provision of a redemption right to shareholders. This feature that – as we saw in Chapter 2 gave rise to SPACs 3.0 – is at the heart of the SPAC revolution in the US.

It is important to note that the redemption right is commonly exercised at the moment of the business combination. In fact, this is the moment when the management submits to the shareholders' meeting the final approval of the proposed business combination, although this approval can also be pursued after the acquisition and specifically at the moment of the successful completion of the business combination. This means that the redemption right is subject to a specific condition: the business combination itself. This scenario is becoming a common trend in Italy. If, on the one hand, it can be a way to facilitate the business combination's approval by the general shareholders' meeting, on the other hand, it imposes a voting decision on minorities. In other words, if those minorities do not vote in favour of a proposed business combination, then they lose their redemption right. This is highly unfair, and can potentially undermine the interests of investors, who do not like impositions, but prefer freedom of choice and "voice". Furthermore, this specific corporate structure is workable only when the sponsor retains a majority of shares or at least it has contributed a substantial amount of "at-risk-capital". If this condition is not met, it is impracticable to provide the sponsors with such a powerful tool to indirectly impose decisions on other people's money.

Additionally, it is also unrealistic to imagine that the redemption right is subject to a future and uncertain event, and especially to limit investors' ability to find a way out immediately after the completion of the IPO. To this end, I shall argue that a lock-up provision of shareholders in the articles of association can be useful only until the completion of the IPO. Then, after this period units must be freely transferable and tradeable on the secondary market, as already happens in the US. Indeed, after the IPO phase, it is useful and wise to give investors the option to sell shares without any specific limitation. This can give shareholders an appealable investment opportunity. Investors can then profit from the increase in share value at the moment of the announcement of the business combination, and at the same time new investors can enter the SPAC by bringing in new equity, this time not necessarily at €10 or £10 per share, but at a higher price.

A clear example of the importance of the redemption right can be seen in Italy. Indeed, SPACs in this jurisdiction faced a series of difficulties in 2020 based on the working mechanism of the redemption right under Italian corporate law. For instance, Value for Italy S.p.A., listed on the AIM in April 2020, did not complete the promised business acquisition, and was wound up upon the decision of its board of directors. Similarly TheSpac, Value for Italy targeted businesses which are well-known for their 'Made in Italy' brand. Value for Italy S.p.A. was promoted by Mr. Marc Gabelli, a well-known Italo-American financier and the son of the famous economist Mr. Mario Gabelli who has Italian origins and is the founder of Gabelli Asset Management Company Investors (Gamco Investors).

Value for Italy S.p.A. had a very good start, but it ended badly. It is not the only SPAC that failed recently on the AIM. We remember the case of the failed business combination of Capital for Progress 2 with ABK Group Industrie Ceramiche S.p.A. or Spactiv which did not merge with Betty Blue S.p.A. (the company run by the famous Italian fashion stylist Elisabetta Franchi), and decided to stop the deal on 30 July 2020.

SPACs in Italy as well as in the rest of Europe are a recent phenomenon and investors are still sceptical. There are three main concerns for the Italian market which still need to be addressed either by the Lawmaker, the Italian Exchange, or financial operators:

1   The redemption right of SPAC shareholders under Italian Law.
2   The role of shareholders.
3   The role of the underwriter (i.e. investment banks or nominated advisers) at the De-SPAC moment.

On point number 1, under article 2437, paragraph 4, of the Italian Civil Code, public companies on the MTA and, therefore, on the MIV market cannot provide investors with a full redemption right. This feature can prevent SPAC investors collecting in full their initial investment unless the SPAC is listed on the AIM. Furthermore, the same provision states that public companies listed on the MTA can only provide redemption rights for the cases established by the law, namely when the SPAC is going to merge, or the certificate of incorporation is subject to changes. The AIM market in Italy is preferred to the AIM market in London, due to its flexibility in modelling the redemption right, although the liquidity reached on this market is lower than that of the MIV market.

On point number 2 the SPAC shareholders' role should be to back up the business combination. For example, on NASDAQ, the shareholders' approval is not required in the case of asset acquisition or shares acquisition unless a direct merger with the SPAC is pursued, and in any transaction where the

SPAC issues more than 20% of outstanding common shares or seeks to amend its certificate of incorporation (for example, in the case of extending the duration period of the company to seek an acquisition or merger). In America there is some flexibility in modelling the shareholders' including within the final acquisition process. For instance, many SPAC prospectuses in the US are exempting shareholders who have more than 15% of the share capital from voting on the proposed business combination. This at least at the start was to avoid the possibility of being 'greenmailed' in the De-SPAC process. Today, we have seen that in the US the decoupling mechanism between voting rights and redemption rights has superseded those original doubts. This should be the way for Europe and Asia to provide SPACs with more flexibility in their corporate law structure.

Italy does not contemplate fully implementing American features in SPACs in any law or regulation of *Borsa Italiana* S.p.A. Furthermore, if we think about the lack of involvement of shareholders to approve a business combination in relation to the purchase of shares or assets, it could even be against Italian corporate law principles. This remark is applicable, in general, to civil law jurisdictions that have a long tradition of investors' protection. This is especially due to the established European legal framework on shareholders' rights (the Shareholders' Directives are a clear example in this regard). However, due to the special nature of SPACs, a change to the law on this point should be highly recommended in order to make the Italian market more competitive, without the need to 'impose' voting decisions on minorities such as in the case of articles of association of TheSpac. Indeed, a recent trend in Italy is making the redemption right of dissenting qualified shareholders (namely, those who hold more than 30% of the share capital) subject to a condition precedent that requires their positive vote to the proposed business combination. It means that a shareholder in Italy can redeem its shares only by voting 'YES' to a business combination. This model was successfully adopted by TheSpac in June 2020. This is a direct suspension of the redemption right that becomes effective only at the moment of the business combination. As I said before, this specific corporate structure might work for sponsors who contribute a substantial amount of funds, such as in the case of TheSpac, but it is not practicable in the case of a sponsor that is, for example, a start-up, for obvious reasons. To this end, a proxy solicitation – although more expensive for issuers – can be seen as a fairer instrument to solicit investors towards a final approval of the business combination or the adoption of recent market practices to consolidate the share capital of the SPAC, such as in the case of the fractional warrant structure (see Chapter 2). The same suggestion applies to European jurisdictions, in general.

Point three can be applied not only to Italian SPACs, but to SPACs more generally. In fact, during the IPO process, investment banks such as JP Morgan, Goldman Sachs, etc., are ready to buy the unlisted shares to complete the IPO. This function mitigates the investment risk (see Chapter 1). However, it would also be very useful to have them involved at the moment of the acquisition / merger process in order to be able to redeem shares more easily and prevent the possible blocking of the business combination. In other words, to back up the issuer in a possible tender offer of shareholders, who sell their shares at the moment of the business combination. This regime could be more sponsor-friendly. For instance, the adoption of this model would have avoided the recent Italian failures. Subsequently, this feature would allow target companies to have a higher reliance on SPACs without being threatened by dissenting SPAC minorities.

Another feature that cannot always be implemented in civil law jurisdictions concerns the so-called redemption price. Sometimes the articles of association of a SPAC can impose a penalty on dissenting shareholders, who will redeem only part of their investment, namely a pre-established value not exceeding a certain percentage. This is usually called the redemption price and can be generally implemented in common law jurisdictions such as the US and the UK. As opposed to those legal systems, in Italy as well as in Europe, in general, the redemption right of shareholders must provide them with reimbursement guarantees of at least a certain percentage. Hence, a redemption price goes against investors' protection, and in some jurisdictions such as Italy can be even prohibited.

Public companies listed on the Italian MIV market are subject to a specific mechanism to assess the value of redeemable shares in accordance with article 2437-*ter*, third paragraph of the Italian Civil Code. Under this legal provision, the market value must be determined with reference to two main parameters: one objective and one temporal. The former imposes that the market value of the shares is determined at the time of market closure; and according to the second parameter, the time to be considered refers to six retrospective months since the shareholders' call notice, which constitutes a ground for the existence of the redemption right. Hence, these mandatory rules of law give rise to two main legal issues: on the one hand, a redemption price cannot be introduced in the articles of association so that the dissenting shareholder can redeem only the total value of the shares; on the other hand, the dissenting shareholder may be negatively influenced by that decision because according to the parameters set forth in article 2437-*ter*, third paragraph of the Italian Civil Code, they might not redeem the entire investment but only part of it, which is determined with reference to the official market value of the securities within six retrospective months since the shareholders' call notice.

However, those concerns do not apply to the AIM market in Italy. Here the issuer can legally derogate to article 2437-*ter* of the Italian Civil Code, and it is not subject to such restrictions. Hence, on the AIM market, it is possible to structure a redemption price, and to enforce it. Generally, the possibility of introducing a redemption price is discouraged. This is because, as I said before, investors have to feel free and have a 'voice' to decide about their investments unless the sponsor does not contribute a consistent amount of funds to the SPAC and, for instance, the free float is only the 15% of the SPAC offered to public investors.

### 4.2.1 Solutions through market practices and self-regulation

Market practices might be a way to overcome the difficulties of the redemption right in Europe. In particular, sponsors can take advantage of regulatory leakage in the legal system in order to implement foreign market practices with self-regulation:

1. The decoupling of the redemption right, and the right of the shareholder to still be the legal holder of the warrant at the moment of the business combination.
2. The fractional one warrant structure that is now a common feature in the US.

Those corporate features can effectively provide European SPACs with workable tools to overcome issues that might arise on the redemption rights of shareholders. Indeed, sponsors and lawmakers should reflect on the enforceability of the redemption right. This is probably one of the key features of SPACs because it directly concerns the success of a SPAC promoter, and the increase in the value of equity on the side of shareholders after the completion of the business combination.

## 4.3 The multilevel SPAC definition

The definition of a SPAC is not currently provided under any statute law, code or capital markets regulation. In other words, with the sole exception of the Korea Exchange and Turkey, there is no compulsory definition of SPACs in terms of positive or written legal provisions.

The Equity Guidelines (EGs) of Bursa Malaysia provide a possible legal definition of SPACs,[15] although they are a form of soft law regulation for the main capital market of Malaysia, so they have no binding effect on the issuers or promoters who seek to list a SPAC on the main capital market. This means the legal nature of such a regulation is not theoretically enforceable and only represents a persuasive recommendation, although the Securities Commission in Malaysia is in charge of delisting powers in case of non-compliance with those listing requirements. Furthermore, such an assessment is carried out on a 'case-by-case basis'. In other words, on the basis of the soft law nature of the EGs, it is not arguable that currently SPACs lack a positive or legal definition under any enforceable law and/or capital markets regulation. This is part of the shell company's game, namely, not to be completely defined,

---

15 According to the Equity Guidelines a SPAC as a: 'a corporation which has no operations or income generating business at the point of initial public offering and has yet to complete a qualifying acquisition with the proceeds of such offering'. For further provisions in relation to SPACs in Malaysia please refer to http://www.sc.com.my/legislation-guidelines/equity/, accessed on 23 December 2015.

because the most important feature every cash-shell company must reflect is its flexible structure beyond any possible definition that could be perceived as an imposed limitation or restriction to its full operation.[16]

However, the lack of a clear legal definition of SPACs does not make a general definition impossible. A dogmatic and general definition of SPACs exists that represents the starting point for understanding the corporate structure of other special purpose vehicles, namely non-operating businesses.

On this point, a possible general definition of SPACs could be constructed in terms of 'multilevel SPAC definition'. It means there is no single possible definition but different ones based on the different qualities or features that a study of SPACs reveals. Indeed, based on the evolutionary track by which blank check companies developed into the modern conception of SPACs in America (namely, NYSE, NASDAQ and NYSE MKT LLC), it is possible to identify a definition based on their customs: an evolutionary definition of SPACs. Other definitions can be derived from their forms of regulation in each capital market. These can theoretically provide a justification for the idea of a 'multilevel SPAC definition' that shall be evaluated on case-by-case basis. Indeed, the acceptance of a multilevel SPAC definition shall not constitute the ground for unreasonable statements on SPACs that goes against their own legal nature. For example, in August 2021, the former securities and exchange commissioner Robert Jackson and Yale Law School Professor John Morley on behalf of a Pershing Square Tontine Holdings (PSTH) shareholder filed a lawsuit that alleges that Ackman's SPAC should be registered as an investment company. Indeed, we have already mentioned in previous chapters as Ackman's original intent was to acquire the 10% shareholding of Universal Music Group as a stock purchase. By contrast, SPAC business combinations are typically structured as mergers in which the operating company merges with and into the SPAC. When a SPAC proposes an unconventional transaction that includes features that deviate from the normal SPAC structure, this cannot constitute the ground to define SPACs as investment companies under the Investment Company Act of 1940 (US) as amended (ICA). The claim that SPACs are investment companies is meritless at least in this specific SPAC deal. As the SEC has recognised for decades, a SPAC is a blank check company whose primary purpose, during its limited corporate lifespan, is to engage in a business combination with an operating company, and therefore is not an investment company. Under Section 3 (a) (1) (A) of the ICA, an investment company is a company that invests in securities. And investing in securities is all the company has ever done or proposed to do with the great majority of its assets. To this end, PSTH has never held investment securities that would require it to be registered under the ICA (see the SEC

---

16 For instance, with reference to the first generation of SPACs that voluntary complied with Rule 419 in the US, although they were not obliged to do so, this fact evidences that a cash-shell company usually rejects any possibility of being defined *tout court*.

130  *International financial regulation of SPACs*

Rule 419 adopting release that establishes that the proceeds held on trust by a blank check company do not qualify this latter as an investment company). Although, the SEC Rule 419 does not apply to SPACs but rather to blank check companies, we have deeply explained in Chapter 2 how SPACs voluntarily complied with Rule 419. Among those listing requirements they adopted the deposit of offering proceeds on trust. Hence, the SPAC is not holding any security.

### 4.3.1 The definition of first- and second-generation SPACs

Previous sections showed that SPACs are connected to their historical development in the US. Their name was changed to Special Purpose Acquisition Companies in order not to be linked with the blank check company phenomenon of the 1980s. They voluntarily complied with provisions set forth in Rule 419 enacted by the SEC although they were not compelled to do so. This was a form of self-imposed restriction.

In other words, modern SPACs comply with Rule 419 on a voluntary basis, and they have developed other features, such as the extension of the company's duration, the involvement of very important managers in the board of directors, etc. This approach should be read as an indirect form of soft law, a bottom-up soft law approach[17] where the SPAC voluntarily complies with having no written rules by accepting a custom or a market practice in order to attract the attention of new investors. For this reason, SPACs in the modern sense were created in the US because after the establishment of these common features, all other listed SPACs started to follow this newly established trend. This contributed to the development of international standards in relation to SPACs and an indirect soft law approach can define them as first-generation SPACs because they were characterised by self-imposed restrictions. In other words, these SPACs represent an instance of bottom-up soft law.

I draw a distinction between those first-generation SPACs and the SPACs of the second generation,[18] namely the SPACs now listed on the main capital markets of Bursa Malaysia. Indeed, for the first time in the history of SPACs, the soft law regulation of the Bursa Malaysia represents a direct form of soft

---

17 Lastra, *Legal Foundations* (n. 25) 462. Furthermore in relation to soft law issues in connection with economical issues please have reference to this non-exhaustive list of readings: Jaye Ellis, "Shades of Grey: Soft Law and the Validity of Public International Law" (2012) 25 (2) Leiden Journal of International Law 313; Thomas Cottier, Rosa Lastra, "The Quest for International Law in Financial Regulation and Monetary Affairs" (2010) 13 (3) Journal of International Economic Law 527; Andrew Guzman, Timothy Meyer, "International Soft Law" (2010) 2 (1) Journal of Legal Analysis 171; Chris Brummer, 'Why Soft Law Dominates International Finance – And not Trade' (2010) 13 (3) Journal of International Economic Law 623.
18 In this sense, I have borrowed the terms 'SPACs of first and second generation' from Daniel S. Riemer, but with a totally new meaning in respect of the different functions that have been exercised by soft law approaches in terms of regulation.

law approach through the enactment of specific EGs adopted in 2009. In other words, it is an instance of top-down soft law.[19]

For these reasons, it is possible to enucleate a definition of SPACs based on their different approach to regulation, namely an indirect and direct soft law approach. It is important to highlight that national corporate law provisions play an essential role, in addition to capital markets regulation. Indeed, the reception of the international standards of SPACs might differ from country to country, depending on the number of mandatory principles and provisions that can constitute a hurdle to the implementation of a fully compliant SPAC (for instance, for the Italian and English law systems).

### 4.3.2 A definition of SPACs based on market practices

It has already been stated above that it is important to study the evolution of SPACs and their development based on capital markets regulations and reforms.

This approach can provide a pragmatic or customary definition of SPACs, rather than a dogmatic one, which does not exist under any enforceable law. It represents the recognition that SPACs are governed by customs; in other words by the codification or reception of market practices that have shaped the configuration of modern SPACs with all the aforementioned international standards concerning the corporate structure of these investment vehicles (the case of SPACs 2.0 in the US).

The conception of SPACs has evolved in this way over the years since the blank check companies' phenomenon in the 1980s. This circumstance provides a definition of evolutionary SPACs.

In particular, the SPAC of the first generation and then the SPAC of the second generation are indirect and direct forms of codification of market practices. Nonetheless, as has been anticipated, when the international standards resulting from a codification of market practices are not implemented in capital markets regulation, then general principles of national law will find application, namely corporate law provisions. In such instances a tension exists between the full application of the agreed international standards and the fulfilment of national law provisions.

### 4.3.3 A definition of SPACs based on legal standardised regulation

A new trend has finally emerged at the international level that takes into account a proper legal standardised regulation for SPACs. It is, for instance, the case of the Korea Exchange. This is the first time that SPACs have received a direct legal regulation through an Enforcement Decree of a primary source of legislation (i.e. the Financial Investment Services and Capital Markets Act).

---

19  Rosa Lastra, Legal Foundations of International Monetary Stability (OUP 2006) 462

This is the first legal, binding and positive definition of SPACs. This regulation approach, which can be defined as a 'by-law approach', is unique because in the majority of cases the financial markets have adopted a regulation based on a reception or rather codification of market practices by virtue of capital markets regulations having a soft law or hard law nature that cannot be strictly assimilated under the law paradigm.

### 3.5.4 SPACs 'without law'

As we said, there are different definitions of SPACs based on their distinguishing features. An evolutionary definition is based on the story of SPACs' origins in blank check companies; a customary definition is based on the evolution of SPACs of the first generation; and a regulatory definition can be traced in the different forms of regulation implemented by each capital market. This definition of SPACs in terms of financial regulation has sometimes followed a standardisation of market practices, so SPACs are investment vehicles that codify market practices into capital markets regulations (such as the NYSE, the NASDAQ, the New AMEX, the EGs of the Bursa Malaysia, the regulation of the Toronto Stock Exchange, etc.). At other times, this regulatory definition of SPACs has followed a 'by-law' approach or the legal standardisation of market practices on the Korea Stock Exchange and Turkey. Within the rationale of this chapter, this is a paternalistic form of regulation, where the state or government acts externally to the market in order to impose a specific legal discipline.

This reception or codification of market practices highlights the peculiarity of the financial regulation of SPACs. It has been seen that SPACs are dominated by a soft law approach which can take either the indirect form of 'bottom-up' codification of market practices, such as in the case of the SPAC of the first generation, or the direct form of 'top-down' reception, such as in the case of the Bursa Malaysia. This can give rise to concerns about whether SPACs are really unregulated investment vehicles.

For these reasons, SPACs are today 'without law', but one could say 'not outside of the law'. Indeed, whenever a SPAC is incorporated in one legal system it must follow the corporate law provisions of the country of incorporation. For this reason, company law becomes a 'legal constant' that will always be applied and cannot be exempted, apart from cases in which exchanges provide for a specific supplementary regulation in relation to SPACs. Another 'legal constant' will be the law applied to the escrow account that especially in common law jurisdictions will sometimes be governed under trust law.

Therefore, it can be seen how the apparent absence of a specific SPAC law is actually supplemented by national law provisions of corporate law and contractual law. On the other hand, this lack of a uniform discipline provides further justification for the original idea of SPACs as 'multilevel' instruments because several disciplines apply to them in respect of their country of incorporation and yet the capacity for living at the margin of the law is also one of the main features of any cash-shell company; cash-shell companies always try to by-pass any possible categorisation, definition or regulation because their flexibility, dynamicity and adaptability are some of their main qualities.

## 4.4 The soft law regulation of SPACs

This first overview of SPACs, to be examined mainly at national level by taking into account the US capital markets, highlights a 'spontaneous' mechanism of self-regulation, especially in relation to what can be defined as SPACs of the first generation. Indeed, although the establishment of national rules can be perceived as an external imposition by a third authority, SPACs have been the prominent instance through which financial regulation has expressed its ability to adapt in order to deal with concrete needs rooted in investors' confidence. In other words, the first concerns that the SEC expressed in relation to blank check companies, with respect to fraud and their cash-shell nature, were addressed by the SPACs of the first generation which, although not obliged to follow Rule 419, did so by following a 'spontaneous' *motus* of adaptation to markets' requirements to attract the investors' attention. This is defined as an indirect soft law approach through which SPACs spontaneously adopted international or market standards initially developed on the PSM by the blank check companies.

For this reason, it is important to understand the new role that soft law plays within financial markets as a potentially effective tool of regulation and governance of markets. The modern financial architecture is the result of the post-World War II economic order, through the institutions created within the Bretton Woods framework in 1944, namely the International Monetary Fund, the International Bank for Reconstruction and Development, and the General Agreement on Tariffs and Trade.[20] Since the establishment of Bretton Woods and its subsequent collapse in the 1970s, the financial industry has dramatically changed, due to its internationalisation, globalisation and the private distribution of financial risk, which has been mainly rooted in private knowledge of the financial industry.[21]

As explained in Chapter 1, there is no clear definition of soft law in financial markets, but here I am working with a possible definition of soft law provided by Snyder under European Union Law, according to which soft law[22] has played a pivotal role within the European Union. For instance, the regional integration of the EU and especially its project of market integration have been carried out by instruments developed in a 'specific kind of soft law' such as the communications of the European Commission (and

---

20 Michael S. Barr, 'Who's in Charge of Global Finance?' (2014) 45 (4) Georgetown Journal of International Law 971, 976. See further Chapter 4.
21 See further Chapters 3 and 4.
22 Francis Snyder, 'Soft Law and Governance: Aspects of the European Union Experience' in Luo Haocai (ed.) *The European Union Experience* (Peking University Press 2009).

also the inclusion of codes of conduct, disciplines, frameworks, etc.), interinstitutional agreements, and the development of the open method of coordination. Therefore, the definition of soft law used here relates to a conception of soft law as a legal instrument or tool capable of supplementing the lack of hard law regulations in the legal system itself, as well as helping the system to coordinate its legal sources and inspire the enactment of new hard legislations. Nonetheless the role of soft law and its apparent non-binding nature has been hardened in international financial regulation where 'races to the top have replaced races to the bottom' in order to guarantee the implementation of minimum standards of regulation where states have taken back control of their regulatory monopoly.[23]

Although I must agree with a general definition of soft law that is directly connected to its non-binding nature and dynamic function, it is important to highlight that in this work there is a specific focus on financial markets, and specifically on SPACs. This gives rise to two different concerns: on the one hand, it raises doubts about the accountability and legality of the new private entities in charge of the enactment of soft law acts, and, on the other hand, it provides explanatory illustrations about the self-regulatory nature of SPACs. The former issue has led to the establishment of a new global administrate law,[24] highly influenced by soft law principles, at least at the start. Within this framework soft law has emerged as a legal instrument capable of influencing market discipline and self-regulation approaches that originated in the financial industry as a spontaneous mechanism to implement the distribution of financial risks. Upon this definition, soft law is informed by the needs of globalisation.

The same definition applies to SPACs where the globalisation of their application is explained in this chapter as a non-legal or non-binding instance. Within this context, it should be argued how 'races to the bottom' rather than 'to the top' have mainly been implemented to develop international financial regulation for SPACs. In fact, instances of 'bottom-up' soft law or self-regulation approaches have replaced 'top-down' instances.[25] The counter trend of self-regulation, as opposed to the hardening of financial regulation

---

23 Barr (n 164) 975. See further Chapter 4 on the role of law in financial crisis and financial markets.
24 Benedict Kingsbury et al., 'Foreword: Global Governance as Administration – National and Transnational Approaches to Global Administrative Law' (2005) 68 Law & Contemporary Problems 1, 5. The authors defined global administrative law as

> the legal mechanisms, principles, and practices along with supporting social understandings, that promote or otherwise affect accountability of global administrative bodies, in particular by ensuring these bodies meet adequate standards of transparency, consultation, participation, rationality, and legality, and by providing effective review of the rules and decisions these bodies make.

25 Rosa Lastra, *Legal Foundations* (n 25) 462. Indeed, according to the Author the "top-down" soft law is different from the "bottom-up" soft law approach, which entails a self-regulation.

*tout court,* has clearly been found in SPACs of the first generation. Additionally, SPACs of the first generation have been perceived as a consolidation of market practices through which a modern conception of SPACs has been developed. The first SPACs to be listed on regulated venues in the US, such as the NYSE, the New AMEX and the NASDAQ, are clear examples of market discipline implemented by private actors, namely the SPAC promoters. The need to attract the confidence of investors has been the catalyst to start this process of private regulation which has manifested itself as an indirect instance of soft law, or in Lastra's terms, as a 'bottom-up' or self-regulation approach. For this reason, this chapter argues that SPACs can effectively represent a unique phenomenon where state regulation, or the paternalistic approach of authoritarian imposition from the top, has changed to softer instruments of discipline which have not been imposed but rather, have been spontaneously undertaken.

It has been seen in Chapter 3 that financial markets are dominated by risk and uncertainty and therefore the role of derivatives has been to allow private actors to diversify risks and hedge against them.

Derivatives are complex financial products that can hardly be defined in law because of the uncertainty of their objects. A derivative product can be seen as a contract whose value is based on the value of underlying assets, which in turn can be a commodity or a financial product, such as interest or exchange rates. The determination of the value of the derivative can be contested because of the impossibility of determining the actual financial and real value of those instruments.[26] This can translate in turn into speculation and betting behaviours that are responsible for the creation of pure risks in subjective terms.[27] Although derivatives can be criticised *per se* for their functioning and their value-assessment, it has been noted[28] that one of the real causes of the financial crisis (2007–2010) was not the inability of the system to keep up with the pace of financial innovations, but the possibility, guaranteed under the law, of trading derivatives on non-regulated and private venues. To this end, it is worth noting that a 'law' consented to the trading of derivatives on a non-regulated venue, namely the OTC market. This created the assumption that a lack of regulation can be responsible for an increase in opportunistic behaviours and inefficient market dynamics. In particular, the lack of regulation in those venues led to a rise in financial speculation, and

---

26 Donatella Alessandrini, 'Regulating Financial Derivatives? Risks, Contested Values and Uncertainty Features' (2011) Social & Legal Studies 1, 2.
27 See Chapter 3.
28 Lynn A. Stout, 'Derivatives and the Legal Origin of the 2008 Credit Crisis' (2011) 1 Harvard Business Law Review 1, 3. The author outlines how the law passed by the Congress in 2000 called the Commodities Futures Modernization Act was mainly responsible for the financial crisis (2007–2010) because it allowed the trading of derivatives on OTC venues. Therefore, according to this view changes in the law have been responsible for the collapse of the system rather than the absence of regulatory guidelines.

in addition, the emergence of a credit default swaps market was critical in the determination of negative outcomes, such as the subprime mortgage and securitisation schemes.

However, regulation itself is often perceived as a limit to a free-market economy where the symbol of the 'invisible hand' is preferred to restrictions and controls. Despite the instincts of human society towards progress and wealth, we have also previously outlined that the absence of perfect competition and perfect information leads to a 'need' for regulatory responses.[29] Among those regulatory instances the Westphalian model of regulation seems to be gaining ground today due to a trend for reinforcement of regulatory controls by public centralised authorities or institutions. Llewellyn has pointed out several of the downsides or negative outcomes[30] to which regulation can lead. Although his critique can be perceived as a statement against regulation itself and the possible negative effects of over-regulation, it should be considered as a pure critique of an 'external' approach to regulation, namely, top-down models or Westphalian approaches. Instead, one can find bottom-up instances of regulation that are market-oriented and represent directly the output of market operators and the financial industry.

This is identified as self-regulation, and it constitutes one of the most important elements of the modern global governance of financial systems, today governed by a mixture of self-regulation and paternalistic approaches. The role of the law is therefore modified towards hybrid models of regulation.

As Coase argues[31] the efficiency of free markets is reliant on considerable internal infrastructure and self-regulation with minimal transaction costs. Although parties can enter into private agreements in order to set interests, the sanctioning of those agreements or their practical enforcement must always be carried out by public laws such as contract law and commercial law. Therefore, looking at free markets through Coase seems to reduce the role of private actors, who in the end must rely on the state, or rather on laws enacted by the state, to enforce their private rules and agreements.

The absence of a serious approach to self-regulation in the modern financial architecture is further justified, according to Omarova, by the unpopularity

---

29 Charles Goodhart, Philipp Hartmann, *et al.*, *Financial Regulation: Why, How and Where Now?* (1998 Routledge) 2. Indeed, famous economists are supporters of free banking such as Dowd, Benston and Kaufman, who theorise how regulation plays a negative role in financial crisis. Before them one can think of Adam Smith's invisible hand that represents a symbol of free markets.

30 David T Llewellyn, 'Re-engineering the Regulator' (1996) 1 (3) The Financial Regulator 21, 23–24. According to the author highly prescriptive regimes of regulation can lead, *inter alia*, to the following downsides: (a) the industry can perceive such regime as excessive and redundant; (b) risks are usually so complex that cannot be covered by mere rules; (c) prevent financial innovation; (d) can cause rules escalation by which new provisions are added into the system, but the old norms are not withdrawn; (e) information loss; (f) over-regulation s not responsive to market conditions.

31 Ronald Harry Coase, *The Firm, The Market and the Law* (University of Chicago Press 1988).

of the concept due to casino capitalism and the negative image of financial markets and Wall Street. A new paradigm of self-regulation is advocated in the form of 'embedded self-regulation'.[32] It has been seen that state regulation can be evaded by financial arbitrage,[33] therefore it seems crucial to take into account the opinions of private actors in regulatory processes, and sometimes even to allow private actors to become rule makers. According to Omarova, self-regulation is vital for achieving two main objectives: 'timely access to market information, on the one hand, and the need to monitor and manage risk across jurisdictional borders, on the other'.[34] Self-regulation must take into account public ends, especially financial stability and social values (this is the 'embedded' conception of self-regulation), but through private enforcement. This new role of self-regulation is, therefore, delicate and requires the imposition of collective self-restraint in order to avoid or limit the unscrupulous profit-oriented activities of private members. This is what Omarova terms 'community of fate': community belief in achieving a common future through self-restriction.

Nonetheless, it has been outlined before in relation to the examples of European and American financial regulation, a macroeconomic approach is more popular today, where no space is left for self-regulation in the financial industry. The financial industry, in contrast to other industries, is permeated by systemic risk and public safety nets, such as bail-outs and deposits schemes, that prevent private and public actors from being seriously interested in the implementation or enforcement of self-regulation approaches within their industry. Indeed, today it seems that there is a lack of practical examples of self-regulation in financial systems; SPACs represent an exception and can therefore be identified as a practical instance of self-regulatory responses. SPACs can be theorised in Omarova's terms as embedded self-regulation instruments, because they aim towards public objectives such as the protection of investors and market stability through the private enforcement that is carried out by the SPAC management.

Soft law is sometimes defined as a form of self-regulation.[35] I shall argue that this is the case especially if one looks at soft law as an instance of

---

32  Saule T. Omarova, 'Wall Street as Community of Fate: Toward Financial Industry Self-regulation' (2011) 159 (2) University of Pennsylvania Law Review 412.
33  Victor Fleisher, 'Regulatory Arbitrage' (2010) University of Colorado Law Legal Studies Research Paper No. 10–11, 1–67.
34  Omarova, Wall Street as community (n 31) 418.
35  Omarova, Wall Street as Community (n 31) 424. Indeed, according to the author there are
   many forms of self-regulation in practice, as well as many definitions of what it is – or should be – in the academic and policy debate. "Self-regulation" is often used interchangeably with other, similar terms, such as "self-governance", "co-regulation", "voluntarism", "private regulation", "soft law", "quasi-regulation", "communitarian regulation", and so on. Each of these terms tends to emphasize a particular characteristic that arguably distinguishes "self-regulation" from regulation – the purely voluntary

bottom-up regulation. Indeed, according to Lastra[36] the 'top-down' soft law differs from the 'bottom-up' soft law approach, which entails self-regulation. Specifically, in the case of 'bottom-up' soft law, it is possible to identify instances of regulation coming from private actors in order to regulate their community as 'community of fate' in Omarova's view. The advantage of having a soft law approach in financial markets reflects the dynamicity of financial innovations, and specifically provides flexibility in order to enforce quasi-legal regimes for complex financial products.[37]

For instance, soft law plays an essential role in relation to SPACs because of the complexity of these investment vehicles. In the first generation of SPACs (namely, the SPACs that came into existence after the disappearance of the blank check companies on the PSM) the 'bottom-up' regulation approach has been identified. Unlike SPACs of the first generation, the second generation of SPACs were provided with a 'top-down' soft law regulation (through the guidelines issued by the Securities Commission of Bursa Malaysia). In this case, SPACs were specifically disciplined through an institutionalised private actor, although in the form of soft law provisions. The guidelines recognise the international standards of SPACs in relation to their corporate features and provide a possible answer to economic concerns.

This codification is the result of the reception of international or market standards that in turn were developed by a 'bottom-up' self-regulation approach. It is the industry and the SPAC promoters that contributed to the formation of corporate standards to imitate. For this reason, I shall argue that without a self-regulation approach that starts with a community of financial operators (in the case of SPACs the promoters or managers), it is harder for institutionalised private actors to impose (such as in the case of exchanges) or to discipline (such as in the case of the Securities Commission in Malaysia) financial innovations. This is why SPACs represent a practical instance of self-regulation in the financial industry that can inspire the enforcement of new private regulations and quasi-legal regimes for new financial products.

It has been seen how the concept of global governance gives rise to intertwined public and private interventions. State and non-state actors sit at the apex of a new financial regulation paradigm where the role of the law is hybrid.

On the one hand, there is a paternalistic approach through state regulation and top-down regulation approaches; on the other there are private actors who are members of the financial industry and can effectively enforce financial regulation due to their control of financial information. Indeed,

---

nature of regulation, the nongovernment actors as the sole rulemaking authority, or the nonbinding or non-legal nature of the rules.

36 Lastra, *Legal Foundations* (n 25) 462.
37 Chris Brummer, 'Why Soft Law dominates International Finance – And Not Trade' (2010) 13 (3) *Journal of International Economic Law* 623. Ibid., *Soft Law and the Global Financial System: Rule Making in the 21st Century* (CUP 2012).

according to global governance scholarship they are capable of taking the regulation debate in the direction of more efficient and practical forms of regulation. This apparent dichotomy becomes even more complex if one recognises that private means are sometimes used by public institutions or governments to achieve public ends. There are certain objectives that a private actor cannot or will not pursue due to public competition concerns. Indeed, competition is one of the core elements informing the new phenomenology of financial markets or financial systems. This is because without competition there cannot be efficient selection and, therefore, efficient classification of risks so they can accumulate in the hands of one single private actor rather than be distributed among participants.

In relation to SPACs, one regulation that is a direct product of the state is the Korean legal system that directly provides investors with a specific discipline. This is because the remarkable story of SPACs has never been a codified one; the financial regulation of SPACs has always been informed by a bottom-up approach as a form of indirect soft law instances. This soft law approach that entails self-regulation practices has been vital in order to set up a modern conception of SPACs. Indeed, since the blank check companies that operated on the PSM, SPACs have developed new corporate features that became international standards to be followed and imitated, as has been outlined in Chapter 2. Rule 419, although not binding, became crucial to preserve investors' interests and SPACs adopted corporate features (such as the escrow account, the right of withdrawal, the winding up procedure, etc.) on non-regulated venues such as the OTC Bulletin, although they were not compelled to do so. This is an indirect soft law approach or self-restraint imposition that in the thinking of Omarova informs self-regulatory practices.

This is one of the many reasons why SPACs can represent the first practical instance of self-regulation, and probably the first practical instance in the financial industry of self-restriction impositions. Market practices are vital for explaining SPACs' evolution towards a modern conception. The standardisation of specific corporate features by the NYSE, the NASDQ and the New AMEX are all practical instances formed on the OTC Bulletin, and beforehand on the PSM with blank check companies.

When the NYSE, the NASDAQ and the New AMEX directly codified those corporate features in their capital markets regulations, they promoted a 'SPAC culture', and from a legal point of view they legitimised a specific form of investment company with specific corporate features. These informed a modern conception of SPACs that also started to be recognised in other legal systems.

As a result, it can be theorised that the financial regulation of SPACs at international level began with a codification, or rather reception of market practices, initially *de facto* enforced on the markets by promoters and managers. Those customs have informed future behaviours and compliance with the SPACs system and generate confidence with investors.

### 4.4.1 The bursa Malaysia

In 2009, the Securities Commission Malaysia enacted a specific regulatory framework dedicated to SPACs (i.e. Chapter 6) in the EGs.[38] The EGs represent an important intuition that has permitted the promoters of SPACs to obtain funding.[39]

The EGs enacted in 2009 by the Securities Commission Malaysia constitute an outstanding example of soft law regulation, namely an instance of 'top-down' soft law, because they are promulgated by an official authority or entity (i.e. the Securities Commission Malaysia).[40] Indeed, the nature of soft law regulation can be seen in the 'Introduction' to the EGs which declares that:

> (…) applicants must observe the spirit and the wording of these guidelines. The principles, on which these guidelines are based, embrace the interests of listed corporations, the provision of investor protections and the maintenance of investor confidence, as well as the need to protect the reputation and integrity of capital markets.

According to the Introduction, the scope of the EGs is to promote the confidence of investors and protect the integrity of the market, namely to create an efficient allocation of resources within financial markets.[41] Furthermore, in the Introduction to Chapter 6 of the EGs (Section 6.02 EQs), the Security Commission Malaysia reserves the possibility of assessing the listing of SPACs on a 'case-by-case basis'. It means that although a SPAC might comply with those principles and guidelines, its application for listing can be still rejected. This approach is reminiscent of the NYSE listing rules, where a broad discretion is used, and it confirms that the memory of blank check offerings is still alive in the minds of regulators.

Following these preliminaries, this section analyses different provisions of Chapter 6 of the EGs, which are conventionally divided into three broad categories: principles enacted in relation to the setting up and capital structure of SPACs; regulations referring to the activities of the management; and sections dedicated to the winding up procedure.

---

38 Securities Commission Malaysia, 'Equity Guidelines', available at http://www.sc.com.my/wpcontent/uploads/eng/html/resources/guidelines/equity/gl_equity_131218.pdf, accessed on 15 September 2016. Indeed, these Guidelines have been amended on the 18th of December 2013.
39 Currently, Malaysia is attracting SPACs listings. Indeed, since 2011 up to 2013 the Malaysia Bursa raised $7.5 billion as reported in the Wall Street Journal, 'Malaysia Attract Blank Check IPOs' (18 April 2013), available at http://blogs.wsj.com/moneybeat/2013/04/18/malaysia-attracts-blank-check-ipos/, accessed on 15 September 2016.
40 Lastra, *Legal Foundations* (n 25) 462. Indeed, according to Lastra the 'top-down' soft law is different from the 'bottom-up' soft law approach, which entails a self-regulation.
41 Louise Gullifer, Jennifer Payne 'Public Offers of Shares' in *Corporate Finance Law Principles and Policy* (Hart Publishing 2011) 407, 416.

First, in order to be listed a SPAC should be incorporated under Malaysian corporate law (Section 6.05 EGs). Currently, the preference for only listing Malaysian SPACs on the main market represents a unique approach which has never been requested by an exchange in the US or Europe. The 'spirit' of this section (to use the initial words of the EGs) is probably enough to show that the Bursa Malaysia considers SPACs to be an investment tool capable of making the national economy grow.

In relation to the capital structure of SPACs, according to Section 6.12 EGs only one class of warrant can be issued during the IPO, and those warrants are callable only after the completion of a business combination. However, a new feature has been introduced in the SPAC anatomy. Under Section 6.15 EGs the investors can purchase the SPAC's equity securities at a lower price before the listing, but in such circumstances a moratorium period applies. According to Section 6.20, EGs the moratorium period will extend from the listing of the SPAC until the effected acquisition, so that investors are prevented from trading their securities during that period. In relation to the proceeds of the SPAC, at least 90% of those must be held on trust[42] until the company has finalised a business combination in accordance with Section 6.21 EGs, and the fair market value of the target company should consist of at least 80% of the amounts held on trust (Section 6.34 EG).

With reference to the voting rights of the SPAC's shareholders, Section 6.25 EGs reads that the dissenting shareholders cannot exercise their redemption right until a business combination is finalised, and the value of the redeemable shares must be determined in the prospectus. On the other hand, the proposed acquisition is approved if it is consented to by a majority of shareholders, representing at least 75% of the nominal value of the share capital (Section 6.39 EGs).

Second, in relation to the management, Section 6.13 EGs introduces for the first time an important concept entitled 'Management credibility' according to which the managers of the SPAC must demonstrate to investors that they have 'experience, qualification and competence' to complete the business combination that the SPAC aims to achieve. This is evidence that the management is the only 'asset', which can be assessed by investors because a SPAC itself is only a cash-shell company. Furthermore, Section 6.14 EGs suggests that the management should possess at least 10% of the equity securities issued by the SPAC on the date of listing on Bursa Malaysia. In particular, the management can hold equity securities of the SPAC before the listing, but in such circumstances according to Sections 6.15 EGs and 6.16 EGs a moratorium period is imposed on those securities. It means that the management will not be able to 'sell, transfer or assign' its securities until a business combination

---

42 Indeed, for the first time Section 6, Part D of the EGs read a series of obligations and features that the escrow agent or trustee must hold, and under section 6.50 EGs describe the possible contents of an escrow agreement or deed of trust. Interesting is the provision, which subordinated the agreement to the governing law of Malaysia.

is completed. This feature confirms that the possible agency costs and moral hazard issues can be controlled by the moratorium period, and the managers will have an incentive to find a profitable target company to sell their securities to a maximum of 50% per annum after the finalisation of a business combination (Section 6.17 EGs).

For the first time, Section 6.18 EGs imposes on the management a special form of moratorium in the case of a business combination connected to specific industries, such as Oil&Gas, and other target companies which are 'not yet income operating' (see Section 6.18 (a) and (b) EQs). In the former circumstance, the moratorium period is extended until the acquired target company commences its commercial production and presents 'one full financial year of audited operating revenue'; in the latter case the moratorium period is extended until the assets of the target company 'have generated one full financial year of auditing operating profits'. In both cases after the moratorium the management will be entitled to sell its securities to a maximum of 50% per annum.

The moratorium period that applies to the management confirms the unique feature of SPACs, and constitutes for the first time a device promulgated in order to make the management refrain from opportunistic behaviours. In particular, to enhance the incentives for management only in case of the completion of a business combination, a ban has been introduced on distributing proceeds which are not being held on trust as a remuneration for managers (Section 6.24 EGs), and also during the winding up procedure (Section 6.42 EGs).

Third, the EGs read a series of provisions in case of the winding up of a SPAC under Section 6, Part C. In particular, the SPAC must be wound up if a business combination is not effected within the 'permitted time framework' (Section 6.41 EGs). According to the guidelines the time frame to complete a business combination is equal to a maximum of 36 months (Section 6.02 EGs). Investors who purchased equity securities before the listing of the SPAC must not receive any distribution of the proceeds raised during the IPO.

### 4.4.2 The Toronto stock exchange

SPACs have found another friendly environment in Canada, where the Toronto Stock Exchange (TSX) has provided investors with guidelines ('Guide to Special Purpose Acquisition Corporations', adopted in 2014, hereinafter referred to as the 'guidelines') and dedicated provisions of listing requirements (i.e. TSX Company Manual – Part X 'SPACs'[43]). The guidelines are not an instance of soft law because they do not contain specific

---

43 TSX Company Manual, available at http://tmx.complinet.com/en/display/display_main.html?rbid=2072&element_id=642, accessed on 16 September 2016. The TSX Company Manual is based on the US regulation of SPACs that can be found in the NYSE and NASDAQ as explained in paragraph 3.

provisions that discipline SPACs, but must be examined from a financial literacy perspective and for promotion purposes. SPACs are a form of financial innovation that is hard to understand and investors need to have them explained by a financial literacy process. Furthermore, the guidelines clearly state that SPACs are designed to allow the public to co-invest with managers and financiers. Canadian retail investors are already familiar with TSX Venture Exchange's Capital Pool Company program, a form of micro-SPAC. Capital Pool Companies ('CPCs') originated in Alberta over 20 years ago. They are cash-shell companies that seek the completion of a qualifying business combination within 24 months of listing. Unlike SPACs, CPCs are not listed through a common IPO process[44] because they are companies set up by private investors to raise a pool of capital through a public equity market, namely the TSX Venture Exchange.[45] The founders of the CPC retain greater control than in a traditional IPO that distributes more of its shareholding among investors. No potential shareholder can purchase more than 2% of the offering and no one purchaser together with its affiliates can purchase more than 4%. For these reasons, CPCs differ from SPACs where the shareholding is variegated through a common IPO process and management ownership is limited to a small percentage of warrants. Additionally, SPACs may have different purposes of acquisition, and acquisition is always total (a SPAC acquires 100% of the shares of the target company), whereas a CPC constitutes a viable route for target companies aiming for public listing through the experience of financiers who acquire an equity share in their companies.

The TSX Company Manual takes into account the main international corporate features of SPACs, but it also includes new provisions that constitute an important instance of understanding the SPAC phenomenon. Under Section 1006[46] of the TSX Company Manual (No Operating Business) a SPAC is prohibited from entering into any written or oral binding acquisition agreement prior to the IPO process. Nonetheless, the SPAC can identify in advance a target business sector or geographic area to make a qualify-

---

44 Guidelines on the CPC have been issued by the Toronto Stock Exchange, available at https://www.tsx.com/resource/en/47, accessed on 17 September 2017.
45 The TSX Venture Exchange is regulated by the TSX Venture Exchange Rule Book, available at https://www.tsx.com/resource/en/1465, accessed on September 2017.
46 Section 1006 TSX Company Manual:

> A SPAC seeking listing on the Exchange must not carry out an operating business. A SPAC may be in the process of reviewing a potential qualifying acquisition, but may not have entered into a written or oral binding acquisition agreement with respect to a potential qualifying acquisition. Every SPAC seeking a listing on the Exchange must include a statement in its IPO prospectus that as of the date of filing, the SPAC has not entered into a written or oral binding acquisition agreement with respect to a potential qualifying acquisition. A SPAC may have identified a target business sector or geographic area in which to make a qualifying acquisition, provided that it discloses this information in its IPO prospectus.

ing acquisition, provided that it discloses this information in the prospectus. This means investors can have access to that information; being informed about the specific characteristics of the future acquisition gives investors a competitive advantage.

Section 1007[47] of the TSX Company Manual expressly regulates the applicable law of the SPAC in respect of its country of incorporation. To this end, the exchange recommends choosing Canadian federal or provincial corporate law, but SPACs can also be set up under a different corporate framework. However, they have to obtain prior approval from the exchange in order to be listed on the TSX. Only if the applicable law of incorporation is considered acceptable is the SPAC listed on the primary market. Indeed, this is a very useful instance to show the mitigation of another uncertainty aspect of SPACs, namely the exogenous factor of the applicable law that have been mentioned in Chapter 1 in terms of national corporate provisions that can conflict or create a tension with the international common standards. The exchange's discretion is vital for avoiding laws of incorporation being selected that might harm the interests of investors due to a different business culture in the country of incorporation.

Having examined the most important provisions of the TSX Company Manual, it should be noted that this regulation is not based on a soft law approach. The listing of SPACs is regulated through the TSX Company Manual, therefore hard law and binding provisions apply to the promoters/sponsors. This is an instance of the standardisation of market practices by virtue of capital market regulations (and it is the case in most SPAC instances on the NYSE, NASDAQ, New AMEX and Bursa Malaysia). It should be noted that Part X of the TSX Company Manual must be read in conjunction with the guidelines illustrated above.

The Canadian market is clearly a competitive one for SPACs. The spread of CPCs in the market shows the potential for micro-SPACs and retail investors are aware of this in Canada, where a 'SPAC culture' seems to be widespread. Financial literacy has mainly been achieved by implementing hard law provisions contained in rule books, or capital market regulations supplemented by guidelines. This technique is the outcome of bottom-up soft law approaches rather than of top-down instances, and again it shows how knowledge of the market and investors' knowledge of investors are the best tools to regulate financial innovations.

---

47 Section 1007 TSX Company Manual:

> The Exchange will consider the jurisdiction of incorporation of a SPAC as part of the listing application process. The Exchange recommends that SPACs seeking listing on the Exchange be incorporated under Canadian federal or provincial corporate laws. Where a SPAC is incorporated under laws outside of Canada and wishes to list on the Exchange, the Exchange recommends that it obtain a preliminary opinion as to whether the jurisdiction of incorporation is acceptable to the Exchange.

## 4.5 SPACs: a 'by-law approach'

The corporate features of SPACs have been recognised and codified not only by direct soft law regulations such as in the case of Bursa Malaysia, but also by hard law provisions. The hard law provisions in the latter case have been identified either through capital markets regulation (NYSE, the NASDAQ, the New AMEX in the US and the TSX in Canada) or by statute law (Korea Stock Exchange).

Both instances represent hard law provisions, but in the case of the Korea Exchange those are contained in a law (the Enforcement Decree of the Financial Investment Services and Capital Markets Act). This is a paternalistic approach to regulation and a form of top-down regulation through the state. For this reason, here the government is acting as external to the market in order to impose a top-down regulation of SPACs that recalls Westphalian approaches to regulation.

In broader terms, there is no definition of SPACs provided by a national legislation apart from two main exceptions: Bursa Malaysia where SPACs are defined within a soft law act, namely the EGs[48] and the Korean Exchange that defines SPACs under Section 6 (4) 14 of the Enforcement Decree of the Financial Investment Services and Capital Markets Act[49] where for the first time we have a 'by-law' approach to SPACs and a first positive definition provided by statute law.

### 4.5.1 The Korean stock exchange

The Korea Exchange (KRX) has implemented for the first time in the history of SPACs a legal and positive definition under Section 6 (4) 14 of the Enforcement Decree of the Financial Investment Services and Capital Markets Act that reads:

> [A SPAC is] a corporation, the sole business objective of which is to merge the corporation with another corporation and issue the stock certificates through a public offering.

The provisions governing collective investments do not apply to SPACs if the investment vehicle fulfils the requirements prescribed under Section 6 (4) 14 of the Enforcement Decree. Essentially, the Enforcement Decree implements

---

48 According to the Equity Guidelines a SPAC as a: 'a corporation which has no operations or income generating business at the point of initial public offering and has yet to complete a qualifying acquisition with the proceeds of such offering'. For further provisions in relation to SPACs in Malaysia please refer to http://www.sc.com.my/legislation-guidelines/equity/, accessed on 23 December 2017.
49 SPACs are defined as 'a corporation, the sole business objective of which is to merge the corporation with another corporation and issue the stock certificates through a public offering'.

146  *International financial regulation of SPACs*

all the international corporate features of SPACs highlighted in Chapter 2,[50] although there are some differences from the NYSE or NASDAQ regulation.[51] In fact, unlike US SPACs, whose funds are mainly raised by institutional investors such as hedge funds or private equity firms, Korean SPACs are mainly financed by individual retail investors. This is because the institutional investor base in Korea is small; clearly a country's legal system and its financial environment can have an influence on fund raising for SPACs, as well as on their profitability.

---

50 Indeed, under section 6 (4) 14 of the Enforcement Decree the following listing requirements are imposed on SPACs:

   a  A corporation shall deposit or trust of not less than the amount which is 90/100 of money collected through the issuance of stock certificates (excluding the securities issued before the initial public offering) with an institution prescribed and publicly notified by the Financial Services Commission, such as a company that obtained authorization under Article 324 (1) of the Financial Investment Services and Capital Markets Act (hereinafter referred to as 'securities finance company'), by the following business day of the deadline for payment of the stock price;
   b  A corporation shall not withdraw or offer as security money deposited or trusted, as provided for in item (a) before registration of merger of a corporation with another corporation is completed: provided that where it is unavoidable for the operation of a special purpose acquisition company, such as the cases where it is necessary to purchase the stocks through exercise of the appraisal rights of shareholders under Article 165-5 of the Financial Investment Services and Capital Markets Act, as prescribed and publicly notified by the Financial Services Commission, the withdrawal shall be permitted;
   c  One or more of promoters shall be the investment trader of equity securities (excluding the collective investment securities), the scale of which is equivalent to or greater than that prescribed and publicly notified by the Financial Services Commission;
   d  An executive shall not fall under any of the subparagraphs in Article 24 of the Financial Investment Services and Capital Markets Act;
   e  A corporation shall list the securities by the initial public offering on the securities market within 90 days from the deadline for payment for stock price;
   f  A corporation shall complete the registration of merger with another corporation within 36 months from the deadline for payment for stock certificates by the initial public offering;
   g  A corporation shall satisfy the guideline prescribed and publicly notified by the Financial Services Commission, as necessary for protecting investors.
51 Kab Lae Kim, 'The Characteristics of SPAC Investments in Korea' (2010) 2 (3) Korea Capital Market Institute 9, 14. He provides a table where difference between US SPACs and Korean SPACs are highlighted. It is interesting that under the Korean securities law a SPAC is not allowed to issue warrants at the IPO stage. It seems, therefore, that managers can be less controlled by shareholders in a moral hazard point of view. Nonetheless, it is possible for managers to buy convertible bonds at the IPO stage. This is not an assumption that SPACs are based on debt, because warrants as well as convertible bonds are hybrid securities. Therefore, cannot be defined completely under the equity or debt securities. However, for our purpose further arguments will be raised in this paragraph taking into account the theoretical framework of SPACs between risk and uncertainty.

The Korea Exchange is an instance of hard law regulation of SPACs, and it is binding on the promoters/sponsors of the SPAC. As SPACs are public listed companies, their securities cannot be traded on an over-the-counter market. To this end, the Korea Exchange has explicitly avoided repeating the history of the blank check companies that, as has been explained in Chapter 2, attempted fraudulent pump-and-dump schemes on the PSM in the US. In Korea there are two stock exchanges, namely the KOSPI market[52] and the KOSDAQ market[53] both being segments of the Korea Exchange (KRX). SPACs are listed as public companies on either the KOSPI or the KOSDAQ.[54]

The effect of the legislation is to determine the corporate features of SPACs in order to protect investors and promote efficiency in the financial market. At least two features of the Korean legislation should be noted. The first is centred on the fact that only authorised promoters – specifically more than one – are entitled to propose a business acquisition. In other words, the management is composed of experts. This feature is completely in line with the EGs of the Bursa Malaysia, where special attention is given to the credibility of the management. Indeed, as has been stated before, one of the endogenous factors the business acquisition depends on is the competence of the management. Managers are non-elected because they are usually the same as the promoters/sponsors of the SPAC. Therefore, it is important for investors to know their competences and expertise in advance. The second point is that SPACs listed on the Korea Exchange are exempted from the provisions governing collective investment securities, confirming that SPACs are not assimilated to private equity or investment companies, and can only be constructed as a species of private equity.[55]

### 4.5.2 The Borsa Istanbul exchange

No SPAC offering has been seen in Turkey, although this jurisdiction is one of the few countries in the world together with the US, Canada, Korea, and Malaysia to have adopted a specific SPAC discipline.

---

52 This is the market for major blue-chip companies. It is essentially a stock market.
53 This is the market mainly designed for start-up companies.
54 Kab Lae Kim, n. 100, 13.
55 Steven M. Davidoff, 'Black Market Capital' (2008) Columbia Business Law Review 175, 225. According to the Author:

> SPACs are a species of private equity: these are capital pools organized to acquire individual businesses. But because the general requirement that the initial acquisition comprise 80% of its assets, SPACs typically only acquire a single privately-held business. Despite these important distinctions, SPACs otherwise attempt to mimic private equity returns by employing comparable structures and practices. For example, SPACs utilize similar leverage to increase the size and potential returns of their acquisitions. The managers of SPACs are also typically provided 20% of the initial share offering at nominal amounts; ownership they are required to maintain until and after consummation of an acquisition. This ostensibly provides them with a similar incentive compensation scheme as private equity advisers.

The definition and requirements for SPACs are listed in the Communiqué No. II-23.2 on Mergers and Demergers issued by the Capital Market Board (CMB) based on the powers the CMB is granted by the Capital Market Law No. 6362.

In particular, a SPAC is defined as a non-operating company which is listed on the primary market for the purpose of merging with a private company and must have a minimum capitalisation of 200 million Turkish liras to complete a business combination within 24 months. Today in Turkey, a SPAC is opened only to qualified investors because it is a cash-shell company, and does not possess balance sheets to be audited before listing. Furthermore, the high level of capitalisation does not allow the SPAC to be a flexible investment vehicle. Once the business combination is completed by virtue of a reverse merger, the targeted private company becomes the newly merged listed entity.

Specifically, in case of failure of an acquisition, the managers are not entitled to any reimbursement, and this provides a Turkish SPAC with more 'skin in the game' on the side of sponsors. Furthermore, only 10% of funds in escrow can be used for running the SPAC. This provision can avoid conflicts of interest on the side of the management and provides SPAC investors with transparency. Finally, 80% of the IPO proceeds must be used to finance the merger at De-SPACing according to the Borsa Istanbul Listing Directive (art. 24), and if shareholders vote against a proposed business combination, the SPAC must buy-back their shares. The buy-back of shares resembles the US rules on tender offers.

Following this brief description of the main listing requirements for SPACs in Turkey, we can clearly recognise features of American rules, such as the release of at least 80% of funds at the De-SPAC moment. However, Turkey could improve its rules if the 'special purpose' were made broader. SPACs could be granted the right to complete a business combination by virtue of direct mergers in addition to reverse mergers as well as acquisition of the majority or minority shareholding of the target company. SPACs can also be used to finance distressed businesses by injecting liquidity into the distressed target entity. They can represent a growth capital opportunity for private companies, the listing of the merged entity being only one of many purposes. This flexibility would make the regulation framework of Turkey more competitive, and unique in the world.

Finally, Turkey and Korea are the only jurisdictions in the world to take a SPAC by-law approach. Here the paternalistic role of the law is emphasised, and SPACs are the product of state legislation. Such an approach is in direct contrast with SPACs of the first or second generation, namely, SPACs that are directly regulated by virtue of indirect or direct soft law. This means that Turkey gives sponsors stricter regulatory requirements and this is not the common playbook for SPACs. Nonetheless, in the silence of the law, Turkish SPACs can take advantage of the many market practices that have soared in America, especially in relation to SPACs 3.0 and 3.5. Those market practices can indeed find a direct application by virtue of self-imposing behaviours or better, self-regulatory practices, on the side of the sponsor.

## 4.6 Conclusions

This chapter has illustrated the evolutionary story of SPACs since their origins as blank check companies on the PSM. Following the adoption of Rule 419, SPACs have evolved by registering the emergence of common corporate features such as the trust, the redemption right, the winding up process, etc. These features were recognised as an agreed form of international standard which started to be codified as listing requirements by other non-American exchanges. Among those, four instances have been examined for their relevance and unicity, namely the Bursa Malaysia, the Toronto Stock Exchange, the Korea Exchange and the Borsa Istanbul Exchange. This phenomenon has for the first time contributed to setting up an international framework in the financial regulation of SPACs.

For this reason, a 'Multilevel SPAC definition' drawing a distinction between first- and second-generation SPACs has been proposed for the first time. American SPACs have a common feature, in that both constitute a reception of market practices by virtue of soft law approaches. Nonetheless, in the case of SPACs of the first generation, their reception is indirect (bottom-up soft law approach) and constitutes only a voluntary form of fulfilment (as in the American case, before the new disciplines of the NYSE and NASDAQ were introduced, and any other instance where the exchange does not impose any listing requirements by virtue of hard law provisions), whereas SPACs of the second generation are subject to a direct regulation of soft law by virtue of a top-down approach (see Bursa Malaysia and Toronto Stock Exchange, although see the latter for the particular form of financial literacy approach). It has been noted that when the exchange does not provide any discipline in terms of listing requirements for SPACs, tension can be created by national corporate law provisions that can essentially limit a full implementation process of the international standards developed in the SPAC's evolution.

Different forms of regulation have also been manifested through the imposition of expressed listing requirements on different exchanges (the new regulation of NYSE, NASDAQ, the New AMEX, the Korea Exchange and the Toronto Stock Exchange). All these instances are cases of reception and/or codification of market practices, namely reception of international standards in terms of corporate features through the imposition of listing requirements which are a form of hard law regulation. They are the codified-codification of market practices.

On the other hand, the reception of market practices that has set up a new international trend, namely a legal standardised regulation of SPACs (see Korea Exchange and Turkey). Those are unique instances that not only take into account the reception of market practices, but impose them by virtue of a 'by-law approach'. This is a new trend in the international financial regulation of SPACs. However, it seems that a standardisation by market practices can effectively overwhelm a 'by-law approach' because it seems more dynamic (namely, it can manifest itself both in the form of hard law as well as soft law regulations), and it is more in line with the evolutionary process of SPACs.

Summing up, this chapter has provided the reader with an overview of the possible international financial regulation of SPACs by outlining the functions that indirect and direct soft law approaches play. To this end, the next chapter deals specifically with a very delicate moment in the lifespan of a SPAC: the business combination. This is where SPACs are most criticised and where the final game will be played to legitimise SPACs as alternative acquisition models.

# 5 De-SPAC

## M&As, regulatory oversight, and securities litigation

### 5.1 Structuring the deal at De-SPACing: the M&A' aspects

This chapter mainly considers the applicable disclosure requirements under US securities law at the De-SPAC phase. However, general remarks related to M&As can be referred more broadly to any SPAC and to any De-SPAC phase.

SPACs are cash-shell companies where the only valuable asset is the management's competence. It is important that the target company is ready to handle the rigour of being a public company with periodic reporting requirements. Generally, SPACs will look for targets whose business has a large market opportunity. The quality of a target's management team will be an important factor too. SPACs also have to evaluate mainly private companies that want to become public. These are high quality targets because they are private companies evaluating a public listing for quite a while.

Time is not a friend of SPACs. The SPAC sponsor(s) from the time that they enter the market, they are under pressure of finding a suitable target within a very limited time period (usually between 24 and 36 months). This time constraint feature can be risky because it can indirectly push sponsor(s) to agree on terms at the moment of the business combination that are not necessarily in favour of SPACs' investors. This is – as we said – in the previous chapters the result of the attractive feature of the promote that can be transformed upon successful completion of the business combination into a generous share of 20% of the newly merged entity. In other words, the sponsor(s) might act against the interests of public investors and stakeholders. However, we saw that this transactional risk can be curtailed with appropriate corporate governance mechanisms, and by creating a compensation scheme for the promote that is directly connected to the performance of the newly merged entity. You cash-in only if you create value for investors and stakeholders. This is not yet a common practice in the US (the reader might remember the definition of the SPAC bonanza), and generally for SPACs Worldwide with few exceptions. However, it might be an improvement that SPACs have to implement in the future in order to create incentives on the side of the promote that are linked

DOI: 10.4324/9781003102779-6

to performance (for instance, the SPAC of Mr. Ian Osborne on Euronext – Amsterdam). The issues concerning valuation of the acquisition target and its existence as a public company were addressed by the SEC on 31 March 2021, in two statements that express concern. Given the accelerated timeline on which private companies can become public through a SPAC, those companies may not have engaged in advance planning and investment in resources necessary to meet their obligations as public companies.[1] The target company does not go through a traditional IPO process. However, this company must meet the "book and records" and "internal controls" provisions of the SEA 1934, the minimum listing standards of the national securities exchanges, and the qualitative standards regarding corporate governance at the time of the De-SPAC transaction. The Division of the SEC observed that: '[t]here is a risk that a private operating company that has not prepared for an initial public offering and is quickly acquired by a SPAC may not have these elements in place'. The statement by Acting Chief Accountant Paul Munter (see Section 5.1.6 below) outlines a similar concern in terms of financial reporting, internal controls and other public company obligations post-merger. Those statements have only one beneficial side: they both understand that the SPAC is not the final merged entity. Hence, they confirm what we said in our introduction to this work: that the lifespan of a SPAC is mainly determined by two different moments, the SPAC IPO and the De-SPAC transaction. Indeed, it is the private company to become public, and it is right that it is subject to higher compliance as in any traditional IPO.

From a transactional point of view entering into a letter of intent (LOI) with a SPAC is always challenging because the sponsor(s) cannot have control over the number of redemptions at the moment of the business combination. Hence, the consequent possible liability of the sponsor(s) is difficult to negotiate in the current SPAC environment, since the SPAC cannot access the trust funds, and redemptions – as said – are beyond its control. Furthermore, a SPAC cannot provide break fees to a target. In fact, if the SPAC reaches an agreement with the target on a De-SPAC transaction, the public investors must approve it. On the one hand, it is true that the current uncodified market practice of the decoupling of the redemption right guarantees investors' money back. On the other hand, a high number of redemptions might cause detriment to the SPAC which will not have enough capital to complete the De-SPAC transaction. A possible remedy to supersede this issue is to seek private investments from institutional investors, including mutual funds and asset managers. These investments are called – as we have seen in Chapter 2 – private investment in public equity (PIPE investments). The PIPE with time has become a crucial feature of every SPAC, at least in the US. Today

---

1 Securities and Exchange Commission, 'Staff Statement on Select Issues Pertaining to Special Purpose Acquisition Companies' (31 March 2021), available at https://www.sec.gov/news/public-statement/division-cf-spac-2021-03-31, accessed on 15 April 2021.

the final vote on the business combination by SPACs' investors is generally allowed only after the SPAC has successfully secured a PIPE investment. This because the PIPE adds the necessary funds to the De-SPAC transaction once the target is selected and the acquisition price is determined. This avoids the possible lack of funds to pay the consideration price at the De-SPAC phase, and it also provides sponsor(s) with more confidence in securing a deal. The PIPE also explains the 'magic formula' by which the SPAC is capable of securing a deal where the target company value is up to four to eight times higher than the value kept in the escrow account. It is important to know that once the SPAC announces a merger, the company gets something like $700 million in cash as a PIPE investment, and sometimes much more than this. For instance, in April 2021, the Singapore-based Grab's agreement with the SPAC Altimeter Growth Corp. secured a valuation of nearly $40 billion. This is one of the biggest valuation ever in SPAC deals. The SPAC in this case had a $4 billion PIPE investment. BlackRock, Morgan Stanley's, Counterpoint Global, T. Rowe Price, Fidelity, Janus Henderson group and Nuveen also participated in the PIPE round. Alongside them were several state-linked funds – including Singapore's Temasek, Malaysia's Permodalan Nasional Berhad, and the UAE's Mubadala – as well as family offices and funds linked to Indonesians conglomerates Djarum, Emtek and Sinar Mas. PIPE investments are a common feature in the US but they might constitute a challenge in Europe, due to regulatory concerns and availability of funds. Hence, at a first glance it might be predicted that Europe will fail to experience the same level of investments or SPAC offerings as has historically occurred in the US between 2020 and 2021.

The transactional risk associated with SPAC deals can be mitigated with traditional M&A contractual tools, such as representations and warranties. Both the SPAC and the target company are expected to make a number of representations and warranties concerning the formation, its good standing, financial statements, liabilities, intellectual property, key contracts, etc. Warranties, indemnities are given by the target shareholders on a no-liability basis (i.e. they do not survive following completion). In the current market a target company will not typically agree to give a SPAC an indemnity for breaches of representations and warranties. Therefore, if in competition with a SPAC, the target may need to forgo any recourse against target company sellers in order to remain competitive with SPAC bidders. The target could obtain a representations and warranties insurance policy in lieu of an indemnity. However, the latter is not common in the SPAC arena with only 4% of 2020 De-SPAC deals referenced insurance policies according to Deal Point Data.

Typical closing conditions to the SPAC business combination include shareholder approval, no material adverse change on the target, and any required regulatory approvals (this latter is also subject to the industry of the target company, for example, acquiring a banking licence from a bank licence provider who might request specific authorisation from the national Central Bank of the country where the target company is incorporated). Most agreements also include a minimum cash condition in favour of the target if a threshold amount of capital is not raised in the transaction. Finally, on a SPAC deal, the target board still runs the business after going public, usually with the addition of one or two directors of the SPAC joining the target/public company board post-closing; if the target is the buyer, it will own and control the target and may need to put into place compensatory arrangements to retain target management.

Having said that, this chapter focuses on M&A aspects of the De-SPAC phase with particular emphasis on due diligence processes, sponsor(s)'ownership, target acquisition valuation, and PIPE investments, as well as disclosure requirements that the de-SPACed entity and the SPAC itself have to satisfy after the SPAC enters into an agreement with a target company (for example, in the US, the SPAC files a proxy statement under Form S-4 registration statement with the SEC or the Form 10 Information, the Form S-8, etc.).

The following sequence shows the main steps that this chapter aims to tackle and explain in depth in order to understand the transactional and regulatory risks at the SPAC IPO phase and De-SPAC phase.

Disclosures apply at the pre-close, close, and post-close phases, whereas SPAC litigation mainly relates to the post-close momentum.

### 5.1.1 Due diligence

In De-SPAC transactions, due diligence is not a one-way street. The target company in a De-SPAC transaction has potentially more work to do before entering into the final transaction. Indeed, as the SPAC conducts due diligence on acquisition targets, likewise the same targets have to conduct due diligence on the SPAC. However, on the SPAC, the due diligence is generally limited but questions may be raised in relation to its capital structure, management's operational and deal expertise, reputation and relationships with potential investors.

On the other hand, preparatory work should be commenced early on vendor due diligence and accounting work streams. The target company should set up data rooms in advance to ensure a quick and efficient due diligence process. To this end, a target should consider to prepare a short form vendor due diligence report which is particularly useful in auction processes and help ensure an efficient process. If the target is operating in certain industries, they might consider to prepare a technical report such as environmental or property. Traditionally, in a typical M&A transaction, sponsor(s) would target companies through an accelerated financial, legal, and tax due diligence process. Although SPACs have historically been focused on positive operating companies, the following shift concerned positive EBITDA companies. In 2020 there was a new divergence from the norm, with pre-revenue "story-stock" companies entering the fray. For instance, in March 2021, the British electric vehicle manufacturer Arrival began trading on the NASDAQ following a merger with a US blank check company. Arrival is still a start-up that is supposed to be trialling its vans with customers in summer 2021, with its van production set to follow in the second half of next year. Arrival secured one of the highest ever valuations for a British company, making its debut on the New York Stock Exchange at a $10 billion valuation.[2] This trend might be risky because if you are not buying an operating company within an industrial sector, you are definitively buying a company that is making a promise, and we all know how things end once promises are broken. However, here is where SPACs can be seen a new development to allow retail investors to bet on promising companies and zero-revenue companies, which have high prospects of becoming either the next Tesla or Apple. In other words, SPACs represent a medium of engagement into late-stage venture capital financing (see Chapter 1).

The acquisition target that is courted by multiple SPACs may not be simply persuaded to accept the highest bid, which pays the highest consideration in cash. By contrast, the target company has to carefully examine the SPAC sponsor(s), their business reputation, their track record, as well as their success or failures in previous De-SPAC transactions. It might be of interest also to consider whether the SPAC board of directors is assisted by an advisory board of SPAC experts or independent directors with extensive experience in public listed companies as well as in SPACs. The identity of major SPAC investors is another crucial detail to agree on the final deal, especially on the identity and share participation of PIPE investors in the deal.

The due diligence of the SPAC must also include a careful consideration of potential conflicts of interest between investment bankers, sponsor(s) and major investors (see Sections 5.2 and 5.3 below). Finally, the target company must be mainly focused on knowing the post De-SPAC transaction management structure and business strategy as well as the SPAC's financial wherewithal to achieve its strategy. This means that if a target company consents to a management rollover stake after the De-SPAC transaction, it is useful to understand when and at what price the target might expect to sell the retained stake (see Section 5.2 below).

---

2 Ryan Browne, 'British Elective Vehicle Firm Arrival Sinks in SPAC Debut' (25 March 2021), available at https://www.cnbc.com/2021/03/25/british-ev-firm-arrival-arvl-goes-public-via-spac-today.html, accessed on 1 April 2021.

A good example of the importance of due diligence in SPAC deals on the side of sponsor(s) is a SEC staff comment letter sent on 5 October 2020, in connection with a SPAC merger between Legacy Acquisition Corp. (Legacy) and Onyx Enterprises Int'l Corp. The legal counsels of the SPAC provided information pursuant to Schedule 14C.[3] The SEC staff requested Legacy Acquisition Corp. to disclose in the background of the merger section a summary of "the financial, business, and legal due diligence questions that arose during its diligence meetings". Legacy, as does every SPAC, has a self-destruct mechanism that requires the SPAC sponsors to locate a private company target to take public usually within 24 months. To "get a deal done", the intent behind the SEC staff's comment might have been probing the diligence process so that investors would have the benefit of comparing it with the rigorous diligence process that occurs in other M&A transactions or with the diligence process undertaken by the underwriters in connection with a firm commitment IPO to establish their due diligence defence under Section 11 of the SEA 1934.

To this end, Legacy's financial diligence also included the analysis of the contents of the Onyx data room, specifically the monthly and quarterly financial reporting, actual results versus budget and forecast, cash management and working capital results to date and projections, capital expenditures and future requirements, gross margin analysis and reasons for changes, taxes and insurance, as well any analysis of SG&A spending. In conducting this diligence, Legacy had several meetings with Onyx management to understand their handling of revenue recognition, accounting policies, key customers, internal control procedures and monthly reporting schedules as well as expected steps to handle public company reporting requirements.

As can be seen, the SPAC has a specific duty of due diligence especially in relation to the ability of the target company to handle public company reporting requirements due to the fact that after the De-SPACing, the former SPAC becomes a public listed company in the form of an operating public company. For example, in De-SPAC transactions in the UK, the target will need to have last three years' audited accounts in accordance with IFRS, which may take several weeks to prepare.

### 5.1.2 The sponsor(s) ownership of the target: higher the risk, higher the return

The sponsor(s) as we said in Chapters 2 and 4 is the 'skin in the game' of SPACs. They buy founders' shares and founders' warrants. These latter are cash net settled and they are not redeemable. A quick glance at S-1 forms in

---

3 SEC, 'Legacy Acquisition Corp. Information Statement on Schedule 14C Filed October 5, 2020, File No 001-38296', available at https://www.sec.gov/Archives/edgar/data/1698113/000121390020034413/filename1.htm, accessed on 1 April 2021.

the US can also show how sponsor(s) are often committed to completing a business combination and there are also specific locked-up agreements that apply to them at the completion of the IPO. For example, lockups are typical for directors, senior officers, and large shareholders of the company following combination (e.g. sponsor, founders and large target shareholders) to enter into lockup arrangements not to sell their shares for a certain period of time.

The share capital of the newly merged entity is usually 30–20% between the SPAC, public investors and PIPE investments, and 70–80% on the side of the acquisition target. This standard proportion is not fixed and regular. It depends on the complexity of the business transaction, and especially on how many founder shares the sponsor is ready to concede to target shareholders. Generally, to mitigate such dilution (the 20% founder shares) and make a De-SPAC transaction more attractive to a target, SPACs often prefer business combination targets that are four to eight times the SPAC's size. Both NASDAQ and NYSE require that the SPAC's charter provides that the business combination must be with one or more targets that have an aggregate fair market value of at least 80% of the value of the SPAC's trust account. For this reason, to mitigate the dilutive effect of the 20% represented by the founder shares, SPACs typically seek a business combination with a target priced at four to eight times the amount of the proceeds from the IPO, with the balance of the acquisition price being funded through debt, forward purchase agreements, PIPE investments in the form of debt or equity or a significant rollover of equity by the target's equity holders. As opposed to a traditional sale, SPACs hold the option for the selling party to maintain a meaningful stake in the new entity post-merger. In a typical M&A process, the seller often surrenders ownership and involvement in the entity once sold. In a De-SPAC merger, the target company is combined with the acquirer and the selling shareholders can retain sizable stakes in the company. For example, in June 2020 Collier Creek's SPAC combined with Utz Quality Food. The funding owners of Utz would retain over 90% of its current equity stake representing more than 50% economic ownership in the combined entity. In this way the founding family (Utz) was able to retain its majority stake in the combined company and use the proceeds from the De-SPAC merger to de-lever its business.

A SPAC is a non-operating company that is created to allow a private company to get listed or to represent a viable growth capital source to restructure businesses. Hence, those who argue about a possible value destruction on the side of SPAC public investors are possibly confusing SPACs with operating companies. A SPAC's main duty is to find an acquisition target and to facilitate its listing. Furthermore, as a general remark, any public listed company always renounces control. This applies to traditional IPOs too. Hence, it is unrealistic to claim that SPAC public shareholders should have a higher return. The reader might remember that SPAC public shares were initially offered at $10 per share to public investors. Until the moment of business combination the SPAC investors do not take any risk. The risk is only taken by the sponsor by virtue of the founder warrants that represent the "at-risk-capital". Hence, if an acquisition is not completed within the settled timeframe the sponsors lose money. In corporate finance there is a saying: the higher the risk, the higher the return. Hence, it seems unreasonable to give SPAC investors a higher return if they do not take a higher risk. One thing we have argued many times is that the SPAC sponsor might be compensated subject to the fulfilment of certain conditions, such as the good performance of the target company. This is surely more reasonable than claiming rights without putting anything at risk. In other words, until the business combination SPAC investors might be depositing money in a bank. The bank in our example is called an escrow account and serves the purpose of financing a business combination. If SPAC public investors redeem their shares, they can have their money back plus a low interest rate that is matured during the lifespan of the SPAC. By contrast, in an ordinary bank account, even this does not always happen.

### 5.1.3 PIPE investment and PIPE engagement letter

In 2020, according to Freshfields Bruckhaus Deringer LLP, 69% of De-SPAC transactions were supported by a PIPE, and only 12% of the deals did not have a PIPE. The average PIPE size for 64 deals closed was $288 million (the median was $160 million).[4] This shows the importance of PIPE investment, as we have already outlined. The certainty of the deal is essential in a De-SPAC phase. As we said, the sponsor(s) might shortfall financing due to the high number of redemptions at the business combination. For this reason, it is essential, *inter alia*, to know whether the PIPE is committed to cover the shortfall. The PIPE can work as an "anchor investor" and a valuation validation of the business combination.

The SPAC will often seek to engage one or more of the same investment banks that assisted the SPAC with its IPO as the placement agents for a PIPE transaction. There is an inevitable need to wall cross investors and maintain the confidentiality of the process. For this reason, is always preferable to have one sole placement agent. The placement agent should follow its normal practice for a private placement engagement and enter into its customary form of PIPE engagement letter with the SPAC, subject to addressing some issues that are SPAC related.

The engagement letter states the fees to be paid by the SPAC in connection with the PIPE transaction. It is key to address any other existing arrangements because various investment banks may be advising the SPAC on capital markets advisory matters or merger and acquisition introductions.

---

4 Freshfields Bruckhaus Deringer LLP, '2020 De-SPAC Debrief' (11 January 2021) Lexology, available at https://www.lexology.com/library/detail.aspx?g=8666d8f2-6a60-4f29-af58-383c24bc7f4a, accessed on 10 March 2021.

If the engagement is not on an exclusive basis, the letter should acknowledge the role of other agent(s) in the PIPE transaction and allocate compensation between the agents to avoid any overlap or dispute.

The acquisition target can also have banking relationships and pre-existing commitments to include an adviser in the PIPE investment. It is common that the PIPE placement agent will consider a fee tail. This shall be included in the engagement letter too. A PIPE engagement letter would include representations and warranties from the issuer relating to the accuracy of due diligence and materials provided by the SPAC to the placement agent. It is convenient if the acquisition target company is included in such representations, since the PIPE placement agent relies on the diligence materials furnished by the private company target including investor presentation and other materials prepared by the private company target to solicit potential PIPE purchasers.

The SPAC is limited to provide indemnification provisions. This because the SPAC's proceeds are deposited in an escrow account, and the account cannot be accessed other than for limited purposes. This is another reason why the private company target has to be a signatory to the engagement letter. Alternatively, the SPAC sponsor can act as a signatory to stand behind the indemnity.

The public announcement of the execution of the business combination coincides with the public announcement of the PIPE transaction. To facilitate a combined public announcement, the PIPE transaction must be secured concurrent with the execution of the business combination agreement. The commitment from the PIPE investors would be irrevocable and conditioned to the consummation of the business combination by a specific date. The majority of PIPE transactions in connection with SPAC business combinations involve the purchase of common shares, without warrants, to the PIPE purchaser. To this end, the PIPE purchaser enters into a securities purchase agreement or subscription agreement with the SPAC where in exchange of liquidity, the PIPE agents are repaid in shares of the new merged entity. The PIPE investors take the pricing risk between the signing of the securities purchase agreement or subscription agreement and the closing of the PIPE transaction.

By contrast, the parties can also announce the execution of the business combination agreement in advance of securing the PIPE financing commitment. In light of this, the PIPE market process would commence when all the details relating to the business combination are already public. This can also be strategic for the SPAC to attract PIPE investors, if other agreements are already in place (for instance, support agreements from SPAC public investors).

On 26 August 2020, the SEC adopted final amendments to the definition of 'accredited investor' and 'qualified institutional buyer'. Those amendments became effective on 8 December 2020. The definition of accredited investor is vital to the regulation of exempt offerings, including PIPE transactions.

Today the category of accredited investor is broader. Any investor can be an 'accredited investor' if the entity has at least $5 million of assets or investments. This means that the cast of PIPE agents has increased significantly. This is to the advantage of SPACs. A PIPE transaction is typically marketed by the SPAC's placement agent to institutional accredited investors that have been 'wall crossed' and have agreed to a securities trading restriction (a wall crossed investor cannot trade in securities of the SPAC and the private company target during the trading restriction period).

### 5.1.4 Equity financing and support agreements

It might happen that a public investor in the SPAC is expected to participate in the PIPE transaction or is affiliated with the SPAC's sponsor. In this circumstance, it is advisable to agree and execute support or non-redemption agreements in support of the business combination and commit not to (or waive the right to) redeem SPAC's shares. These agreements are signed at the execution of the business combination agreement. It is logical that if there is a high number of supporting shareholders in the SPAC, then the redemption risk and the need for a PIPE transaction is lowered. However, the percentage of public investors that have entered into a no-redemption agreement must be disclosed. The public announcement of the business combination can include these commitments to attract, for instance, the PIPE transaction. Those commitments must also be disclosed in the proxy statement given to the SPAC's shareholders once they express their vote on the business combination.

Other SPAC shareholders might sign lock-up agreements restricting their ability to transfer securities in the acquisition target for a specified period of time following the business combination. A high number of locked-up shareholders can reduce the risk of selling at completion of the business combination. To this end, PIPE investors in the US must ensure that the resale registration statement covering the resale from time to time of securities bought in the PIPE transaction becomes effective prior to the release of the lock-up agreement of the SPAC's shareholders.

Finally, SPAC sponsors can secure additional funding by directly asking for bank financing through specific facility agreements as well as entering into a forward purchase agreement with the SPAC where the sponsor commits to buying shares in the newly merged entity at the execution of the business combination. Forward purchase agreements (if secured at the time of the IPO) must be disclosed in S-1 forms. Essentially, in a forward purchase agreement, affiliates of the sponsor or institutional investors either commit or have the option to purchase equity in connection with the De-SPAC transaction. The proceeds of the forward purchase agreement are used to finance a portion of the purchase price for the business combination, meet minimum cash conditions required to consummate the business combination and fund the working capital needs of the surviving entity.

## 5.1.5 Valuation of the acquisition target

A SPAC transaction can offer target companies several benefits. First, a SPAC acquisition allows a private company to become public without making arrangements with underwriters, conducting roadshows, or preparing a prospectus to sell its securities to the public. Second, a target company is able to privately negotiate a fixed valuation with the acquirer by setting a fixed dollar "purchase price" that is usually greater than what an operating company could or would offer. For this reason, the valuation is locked-in at the time the merger agreement is executed and announced (often with a PIPE set to close concurrently). Therefore, the target company can avoid the potential hit to valuation that is associated with the pricing of traditional IPOs. Third, a SPAC acquisition typically provides significant liquidity for a target's shareholders by giving them access to public markets, even during periods of market instability such as Covid-19 in 2020. These may include secure upfront capital, greater confidence in the execution of the deal, and potentially greater ownership retention in comparison to a traditional strategic sale.

Finally, SPAC transactions often present an opportunity to simplify deal terms by using a public-company-style acquisition approach based on an enterprise value without negotiating working capital, cash, debt, or transaction expense adjustments.

A critical distinction between a De-SPAC transaction and a traditional IPO is the ability to include forward-looking financial projections in a proxy or registration statement, rather than historical financial results. Financial projections made in relation to a De-SPAC transaction fall within the Private Securities Litigation Reform Act (PSLRA) 1995 safe harbour for forward-looking statements. However, there is a risk in relying on such projections because the safe harbour rule does not apply to knowingly false or misleading projections. Having said that, the elaboration of projections is purely discretional and subjective. Hence, it is tricky.[5] This is the ground on which lie disgruntled investors and litigation is on the rise (see Sections 5.3 and 5.4 below). Indeed, the US House Committee on Financial Services held a hearing regarding SPACs, direct listings, public offerings and investor protections associated with these offerings. In advance of the hearing, the committee released a draft legislation amending the Securities Act of 1933 and the Securities Exchange Act of 1934 to specifically exclude all SPACs from the safe harbour for forward-looking statements. This move of course can create

---

5  An example is *Jensen v GigCapital 3, Inc. et al.*, where the claimant alleges that the SPAC and its board members authorised the filing of a proxy statement containing "materially incomplete and misleading" financial projections and valuations for the planned target company. Among other issues, the plaintiff accused the defendants of selectively revealing certain metrics (such as projected EBITDA) while allegedly concealing more relevant cash flow projections and earlier versions of these figures, which had been revised in anticipation of the De-SPAC transaction.

further potential liability for inaccuracies in forward-looking statements for companies looking to go public through a SPAC.[6]

It is frequently said that the private company audit is about what the numbers are (revenues, operating costs, etc.), whereas in a public company, the audit is more about how and why those numbers are there. It is the reporting methodology that counts. Hence, in a public listed company the quality of the auditors and the quality of the audit opinion is essential. In other words, you want to make sure that your company is ready to go public. This is also in line with the SEC's concerns that we outlined at the start of this chapter. To this end, SPACs can use projections to determine the value of the target company. However, those projections must be reliable and drafted in good faith. Hence, the assessment of the accounting acquirer in a SPAC merger should be performed prior to the evaluation of earnout arrangements (see Section 5.1.6).

A SPAC acquisition can require an extended timeline given the hybrid "M&A/IPO" nature of the transaction and extensive transaction costs. Targets may need to negotiate a definitive acquisition agreement alongside preparation of the Form S-4 (proxy statement, see Section 5.2 below), and other filings, which may require extra resources. Although such documents might be successfully negotiated, SPAC shareholders still have the right to redeem their shares and receive their pro rata portion of the IPO proceeds, which can trigger uncertainty about the amount of capital the SPAC will have at closing. Additionally, the sponsor(s) equity will be dilutive to the private company shareholders (see Section 5.1.2 above). SPAC sponsor(s) and the operating company must sell the deal to current private shareholders, public shareholders, and PIPE investors to implement a capital structure that is aligned with the company's profile and business plans.

Under NY stock exchange rules, the business combination must be with one or more targets that together have an aggregate fair market value of at least 80% of the assets held in the SPAC's trust account. Acquisitions are completed usually through a merger agreement with a joint Form S-4 registration statement, proxy process, or tender offer. Under the SEC proxy rules, a proxy statement must include two or three years of financial statements of the target, plus interim financial statements. The financial statements and the target's auditor have to meet certain requirements, and thus the necessary audit or re-audit of the target's financial statements can be a gating item for the business combination.

Valuation of the target in a SPAC combination is subject to negotiation, and it is not always focused on a positive EBITDA, but rather – as we said – on

---

6 Ran Ben-Tzur, Jay Pomerantz, 'House Releases Draft Legislation Eliminating SPAC Safe Harbor for Forward-Looking Statements' (7 June 2021) Harvard Law School Forum on Corporate Governance, available at https://corpgov.law.harvard.edu/2021/06/07/house-releases-draft-legislation-eliminating-spac-safe-harbor-for-forward-looking-statements/?utm_content=buffer848d7&utm_medium=social&utm_source=linkedin.com&utm_campaign=buffer, accessed on 10 June 2021.

pre-revenue companies. Since SPAC shareholders' approval is necessary for the completion of the business combination, and SPAC shareholders may elect to redeem, the valuation must be viewed as appropriate by those shareholders or the deal could result in increased redemptions, and therefore in less operating cash for the newly merged entity. In other words, dissenting shareholders have the right to redeem shares, and therefore the final amount of cash available to pay the target's shareholders can be uncertain. For these reasons, SPACs and targets often negotiate a "minimum cash" closing condition, and SPAC acquisitions often include a simultaneous PIPE investment upon consummation of the merger (see Chapter 2, and within this chapter Section 5.1.3).

### 5.1.6 Earnout provisions

On 31 March 2021, the SEC Acting Chief Accountant Mr. Paul Munter issued a public statement[7] regarding SPAC transactions. The statement establishes that SPAC transactions are subject to the same review process by the SEC as traditional IPOs. Specifically, one of the points raised concerned the financial reporting and accounting standards to be followed in the case of earnout arrangements and complex financial instruments.

There are instances where the value of the operating company is uncertain. A possible transactional tool to mitigate uncertainty in relation to the acquisition target is for the SPAC to enter into agreement with its sponsor(s), the selling shareholders of the target company, or employees, whereby the SPAC will issue additional shares (or release existing shares from escrow) post-merger if certain performance measures (usually based on stock price) are met. Those agreements are defined as earnout provisions and are based on the following characteristics: the merged entity is required to issue additional common shares if, during a specified period after the merger date, its shares price equals or exceeds a stated amount or amounts; second, some or all of the shares not previously issued are issuable upon the occurrence of a specific event (change of control of the newly merged entity); finally, the settlement must occur in shares (the newly merged entity or holder cannot elect cash settlement). In other words, earnouts can bridge a valuation gap unlike in a traditional IPO. Tendentially, the emerging market practice in this sector is that the average size of the earnout component on De-SPACs is decreasing whilst the average length of the earnout period is on the rise.

If the SPAC is the accounting acquirer and the earnout agreement is with the acquisition target, it can be considered contingent consideration. Hence, there are accounting rules to assess whether a contingent payment should be accounted as contingent consideration or recognised as a post-combination

---

7 Securities and Exchange Commission, 'Financial Reporting and Auditing Considerations of Companies Merging with SPACs' (31 March 2021), available at https://www.sec.gov/news/public-statement/munter-spac-20200331, accessed on 15 April 2021.

compensation cost. The contingent consideration is measured at fair value. The obligation to pay the contingent consideration is classified as liability or in shareholders' equity, or other applicable US GAAP. On the other hand, the accounting on contingent consideration paid in the post-combination period is classified as an asset, liability, or equity, and it is determined by the nature of the instrument. Finally, contingent payments to selling shareholders that remain employed and are linked to future services are considered a compensation cost and recorded in the post-combination period.

### 5.1.7 Place of incorporation, growth capital, and high growth companies

An important element that people often forget in SPAC markets relates to the country of incorporation. The vast majority of SPACs in the US are incorporated under Delaware corporate law. However, this depends on the geographical area where the acquisition is going to take place. For example, tendentially any SPAC listed in the US that seeks an acquisition opportunity in Europe as well as in other countries except America, they usually prefer to be incorporated either in the Cayman Islands (most commonly used jurisdiction) or elsewhere, such as the British Virgin Islands. This is done mainly for tax reasons and to avoid the complex burden of American tax rules once the De-SPAC moment is approached (as the assets of the SPAC have increased due to the business acquisition or combination). This can be seen as a further evolution of the SPAC regime, and it has been adopted in the US by many SPACs such as Galileo Acquisition Corp., Malacca Straits Acquisition Corp, Ascendant Digital Acquisition Corp., HPX Corp., Jaws Acquisition Corp., D8 Holdings Corp., etc. For instance, on 25 March 2021, Malacca Straits Acquisition Corp. reported a deal to merge with Netflix Indonesia (PT Asia Vision Network), or in April 2021, Ajax I Acquisition Corp. which was incorporated in the Cayman Islands and acquired Cazoo, the UK's leading online car retailer.

Hence, the country of incorporation of a SPAC matters and the country of incorporation sometimes also follows the country of listing. There is a tendency to prefer European SPACs to be listed in Europe. For example, Italian investment banks sometimes seem reluctant to list sponsors that are not incorporated in the form of an Italian joint stock company. This is also due to anti-money laundering provisions that require certainty of individuals' identities and corporate entities. Furthermore, the underwriter might require the SPAC to have some well-known executives and to target national companies where the SPAC is seeking the offering. This is because the capital is raised by virtue of public investors, which are mainly national institutional investors. Indeed, national public investors seem reluctant to invest in a SPAC mainly formed by foreign managers and pursuing a cross-border acquisition. Having said that, the US has a different standing and it is more flexible as the De-SPAC transactions of Grab and Zegna can show. Such lack of flexibility can constitute a possible hurdle for European SPAC listings.

A business trend in SPACs that has been mainly imposed by the circumstances of Covid-19 relates to SPACs that target distressed entities. This is possibly the start of a larger phenomenon that goes under the name of growth capital. Essentially, this is a type of private equity investment, usually a minority investment, in relatively mature companies looking for capital to expand or restructure operations without a change of control of the business. SPACs are also exploring these alternatives. For instance, in August 2020 a possible new trend has emerged with the incorporation of Broadstone Acquisition Corp. (Broadstone): a SPAC sponsored by Sun Capital Partners. Broadstone is incorporated as a Cayman Islands company, listed in New York and headquartered in London. It seems that since then there has been a swift change in the purpose of SPACs, i.e. distressed opportunities. Indeed, Broadstone is targeting companies either in the UK or Europe that are in distress. This is evidenced by the S-1 Form filed with the SEC on 13 August 2020 which reads that the main focus of the SPAC is on "sound but stressed businesses". This is because the management of Broadstone believes that the pandemic is creating an unusually large number of undervalued acquisition opportunities, as target businesses suffer from financial indebtedness and a lack of equity funding alternatives. Specifically, Broadstone can be an ideal liquidity solution for vendors that suffer a lack of alternative sources of equity available for private companies, and at the same time shareholders may get share exchange deals. Indeed, under the right circumstances (di) stressed businesses can be viable targets for SPACs.[8] Finally, as we have already mentioned, SPAC targets promising companies or better zero-revenue companies. Those are high growth companies usually operating in emerging sectors such as electric vehicles, FinTech, digital media, more broadly technology companies.

## 5.2 Structuring the deal at De-SPACing in the US: the regulatory challenges[9]

As we explained a SPAC is a blank check company that conducts an IPO to raise funds for use in a future business combination transaction involving a company in a previously identified industry or geographic area.

Once an appropriate target company is identified for a business combination, the SPAC and the target undertake a merger, acquisition or other transaction that results, in most cases, in the operating business becoming a publicly traded company that effectively "takes over" the public company status of the SPAC, and as a result, the SPAC is "De-SPACed" and continues its life as a public company.

---

8 Michael Levitt, Madlyn Primoff, 'Distressed Businesses Can be Good Targets for SPACs' (3 March 2021) Bloomberg Law Insights.
9 Some parts of this section have been consolidated through a report written by the law firm Allen & Overy titled 'The Journey to De-SPACing and Beyond' (2020).

Upon the completion of the business combination, the newly De-SPACed public company, and the board of directors often find themselves in uncharted territory, especially those individuals who have not previously been part of a De-SPACing transaction or a company that is a former SPAC. SPACs have to satisfy a number of unique challenges and obligations upon completing the De-SPACing process. In some cases, SPACs have a special regime under US federal securities law that is not reserved to most 'normal' public companies. The following sections illustrate the main forms to be completed by a US SPAC.

### 5.2.1 Form 10 information

This form refers to the requirement that public companies must provide robust disclosure to the market similar to what is required by registration statements on Form S-1, including financial statements, disclosures about the company, its management and its securities, following the business combination transaction.

This requirement is usually met by newly De-SPACed companies through the filing by such companies of a Current Report on Form 8-K that includes the Form 10 Information (a 'Super 8-K'). Indeed, if an affirmative vote is obtained from the proxy process, the business combination can be completed, and the target company becomes a publicly traded entity. Hence, a Super 8-K Form must be filed within four days of the acquisition and must contain substantially the same information that would be required in a registration statement for companies that go through a traditional IPO.

As the company continues its public company life, a number of securities law restrictions are applicable to it, as a former SPAC, are tied to the timing of the filing of the Form 10 Information. In other words, the De-SPACing process relates to the day on which the SPAC ceased to be a shell company. This date is generally a few days before the filing date of the Form 10 Information on the Super 8-K and is the date of the closing of the business combination transaction. Subsequently, the sponsor's founders' shares and warrants are locked-up for a specified period starting from the date of the Super 8-K Form. The lock-up period is typically one year, subject to negotiation at the inception of the SPAC, but the agreement might include exceptions for gifts, transfers to affiliates or trusts, or estate planning. Some or all of the target's security holders will also be expected to sign a lock-up agreement, which is typically 180 days from the closing of the merger.

### 5.2.2 Form S-8

After the completion of the business combination and the filing of the Form 10 Information, recently De-SPACed companies have to make incentive awards to members of the new company's board of directors. These grants, as with many other public companies, are conducted pursuant to an equity incentive or similar award plan and registered on Form S-8 with the SEC.

The Form S-8 is a SEC registration statement, and it is, for instance, used by many companies to register securities to be offered to employees of the company under any employee benefit plan, or it is available for reoffers and resales of securities owned by affiliates of the company. The Form S-8 is not reviewed by the SEC and it is effective immediately upon filing. It is straightforward and inexpensive to use.

However, the Form S-8 is raising issues in relation to SPACs. This form is available to shell companies only if: (a) the company has not been a shell company for at least 60 calendar days prior to the filing of the S-8 registration statement; and (b) the company has filed current Form 10 Information with the SEC at least 60 calendar days prior to the filing of the S-8, reflecting its status as an entity that is not a shell company. This means that SPACs face a 60-day delay between closing the business combination and filing the Form 10 Information. This directly affects the SPAC's ability to file a S-8 registration statement. Hence, SPACs frequently experience a delay in the company making certain incentive grants to its directors and officers, due to the need to register the relevant grants with the SEC.

### 5.2.3 Rule 144

Once the former SPAC continues its life as a public company, it will get questions from employees and investors who hold "restricted securities" or "control securities" in the company and are interested in selling those securities and/or transferring them to their brokerage or other investment accounts. Generally, those questions arise after six months of De-SPACing. The questions of such security holders are directed to the company, and their transfer agent, to remove the restrictive legends on their securities. This is when Rule 144 is usually invoked as the basis for their request.

Rule 144 provides an exemption from registration of certain resales of restricted or control securities if a number of conditions are met, including a holding period for the relevant securities and restrictions on the volume and manner of sales.

For SPACs, Rule 144 imposes additional requirements including that the company:

- has ceased to be a shell company as defined in the rule;
- is a SEC reporting company;
- has filed all reports required to be filed with the SEC during the preceding 12 months and
- has filed current Form 10 Information with the SEC reflecting that the company is no longer a shell company and at least one year has elapsed from the filing of this Form 10 Information.

The requirement for current SEC reporting included above is referred to as the 'evergreen provision'. In other words, it means that the current Securities

Act 1933 reporting requirement for former SPACs is perpetual. Notwithstanding, holders having met the holding period and other requirements to sell the former SPAC's securities under Rule 144, no sales can take place, unless the company is current in its Securities Act 1933 reporting. If the company, for instance, is missing a required Exchange Act filing covered by the requirements of the rule, it will cease to be current in its Exchange Act reports and will not meet this requirement for the use of Rule 144. This means that the restrictive legend on "restricted securities" of the former SPAC cannot be removed in advance of a sale. This is possibly inconvenient for many SPAC shareholders because it can limit the transferring shares and efficiency of potential sales.

### 5.2.4 Form S-3 eligibility

As has been explained in the previous section, the evergreen provision of Rule 144 is unavailable for 12 months following the provision of Form 10 Information and the completion of the business combination. Hence, resale registration statements and the right to such registration statements is often a critical part of the business combination negotiations. This is likely to become of even greater significance after the recent SEC's C&DIs (Compliance and Disclosure Interpretations)[10] for former SPACs.

As we said, SPACs face large limitations on the use of Rule 144 and the eligibility question is likely to present challenges in negotiating registration rights in SPAC transactions. On 21 September 2020, the SEC issued new guidance limiting the ability of former SPACs to satisfy the eligibility requirements of Form S-3. Former SPACs cannot use Form S-3 during the 12 calendar months following the completion of the SPAC business combination transaction. Hence, it is vital for a former SPAC to understand whether the SPAC pre-business combination SEC reporting history can be used for the purpose of determining S-3 eligibility following the business combination.

In September 2020, the SEC indicated that a former SPAC may not use the Form S-3 in situations in which the post-business combination company is a new entity or successor registrant to the SPAC. In both cases, the SEC provides that the company will not be eligible to use Form S-3 for 12 months following the business combination. Furthermore, in cases in which the post-business combination entity is neither a new entity nor a successor registrant to the SPAC, the entity would have less than 12 months post-combination reporting history and therefore the SEC staff would be 'unlikely' to accelerate effectiveness on a registration statement on Form S-3.

Hence, it means that because SPACs are non-operating companies seeking to acquire private operating businesses, this has a significant impact on

---

10 SEC, 'Securities Act Forms Last Update: September 21, 2020', available at https://www.sec.gov/corpfin/securities-act-forms.

increased costs and time required in using Form S-1 for the first year following the business combination transaction.

*5.2.5 Ineligible issuers*

After De-SPACing, many former SPACs are active public companies. They return to public securities markets for acquisition financing, general capital raising or other transactions conducted through the SEC's registration regime, all of which are likely to be affected by the SEC's recent guidelines and limitations on the use of Form S-3.

Furthermore, public listed companies frequently use 'free writing prospectuses' (FWPs) or written communications that constitute an offer to sell or a solicitation of an offer to buy registered securities and are not a statutory prospectus under Section 10 of the Securities Act of 1933, as amended. FWPs can take many forms, such as electronic graphic media, television broadcasts and printed materials, and they may include information not contained in the company's registration statement as filed with the SEC. FWPs are frequently used by American public companies due to their flexibility in conveying information to the market. However, FWPs might not be used by companies who are defined as ineligible issuers.

According to Rule 405 of the Securities Act of 1933, ineligible issuers are issuers that are or, during the past three years, have been, blank check companies. This includes SPACs and, therefore, former SPACs are deemed ineligible issuers for a period of three years from the completion of the De-SPACing process. This precludes former SPACs using FWPs during this time frame. This, along with the challenges related to S-3 eligibility for former SPACs, may result in a more restrictive and less fluid opportunity for capital raising through the SEC's registration process in the early years following De-SPACing.

It means SPAC sponsors must always take into account alternative strategies and/or invest additional time and resources to address these challenges.

## 5.3 Disclosure duties of the sponsor and underwriters in the US

In September 2020, Mr Jay Clayton commented about SPACs on CNBC's Squawk Box and expressed his views that SPACs provide 'healthy' competition to traditional IPOs, but he went on to stress that 'for good competition and good decision-making, you need good information', and signalled that the SEC would be looking more closely at disclosure related to sponsors' equity and the related incentives of SPAC sponsors.

Specifically, Mr Clayton highlighted that the SEC is not going to dictate managers' compensations, but it will make sure that those compensations are fully disclosed to investors. Mr Clayton did not specify where disclosure practices might fall short, other than noting that the SEC wants to make sure that investors have the benefit of the same level of rigorous disclosure they would have in a traditional IPO.[11]

Mr Clayton outlined how SPAC retail investors might have limited knowledge of potential acquisition targets, whereas institutional investors, which provide the bulk of financing, are typically given confidential information on the vehicle's strategy. In December 2020, the SEC published its C&DIs bulletin[12] with new guidance on disclosures, and as we said before, in March 2021 further statements were made. The SEC also initiated an informal enquiry addressed to underwriters concerning how they manage the risks involved in SPAC transactions.[13] Specifically, the inquiry was focused on SPAC deal fees and volumes, controls over regulatory compliance, including reporting and insider trading; De-SPAC due diligence; and disclosure of compensation of SPAC sponsors. For instance, as SPACs are publicly traded companies, certain information about a potential acquisition can create issues related to securities laws and disclosures. It is therefore vital that companies keep confidentiality between the signing of a letter of intent and the consummation of the business combination agreement to avoid situations in which the SPAC has to make a public disclosure that potentially taints the process, and trading in the stock of the entity with non-public information could potentially violate insider trading rules. Target shareholders have to understand that trading in the SPAC's shares on the basis of confidential information can be considered insider trading.

### 5.3.1 Conflict of interests between sponsor(s) and investors

A SPAC is a non-operating company that is directed by managers. The management team that form the SPAC sponsor(s), the directors and affiliates of a SPAC often have economic interests different to those of public shareholders. This potential conflict of interests that arise in identifying and decide whether to recommend a business combination transaction to shareholders must be clearly disclosed. The disclosure must contain the sponsors', directors' and affiliates' potential conflicts of interest and their economic interests in the SPAC because those actors will negotiate the SPAC's business combination transaction. In other words, managers decide the value of the target company and the consideration that is paid, unlike a traditional IPO where a

---

11 Katanga Johnson, 'The U.S. markets watchdog says blank-check IPOs offer "healthy competition"' Reuters (24 September 2020), available at https://www.reuters.com/article/us-usa-sec-clayton-spac-idUSKCN26F2II, accessed on 1 January 2021.
12 SEC's C&DIs (22 December 2020), 'CF Disclosure Guidance: Topic No. 11', available at https://www.sec.gov/corpfin/disclosure-special-purpose-acquisition-companies#_edn2, accessed on 3 January 2021.
13 Jody Godoy, Chris Prentice, 'Exclusive-US Regulator Opens Inquiry into Wall Street's Blank Check IPO Frenzy – Sources' (25 March 2021), available at https://www.reuters.com/article/usa-sec-spacs-idUSL1N2LM3CH, accessed on 1 April 2021.

private company sells its securities to the public through market-based price discovery.

Hence, SPACs should consider disclosing such conflicting interests pursuant to Regulation S-K and the requirements of Form S-4, Form F-4, Schedule 14A, Schedule 14C and Schedule TO, as applicable. For example, as we said, on 5 October 2020 a SEC staff comment letter in connection with a SPAC merger between Legacy Acquisition Corp. (Legacy) and Onyx Enterprises Int'l Corp. gave information pursuant to Schedule 14C.[14] This shows the importance of disclosure at the De-SPAC phase.

This disclosure obligation at the De-SPAC phase is furthermore well connected with another disclosure that should be implemented at the IPO phase through the registration statement S-1 Form. For instance, sponsors and directors may work for other entities and may have fiduciary or contractual obligations to other entities. Those obligations must be disclosed where they might lead to conflicts of interest, including conflicts involving entities that might compete with the SPAC for business combination opportunities.

### 5.3.2 Conflict of interests on sponsor(s) proxy statement and redemptions

In the De-SPAC phase, the SPAC's sponsors are potentially liable under Section 10 (b) and 14 (a) of the SEA 1934 for misleading statements included in a proxy statement. If there is a registered offer, the SPAC is also liable under Section 11 of the Securities Act of 1933. SPACs have seen a number of recent litigations for misstatements at the time of the merger or post-merger, such as the case of *VectoIQ vs Nikola*, *Landcadia vs Waitr*, or *MMAC vs Akazoo* (see Section 5.4 below). In August 2021, the Department of Justice and the SEC charged Nikola founder Mr. Trevor Milton with criminal charges for defrauding investors. Specifically, this case can show how SPAC corporate officers like Milton shall provide complete, truthful and accurate information at all times when discussing their company's affairs. There are no exceptions to those obligations and all public companies including those that have recently entered the markets through SPAC transactions shall be in compliance.

A SPAC proxy statement is a communication by which the issuer notifies the investors how much equity is held by the sponsor pre-business combination in the SPAC, as well as the fact that the sponsor does not possess or own any publicly traded share if a business combination is not completed. Specifically, once a SPAC shareholder votes in favour of the business combination or redeems shares, that shareholder is not aware of how many shares will remain outstanding or how many shares the sponsor will own. This can

---

14 SEC, 'Legacy Acquisition Corp. Information Statement on Schedule 14C Filed October 5, 2020, File No 001-38296', available at https://www.sec.gov/Archives/edgar/data/1698113/000121390020034413/filename1.htm, accessed on 1 April 2021.

create a potential conflict of interest between the sponsor(s) and the investors. Essentially, the amount of equity owned by managers, public investors, and target shareholders at the De-SPAC phase will vary upon redemption levels. This is also influenced by the mix of shares and cash consideration paid to target shareholders.

Currently, SPACs disclose in the proxy statement the pro forma capital structures and ownership under minimum and maximum levels of redemptions. Although neither scenario ends up representing the actual outcome, investors know that the final results will be close to the disclosed range.

The disclosure to elect redemption is the most important decision for investors. However, the model of SPAC 3.0 makes disclosure more complex. Indeed, the decoupling allows a shareholder to approve a business transaction and still exercise redemption rights (see Chapter 2). This practice is also incentivised because the warrants have value if the business combination is completed. The level of redemptions is not known until after the redemption deadline. If a SPAC shareholder votes in favour of the business combination and the redemption is made in connection with the distribution of a proxy statement, the SEC treats the SPAC's purchase of its shares as a redemption in accordance with the SPAC's bylaws rather than an issuer tender offer.

The SEC has always treated the redemption process as an ancillary part of the proxy voting process. The redemption of shares in connection with a shareholders' meeting is not an issuer tender offer. The rule of a tender offer simply does not apply. For this reason, the exact disclosure of sponsor(s) ownership at the De-SPAC phase is destined to be complex, and as we said it shall be illustrative rather than definitive because subject to negotiations (see Chapter 4 and the addendum with reference to the remarks on the UK SPAC reform and the ESMA public statement issued in July 2021).

To this end, the SEC might re-examine, in connection with the IPO, the exercise of the redemption rights and voting on the business combination, although it will never be possible to predict the future outcome of a shareholdings' meeting at the De-SPAC phase, and consequently a clear disclosure in the proxy statement would never be realistic unless shareholders are not required to vote and a tender offer applies in accordance with the 2011 codified rules (see Chapter 2).

### 5.3.3 Conflict of interests between sponsor(s) and underwriters

The underwriter of the SPAC IPO can agree to defer its compensation until the closing of the business combination. If an underwriter provides the sponsor(s) with additional services such as identifying potential targets, providing financial advisory services, acting as a placement agent in a private offering or arranging debt financing, the SEC has outlined that those potential services must be disclosed as well as the fees that the SPAC is due to pay for those services, and whether the consideration is paid in something other than cash.

Furthermore, potential conflict of interests of the underwriter must be disclosed in providing such services given any deferred IPO underwriting compensation as we have seen in the PIPE investment and engagement letter section.

## 5.4 SPAC securities litigation in the US

Between September 2020 and March 2021 there were at least 35 SPACs under litigation attack with one or more shareholder lawsuits filed in New York state court. Those proceedings generally allege that SPAC directors breached their fiduciary duties due to inadequate disclosures (see Section 5.3 above) regarding the De-SPAC execution of merger agreement. Some of those lawsuits claim against the SPAC itself, as well as the target company and its board of directors for abetting the SPAC director's breaches. It is important to note that those lawsuits are in an early stage and are limited in scope. However, a significant amount of data asserts that the plaintiffs' bar is pursuing SPACs. Hence, at the time merger agreements are executed, SPAC shareholder lawsuits are likely to multiply, although with some pointers that this section would like to outline.

As we said, in December 2020, the Division of Corporate Finance of the United States Securities and Exchange Commission issued guidance regarding disclosure considerations for SPACs. Since then, the plaintiffs' attorneys have seized upon this roadmap, building an initial wave of New York state court shareholder lawsuits. Some lawsuits were filed on an individual basis and others on behalf of a putative class. The actions share key similarities. The vast majority of complaints were filed after the SEC's December 2020 disclosure guidance. The complaints track the SEC's disclosure guidance regarding, for instance, the continued relationship, if any, the SPAC's directors or officers may have with the combined company, potentially giving rise to conflict of interests with public shareholders (for instance, *Ezel v GigCapital 3, Inc., et al.*). At other times the litigation was focused on the inadequate disclosures relating to the SPAC's financial advisor's compensation, including whether any portion is contingent upon consummation of the De-SPAC transaction, and the potential conflict of interest arising from the financial advisor's past services for any parties to the transaction (see *Quarles v InterPrivate Acquistion Corp.*). As we said, those lawsuits were filed after the De-SPAC transaction was announced, but prior to the shareholder vote and subsequent closing. To date those lawsuits have not resulted in any substantive proceedings. The claimants voluntarily discontinued a number of these lawsuits.[15] In these instances, the SPAC simply filed supplemental amended disclosures regarding De-SPAC transaction, mooting the allegations in the complaint

---

15 See Notice of Voluntary Discontinuance, *Bushansky v Haymaker Acquisition Corp. II*, et al., Index No. 656268/2020 (Supreme Court of NY Cnty. 14 January 2021).

in advance of the shareholder votes and closings (for instance, see the definitive proxy statement relating to a merger or acquisition issued by Haymaker Acquisition Corp. II).

A claimant prefers to sue SPACs in New York Courts. This is because it can try to avoid unfavourable precedent in Delaware relating to disclosure-only class settlements. In such circumstances, a target company provides the shareholders with supplemental disclosures prior to the closing of the transaction and the plaintiffs' attorney with a substantial award of attorney's fees to resolve the class claims. These class settlements were popular until Delaware Court of Chancery made clear in 2016 that disclosure-only settlements would not be approved absent certain conditions.[16] The New York courts were critical of disclosure-only settlements too, given that those settlements provide the allegedly injured shareholder(s) with little value. However, a disclosure-only settlement may still also be a viable option in New York (see *Gordon v Verizon Commc'ns Inc.* (2017), that reversed denial of final approval of disclosure-only settlement; or *City Trading Fund v Nye* (2018)). It remains to be seen whether any of those lawsuits pending in NY will take advantage of this practice.

Technically speaking it is correct to say that there is no SPAC specific litigation risk. I define it as non-SPAC specific because there are always federal securities claims whether they relate to misstatements in the IPO and/or claims against directors and officers or security litigation against the operating company post De-SPAC.

A SPAC specific litigation risk might arise at the redemption right phase. A significant reduction in shareholders could lead to involuntary delisting under exchange rules, which generally require a minimum shareholder numbers. This can lead the SPAC to attempt a renegotiation of its deal with the target company and to litigation between the SPAC and the target on that basis (see *Manichaean Capital LLC v SourceHOV Holdings, Inc.*[17]).

The most SPAC specific litigation risk relates to the breach of fiduciary duty against SPAC's directors and officers under Delaware law, or more broadly any company law provision under which the SPAC is incorporated. This latter form of litigation is still in its embryonal phase in the SPAC arena. It is normal. When there is a new deal structure or a new capital structure it might take several years before fiduciary duty litigation is filed or ascertained. This does not mean that SPACs are not subject to this, but that the majority of filings might be seen in ten years' time. Historically, fiduciary duty litigation involves more risk than securities litigation, which is often manageable.

---

16 *In re Trulia, Inc. Stockholder Litig.*, 129 A.3d 884, 899-907 (Del. Ch. 2016).
17 *Manichaean Capital LLC v SourceHOV Holdings, Inc.*, No. CV 2017-0673-JRS (2020) WL 496606. Target company shareholders brought a claim that redemption rights "can result in last-minute re-negotiations of SPCA deals when there are more redemption than anticipated".

### 5.4.1 Securities litigation related to the De-SPAC transaction

In theory, SPAC litigation can emerge at any time in the SPAC lifespan. However, it has been seen that the moment where SPACs litigation is more frequent is the moment of the De-SPAC. Any sizeable merger is likely to draw a federal securities lawsuit challenging the merger disclosures, and De-SPACing transactions will prove no exception.

SPACs – as we said – are subject to the same securities law provisions and principles as other public companies, but they do have a unique structure that provides heightened disclosure considerations. The vast majority of claims related to De-SPAC transactions relates to the financials of the target company projections that the SPAC carried out at the time of the due diligence pre-business combination. This type of responsibility on the side of the SPAC relates to two different moments:

1. Merger disclosure
2. Disclosure pre-merger (such as statements that are directly made at the time of the IPO)

For merger disclosures, challenges relate mainly to proxy statements soliciting shareholder approval of the De-SPACing transaction. This claim can be brought either under Section 10 (b) or Section 14 (a) of the Securities Exchange Act 1934. A material misstatement or omission (most commonly target projections and descriptions, conflict of interest, etc.) is requested. Materiality relates to whether a reasonable investor would consider the piece of information important in determining whether or not to approve the transaction.

One notable distinction is that under Section 14 (a) of the SEA 1934, unlike Section 10 (b), it is not necessary to show an intent to defraud. It is essentially a negligence standard.

Turning to pre-merger disclosure, this concerns challenges under Sections 11 and 15 of the Securities Act 1933 that are brought to the IPO, but can also relate to a registration statement issued in connection to the merger. Like Section 14 (a) of the SEA 1934, it requires material misstatement or omission, but not intent to defraud. The scope is broader, and it might cover also other disclosure documents by the SPAC such as press release, interviews, etc.

These lawsuits, while an inconvenience, are usually quite manageable. Typically, they are brought before the merger has closed, threatening an injunction in order to extract a settlement of the dispute. Those claims are often quickly dismissed or settled for non-monetary relief, such as an additional disclosure, and a modest attorney's fee. However, some lawsuits are more serious, specifically, those that relate to a lawsuit plausibly alleging material deficiencies in disclosures that can introduce delay and uncertainty for the closing of the merger. Or post-closing, the lawsuits can seek damages caused by the alleged misstatement or omission. For example, it is particularly dangerous if the pro forma entity struggles after the De-SPACing transaction. Shareholders with buyer's remorse can allege that the merger would not have gone forward but for the alleged misstatement or omission.

### 5.4.2 Litigation based on reports of short selling

Nikola Corporation is a zero-emissions vehicle company that went public in June 2020 by merging with VectoIQ Acquisition Corp. Nikola's market capitalisation more than doubled to $30 billion the week after the De-SPAC transaction. The share price moved around, but increased almost 40% after the company announced a partnership agreement with GM to produce an electric truck. Subsequently, the short seller firm Hindenburg Research announced that it had taken a short position on Nikola's shares arguing that Nikola's last partnership was an "intricate fraud".[18]

Actions against Nikola Corp. were brought under Section 10 (b) and Rule 10b-5 of the Securities Exchange Act 1934 by claiming false statements reported by individual directors and officers who participated in making those false statements. These complaints relied on the report by Hindenburg Research. This case shows that the release of information by short sellers can have a high impact on share price. This can lead to litigation, and Jay Clayton (Chairman of the SEC in 2020) highlighted that the SEC will look to examine "incentives and compensation to SPAC sponsors" to make sure that "investors understand those things" at the time of both the SPAC IPO and the De-SPAC transaction.[19]

Another company that has similarities with Nikola's litigation is Multi-Plan Corp. that went public via merging with Churchill Capital Corp. III in October 2020. Multiplan is a healthcare cost management company. The transaction was one of the largest SPAC deals of 2020, worth approximately $11 billion. Before the closing, a class action litigation alleged false statements in the proxy statement under Section 14 of the Securities Exchange Act to block the merger. The De-SPAC transaction still closed. At that time Carson Block of the short seller firm Muddy Waters released a report that claimed the weakness of MultiPlan's business model. As a result, MultiPlan was close to losing its largest client, UnitedHealth. Multiplan stock dropped 20% on the release of the report. This brought a claim to assess whether MultiPlan made materially false or misleading statements to investors.

In September 2020 Akazoo S.A. was the defendant of a lawsuit by shareholders who filed an amended consolidated securities class action. Akazoo

---

18 Hindernburg Research, 'Nikola: How to Parlay an Ocean of Lies into a Partnership with the Largest Auto OEM in America' (10 September 2020), available at https://hindenburgresearch.com/nikola/, accessed on 10 April 2021.

19 CNBC, 'SEC Chairman Jay Clayton on Disclosure Concerns Surround Going Public through a SPAC' (24 September 2020), available at https://www.cnbc.com/video/2020/09/24/sec-chairman-jay-clayton-on-disclosure-concerns-surround-going-public-through-a-spac.html, accessed on 10 April 2021.

operates a music streaming platform, and it was the result of a merger with Modern Media Acquisition Corp. The shareholders claimed that the company made numerous false statements as to Akazoo's financial results as well as the number of subscribers to the service, etc. The lawsuit was based on the investigative report issued by short sellers Quintessential Capital Management. Akazoo was delisted in June 2020 and in September 2020 the SEC filed a civil case against Akazoo alleging fraud and misleading statements and omissions.

Triterras Inc. is a fintech company that operates a blockchain-enabled commodity trading platform known as Kratos. It went public in November 2020 by merging with Netfin Acquisition Corp. In December 2020, Rhodium Resources Pte Ltd (a related party to Triterras) sought a moratorium on creditor actions to restructure its own debt. In this case short sellers claimed ties between Rhodium and the CEO of the SPAC that merged with Triterras. Those ties were suspicious, and investors were not told about the weakened financial position of an important related party. A shareholder filed a class action under Section 10 (b) and Rule 10b-5 of the Securities Exchange Act 1934.

A quick glance at those filed claims can provide evidence on the importance of disclosure. In SPACs disclosure matters, short seller companies can play an even more essential role if such disclosures are not there.

### 5.4.3 Breach of fiduciary duty claims

While, thus far, they are less common than disclosure claims under federal securities laws, breach of fiduciary duty claims against the SPAC's directors and officers for approving the De-SPACing transaction pose a potentially more significant threat. The level of threat posed by fiduciary duty claims principally depends on the standard of review applied by the court. To this end, the appropriate standard of review for the De-SPACing transaction is an unsettled question.

Surely many shareholders will try to argue for the application of the 'entire fairness' standard. However, there are strong policy arguments against applying an entire fairness review to the typical De-SPAC transaction. Even assuming entire fairness would otherwise apply, SPACs can often take steps to lower that standard. In Delaware Courts, the default standard of review for approval of a transaction is called business judgement of review. Essentially, the court and the judge will not second guess the business judgement of directors and officers of the corporation. This is a highly deferential standard that almost always defeats the shareholder challenge. However, when there is a material conflict between directors, then the Delaware Courts will refer to Delaware's most exacting standard of review: the entire fairness review. Entire fairness applies in certain circumstances where the transaction poses a material conflict of interest, mainly where:

– a majority of the board received material personal benefits not shared generally by shareholders;

- a majority of the board were beholden to a controller or another director who was pursuing the transaction for such a purpose or
- a majority of the board or a controller competes with the common shareholders for consideration.

The application of the entire fairness review is consequential not only because it increases the risk of liability but also because it decreases the chances of dismissal at the lawsuit's early stages. Shareholders can argue that entire fairness applies to conflicts implicated by the founders' units to be received by the SPAC's founders and directors only upon the completion of the De-SPAC transaction. Essentially the theory is that founders' units incentivise the recipient to close any transaction possible, even if it means overpaying or pursuing a transaction that is not in the SPAC shareholders' best interests. This theory is sustained in *AP Services (LLP v Lobell)*, a 2015 New York state court opinion that refused to dismiss Delaware entire fairness claims against a SPAC and its directors alleging such a conflict. However, this judicial decision has not yet led to additional litigation espousing this theory. Delaware Courts have not ruled upon this theory in De-SPACing transactions, and *AP Services* court noted that the defendants did not raise arguments regarding "a requirement that a majority of IPO shareholders approve a business combination".

The current trends show that fiduciary duty actions represent a vehicle for shareholders of target companies who contend that the company has been undervalued. However, in the current environment the risk is more on target companies that have been overvalued. Indeed, most SPAC litigation occurs post-merger when the new company has performed poorly. Whether the combined company is a success or not, there may be an incentive for sponsors to aggressively pursue questionable transactions. The litigation risk on this side can only increase, especially if we consider recent SPAC trends that focus on the acquisition of pre-revenue companies. Again, if you are not taking an operating company, you are taking a company that is making a promise, and this makes SPAC life more complex, although definitively more interesting.

### 5.4.3 D&O insurance

The previous sections have highlighted the main transactional risks and regulatory risks that can be challenging for SPACs both at the IPO phase and De-SPAC phase. It is obvious that a from a risk mitigation perspective, SPACs can mitigate those risks by virtue of contract law by, for example, entering into supporting agreements or securing a PIPE investment to back up the possible high numbers of redemptions. Additionally, the classic tool to cover risks and to shift risks to a third party is insurance. In Chapter 3 we outlined how insurance is a fundamental activity in contemporary financial markets (think of the hedging nature of derivatives contracts). SPACs are not exempted. They can and they must cover the litigation risk through a specific and SPAC-tailored Directors and Officers Insurance (D&O Insurance).

As we said in Chapter 2, the SPAC will have two separate accounts. One is the operating account for expenses such as due diligence, closing costs, legal, accounting and tax services; and the other is the escrow account where the IPO proceeds are deposited for the purpose of completing a business combination. It is very important to highlight that funds in the escrow account cannot generally be used to indemnify D&Os. As a result, the small operating account (usually only $2 million sit in this account) may be the only funds available to indemnify in a D&O claim.

The sponsor is responsible for finding the target, negotiating the transaction, and making the company public. If this is not done or it is done incorrectly, then the key risks for a sponsor are the loss of the "at-risk-capital" and reputational damage. On the side of investors, they do have a lucrative investment opportunity with downside protection (redemption rights). However, we saw how the SPAC has to provide investors with better information than they would get from a traditional IPO, including forward-looking projections. Once they buy units, the public investors of the SPAC are buying a fraction of a warrant with limitations on exercise timing and price. Therefore, public investors can face the risks of excessive valuation and failure of due diligence on the part of the target.

Finally, on the side of the target company, SPACs de-risk traditional IPOs. Market risk is reduced compared with traditional IPOs, given the ability to lock-in PIPE commitments before market disclosures or secure forward purchase and non-redemption agreements, as we said. The target company may benefit from the experience and relationships of the SPAC sponsor once it goes public. Here the key risks are dilution of the sponsor's promote, the exercise of warrants and market execution risk.

To cover those risks that are SPAC specific, the D&O insurance for the SPAC period (pre-combination) aligns with the search period, and unlike traditional public D&O, policy terms are often signed for two years. The SPAC industry has developed an interesting market practice in this regard by dividing the insurance offer into 18 months terms plus 6 months extensions to save premium. This is because the majority of deals are usually secured within the first 14 months of the SPAC's existence. Hence, it seems unfair for the sponsor to pay upfront a consistent sum of money to secure insurance coverage. Furthermore, tail coverage is pre-negotiated to cover claims against the SPAC brought after the completion of the business combination and usually allows for six years to report a claim arising from any misbehaviour by the sponsor that occurred pre-combination. Generally, a new D&O insurance can be put into place for the newly merged entity that is a public company post-combination.

Most SPACs continue to purchase a blend of primary ABC D&O with excess Side-A D&O coverage dedicated to protecting individual insured persons. A notable change is that Side-A excess layers no longer have "DIC" features. The following table summarises the main insurance categories.

| SIDE-A | SIDE-B | SIDE-C |
| --- | --- | --- |
| Claims against Officers and Directors Individually. No Indemnification. Personal Asset Protection $0 Retention. | Claims against Officers and Directors individually. Indemnification of permitted company asset protection. Retention Applies. | Claims against the Insured Organisation (SEC claims only if public) Company Asset Protection Retention Applies. |

Finally, Representations & Warranties Insurance (RWI) is also employed in the vast majority of acquisitions of private companies. SPACs are the acquirer of a privately held company and RWI serves the same function it would serve in a traditional transaction. RWI insurance is valuable in transactions in which the acquirer is a SPAC because of the risk of securities litigation and challenging statements made in the proxy statement. Indeed, some claims may relate to the breaches of representations and warranties in the underlying agreement, potentially giving rise to RWI coverage.

## 5.5 Conclusions

This chapter has pointed out some of the most important aspects and profiles that SPAC sponsors, investors and regulators have to take into account in relation to the De-SPAC transaction. The lifespan of a SPAC is complex. From the point of the IPO and even before the IPO the SPAC is a cash-shell company. This makes the SPAC unique and subject to specific disclosure duties. The chapter has examined those duties with specific reference to the legal system of the US which is today the country with the highest number of SPAC offerings. In the end, the SPAC is an investment vehicle with one single purpose, namely to facilitate the IPO process of a private company. SPACs are risk-free investment vehicles until the moment of the business combination, then once the reverse takeover happens, the newly merged entity is subject to the same reputational and operational risks as any other public company.

It is not the task of the SPAC to increase the value of the target company, but it is – as we saw – the duty of the sponsor to make reliable projections and to make them in good faith to keep the valuation projections of the target company close to reality. SPACs de-risk the traditional IPO, reduce adverse selection, and can settle the valuation of private companies through negotiations. Indeed, as we said, a critical distinction between a De-SPAC transaction and a traditional IPO is the ability to include forward-looking financial projections in a proxy statement rather than historical financial results. The draft legislation that has been proposed in May 2021 to exempt SPACs from the safe harbour rule might be misleading. Indeed, the draft legislation defines the SPAC as a "development stage company". This gives rise to a possible confusion with search funds. The main objective of a SPAC is to list a target company. SPACs are investment vehicles, which entail risks, like any other investment. The De-SPAC phase relates to M&As transactions, and operational risk can be properly curtailed by adopting appropriate contractual tools such as earn-out arrangements. This is often the case in the acquisitions of zero-revenue companies or pre-revenue companies, as it is difficult to make a valuation. The buyer (the SPAC) might want to protect itself against overpaying for a new company that does not grow in the original seller's direction. In other words, if a target is not ready to get public, or if the corporate valuation is inflated, this final responsibility rests with the target company itself rather than the SPAC. Nonetheless, in this case SPACs are not buying into an operating company, but a company that's making a promise. Hence, the promise of a pre-revenue company (i.e. future sales) of a promise (i.e. forward-looking statements) might constitute the anti-room of misleading statements. A SPAC reform (if ever) shall beware of market practices and efficiently and fairly discern between less risky SPACs (those targeting operating and positive EBITDA companies), and more risky ones (SPACs whose targets are pre-revenue companies). The safe harbour rule should be still available to SPACs due to a fundamental legal principle of common law systems (at least): *caveat emptor*. In civil law traditions translated as the principle of good faith. Furthermore, the valuation of the equity value is always tricky and subjective in any type of acquisition. Nonetheless, contractual mechanisms and private negotiations can mitigate those risks. Market practices matter in the SPAC arena, and a consistent valuation of the target shall be rendered possible by virtue of enforced disclosure duties on the side of pre-revenue target companies.

The chapter examined the transactional risks that a SPAC must face at the De-SPAC phase. One of them relates to the possible high number of redemptions. This risk can be mitigated by securing a PIPE investment that can take a transaction risk early on in the process. Other contractual terms are related to support agreements and non-redemption clauses. As can be seen, SPACs can be risky investments, but financial risk can be mitigated through proper corporate governance mechanisms and private negotiations. Finally, the last section of this chapter has dealt with the raising role of litigation in SPACs. Indeed, SPAC sponsors shall avoid rushing due diligence to mitigate potential litigation risks as well as ensure sufficient time is given for Public Company Accounting Oversight Board (PCAOB) audits, as this is a common cause for delayed mergers. On the side of the target companies, public company readiness is vital and an accounting team should be involved early on in the transaction to be able to fulfil the strict financial reporting requirements of a public company. Furthermore, the disclosure of potential conflicts by the SPAC sponsors in the context of their fiduciary duties may mitigate conflicts liability. We might add that SPAC sponsors shall pay attention to cross-border transactions including potential delays in filings due to PCAOB audits, and difference in reporting standards between US and Asia or US and Europe (namely, Generally Accepted Accounting Principles vs. International Financial Reporting Standards). In such cases internal controls and financial and legal due diligence become even more critical to mitigate the risk of litigation later on.[20]

---

20 Robert Malionek, Ryan Maierson, Beth Junell, 'SPAC-Related Litigation Risks and Mitigation Strategies' Harvard Law School Forum on Corporate Governance available at https://corpgov.law.harvard.edu/2021/08/09/spac-related-litigation-risks-and-mitigation-strategies/?utm_content=buffer44b42&utm_medium=social&utm_source=linkedin.com&utm_campaign=buffer, accessed on 20 August 2021.

# 6 SPACs
## Law, uncertainty and the market

### 6.1 Financial markets as financial systems

Chapter 3 described a theoretical and philosophical distinction between risk and uncertainty. In particular, the epistemological and ontological dimensions of risk were described, together with the connected concept of uncertainty. By contrast, the aim of this chapter is to analyse how the concepts of risk and uncertainty relate to financial systems rather than financial markets. It will be theorised for the first time how biological conceptions of autopoiesis can effectively influence regeneration processes in financial systems where uncertainty dominates free markets.

To start with, it is important to introduce the environment in which the economic agent faces financial risks today, and consider how financial operators deal with uncertainty. This position paves the way for a new contemporary phenomenology of financial markets – anticipated in Chapter 1 – that can be defined as complex systems[1] dominated by risk and uncertainty and especially by competition in terms of financial innovation and adaptability. As in physics the concept of the disorganisation of the universe is measured as entropy, the uncertainty of a system is measured in the same way, so free markets that are a form of economic system always look disorganised, but uncertainty produces competition, which is the equilibrium feature of the system itself.

However, before theorising this provocative idea it is useful to establish what a system is, and then assess whether financial markets can be assumed under the concept of systems theory. Finally, this analysis will introduce a connection between complexity and financial markets.

---

1 John H. Holland, *Complexity A Very Short Introduction* (OUP 2014) 4. Complex systems are not complicated systems. Indeed, the distinction between the two is centred on the concept of

> emergence (the whole is more than the sum of the parts) (...) hierarchical organization is thus closely tied to emergence. Each level of a hierarchy typically is governed by its own set of laws. (...) emergent properties at any level must be consistent with interactions specified at the lower level(s).

DOI: 10.4324/9781003102779-7

The concept of system is vague and there is no clear definition. According to Luhmann[2] – who is a sociologist – a possible reflection on a general systems theory must start by introducing the metaphor of balance and equilibrium. This is because Luhmann aims to provide the reader with an intuitive image of what a system is, especially if one takes into account the system's entropy under the thermodynamic law of physics. Equilibrium is a symbol that is justified by mathematical functions, and in thermodynamics this balance is expressed through the Boltzmann constant; intuitively our idea of balance is not directly related to thermodynamics, but rather, it refers to the image of a living organism or to a system in the form of an organisation that tries to respond to deviations to re-establish order or achieve a new equilibrium. The concept of balance can be achieved directly in the form of responses to deviations and disturbances that are external. Figuratively, this is the image of a football player who loses his balance due to the speed at which he runs to avoid contact with another football player who is trying to get hold of the ball. In this example the deviation in his balance comes from outside, namely from the possible encounter with another football player, which represents the element of deviation of the original balance of the first football player.

However, such an idea is erroneous if one examines how the economic system works. Here it seems that the same concept of disequilibrium represents a condition of stability,[3] and uncertainty, particularly from competition and financial innovation, constitutes the measure of stability in free markets. In other words, it is not the balance of the natural condition of the system but the imbalance that characterises the ontology of such a system. Therefore, our initial idea of balance as well as our image of a system is overturned in relation to the economic system.

Nonetheless, this natural condition of imbalance can – at the same time – make the economic system resemble the entropy of closed systems in physics. Indeed, if we look at financial markets in terms of isolated or closed systems, we turn again to the concept of entropy in thermodynamics. Entropy presupposes a closed or isolated system where no distinctions are produced because no interactions occur between the system and the environment. In thermodynamics the structure of a macroscopic system is in disorder, and such chaos is measured by entropy. Therefore, entropy constitutes a unit of measurement for the disorder of a macroscopic system. The second law of thermodynamics states that an isolated system's entropy never decreases. Such systems spontaneously evolve towards thermodynamic equilibrium, which is the maximum state of entropy. This means that closed systems tend to achieve the maximum state of entropy where in terms of physics no usable energy is left. Indeed, non-isolated or non-closed systems may lose entropy because they exchange and disperse energy in the environment.

---

2 Niklas Luhmann, *Introduction to System Theory* (Polity Press 2013) 26.
3 Janos Kornai, *Anti-equilibrium: On Economic Systems Theory and the Task of Research* (North-Holland 1971).

Likewise, if one examines free markets as a form of closed system they can be conceptualised as systems dominated by disorder, and disequilibrium becomes their natural condition for balance. Free markets are a perfect instance of a closed system dominated by uncertainty, which in turn measures the entropy of that closed system. In this system the maximum level of uncertainty is also the maximum level of balance and equilibrium. In other words, financial markets start in a position of disequilibrium and evolve spontaneously towards a new equilibrium determined by the maximum level of uncertainty. Therefore, in such a system uncertainty must not be seen as a negative quality of the system itself, but as a fundamental element that is capable of constituting the same ontology and essence of the system. It is only through uncertainty that the regenerating processes of the system are activated, especially in the form of self-regulation, which becomes an evolving feature of the market. For this reason, a first level of paradox is determined, by which uncertainty has a positive quality in the common understanding of a human being who wants to dominate and control uncertainty to reduce their anxiety (see Chapter 3). Here, there is no space for the human being, because markets are closed systems, and these can only be studied if the observer can objectivise them as separate entities. In the same way, science can justify its research outcomes only if the scientist is able to objectivise what exists in the world in the form of substance or essential elements or parts of a living system.

In a modelling theory, financial markets are models, and are therefore isolated; they appear to the external observer as forms of closed systems that exist without internal information exchange or external interference. Although it might appear obvious that this model does not exist in real life, the recognition of this status of the world as objectification of elements or parts of the system constitutes an important starting point in our philosophical discourse for explaining the importance of uncertainty in financial markets. In other words, in thermodynamics, closed systems spontaneously evolve towards their own equilibrium, which is also the maximum state of entropy; in the same way, uncertainty plays a vital role in financial markets because it is the spontaneous element or mechanism by which financial markets reach their equilibrium, and it also corresponds to the maximum level of uncertainty.

On this basis, I shall argue that, in contrast to a model theory of financial markets, it is important to consider a pragmatic definition of markets in terms of financial systems that are not construed as forms of closed systems, insofar as the world is not an instance of a closed system, although its objectification can be important for study purposes. Indeed, in free markets we can effectively experience an exchange of information between their systems and the environment. We have said in Chapters 1, 3 and 5 that information is a vital component in financial markets (to this end, look at the many disclosures to which SPACs are subject), and that it can take either the form of research information or financial knowledge (i.e. financial literacy) or investment information (i.e. economic news, financial reports, balance sheets, etc.): the latter in the sense of information that can be useful to investors for making a reasonable investment choice between financial products. The opposite side of the coin is the absence of information, or rather the disproportionate balance between the agent and the principal in terms of who has more information to trade. This last concept is expressed in financial markets and within the economy as 'financial asymmetry' or 'information asymmetry'. Thus, it is possible to reaffirm that the disequilibrium of the economic system, which is based on information asymmetry, represents the necessary condition for its balance, especially if the system is studied as a model system.

By contrast, financial markets are forms of open systems. For this reason, the concept of negentropy becomes central for a sociological and phenomenological representation of free markets as non-isolated and open systems. It means that in Luhmann's conception, a system is defined as open when an exchange with the environment takes place. Such an exchange can actually transform the structure of the system; it means that an unexpected event, such as a financial crisis, can actually modify the structure of markets and negatively affect those markets, with potentially adverse effects. Indeed, each market system is integrated in a network of connections and interdependence that can fundamentally influence different structures (the spill-over effect of a bank crisis is a self-evident sign of this discourse). However, at the same time if one imagines financial markets in terms of open systems, a financial crisis is seen as a vital event which contributes to the dispersion of market disorder directly into the environment, and the achievement of a new equilibrium status. Yet in thermodynamics, irreversible operations are capable of affecting the entropy of both the system and the environment. For this reason, a new balance can be achieved.

On such a basis, it is possible to differentiate between a system-environment paradigm, through which the theory of open systems is introduced (in this sense, it is the very moment of differentiation between the system and the environment that initiates a system theory and defines what a system is), and a system-to-system relation that effectively reflects this idea of interdependence between different systems, and in our case between different markets (such as the equity market, the debt market, the derivative market, the forex market, etc.). All these different markets potentially have interactions and relations, but they are also influenced by input from their environment, otherwise they would be described simply as closed systems and model paradigms.

### 6.1.1 Self-organisation and autopoiesis of systems

The previous section introduced the concept of operational closure, namely a system that relies on its own operations and activities, both to distinguish itself from the environment and specifically to self-organise. Indeed, the only exchange that can occur between the system and the environment is in the form of meaning and, therefore, of information rather than operation. However, information in turn can be conceptualised as the output of the operational function of communication. This can again confirm the importance of operational closure inside each system. Every operation that occurs within the system is capable of developing different structures within the system itself, yet no structures can be imported from the environment and no operation can be translated into every system (i.e. operational closure).

This means that when a system is going to self-organise it carries out different operations to determine the existence of different structures. For instance, self-regulation is an evident example of self-organisation in financial markets. Indeed, as has been seen in Chapter 4, state regulation can be evaded by financial arbitrage,[4] therefore it seems crucial to take into account the opinions of private actors in regulatory processes, and sometimes even to allow private actors to become rule makers. According to Omarova, self-regulation is necessary to achieve two main objectives: 'timely access to market information, on the one hand, and the need to monitor and manage risk across jurisdictional borders, on the other'.[5] This self-regulation approach in financial markets represents one of the best justifications for the existence of markets as financial and autopoietic systems.

The self-organisation of a system is intimately connected to its autopoiesis, and consequently, in order to explain for the first time why a market can implement autopoietic operations, we should first introduce the theoretical background and practical application of a type of regeneration process that is typical of living organisms. Therefore, we come back again to that intuitive conception of systems as living organisms that are a form of closed system in terms of physics' laws of thermodynamics.

The term 'autopoiesis' was first introduced by the biologists Humberto Maturana and Francisco Varela. According to them,[6] living systems represent forms of self-contained unities whose only reference is to themselves. They are closed systems but with special features that can stop the observer from observing them. This means that they cannot be either objects of observation or interacting systems, and observation by an external observer represents a violation of the fundamental requirements of such systems. Indeed, these living systems are autonomous, self-referring and self-constructing; in short, autopoietic in their terms. This means that a living organism, if it is autopoietic, is capable of sustaining its own system boundaries and system maintenance. These are, in the view of Maturana and Varela, 'first-order autopoietic systems'. In other words, there can be destruction of the system by the environment, but the environment cannot maintain a system that is always going to regenerate itself in order to survive. It means either the autopoiesis is active or it is not. This is defined by Maturana as 'structural coupling'. Essentially,

---

4 Victor Fleisher, 'Regulatory Arbitrage' (2010) University of Colorado Law Legal Studies Research Paper No. 10–11, 1–67.
5 Omarova, "Wall Street as community of fate: toward financial industry self-regulation' (2011) 159 (2) University of Pennsylvania Law Review, 418.
6 Humberto R Maturana, Francisco Varela, *Autopoiesis and cognition: the realisation of the living* (Reidel 1980) 59–134.

the system is autonomous, and a system can develop in different structures by virtue of autopoietic activities (for instance, regenerating structures differ between mammals and birds because they are two different living systems with different characteristics, but they both implement auto-regenerating processes to guarantee their survival).

However, Luhmann rejected such an explanation of autopoiesis and adapted it to his social theory, by which systems and environment can interact because systems are open, and the environment can influence them. Nonetheless, the structures of the system – as we have seen in the previous section – cannot be imported from the environment, otherwise the system cannot be autopoietic in Luhmann's conception, and a system theory cannot come into existence. Indeed, differentiation, namely the difference between the boundaries of the system and the space of the environment but also between the relations between system-to-system activities, is the primary element of every system theory.

### 6.1.2 The structures of financial systems and liquid autopoietic markets

To translate Luhmann's theory to financial markets, one must re-define markets as the space where risk and uncertainty exist and where competition and financial innovations operate in order to determine different structures. The operational closure of the system can allow the entire economy to re-generate itself. I define such financial systems as 'liquid markets or liquid financial systems' because their dynamic activities tend towards the function of regeneration, and they can take as many forms as there are different structures developed inside each system. Furthermore, the operational closure of financial systems is in structural coupling with their environment.

Thus, financial markets are financial systems with autopoietic mechanisms and self-organisation features that create different macro structures, such as bond markets, equity markets, derivative markets, etc., and microstructures such as financial innovations, in order to appear more competitive (e.g. Co-Cos, SPACs, credit swaps, etc.). Furthermore, the structural coupling between the environment and financial systems is expressed in terms of meaning. The environment is capable of influencing the creation or modification of system-structures, but they cannot introduce or import their own structures. Therefore, the risk and uncertainty always present in every financial system are particular to that market and can be classified into different levels of risks and uncertainties with different features depending on the market of enquiry, such as the equity market or the debt market. This is the reason why debt markets are less risky than equity markets: a different level of risk is embedded. For instance, the level of risk embedded into bond markets or equity markets is due to the conditioned observation of investors who are willing to take different levels of risk depending on the markets in which they operate.

### 6.1.3 The 'metamorphosis of subjects': financial markets as open systems

If we observe the observer, the latter is described under a second level of observation, through which investors can be identified through their risk-averse tastes and behaviour.

To clarify, the real difference between observing and the observer is based on the fact that the former is understood as a type of operation or action related to the observer and is closed to the system. The observer is viewed as a system because it is going to carry out different operations, or rather, different kinds of observations, able to distinguish the observer-system from the environment that becomes the object of its observation, as well as from other systems that can also be studied as forms of a second-level observation. It is possible to say that the observation of the observer is the starting point of open systems theory. In figurative terms, it is the unity of subject and object, although it can be paradoxical to discover unity through diversity, or rather through differentiation. Nonetheless, these are Luhmann's terms for a sociological construction of the world and they will in turn be re-used and re-invented to theorise a new phenomenology of contemporary financial markets (see Section 6.2 below).

Turning back to our investors, they need to take risks if they wish to make profits. For this reason, in financial markets the investors will necessarily turn into speculators, who are fundamentally risk-takers. This is what I shall define as the 'necessary translation' of the subject, who will be translated from first to third level. The direct observation of financial systems represents a first-level observation through which causality dominates the objectification of the markets. For instance, an investor within this first-level observation will necessarily evaluate risks under a causality model description of the markets. This means that causes and effects dominate his thinking. If I take certain risks in the equity markets, I can statistically make a certain amount of profit by implementing specific risk management tools. This is the first-level observation of the market from the point of view of an investor-observer. Subsequently, when we observe the observer, we necessarily take into account a second-level observation through which markets are no longer models, but are at the same time both objects and subjects. Markets become open systems where it is understood that the direct observation of the markets by first-level observers is relative and subjective. This fusion or union of subject and object is the real essence of financial systems.

Nonetheless, I shall argue that a third-level observation exists in financial markets and it is identified by the necessary translation of subjects. So, in financial systems, objects of observation (i.e. the markets and financial products) and subjects (i.e. investors/speculators) are not static but dynamic elements. This means that the investor of today must necessarily turn into the speculator of tomorrow. In other words, the risk-aversion paradigm of the lender is translated into the risk-taker paradigm of the borrower. This is a necessary 'translation' of subjects because in financial systems, the figures of lender and borrower can be interchangeable (for instance, imagine a bank, typically a lender, that translates into a borrower when it invests part of its deposits into buying shares of companies), so that the lender of today can be the borrower of tomorrow, but the same essence of translation calls for a transformation and regeneration of markets. This philosophical discourse means that the speculator of tomorrow is a necessary feature for transforming market operations and perspectives under a third-level observation which is the expression of translations and trans-figuration, or metamorphosis, of subjects.

It is with reference to this new feature of metamorphosis of subjects that financial markets are financial systems, and they are an instance of open systems. They share meanings among themselves and their environments, but they never translate operations into other systems in order to determine new structures. Each structure of the system or market is created with its own meanings and operations. Thus, a collapse might occur in the debt market and affect borrowers' trust, but that failure cannot at the same time be translated into a corresponding collapse of the equity market, where borrowers take more risks through share investments. This is because equity and debt are two different markets and, therefore, two different financial systems. Nonetheless, the structural coupling within the system-to-system relationship can produce an effect in those systems. For instance, a collapse in the mortgage subprime market, such as the notorious debt market of the 2007 financial crisis in the US can be translated into a selling panic effect by borrowers who own shares and try to avoid a negative credit score. This is why financial systems are 'liquid markets': they can influence each other by virtue of structural coupling and are characterised by a third-level observation through which we assist in the translation or metamorphosis of subjects. I define this as the 'necessary translation' of subjects.

### 6.1.4 Financial systems and complexity

It has been shown that financial markets are financial systems and that they are open systems, characterised by operational closure and by structural coupling. It is now time to discover whether financial systems are also forms of complex systems.

Complexity gives rise to a spontaneous order, but at the same time complexity can also generate uncertainty. Indeed, the co-existence of those two opposite features, namely order and uncertainty, is justified by the different spatial dimensions in which order and uncertainty are placed. Order is always placed at a global level, whereas uncertainty is the vital feature of the local level. For instance, if we think biologically of a living organism, such as a pine tree, the main features, or functions, that allow us to identify it are usually constant and statistically common (every pine tree grows from a pine cone so long as the area in one tile radius remains clear; the time to maturity is about

18 days with over 90% of seeds maturing in less than 32 growing days; etc.), but the specific features of each pine tree can change constantly, such as the length of its leaves, the diameter of its trunk, and so on. Uncertainty is in the details and specifically it emerges at the local level.

In the same way free markets are characterised by two levels of risk and uncertainty: global uncertainty which is encountered by the financial system as a whole and can give rise to macroeconomic effects and local uncertainty, which characterises every single financial system, and is a vital characteristic of each market (for instance, the uncertainty of the debt market in the aftermath of the global financial crisis in 2007–2010 did not have the same features as the local uncertainty of the equity market in the same period of time). A global risk is commonly associated with systemic risk and spill-over effects, and a local risk is related to investment risk.

Indeed, financial systems are based on a duality: the global level and the local level. The global level should be observed by a global observer, but the latter does not exist. The global level should be governed by global law such as a global or universal insolvency procedural law, but it does not exist. There is no global lawmaker, as we have seen in Chapter 4. For this reason, the existence of a local observer and a local investor is vital for determining financial outputs, but they are often influenced by randomness at the local level and conditioned by subjective opinions, whereas the global level tends towards objectivity and order. It is not by chance that scholars use the expression 'global governance' in order to identify this dual dimension of the markets that are characterised by randomness at the local level, and order at the global level. This tension between opposites can lead us to think that the global level influences the local. Despite this logical conclusion, financial markets are irrational and today the local level is frequently able to influence the global (i.e. the collapse of the subprime mortgage market in 2007 gave rise to spill-over effects throughout the whole economy and most markets). In other words, globalisation is a phenomenon that has a local basis and justification. The privatisation of financial risk would not have been possible without the local domestic policies enacted by every single individual state through liberalisation.

For this reason, it can be said that unlike physical or biological systems, where complexity is seen as a means of creating order, in financial markets order is not always connected to the global level but can and should be first achieved locally. Only in this way can the local order influence the establishment of a global order in a new integration of global and local through the expression of glocalisation.[7] Here, the term 'glocalisation' is re-used and re-interpreted to include the concept of markets in the new contemporary

---

7 Philip Young P Hong, In Han Song, 'Glocalization of Social Work Practice: Global and Local Responses to Globalization' (2010) 53 (5) International Social Work 656–670.

phenomenology of financial markets, in order to highlight the importance of the role of the local level as opposed to that of the global.

The distinction between the global and local level of financial systems can also be justified by what I have defined in Chapter 1 as complexity thinking, which Anderson first theorised in 1999.[8] Following an Introduction using complex theories, we should now assess whether financial systems, as we have conceptualised them above, can effectively represent an instance of complex systems. I shall assume financial systems to be complex systems not only because they are characterised by the duality global/local, but also because they have a self-organising network, and their structures are based on nonlinear behaviours that tend to follow autopoietic mechanisms (see Chapter 4 on the self-regulation of markets as an instance of autopoiesis).

In other words, financial systems try to reduce disorder and complexity through information. In economics, risk and uncertainty are also defined as information economics or informed economics. This reflection is also capable of justifying the existence of markets as financial systems because they are represented directly in the form of system-meaning. In other words, their relationship with the environment is constituted by information, and how such information is interpreted. The meaning of that information can change the structure of each financial system and the meaning of one system-structure can influence the meanings of other systems. This is why legislation or financial regulation in financial markets are capable of causing effects within the network of market systems. For instance, European legislation on derivatives – the so-called EMIR regulation – although designed to influence the system of derivatives, can also have effects on bond and equity markets because investors may decide to hedge their position against specific market risks that will be dependent on specific financial systems. Another example could be a financial crisis; an unexpected event that occurs in the environment has a negative cascades failure effect on each financial system, leading to notorious banking collapses such as that of Lehman Brothers in 2008. Complexity and autopoiesis are characteristics of financial markets that justify their structural coupling in the form of information sharing.

## 6.2 The phenomenology of contemporary financial systems

The previous sections theorised the existence of markets in the form of systems; but now I will discuss financial systems. Society is not inside the markets – it is external to them. Society is an important system, but it does not communicate with markets in the form of closed systems; rather, it does so exclusively in the form of open systems where effective communication

---

8 Philip Anderson, 'Complexity Theory and Organization Science' (1999) 10 (3) Organization Science, 216–232.

between financial systems and the environment exists and is active (i.e. structural coupling).

The structure of the markets and of their environment can effectively contribute to a new phenomenology of contemporary financial markets. Indeed, under this phenomenology, markets can be seen both as closed systems where the role of uncertainty is privileged and justified, and as open systems where interactions and network effects play a vital role (i.e. structural coupling). It is the distinction between model systems and metaphysical systems.

In the case of markets as closed systems, uncertainty is the measure of the entropy of the system. A maximum level of uncertainty can correspond to a maximum level of balance, so financial markets are examined in terms of 'what a financial market is'. It is the exploration of the ontology of markets, the characterisation of their being, that is the object of our enquiry. Here, markets are seen as a living organism where autopoietic mechanisms of regeneration contribute to a spontaneous balancing of the system itself. This spontaneity is achieved through risk, uncertainty, competition and financial innovations. These are essential elements of the system that can determine different structures.

Therefore, rather than perceive society as a form of closed system which is outside the market, we must begin to think of financial markets and society as forms of open systems, to study the interconnections and the sharing of meanings that occur between those systems. Indeed, in order to understand the feature of risk and the negative outcomes that are connected to those interactions, namely those between society and the market, or better, between the environment and the system, it is useful first to argue the importance of determining the existence of a closed system inside this new phenomenology of financial markets.

Inside a closed system there are no differentiations because closed systems are characterised by entropy-disequilibrium, but this does not mean that subject and object are not differentiated. There is a difference between subject and object but there is no form of communication between systems and environment. Therefore, the society in such a model is not affected negatively by the market's own structures, such as risk, uncertainty, competition and financial innovation. If a financial crisis affects the market this does not necessarily have negative welfare effects, because both the society and the markets are closed systems. This is the reason why uncertainty cannot be blamed as the catalyst of financial crisis and by contrast, in a closed system, uncertainty becomes the leading feature of stability under disequilibrium positions. This not only because – as we have seen in Chapter 3 – without uncertainty there is no profit, but specifically because uncertainty is the measure of the entropy of the system. Therefore, uncertainty is the essential feature through which financial systems can achieve their spontaneous balance and equilibrium, generating in turn spontaneous regeneration processes in the system itself (i.e. autopoiesis).

The description of financial systems as closed systems is a model level of observation that helps to construct model theories that are necessarily abstract.

Here the observer is differentiated from the object of his observation. The difference between subject and object is self-evident. In other words, financial markets are studied through the lens of the ontology of being, namely 'what financial markets are' and 'what society is' as forms of isolated and auto-referral systems without experiencing any sort of interaction and interconnection.

Therefore, first it is important to study society through the lens of closed/open systems, and if one looks at society as a form of closed system, a fundamental distinction between investor/lender and borrower/speculator can be found. On the one hand, there are those who are decision takers, and on the other, the subjects or objects of decisions. Yet it is possible to imagine this duality in terms of risk-aversion and risk-taking (see sections above and Chapter 3). However, in a closed system such a duality is static; it cannot directly influence markets that are isolated and separated. Therefore, differentiation must again become real unification of subject and object where society and markets are parts of the same universe.

Indeed, if one examines financial markets as open systems where the influences or disturbances present in the environment can affect financial systems, and the disturbances created under a system-to-system paradigm can develop into network effects, one can be persuaded that this is not a model theory. It is a practical expression of being. In other words, it is 'what is experienced in financial systems'. Here the difference between a system and the environment is the starting point for the characterisation of the system. In other words, the definition of the system begins with a differentiation. Open systems are not centred on the role of the observer and the role of the object of observation. Here subject and object are unified. This is because the observer itself is a system and the operation of observing is a material activity that can influence the subjectivity of the observer. In fact, we outlined in the previous section that a third level of observation exists, characterised by what I defined as the 'necessary translation', or the metamorphosis of subjects (to this end, the lender becomes the borrower and *vice versa* as well as the investor becoming the speculator). Therefore, in a theory of open systems both the system-environment paradigm and the relations of the system-to-system paradigm are reciprocally influenced and affected in the form of a system of networks and interactions.

This can cause a natural paradox because it is possible to justify a unity by virtue of a difference; however, this is how financial markets will be seen, especially in the case of the unification of subject and object. In those circumstances, risk can be introduced either as a quality of the environment or as a quality of the system, but as one that is capable of directly affecting the structure of free markets. Indeed, when processes of privatisation of risk emerged in societies after the collapse of the Bretton Woods agreement, it immediately became clear that interactions between the environment and financial systems could bring about a re-interpretation of financial risk, and begin its irreversible evolution towards systemic risk, socialisation of risk and under-pricing. For this reason, the re-interpretation of financial risk has profoundly influenced markets, and the differentiation between those who took the decisions and those who had to bear the consequences of those decisions contributed to the fuelling of credit bubbles and the creation of financial crises. Indeed, financial crises, in this distorted vision of markets and society, are no longer seen as an essential element of the market, namely a part of the necessary disequilibrium of the markets, but as a categorisation of financial risk in terms of credit expansion and privatised debt. This phenomenon contributed to a socialisation of financial risk, with severe consequences for the welfare state, where unemployment became the central feature of each market-environment, or if preferred, market-society paradigm.

This understanding of financial systems as financial open systems can determine a new phenomenology of contemporary financial markets, where the differentiations of their qualities can be understood directly through the examination of their unity. Financial crises are processes that are the result of the meaning that is attributed to risk by the system-society where it is possible to differentiate between decision takers and the subjects of decisions and where a process of 'necessary translation' of subjects is in continuous evolution. The meanings of risk transmitted to the market system and society-to-market relations are able to influence each system and its environment. Indeed, we have said that open systems are determined by unity of subject and object. The observer is a system itself. For instance, an investor can study the bond market and try to evaluate how much risk he or she can take and still be risk-averse. Here a possible devaluation of debt or expectations of risk assessment of the debtor can influence not only the behaviour of the borrower/speculator, but also that of the investor/lender. This is a vital point because it can show practically how financial systems are open systems that are influenced by their environment, and specifically by the risk approach that each investor in each market can take. Here risk is not an element of the market, whereas uncertainty is an essential element. Nonetheless, it is not excessive uncertainty that stops people investing, but actual financial risk. This is because financial risk has influenced the operations of markets because free markets are forms of open systems, and are therefore in continuous communication with their environment and with other systems, such as society. Structural coupling is an effective feature of those relations.

For this reason, while closed systems are an important paradigm for describing the object of our enquiry – for instance, the feature of uncertainty in financial systems – open systems are the dynamic element by which can be appreciated the real mechanisms of activities and influences that each system can produce on other systems as well as on the environment. This leads us to define an ontological realism through which the unity of subject and object can be discerned through its differentiation, but at the same time that differentiation can merely constitute a description and it cannot give rise to new meanings. To identify those new meanings, we must take into account financial systems in the form of open systems and recognise the existence of a third-level observation where the 'necessary translation' of the subjects contributes to the creation of new meanings by shifting approaches from a risk-averse to a risk-taking position, or from a lending position to a borrowing one. This is the metamorphosis of subjects that confirms the high dynamicity of financial systems. I previously defined financial systems as 'liquid markets' in order to provide the reader with an intuitive image of constant change (liquids change their shape and form in respect of their recipients). Likewise in financial systems the second-level observation seems to describe the unity of subject and object but actually reveals the existence of a third-level observation where the reciprocal influence of the system-environment and the system-to-system relation is also characterised by metamorphosis of subjects that necessarily complicates the discourse on financial systems. Thus, according to Luhmann, the second-level observation has allowed us to achieve a new stage of thinking that is in our case peculiar to markets, and characterises them as products of the metamorphosis of subjects. According to this view, the 'necessary translation' of subjects prevents us from identifying a fixed model for the observer or subject. It is in continuous evolution in financial systems, and it cannot be predetermined, so from an ontological point of view the 'necessary translation' of the subject is seen as a qualified process of transformation; we must observe the observer in each contextualised financial system. This is because the observer can change his qualification and can subsequently influence the object of our observation in a phenomenology of financial systems which is also in continuous evolution.

We cannot find a real unification of subject and object in financial systems because the changing nature of the subject prevents us from identifying such a unity. Nonetheless, Luhmann's open system theory has been vital in our case to discover the metamorphosis of subjects and the open nature of financial systems.

### 6.2.1 SPACs as financial innovations and observers of the markets

As explained before, the system-environment and system-to-system constitute the point where system theory starts. A system is a system because it is different from its environment. It is capable of drawing its own borders and of distinguishing itself from its environment: this is what Luhmann defines as operational closure.[9] In other words, the operations that are carried out by and inside the system are capable of distinguishing it from the environment. For this reason, systems theory begins with a difference, or duality, such as in system-environment or system-non-system relations; none of the operations inside the system can be translated into the environment, and *vice versa*. Nor can any operation of the system be transplanted to other systems. It is common to speak of operational closure to express this idea of embeddedness. In other words, the difference between a system and the environment is at the

---

9 Ibid., 63.

system's disposal, and any interaction that can occur between the system and the environment is based on the level of meaning, but in economic terms one could speak of economic news or financial literacy or simply of possession of financial information in terms of information asymmetry. It is the exchange of information that contributes to the formation of specific meanings which are elaborated by different systems, or by different markets.

Nonetheless, the reference to operational closure is not a direct reference to the theory of closed systems, nor, therefore, to entropy. Indeed, the concept of operational closure deals with the difference between operation and causality. The operations are the activities that occur inside a system, whereas causality is based on the observation of the observer. Thus, causality is the schema of observation of the world, and it is relative because it depends on each single judgement of each different observer, and this latter is an entity that is already conditioned. For this reason, as Luhmann suggests, we must 'observe the observer' in order to understand how certain causes have been ascribed to certain effects due to the relativity of the observer's view. However, it is only possible to observe the observer if we consider the observer as a system that distinguishes itself from its environment and can consequently also be differentiated from other systems. This is a second-level, as opposed to a first-level, observation that is constituted by the direct observation of a closed system by an observer. This is where the outcomes of scientific research can be disseminated due to first-level observations that are independent from each other.

SPACs can be characterised in general terms as a form of financial innovation because they originated from the creativity of promoters and managers (see Chapter 2). Indeed, as we have seen in the previous sections, financial innovations constitute one of the main features or structures of closed systems and specifically of financial systems. Only through financial innovations can the market regenerate itself because financial innovations are the product of uncertainty.[10] Furthermore, SPACs in corporate terms do not always follow the main international corporate standards of incorporation, therefore when imitation is not applied, variation is implemented. This is also a reason why specifically SPACs can be characterised in terms of financial innovation. For instance, when SPAC issues a unit composed of common shares and convertible bonds during the IPO process, it is acting as a form of financial innovation because it is not strictly following an international corporate standard that wants it to issue warrants in addition to common shares (see Chapter 2). The same happens when SPACs are only financed by virtue of common shares and they are warrantless.

Finally, SPACs are observers of the markets because they are private actors in the markets and they are characterised by 'private' purposes that are

---

10 It is useful to recall the main structures of financial systems as closed systems: risk, uncertainty, financial innovation and competition.

commonly connected with acquisition processes, restructuring activities (the growth capital function) and financing. In turn if we 'observe the observer', namely the SPACs, we can also characterise them in terms of risk and uncertainty (see Chapters 1, 3, 5 and the following Section 6.4).

## 6.3 Law and globalisation

In the post-modern economy the role of law has changed. Globalisation has been seen as a common challenge for law, but this is only one side of the coin. Indeed, if globalisation is seen as a process rather than an effect, society can be seen in non-hierarchical relations. In particular, in Chapters 1 and 4 we saw how global governance, as opposed to international governance, represents a new stage of thinking in financial markets. Essentially, for our purposes, financial globalisation began after the collapse of the Bretton Woods system. Since that time, financial risk has been privatised, and consequently the law has evolved from a positive conception embedded into state legislation or authoritative decisions of judges into a hybrid combination of knowledge that is neither public nor private. The law has been the result of a process of interactions among multiple actors of different, and sometimes opposing, spheres of influence, but the indirect, or side-effect of their cooperation has been vital to the development of the law. Furthermore, self-regulation has become widespread recently, due to the emergence of non-state actors in financial markets and the absence of a global lawmaker. Indeed, the absence of perfect information in markets can further justify the vital contribution that private actors can bring to the legislation process.

Therefore, in contemporary financial systems the role of law has been pushed by globalisation towards self-regulation approaches, which are in turn the clear instance of cooperation mechanisms between private and public actors (see Chapter 4).

### 6.3.1 The lack of a central planner

Self-regulation becomes the direct instance of the fragmentation of knowledge, according to Ladeur, who argues "from a legal theory perspective, the new shift towards the 'society of networks' and its transformed knowledge basis"[11] is one of the clearest signs of the financial revolution that has occurred in the last 40 years. Indeed, according to Ladeur, markets are no longer places where financial resources are efficiently allocated between lenders and borrowers, but experimental venues where risk is optimised. Therefore, welfare effects are completely abandoned in this new conception

---

11 Karl-Heinz Ladeur, The Financial Market Crisis – a case of Network Failure?' in Kjaer, Teubner, Febbrajo (eds.), *The Financial Crisis in Constitutional Perspective: the dark side of functional differentiation* (Hart Publishing 2011) 78.

of markets. Furthermore, companies as well as the banking sector are evolving continually, and this is an instance that directly shows, in Ladeur's view, the difficulty of regulating a dynamically changing environment in the way the economy was regulated, for instance, in the 1800s.

I shall add that this is one of the central features of contemporary financial systems, which lack central planning and a central planner. Indeed, decentralised processes and operations characterise free markets.

To this end, the law in relation to financial systems becomes a 'form' for trying to optimise financial risk for the benefit and protection of investors. Indeed, because epistemologically the knowledge of risk is knowledge of a lack of knowledge, the law becomes the 'form' through which knowledge is transmitted and information is shared through the financial system and the environment, as well as among financial systems. In the end, systems can communicate through meanings, and the form through which the meaning is conveyed is the law.

The law can assume different forms, such as state regulation, private rules and judicial decisions. From a comparative law perspective, those forms are identified as legal formants.[12] In financial systems the most important function for the law to explain is in the form of self-regulation or private rules. Yet in respect of such private rules, the conception of enforcement can always characterise a limit for practical application. It means that neither indirect soft law approaches to regulation nor direct soft law provisions are binding, nor, therefore, are they enforceable. For this reason, one of the functions of public law, at least when we conceptualise it in the form of the law of the state, must be the legitimisation of private institutions to enhance private enforcement. Cooperation is needed between private and public spheres, and between private actors too, to promote an effective enforcement of social norms and legal rules. Nonetheless, it is also possible to conceptualise the existence of a meta-norm capable of sanctioning breaches to lower-level norms without the need for cooperation, due to some innate spirit of observance and obedience of the law.[13] However, this latter hypothesis must be rejected due to the fact that cooperation processes are installed as the result of the fragmentation of knowledge determined by the absence of a central planner. To this extent, the existence of a meta-norm must always be idealised as a materialisation of the will of a central planner that influences the behaviours of private and public actors.

For this reason, the law in the contemporary phenomenology of financial markets is seen as a form without contents, because the contents of the law will be determined by the form that the law takes each time. This is a clear instance of observers observing markets without taking into account their interactions.

---

12 Rodolfo Sacco, 'Legal Formants: A Dynamic Approach to Comparative Law' (1991) 1 American Journal of Comparative Law 39.
13 Robert Axelrod, 'An Evolutionary Approach to Norms' (2006) 100 (4) American Political Science Review 1095.

Indeed, the analysis of markets in the form of closed systems is useful to assert the reason why at first glance financial law does not take into account welfare concerns. This is not due to the absence of social justice, but because a first-level observation relates to an epistemological view of the law. Essentially, the law is looked at in this way only from the point of view of epistemology. For this reason, if we speak of the knowledge of the law, we have to focus our attention on its form. In a closed system view, it is not the content of the law that is important, but the processes through which law is adopted and legitimised, whether we take into account either public or private law.

It thus becomes clear that a fictitious feature of being, without specific contents, characterises financial law. Indeed, the contents of financial law are determined by the structural coupling of every financial system with its environment as well as system-to-system relations. Indeed, if private and public actors cooperate within a heterarchical network of relations, the law becomes the product of multiple interactions that must reflect the interests of different stakeholders. Therefore, the contents of financial law are not necessarily characterised by welfare concerns but are highly influenced by market discipline and supervision concerns. The latter aims are endemically characterised by a need for regulation of the market and selection of the best financial products to optimise profit-making and inspire financial actors to pursue virtuous behaviours. Welfare effects may be a side-effect of such aims, but they are not necessarily the main concern of market policy regulation. Indeed, financial self-regulation is a direct instance of financial industry knowledge as opposed to public concerns for investor protection which should be pursued by the state.

For this reason, there is a lack of specificity and of specialisation of contents in financial law. This is in part a result of the crisis of Westphalian models of legislation, in addition to a complex way of thinking about financial systems. If markets are able to influence each other in structural coupling, in the same way the law cannot be exempted, and it must reflect the web of interactions among these networks.

### 6.3.2 SPACs as market-driven instruments

As stated in the previous section, the current financial systems are not regulated by a central planner. It means that the heterarchical relationships among the market participants inform markets in terms of cooperation and self-regulation.

An important instance of this discourse can be found in SPACs. They are mainly self-regulated instruments governed by market practices rather than legislative impositions, so SPACs are market-driven instruments following a customary law that has been developed in the form of either indirect or direct soft law approaches (see Chapters 2 and 4). Furthermore, the market-driven features of SPACs that are directly connected to international corporate standards have also determined the evolution of SPACs as self-regulated instruments where imitation of standards constitutes the rule of such evolution, and variations are limited and rare.

Nonetheless, as mentioned before, SPACs are a form of financial innovation of the market. Therefore, variations in corporate standards can be found. Yet in such circumstances the variations are always related to market practices rather than legislative inventions. Specifically, the next section explores this feature of SPACs in terms of non-legal instances.

## 6.4 SPACs as a non-legal instance

It is in this context, previously described as a new phenomenology of contemporary financial markets, that SPACs represent a remarkable instance of financial innovation which can provide the equity market with competition as well as promote the expansion of the same market under auto-regenerating processes. These will take the legal forms of self-regulation with either direct or indirect soft law expressions. In the last instance, the law is an operational process of the system and can determine the existence of new structures that can in turn influence both the environment and the other systems. This is because we believe in an open system theory.

SPACs in this manifestation are the non-legal expression of the law – the non-binding image of legislative processes. In Chapters 1, 2 and 4 we spoke of 'SPACs without law'. Those processes are the same as in the equity market, in the sense that promoters of SPACs were initially aware of the main characteristics of SPACs on the PSM, as explained in Chapter 2. This is because the modern conception of SPACs is the product of an evolutionary process that has been developed over decades in different financial systems, such as the PSM, the OTC market, the AMEX, the NYSE, and the NASDAQ in the US SPACs proliferated especially in markets where legislative processes did not take the form of an authoritative third figure that is the state, but rather an indirect form of soft law. Furthermore, there is nowhere in the world a compulsory SPAC definition, with the exception of the Korean Exchange and Turkey, which have adopted a positive law with a clear definition of SPAC. Nonetheless, as has been seen in Chapters 2 and 4, positive law and the Westphalian model of legislation have been reduced in importance in contemporary financial markets, where the rise of non-state actors has transformed the enactment of law processes. For this reason, SPACs stand at the apex of non-legal instances and the law. Sometimes markets require SPACs to satisfy particular features to be listed (for instance, the NYSE, the NASDAQ, etc.), whereas in other cases, the market does not provide any specific and detailed discipline for SPACs (such as in the case of *Borsa Italiana* in Italy or Euronext in Europe). Yet it is the need of regulation that can be seen as a threat by SPACs unless it is aimed at the discipline of common and international corporate standards (such as the winding up procedure, the escrow account, etc.). This is because SPACs are cash-shell companies and, therefore, dynamic vehicles of profit.

## 6.4.1 SPACs and market spontaneity

In relation to markets, SPACs stand as an instance of financial innovation. Therefore, as we have pointed out in the previous sections of this chapter, markets are instances of financial systems. Financial markets are financial systems. Furthermore, it has been shown in the previous sections that financial systems are complex systems because they directly experience a structural coupling between system and environment as well as system-to-system relations. For this reason, when financial systems need to re-organise themselves, competition plays an essential role. Competition serves a fundamental role in the market, not only in respect of sustaining the creativity of new financial innovations through the imagination and entrepreneurial instinct that can transform risks into opportunities, but specifically in selecting the best financial tools or innovations to turn a crisis into a profitable occasion. SPACs are a product of market collapses where uncertainty about the future is seen as a spontaneous organisation of the complexity of the markets. Spontaneity, as opposed to the rigid pre-qualifications of a central planner, is the right term to identify the mechanisms of cooperation among actors within the markets. Indeed, cooperation among market participants aims at achieving a new equilibrium of the market, so SPACs contribute to the processes of spontaneous re-creation and regeneration of the market known as autopoiesis (see sections above).

## 6.4.2 SPACs and uncertainty

SPACs are a product of uncertainty not only because they are a financial innovation, but because they represent the creation of profit as a form of uncertainty absorption through the taking of risk opportunities. The system has responded to demand for risk management tools with the creation of an investment vehicle that can satisfy the needs of both investors and market. Indeed, investors pursue risk-aversion and consistent profits, whereas the market is concerned with liquidity. SPACs as forms of equity investment can directly provide markets with a boost of liquidity, and at the same time supply investors with a high-risk profit investment vehicle. That it is impossible for any investor to be aware of the profile of the target company the SPAC is going to acquire or merge with can itself be seen as high-risk. An acquisition might not occur, or once signed, it might not be closed due to balance sheet concerns in the target company. For this reason, the high risk that investors are willing to take at the time of the IPO through common shares purchase must be counterbalanced by a 'sweetener' that can either be identified in warrants' purchase or convertible bonds' purchase. In other words, the commitment to a future plan of investments that might occur after the business combination is one of the keys to mitigate the high-risk perspective of the initial investment.

Uncertainty plays a vital role in identifying which target company might constitute the objectification of a rightful risk opportunity. These decisions are taken by the management of the SPAC. Therefore, it is vital for the managers of the SPAC to be expert in the industry of the target company as well as used to directing a SPAC or cash-shell company. This is because information sharing will play a vital role in selecting the right target company to make the maximum profit and absorb the uncertainty of the market.

## 6.5 Conclusions

In this chapter, a possible re-definition of free markets has been described for the first time in the new paradigm of the phenomenology of contemporary financial markets. We have identified markets as systems under Luhmann's system theory, so financial markets are financial systems and specifically they are open systems. However, to identify financial markets as financial systems is not enough because this is only a partial description of the object of our enquiry. We must now adopt a second- rather than a first-level observation to observe the observer. The subject and object are then unified, although through a paradoxical differentiation of system and environment as well as system-to-system relations. Nonetheless, it seems that the unity between subject and object cannot be completely achieved, at least in financial systems, because of what I defined as 'necessary translation' or metamorphosis of subjects. Indeed, according to this view, subjects of financial systems are continuously evolving and shifting their roles (i.e. investor to speculator and lender to borrower and *vice versa*). This is a third-level observation of the markets where subjects are in continuous evolution.

Within a first and second level of observation in Luhmann's conception I have re-interpreted the manifestation of financial systems in their original forms as closed systems. Here, it is possible to identify 'what financial markets are', and I have argued that markets are determined by three main features: uncertainty, competition and innovation. However, this is only a model theory and cannot actually reflect the complexity of the reality. For this we need a metaphysical description of markets under the heading 'what is experienced in financial systems'. This reveals a new stage of thinking where financial systems are open systems and financial risk dominates the scene. Financial risk has been privatised and under-priced, giving rise to credit bubbles, but it is that same experience of financial risk that creates profit; so the risk-taker or entrepreneur is a profit-maker, and his willingness to make a profit turns the uncertainty that permeates the markets into risk opportunity, so that profit becomes a way of absorbing uncertainty.

I define the financial systems that are open systems as 'liquid markets' because they can influence each other by means of structural coupling. Nonetheless, each financial system's operation is strictly confined within the same system and it cannot be transferred into the environment or into another system. Operational closure is the right term, in the view of Luhmann, to identify this feature of modernity. Indeed, in modern economies liquid autopoietic markets are determined by a web of connections and mechanisms of cooperation because of their open systems, but at the same time the environment cannot influence the markets' operations. In other words, markets can regenerate themselves as a response to external stimuli through operational closure and effectively implement a process of autopoiesis where financial structures are reformed and spontaneously re-created to achieve new economic equilibria.

Within this context SPACs are a form of financial innovation and they are therefore a product of the competition to respond to stimuli created by market uncertainty. SPACs deal mainly with financial risk because they are a form of risk management where the interests of different stakeholders coexist for a special purpose, namely the acquisition of a target company. Any lost deal or less than profitable transaction becomes part of a risk opportunity discourse that can lead to a profit lost, and therefore, it is for the management which represents that entrepreneurial instinct to confront uncertainty and turn it into profit. In the end, SPACs are financial innovations for controlling uncertainty and absorbing it through profit creation.

# Conclusions

In January 2012 when I was working for Dewey & Leboeuf in Rome, one of the NY partners wrote me an email saying: "in good faith, and in the best interest of the firm". Dewey & Leboeuf filed for bankruptcy under Chapter 11 of the US Bankruptcy Code just a few months later in May 2012. It was one of the biggest collapses of American law firms in history. This shows the asymmetry of knowledge that exists between insiders and outsiders of the firm. SPACs are no different. They must and will disclose information to the public. In financial markets, information is key. Misinformation can be fatal. The role of a financial regulator must be to preserve information and protect investors. Volatility is an intrinsic quality of market economies, and the role of any financial regulator must be first to preserve investors' confidence, as well as to guarantee transparency and disclosure of correct information. It feels as though a SEC warning sign on warrants without an implementation date and legal force sits well beyond such objectives, and just looks like an unjustified activism. This is not a sound decision and represents an attempt to stop the SPAC-frenzy. And in April 2021, it did, unfortunately. Nonetheless, this is also a progressive approach to regulation, and it might constitute the starting point of a full legitimisation of the SPAC model. Indeed, a new consistent reform on SPACs is expected to take place in the US in 2022, this time with a higher degree of protection in relation to retail investors and of those who do not redeem their shares facing a dilution risk.

Many would say the bubble in SPACs has burst in June 2021. Only 30 SPAC floatation took place in April and May compared to 299 in the first three months of the year, while total Wall Street investment bank revenues derived from these vehicles has fallen from over 20% to under 5% over the same period. Finally, in June 2021, the two largest US exchange-traded funds focused on SPACs (SPAK and SPCX) were down 26% and 12% in value, respectively, from their February highs. This is linked to US regulator the SEC beginning to rein in the sector to protect retail investors. Retail investors are only a few marginal side of the SPAC arena that is mainly populated by institutional investors.

Though in my view the rate of SPAC creation would have slowed down to reach a lower equilibrium anyway, the SEC intervention is reducing some of the benefits to using SPACs as a way of accessing the capital markets. Indeed, the Biden era is corresponding to a tougher period of enforcement and regulation. We saw how the SEC has made it harder for SPACs to reward early investors with shares in a company after an acquisition, and is looking at preventing the management from making statements about future profitability. Regulators often resit financial innovation in the hope of reducing uncertainty in investing. It is not by chance that Gary Gensler, the new SEC chair under the Biden administration, recently associated SPACs and bitcoin[1] when he spoke of the need for better investor protections. As with SPACs, regulatory moves to restrict the use of bitcoin and other cryptocurrencies have probably contributed to price falling lately (along with other worries such as bitcoin's carbon footprint).

The SEC decisions may be based on an apparent misconception of SPACs. The SEC's concern about competition issues involving business combination opportunities is unrealistic. A closer look at S-1 forms clearly shows that today we do have sector-focused or multi-sector-focused SPACs. Competition might only emerge in the latter, although the number of potential targets is infinite, and competition (if it exists) extends far beyond American borders to Europe (see Arrival and Cazoo in the UK or Zegna in Italy) and to Asia (see Grab in Singapore). On the SPACs' promote (founder shares): sponsors often invest further cash into the SPAC at the De-SPACing phase and sometimes they decide to align themselves with the target shareholders by giving up a portion of their promote. The PIPE process takes on the transaction risk early in the De-SPAC process; consequently, today's SPAC investors do not sustain any particular cost. The promote is the skin in the game, although the sponsor's compensation scheme must be directly connected to the SPAC's performance. Ultimately, it would be worth questioning why the SEC or other market operators are not suggesting any improvement for the traditional IPO in terms of price discovery mechanisms. The SEC's warnings are not beneficial either for SPACs or their investors.

SPACs are an American invention. We have seen how SPACs 2.0, 3.0 and 3.5 show the dynamicity of these investment vehicles, and how they can increase markets' liquidity despite the austerity and price volatility imposed in the Covid-19 era. SPACs' numbers demonstrate that there is an actual market for SPACs with liquidity and proper volumes, and that they are money creation vehicles. Indeed, the Covid-19 pandemic has imposed a dramatic re-formulation of the rule of law, giving way to a more flexible and dynamic form of regulation where traditional instances of statute law are unable to provide answers to new legal issues. Since their origin, SPACs have never been regulated by a statute, but rather by market practices. A practical

---

1 Gary Gensler, "Testimony before the subcommittee on Financial Services and General Government U.S. House Appropriations Committee" available at https://www.sec.gov/news/testimony/gensler-2021-05-26, accessed on 23 June 2021.

evidence of this statement is not only provided by the emergence of SPAC 3.0 and SPAC 3.5 but also by a new conception of financial innovation that has been introduced by Ackman in summer 2021: the Special Purpose Acquisition Rights Company (SPARC). Unlike a SPAC, where investors pledge capital to acquire an unknown company, the SPARC won't ask for money just yet. The SPARC will only collect cash from investors once it is identified a target and published a prospectus. Without further complicating the life of the reader, the SPARC is the right example to directly provide a concrete evidence to the theory of this book. Financial innovation is a structure of contemporary financial markets or better financial systems. SPACs invest in innovation through high growth companies or pre-revenue companies, and financial operators further expand the market segment of alternative investments through new financial products. The SPARC is one direct instance. Uncertainty is a friend of markets. More regulation equals to a reduction of uncertainty and therefore of competition and creativity. Less competition equals to less financial innovation. This is the reason why profit is threatened and individual income is lost.

By contrast, some argue that SPACs constitute a potential risk to markets and the whole economy, despite their risk-free nature, due to their lack of strict regulatory requirements. Over-regulation is a killer not just in SPACs but generally. As long as the parties understand the risks associated with free-rein powers granted to the management (which can be limited if need by establishing a narrower purpose), there is no need to regulate SPACs further; they have re-emerged as a result of their *laissez-faire* nature combining different aspects (tax advantages, no-history-no-liability status and multiple exit/redemption strategies) in ways similar to other alternative investment vehicles such as private equity funds and hedge funds.

I argue that in a financial crisis, unregulated market practices are often seen as a trigger (or at least as an amplifier) but regulators have mostly focused their attention on managing the effects of crises rather than on regulating triggers. A direct instance of this is the 2007–2010 crisis when the lack of proper regulation of the OTC derivatives market and subprime mortgages prompted the enactment of legislation focused on financial stability effects rather than on trigger profiling. Regulation is not the final answer to financial crisis, but it is an instrument to mitigate financial risk, and it should be properly and carefully used.

As opposed to the 2007–2010 financial crisis, SPACs' main evolutionary market trends are disciplined by the regulator (so far mainly the SEC) and listing standards (i.e. the exchanges where they are listed). Hence, the trigger has been expressly codified. However, we have seen that market practices are not necessarily codified by exchanges, and they still follow a self-regulatory approach (namely, SPAC 3.0 and SPAC 3.5 models). To this end, SPACs represent one of the most prominent instances of voluntary compliance and self-regulation in financial markets. It cannot be denied that, like other similar investment vehicles, SPACs pose a risk as risks cannot be completely eradicated. However, these risks can be curtailed through proper contractual risk allocation and enhanced corporate governance mechanisms. For instance, the PIPE investment mitigates the risk of high redemptions; the earnout provisions make the uncertain valuation of the acquisition target more predictable; the support agreements (such as the lock-in provision of SPAC shareholders) give target companies more certainty of closing a deal, etc. This is only part of SPACs' secret success story and, one might say, of a possible reshaping of financial markets *tout court*.

To this end, the 'human-humanity' feature of risk, and specifically of financial risk, has totally reshaped financial markets because risk itself, since the time of Galileo Galilei, has been perceived as substituting the will of God with man's desires. Since that moment, risk and the figure of the risk-taker have been the catalysts of progress and development for society. In other words, only risk-takers are brave enough to confront uncertainty; risk calculation, based on the laws of probabilities, has met the uncontrollable limit to measuring a new subjective feature of risk, which is identified in uncertainty. Uncertainty is not only the subjective characteristic of risk in terms of the desirability of the risk-taker's choices, but it is an unmeasurable entity that can cause either anxiety or profit in society. Indeed, according to Knight[2] profit, when it is achieved, represents the absorption of uncertainty. However, to make a profit one has to take more risks and, therefore, to confront more uncertainties. The common aphorism in corporate finance is, the higher the risk, the higher the profit.

To this end, the 'human-inhumanity' of risk has started to dominate the world because uncertainty represents the domain that is beyond 'open human control'.[3] To counterbalance, uncertainty societies have developed symbols such as Smith's 'invisible hand'. This invention initially reduced the anxiety of living in an uncertain world, but it has not completely solved the issue of 'control'. It is useful to highlight once again that uncertainty is an uncontrollable and ungovernable element of our own existence, both because we cannot anticipate with certainty the occurrence of future events and because we cannot manage all the risks that are hidden in financial operations. Furthermore, the nature of our own existence has been irremediably changed by the emergence of complexity as a new main feature of the world. The world is complex, and our judgements are only relative and subjective.

One practical instance of the relativity of judgements as well as of complexity, especially in terms of interconnections between negative economic effects, was the recent financial crisis (2007–2010). The collapse of Lehman Brothers in 2008 showed how contagious effects could come from the collapse of a major investment bank. After Lehman, almost every sector of the financial industry was affected. A global crisis required global answers. Hence, the

---

2 Frank Knight, *Risk, Uncertainty, and Profit* (first published 1921, Martino Publishing 2014).
3 Anthony Giddens, *Modernity and Self-identity* (Stanford University Press 1991).

rhetorical question was: where did the contagion come from? How could the world allow something of that magnitude to happen?

Uncertainty is the answer, a financial regulator would say, and the answer of a 'private' banker in Canary Wharf or Wall Street would be that the privatisation of financial risk is the cause. Capitalism is the technical specification of the theoretical background I have just presented. Specifically, the devastating social effects of the crisis have shown what a 'private' connotation of financial risk means. That privatisation was the result of liberalisation policies after the collapse of the original Bretton Woods system. Private actors such as banks and financial intermediaries introduced a new collective good, namely moral hazard as a form of 'privatised Keynesianism'.[4] Post-war consumer society was kept going by immorality and excessive risk-taking. To enable private actors to take unreasonable forms of investment risks, credit rating agencies such as Moody's, Fitch, and Standard & Poor's (essentially private companies) were empowered with evaluation prerogatives to rate the solvability of financial intermediaries and the quality of the financial products that were issued, such as bonds, shares, etc. For this reason, the 'private' nature of the financial environment was one of the grounds on which moral hazard was produced and became widespread.

However, since that moment academics and financial operators as well as regulators have begun to single out uncertainty as one of the main causes of the financial crisis (2007–2010). This view is possibly misleading, especially if uncertainty is used to justify the existence of morally hazardous behaviours on the basis of 'black swan' events. Uncontrollability is not synonymous with the legitimation of wrongful and immoral actions and must not be constructed as such.

Indeed, in the view of Knight, and as we have seen in this work, uncertainty is connected to profit, and without uncertainty there is no profit. Uncertainty underpins money creation processes rather than undermining them. This work aims to show that the real cause of the recent financial crisis (2007–2010) can be identified in the 'private' nature of risk and in under-pricing movements (for example, banks did not accurately carry out a credit risk assessment of the borrowers and their activities). Systemic risk is therefore seen as the shifting of costs onto society rather than onto banks and financial operators. In other words, financial risk was not efficiently distributed, classified or managed, and moral hazard was not prevented but promoted by the same markets' private actors.

Reacting to this misleading reading of uncertainty, governments enacted macroeconomic legislations aimed at confining uncertainty by reducing risk-taking activities (Chapter 4). This can be conceptualised as a real uncertainty-aversion paradigm. However, this approach did not have positive results; instead, it resulted in a wrong conception of markets and uncertainty *tout court*.

---

4 Colin Crouch, *The strange non-death of neo-liberalism* (Polity Press 2011).

The main point is that uncertainty is neither the cause nor the effect of a financial crisis, but it is simply a remarkable concept that cannot be erased from our own experience or from financial markets. Uncertainty can be the product of internal shocks such as the collapse of a major investment bank as it happened back in 2008–2010 or can be the result of an external factor such as in the case of Covid-19.

For these reasons, uncertainty must be seen and studied from a system perspective in which financial markets can be conceptualised for the first time as financial systems. Specifically, if financial systems are instances of closed systems, they are characterised by four structures or elements: risk, uncertainty, financial innovation and competition. Those structures are also capable of regenerating markets by creating new structures. Indeed, uncertainty in this context is the catalyst for autopoietic systems independently from the cause that has generated it being either an internal shock of the system or external factor. Uncertainty, with its connotation of profit, pushes the risk-taker into taking risks, then in order to compete with other market operators new, creative ideas are developed as financial innovations. That cycle can be a virtuous process of market renovation, where uncertainty is seen as the main element activating the momentum. This has also been theorised as a new contemporary phenomenology of financial systems. Financial systems should be seen as open systems where markets and financial operators are connected by networks. Ladeur identifies them as 'networks of networks': the spill-over effect of investment bank collapse represents the most direct instance of these. This identification of markets as networks is also justified by a 'complexity' that rejects Newtonian cause and effect. In other words, linear thinking has been suppressed by the contingencies of financial markets and their 'private' nature.

Within this context and interpretation of financial markets as financial systems, SPACs are studied for the first time as alternative investment vehicles capable of replacing private equity deals and structures as well as being market-driven vehicles for money creation. Money creation processes, as has been explained above, are underpinned by uncertainty and risk. SPACs are vehicles of risk and uncertainty. They convey uncertainty as money creation processes, and they are instances of financial risk because they are risk-takers, namely, borrowers. The conceptualisation of SPACs as risk-takers gives rise to the classic economic issues of information asymmetry, moral hazard and agency costs. These economic issues are still present in many corporate structures but in the case of SPACs, there is a connotation with cash-shell companies. It means that SPACs do not have balance sheets because they are non-operating companies. For these reasons, the classic economic issues of corporations become even more complex in relation to SPACs. However, this work has shown how specific corporate governance mechanisms, such as the issuance of units, as well as policy interventions (for instance, the soft law approach of the Malaysian markets) can mitigate the aggression embedded in this kind of risk-taking.

Furthermore, SPACs can be constructed under a complexity thinking approach where financial systems are characterised by financial innovations.

SPACs are a vehicle for innovation, and from a system perspective they are able to master the complexity of the system through a form of self-regeneration: namely, what I have defined as the direct and indirect soft law approaches of SPACs, and as the codified-codification and uncodified-codification of market practices (Chapters 2 and 4). From the point of view of the law, current circumstances in financial markets have indeed dramatically changed the role of both law and global governance. Law in financial markets has become a hybrid entity where cooperation processes have seen the involvement of private and public actors, due to the 'heterarchical' nature of market participants and the interconnections, networks, and regulatory networks that inform financial markets today.

In the post-crisis regulatory environment, SPACs emerge as a market-driven force that can provide scholars and market operators with an outstanding example of soft law approaches. Indeed, SPACs are informed either by an indirect soft law approach or by a direct soft law policy. The former is the result of the adaptation of SEC Rule 419 when SPACs began being listed on less-regulated venues. Nonetheless, regulated venues such as the NYSE, NASDAQ and the New AMEX have started since 2008 to receipt those market practices in their market regulations. This is an instance of hard law and the codification of market practices. Those regulations are the product of private actors (SPACs and exchanges) but in contrast to those private instances, a 'by-law' approach has been implemented in Korea and Turkey where for the first time the state, and therefore a public actor, has directly imposed a SPAC law.

For these reasons, SPACs are today 'without law' but not 'outside the law' because corporate law provisions will always be applied as a general rule to any SPAC incorporation in any country. The lack of a European law discipline has not avoided the possibility of configuring SPACs as collective investment undertakings, due to their close similarity to alternative investment funds. A final guidance has not yet been provided in this sense.

This work has examined SPACs in their 'private' nature; a comparative study has revealed three main outcomes: first, common law jurisdictions are more SPAC-friendly because of their greater compliance with international corporate standards developed from the reception and codification of market practices (this is also because of the flexibility of the law in common law traditions, as opposed to civil law countries); second, the market venues that have implemented a SPAC regulation by the reception of market practices are able to attract greater investment because of the transparency of their listing procedures and the corporate governance standards that must be followed; third, indirect or direct soft law regulation is preferred to hard law instances because SPACs are cash-shell companies and they have a highly flexible structure.

SPACs have a promising future because they are a potential alternative to private equity, being based on equity rather than on debt. Thus, if the cause of the previous financial crisis is seen as the under-pricing of private debt, SPACs constitute a possible way to boost liquidity in markets, regenerate the M&A industry, and provide private companies with new forms of financing. At the same time – we have seen – how SPACs are also an alternative investment for private equity firms either when private equity managers sponsor a SPAC or sell to a SPAC some of their portfolio assets as an exit strategy. On the other hand, as a security equity is riskier than debt, so SPACs must always find ways to protect investors through risk management tools with the aim of mitigating the downside effects of equity. It is undeniable though that SPACs are a great financial innovation, and at least in the US are definitively here to stay. We have seen that SPAC markets are also expanding beyond the US borders, to Europe and Asia. Through SPACs, private companies gain access to public funds and have an opportunity to be directed by reputable managers who can bet on innovative ideas. What is not often said is that SPACs believe in other people's entrepreneurship dreams. That's true. Dreams may end, but until then, SPACs matter, and the world is their oyster.

# Bibliography

Abraham K S, *Distributing Risk: Insurance, Legal Theory and Public Policy* (Yale University Press 1986)

Akerlof G A, 'The Market for "Lemons": Quality Uncertainty and the Market Mechanism' (1970) 84 (3) Quarterly Journal of Economics 488

Aldohni A K, 'The Quest for a Better Legal and Regulatory Framework for Islamic Banking' (2015) 17 (1) Ecclesiastical Law Journal 15

Alessandrini D, 'Regulating Financial Derivatives? Risks, Contested Values and Uncertainty Features' (2011) Social & Legal Studies 1

Allen F, Gale D, 'Financial Contagion' (2000) 108 (1) Journal of Political Economy 1

Al-Saati A, 'The Permissible *Gharar* (Risk) in Classical Islamic Jurisprudence' (2003) 16 (2) Journal of King Abdul Aziz University: Islamic Economics 7

Anderson P, 'Complexity Theory and Organization Science' (1999) 10 (3) Organization Science 216

Arnold G, *Modern Financial Markets and Institutions – A Practical Perspective* (Pearson Education 2012)

Autore D M, Kovacs T, 'Equity Issues and Temporal Variation in Information Asymmetry' (2010) 34 (1) Journal of Banking & Finance

Axelrod R, 'An Evolutionary Approach to Norms' (2006) 100 (4) American Political Science Review 1095

Aydogdu M, Shekhar C, *et al.*, 'Shell Companies as IPO Alternatives: An Analysis of Trading Activity around Reverse Mergers' (2007) 17 (16) Applied Financial Economics 1335

Ayotte K, David Skeel, 'Bankruptcy or Bailouts?' (2010) 35 Journal of Corporation Law 35

Bachmann S H, 'Serbanes-Oxley Act: Have the Americans Set Capital Market Standards?' (2006) 27 (2) Company Lawyer 35

Bain B, Tse C, 'Silicon Valley Wins as SEC Allows New Direct Listing' (22 December 2020) Bloomberg

Balala M H, *Islamic Finance and Law: Theory and Practice in a Globalized World* (I.B. Tauris 2010)

Balleisen E J, Moss D A (eds.) *Government and Markets toward a New Theory of Regulation* (CUP 2010)

Barnhart C L, Barnhart R K (eds.), *The World Book Dictionary L-Z* (World Book Inc. 1987)

Barr M S, Miller G P, 'Global Administrative Law: The View from Basel' (2006) 17 (1) The European Journal of International Law 15

———. 'Who's in Charge of Global Finance?' (2014) 45 (4) Georgetown Journal of International Law 971

Beck U, *Risk Society: Towards a New Modernity* (SAGE Publications 1992)

Berger C, 'SPACs: An Alternative Way to Access the Public Markets' (2008) 20 (3) Journal of Applied Corporate Finance 68

Bernstein P L, *Against the Gods: The Remarkable Story of Risk* (John Wiley & Sons 1996)

Billes S, Erpf E, *Langenscheidt Handwörterbuch Englisch*, vol. 1 (2nd ed., Langenscheidt KG 2010)

Bishop S, Walker M, *The Economic of EC Competition Law: Concepts, Application and Measurement* (Sweet & Maxwell 2010)

Black J, 'Decentring Regulation: Understanding the Role of Regulation and Self-Regulation in a "Post-Regulatory" World' (2001) 54 (1) Current Legal Problems 106

Borio C, Zhu H, 'Capital Regulation, Risk-taking and Monetary Policy: A Missing Link in the Transmission Mechanism?' (2008) 268 BIS Working Papers 3

Boyer C, Baigent G, 'SPACs as Alternative Investments: An Examination of Performance and Factors that Drive Prices' (2008) 11 (3) Journal of Private Equity 8

Bruner J, Goodnow J J, Austin G A, *A Study of Thinking* (Wiley 1956)

Brunnermeier M K, *Asset Pricing under Asymmetric Information: Bubbles, Crashes, Technical Analysis and Herding* (OUP 2001)

Buckley R P, *International Financial System: Policy and Regulation* (Kluwer Law International 2008)

Castelli T, 'Not Guilty by Association: Why the Taint of their 'Blank Check' Predecessors Should Not Stunt the Growth of Modern Special Purpose Acquisition Companies' (2009) 50 (1) Boston College Law Review 237

Chancellor E, *Devil Take the Hindmost: A History of Financial Speculation* (Plume 2000)

Chemmanur T J, Fulgheri P, '"Why Include Warrants in New Equity Issues?" A Theory of Unit IPOs' (1997) 32 (1) Journal of Financial and Quantitative Analysis 1

Coase R H, *The Firm, The Market and the Law* (University of Chicago Press 1988)

Collins H, 'Methods and Aims of Comparative Contract Law' (1991) Oxford Journal of Legal Studies 396

Corby B, 'On Risk and Uncertainty in Modern Society' (1994) 19 (72) The Geneva Papers on Risk and Insurance 235

Cottier T, Jackson J H, Lastra M R (eds.) *International Law in Financial Regulation and Monetary Affairs* (OUP 2012)

Crouch C, *The Strange Non-death of Neo-liberalism* (Polity Press 2011)

Cumming D, Hab LH, Schweizer D, 'The Fast Track IPO-Success Factors for Taking Firms Public with SPACs' (2014) 47 Journal of Banking and Finance 198

D'Alvia D, '(Legal) Uncertainty: Takaful between English Common Law and Shari'a Law' (2017) 10 (1) International Review of Law 1

Dali N R S M, *Introduction to Muamalat* (McGraw Hill 2008)

Davidoff S M, 'Black Market Capital' (2008) Columbia Business Law Review 175

Davies H, Green D, *Banking on the Future: The Fall and Rise of Central Banking* (Princeton University Press 2010)

Dawson M, Enderlein H, Joerges C (eds.) *Beyond the Crisis: The Governance of Europe's Economic, Political and Legal Transformation* (OUP 2015)

Demyanyk Y, Van Hemert O, 'Understanding the Sub-prime Mortgage Crisis' (2011) 24 (6) The Review of Financial Studies 1848

Dewatripont M, Freixas X, Portes R (eds.), *Macroeconomic Stability and Financial Regulation: Key Issues for the G20* (Centre for Economic Policy Research 2011)

Dimitrova L (2017) 'Perverse Incentives of Special Purpose Acquisition Companies, the "Poor Man's Private Equity Funds"' (2017) 63 (1) Journal of Accounting & Economics 99

Eichengreen B, Mussa M, *et al.*, 'Capital Account Liberalization: Theoretical and Practical Aspects' (1998) IMF Occasional Paper n. 172

Esposito E, *The Future of Futures: The Time of Money in Financing and Society* (Edward Elgar 2011)

Fabozzi F, Modigliani F, *Capital Markets: Institutions and Instruments* (2nd ed., Prentice Hall 1996)

Figlewski S, 'Viewing the Financial Crisis from 20,000 Feet up' (2009) 16 Journal of Derivatives 53

Fisher I, *Nature of Capital and Income* (Macmillan 1906)

Fleisher V, 'Regulatory Arbitrage' (2010) University of Colorado Law Legal Studies Research Paper No. 10–11, 1

Floros I, Sapp T, 'Shell Games: On the Value of Shell Companies' (2011) 17 (4) Journal of Corporate Finance 850

Frenz W, *Handbook of EU Competition Law* (Springer 2016)

Gadinis S, 'From Independence to Politics in Financial Regulation' (2013) 101 (2) California Law Review 322

Geradin D, Layne-Farrar A, Petit N, *EU Competition Law and Economics* (OUP 2012)

Giddens A, *Modernity and Self-identity* (Stanford University Press 1991)

Goode R, *Principles of Corporate Insolvency Law* (4th ed., Sweet&Maxwell 2011)

Goodhart C, *The Evolution of Central Banks* (MIT Press 1988)

———. *The Regulatory Response to the Financial Crisis* (Edward Elgar 2009)

Goodhart C, Hartmann P, *et al.*, *Financial Regulation: Why, How and Where Now?* (Routledge 1998)

Grote R, Marauhn T, *The Regulation of International Financial Markets: Perspectives for Reform* (CUP 2006)

Gullifer L, Payne J, *Corporate Finance Law Principles and Policy* (Hart Publishing 2011)

Guttentag J, Herring R, 'Disaster Myopia in International Banking' (1986) Essays in International Finance No. 164, Princeton University Press

Haas E B, 'Why Collaborate? Issue-linkage and International Regimes' (1980) 32 (3) World Politics 357, 380

Hale LM, 'SPAC: A Financial Tool with Something for Everyone' (2007) 18 (2) Journal of Corporate Accounting & Finance 67

Hallaq W B, *An Introduction to Islamic Law* (Cambridge University Press, Cambridge 2009)

Hardy C O, *Risk and Risk-Bearing* (Risk Books 1923)

Hassan M K, Mervyn K, Lewis, *Handbook of Islamic Finance* (Edward Elgar 2007)

Heyman DK, 'From Black Check to SPAC: The Regulator's Response to the Market, and the Market's Response to the Regulation' (2007) 2 Entrepreneurial Business Law Journal 531

Hindelang S, *The Free Movement of Capital and Foreign Direct Investment* (OUP 2009)

Hockett R C, 'A Fixer-Upper for Finance' (2010) 87 (6) Washington University Law Review 1213

———. 'Recursive Collective Actions Problems: The Structure of Procyclicality in Financial and Monetary Markets, Macro Economies and Formally Similar Contexts' (2015) 3 (2) Journal of Financial Perspectives 36

Hockett R C, Omarova S T, '"Private" Means to "Public" Ends: Government as Market Actors' (2014) 1016 Cornell Law Faculty Publications 54

## Bibliography

Holland J H, *Complexity A very Short Introduction* (OUP 2014)

Howe JS, O'Brien SW, 'SPAC Performance, Ownership and Corporate Governance' (2012) 15 Advances in Financial Economics 1

Iqbal M, Llewellyn D T, *Islamic Banking and Finance: New Perspectives on Profit Sharing and Risk* (Edward Elgar 2002)

Jenkinson T, Sousa M, 'Why SPAC Investors Should Listen to the Market (Digest summary)' (2011) 21 (2) Journal of Applied Finance 38

Jensen M, 'The Agency Cost of Free Cash Flow, Corporate Finance, and Takeovers' (1986) 76 (2) American Economic Review 323

Jensen M, Meckling W H, 'Theory of the Firm: Managerial Behaviour, Agency Costs and Ownership Structure' (1976) 3 (4) Journal of Financial Economics 305-360

Jog V, Sun C, 'Blank Check IPOs: A Home Run for Management' (2007), available at SSRN: http://ssrn.com/abstract=1018242, accessed on 18 April 2019

Kelsen H, *General Theory of Law and State* (The Lawbook Exchange 1945)

Kern A, Rahul D, John E, *Global Governance of Financial Systems: The International Regulation of Systemic Risk* (OUP 2006)

Keohane R O, Nye J S, 'Globalisation: What's New? What's Not? (And So What?)' (2000) 118 Foreign Policy 104

Kettell B, *Introduction to Islamic Banking and Finance* (Wiley 2011)

Khan M, Mirakhor A, 'Islam and the Economic System' (1992) 21 (1) Review of Islamic Economics 1

Kim H, *Essays on Management Quality, IPO Characteristics and the Success of Business Combination* (2009, Doctoral dissertation, Louisiana State University)

Kindleberger C, *Manias, Panics and Crashes. A History of Financial Crises* (3rd ed., John Wiley & Dons 1996)

Kingsbury B, Krisch N, Stewart R B, 'The Emergence of Global Administrative Law' (2005) 68 Law and Contemporary Problems 15

Knight F, *Risk, Uncertainty and Profit* (first published 1921, Martino Publishing 2014)

Knozelmann S, Fovargue-Davies M, *Banking Systems in the Crisis – The Faces of Liberal Capitalism* (Routledge 2013)

Kokkoris I, Olivares-Caminal R, *Antitrust Law Amidst Financial Crises* (1st ed., CUP 2010)

Kolb J, Tykvová T, 'Going Public via SPACs: Frogs Do Not Turn into Princes' (2016) 40 Journal of Corporate Finance 80

Kornai J, *Anti-equilibrium: On Economic Systems Theory and the Task of Research* (North-Holland 1971)

Krimsky S, Golding D (eds.), *Social Theories of Risk* (Praeger Publishers 1992)

Labrosse J R, et al. (eds.), *Financial Crisis Management and Bank Resolution* (Informa 2009)

Ladeur K H (ed.) *Public Governance in the Age of Globalisation* (Ashgate 2004)

Lakicevic M, Shachmurove Y, Vulanovic M, 'Institutional Changes of Specified Purpose Acquisition Companies (SPACs)' (2014) 28 (C) North American Journal of Economics and Finance 149

Lakicevic M, Vulanovic M, 'A Story on SPACs' (2013) 39 (4) Managerial Finance 384

Lastra R, *Cross-Border Bank Insolvency* (OUP 2011)

———. *International Financial and Monetary Law* (2nd ed., OUP 2015)

Lewellen S M, 'SPACs as an Asset Class' (2009) working paper, Yale University, available at http://ssrn.com/absract=1284999, accessed on 18 April 2019

Lianos I, Kokkoris I, *The Reform of EC Competition Law* (Wolters Kluwer 2010)
Llewellyn D T, 'Re-engineering the Regulator' (1996) 1 (3) The Financial Regulator 21
Luhmann N, *Risk: A Sociological Theory* (Transaction Publishers 2008)
———. *Introduction to Systems Theory* (Polity Press 2013)
Markowitz H, 'Portfolio Selection' (1952) 7 (1) The Journal of Finance 77
Masters B, 'Year in a Word: SPAC' (1 January 2021) Financial Times
Maturana H R, Varela F, *Autopoiesis and Cognition: The Realization of the Living* (Reidel 1980)
Mitchell M, Pulvino T, 'Arbitrage Crashes and the Speed of Capital' (2012) 104 (3) Journal of Financial Economics 469
Moloney N, 'EU Financial Market Regulation after the Global Financial Crisis: "More Europe" or More Risks?' (2010) 47 (5) Common Market Law Review 1317
Monti G, *EU Competition Law* (CUP 2007)
Moore S, "New Direct Listing Rules Challenge SPACs" (28 December 2020) Forbes
Mulbert P O, Wilhelm A, 'Reforms of EU Banking and Securities Regulation after the Financial Crisis' (2010) 26 Banking and Finance Law Review 187
Murray J, 'Innovation, Imitation and Regulation in Finance: The Evolution of Special Purpose Acquisition Corporations' (2017) 6 (2) Review of Integrative Business and Economics Research 1
Neal J (eds.), *Handbook of Faith and Spirituality in the Workplace* (Springer 2013)
Noam E M, *Interconnecting the Network of Networks* (The MIT Press 2001)
Omarova S T, 'Rethinking the Future of Self-regulation in the Financial Industry' (2010) Cornell Law Faculty Publications Paper 1022
———. 'Wall Street as Community of Fate: Toward Financial Industry Self-regulation' (2011) 159 (2) University of Pennsylvania Law Review 412
Passet R, 'The Paradigms of Uncertainty' (1984) 9 (33) The Geneva Papers on Risk and Insurance 370
Pidgeon N, Kasperson R E, Slovic P (eds.), *The Social Amplification of Risk* (CUP 2003)
Rechtschaffen A, Trichet J C, *Capital Markets, Derivatives and the Law: Evolution after the Crisis* (OUP 2014)
Riemer D S, 'Special Purpose Acquisition Companies: SPAC and SPAN, or Blank Check Redux?' (2007–2008) 85 (4) Washington University Law Review 931
Rodrigrues U, Stegemoller M, 'Exit, Voice, and Reputation: The Evolution of SPACs' (2011) 11–12 University of Georgia School of Law – Legal Studies Research Paper Series 2
———. 'What All-cash Companies Tell Us about IPOs and Acquisitions?' (2014) 29 Journal of Corporate Finance 111
Sacco R, 'Legal Formants: A Dynamic Approach to Comparative Law' [1991] 1 American Journal of Comparative Law 39
Schultz P, 'Unit Initial Public Offerings' (1993) 34 (2) Journal of Financial Economics 199
Schwarcz S L, 'Controlling Financial Chaos: The Power and Limits of Law' (2012) 3 Wisconsin Law Review 816
Shachmurove Y, Vulanovic M, 'Specified Purpose Acquisition Companies in Shipping' (2015) 26 (C) Global Finance Journal 64
———. 'US SPACs with a Focus on China' (2016) 39 (C) Journal of Multinational Financial Management 1

———. 'SPACs IPOs' in Duglas Cumming and Sofia Johan (eds.) *Oxford Handbook of IPOs* (OUP 2017)
Sjostrom W K, 'The Truth about Reverse Mergers' [2008] 2 Entrepreneurial Business Law Journal 743
Snyder F, 'Soft Law and Governance: Aspects of the European Union Experience' in Luo Haocai, *The European Union Experience* (Peking University Press 2009)
Sookhdeo P, *Understanding Shari'a Finance, The Muslim Challenges to Western Economics* (Isaac Publishing 2008)
Soros G, *The New Paradigm for Financial Markets – The Credit Crisis of 2008 and What it Means* (PublicAffairs 2008)
Stout L A, 'Derivatives and the Legal Origin of the 2008 Credit Crisis' (2011) 1 Harvard Business Law Review 1
Tabari N M, 'Islamic Finance and the Modern World: The Legal Principles Governing Islamic Finance in International Trade' (2010) 31 (8) Company Lawyer 249
Taleb N N, *The Black Swan: The Impact of the Highly Improbable* (Penguin 2008)
Tennekoon R, *The Law and Regulation of International Finance* (LexisNexis 1991)
Tran A, 'Blank Check Acquisitions' (2012) available at SSRN http://ssrn.com/abstract=2070274, accessed on 18 May 2019
Valdez S, Molyneux P, *An Introduction To Global Financial Markets* (8th ed., Palgrave Macmillan 2016)
Visser H, *Islamic Finance: Principles and Practice* (2nd ed., Edward Elgar Publishing 2014)
Voegelin E, *Order and History* (Baton Rouge: Louisiana State University Press 1956)
Vulanovic M, 'Post-merger Survival' (2017) 43 (6) Managerial Finance 679
Weiss B G, *The Spirit of Islamic Law* (The University of Georgia Press 1998)
Weiss T G, 'Governance, Good Governance and Global Governance: Conceptual and Actual Challenges' (2000) 21 (5) Third World Quarterly 795
Weisskopf W A, 'Reflections on Uncertainty in Economics' (1984) 9 (33) The Geneva Papers on Risk and Insurance 335

## Legislations and Capital Markets Regulations

**Malaysia**
Equity Guidelines 2009
**Canada**
TSX Venture Exchange Rule Book
TSX Company Manual
**Korea**
Enforcement Decree of the Financial Investment Services and Capital Markets 2008
**Europe**
Directive 2011/61/EU on Alternative Investment Fund Managers (AIFMD)
**Turkey**
Communiqué No. II-23.2 on Mergers and Demergers 2013
**US**
NYSE Listing Company Manual
NASDAQ listing rules
NYSE AMEX Company Guide
Securities Act 1933
Securities Enforcement Remedies and Penny Stock Reform Act 1990
Dodd-Frank Act 2010

# Index

Note: **Bold** page numbers refer to tables; *italic* page numbers refer to figures and page numbers followed by "n" denote endnotes.

ABK Group Industrie Ceramiche S.p.A. 125
Accor Acquisition Company (ACC) 4
Ackman, Bill 32, 59
acquisition: asset 125; and negotiation process 38; and redemption right 38–39; shares 125; valuation of the acquisition target 161–163; *see also* merger
Akazoo S.A. 176–177
Alternative Investment Fund Manager (AIFMD) 30–31, 111
Alternative Investment Funds 112
Alternative Investment Market 112
American modern SPACs 53–55
Ant Group 2
*AP Services (LLP v Lobell)* 178
Ascendant Digital Acquisition Corp. 53
'autopoiesis' 187

Basel III Committee on Banking Supervision 103
Bernoulli, Daniel 72–73, 87
Bernstein, Peter L. 68, 69
blank check companies 4, 44–45; *vs.* cash-shell companies 61; to modern SPACs 47–55; purpose of 28; and SEC 29, 40; *see also* Special Purpose Acquisition Companies (SPACs)
blind pools 1
Borromeo-Arese, Vitiliano 120
'borrowers' 78n40
Borsa Istanbul exchange 147–149
*Borsa Italiana* S.p.A. (Euronext Group) 36, 116, 118, 121, 126; SPACs and 119–121

breach of fiduciary duty claims 177–178
Bretton Woods agreements 93–95, 194
Broadstone Acquisition Corp. (Broadstone) 165
Buckley, Ross Philip 96; *International Financial System: Policy and Regulation* 93n84
Bursa Malaysia 39n91, 110, 140–142; Equity Guidelines (EGs) of 128

Capital for Progress 2 S.p.A. 125
cash-shell companies 23, 28, 31, 37, 43–45; *vs.* blank check companies 61; *see also* Special Purpose Acquisition Companies (SPACs)
caveat emptor approach 55
caveat venditor approach 55
Central Banks 14–15
Churchill Capital Corp. III 23, 176
Churchill Capital Corp. IV 8, 23, 33
*City Trading Fund v Nye* 174
Clayton, Jay 169–170, 176
Coase, R. H. 105, 136
common shares 61
competition 18–22; and liberalisation 20
complexity: and financial markets 85–92; and financial systems 190–192; risk-aversion 87–90; uncertainty-aversion 87–90
conflict of interests: between sponsor(s) and investors 170–171; between sponsor(s) and underwriters 172–173; on sponsor(s) proxy statement and redemptions 171–171
corporate structure 61–63
corporate valuation 38, 181

Covid-19 161, 206; and SPACs 22–25
credit-fuelled asset price bubble 15
credit risk 18
Crown Corporation 113

D8 Holdings Corp. 53
debt securities crisis *see* financial crisis (2007–2010)
Deliveroo 2
derivatives: defined 104; OTC 103
De-SPAC/De-SPACing 3, 7, 8–9, 23, 151–182; disclosure duties of sponsor and underwriters in US 169–173; Form 10 information 166; Form S-3 eligibility 168–169; Form S-8 166–167; ineligible issuers 169; M&A' aspects 151–165; regulatory challenges 165–169; Rule 144 167–168; and shareholders 53; SPAC securities litigation in the US 173–180; structuring the deal at 151–165, 165–169; structuring the deal at De-SPACing in US 165–169
De-SPAC transactions: due diligence 154–156; earnout provisions 163–164; equity financing and support agreements 160; growth capital 164–165; higher the risk, higher the return 156–158; high growth companies 164–165; PIPE investment and PIPE engagement letter 158–160; place of incorporation 164–165; securities litigation related to 175–176; sponsor(s) ownership of the target 156–158; valuation of the acquisition target 161–163
DFP Healthcare Acquisition Corp. 53
Diamond Eagle Acquisition Corp. 7
Dimitrova, Lora 27
direct soft law regulations 145, 211
disclosure duties: of sponsors 169–173; of underwriters 169–173
D&O insurance 178–180
Double Eagle Acquisition Corp 53
due diligence and De-SPAC transactions 154–156
Dutch Star Companies ONE (DSC1) 122
Dutch Star Companies TWO 122

earnout provisions 163–164
Ellenoff, Douglas 53, 67
embedded self-regulation 105

E. Merge Technology Acquisition Corp. 23
enterprise value 161
epistemology of risk 70–71
equity financing and support agreements 160
Equity Guidelines (EGs) of Bursa Malaysia 128
escrow account 47, **63**, 63–64
ESG Core Investment B.V. 122
Euronext Group 34, 36, 119–121
Euronext N.V. 121–122, 123; and SPACs 121–123
European Commission 133
European Private Equity and Venture Capital Association 14
European regulation of SPACs 111–113
European Securities and Markets Authority (ESMA) 30, 111, 172
European Union 14, 111, 133
European Union Law 133
exchanges and SPAC 35–36

fiduciary duty claims, breach of 177–178
Financial Conduct Authority (UK) 113
Financial Conduct Authority Listing Rules 114
financial crisis (2007–2010) 12–17
financial innovations 18–22
financial markets: competition 18–22; and complexity 85–92; as financial systems 183–192; financial systems and complexity 190–192; 'metamorphosis of subjects' 189–190; as open systems 189–190; risk-aversion 87–90; and risks 17–18; self-organisation and autopoiesis of systems 186–188; structures of financial systems and liquid autopoietic markets 188; and uncertainty 17–18; uncertainty-aversion 87–90
financial regulation 99; between macroeconomic stability and microeconomic objectives 102–103
financial risk 18, 77–84; classification 80–81; defined 78; and government failure 99–102; and knowledge 84; (no)-classification of 79–81; and uncertainty 82–84; *see also* risk
Financial Service Market Authority 5
financial systems: and complexity 190–192; financial markets as 183–192; phenomenology of contemporary

192–198; SPACs as financial innovations and observers of markets 196–198; structures of 188
FinTech Acquisition Corp. IV 24
first-generation SPACs 48, **48–49**, 130–131
Flipkart 5
Form 10 information 166
Form S-3 168–169
Form S-8 166–167
'founder shares' 59
'founder warrants' 59
Franchi Umberto Marmi S.p.A. 120
free markets 19, 86, 91–93, 105, 107–109, 183–186, 191, 194–195, 199, 203
'free writing prospectuses' (FWPs) 169
Freshfields Bruckhaus Deringer LLP 158

Gabelli, Marc 125
Galateri, Marco 120
Galileo Acquisition Corp. 120, 164
Galileo Galilei 120, 208; *Sopra la Scoperta dei dadi* 72
*gefahr* 82
General Agreement on Tariffs and Trade 133
*The General Theory of Employment, Interest and Money* (Keynes) 88
Gensler, Gary 206
G.F. Group S.p.A. 119
*Gharar* 11, 39, 75–77, 75n28
Giacometti, Luca Fabio 119–120
Giddens, A. 69–70, 92, 108
Glenalta Food S.p.A. 119
globalisation and law 198–201
global markets 98, 108
Go Acquisition Corp. 53
Goldman Sachs 126
Gores Group 32
government failure: and financial risk 99–102; and public-private divide 99–102
Grab holdings Inc. (Grab) 4
Great Depression 80, 93
Group Accor 4
growth capital 164–165
GSME Acquisition Partners I 53
Guttentag, Jack 82n54, 88

H.D. Partners Acquisition Corp. 25
Heisenberg's principle 86
Herring, Richard 82n54, 88
high growth companies 164–165

Highlands Acquisition Corp. 25
Hill, Lord Jonathan 116
Hill Report 116–118
Hindenburg Research 176
*homo economicus* 85
homogeneity: and financial risk 81; of risk classes 79
*homo stocasticus* 85
*homo stocaticus* 91
*homo technologicus* 91
Hong Kong 5
HPX Corp. 53
human-humanity of risk 91–92
human-inhumanity of risk 91–92

India 5
indirect soft law regulations 211
Indonesia 5
initial public offerings (IPOs) 2; *vs.* SPACs 6–7; traditional 6, 24
insurance: defined 79; and financial risk 79
International Bank of Reconstruction and Development (World Bank) 93–94, 133
international financial regulation of SPACs 110–150
*International Financial System: Policy and Regulation* (Buckley) 93n84
International Monetary Fund (IMF) 93–94, 96, 133
Investment Company Act of 1940 (US) 129
investor(s): conflict of interests between sponsor(s) and 170–171; objective of 78; risk factors for 45
'invisible hand' 86, 99, 99n106
IPO "pop" 24
Italian Civil Code 127

Jackson, Robert 129
Jaws Acquisition Corp. 53
Jenkinson, Tim 27
Jog, Vijay 27
JP Morgan 126
J2 Acquisition 116

Keynes, J. M. 19, 87–89; *The General Theory of Employment, Interest and Money* 88
Klein, Michael 8, 23, 33
Knight, Frank 73, 81, 83–84, 89, 90; *Risk, Uncertainty and Profit* 18, 83

knowledge 70–71; and financial risk 84; and risk 79
Kolb, Johannes 27
Korea Exchange (KRX) 110, 145–147
K Road Acquisition Corp. 25

Ladeur, K. H. 21–22, 198–199, 210
*Landcadia vs Waitr* 171
Landscape Acquisition Holding 116
Lastra, R. 106, 135, 138
law: and globalisation 198–201; lack of a central planner 198–200; and self-regulation 104–106; and SPACs 93–107; SPACs as market-driven instruments 200–201; and systemic failure 104–106; *see also* soft law
Legacy Acquisition Corp. (Legacy) 156, 171
Lehman Brothers 14, 83, 90, 192, 208
lender 78n41; risk assessment of 87
Lewellen, Stefan 27
L.F. Capital Acquisition Corp. 25
*Liber Abaci* (Fibonacci) 72
*Liber de Ludo Aleae* (Cardano) 72
liquidation procedure 64–65
liquid autopoietic markets 188
litigation based on reports of short selling 176–177
Llewellyn, David T. 105, 136
Lobao, Jeff 10
London Stock Exchange 5, 114, 121; SPACs and 113–119
Lugli, Gino 119
Luhmann, N. 184, 186, 188–189, 196–197, 203–204
Luhmannian paradigm of system theory 17

Made in Italy 1 S.p.A. 119, 125
Malacca Straits Acquisition Corp 53
Malagoli, Stefano 119
Malaysia: regulation of SPACs 10–12; Securities Commission in 107
management competence 37
Marenco, Silvio 119
market failure: preventing 20; and systemic risk 96–99
markets: endemic failure of 99; free 19, 86, 91–93, 105, 107–109, 183–186, 191, 194–195, 199, 203; global 98, 108; SPACs as financial innovations and observers of 196–198
market spontaneity and SPACs 202

Matrix Capacity Petroleum Bhd 10
Maturana, Humberto 187
*Mercato Telematico Azionario* (MTA) market 119
merger 28; agreements 60, 161–162, 173; reverse 28, 31, 33, 148
merger and acquisition (M&A) 151–165
Merge Technology Acquisition Corp. 23
'metamorphosis of subjects' 189–190
Milton, Trevor 171
Mitchell, Mark 27
*MMAC vs Akazoo* 171
Modern Media Acquisition Corp. 177
modern SPACs 49–52
moral hazard 80
Morgan Stanley 34
Morley, John 129
*Muamalat* 74
multilevel SPAC definition 128–133
MultiPlan Corp. 23, 176
multi-sector-focused SPAC 4
Munter, Paul 152, 163

National Association of Securities Dealers Automated Quotations (NASDAQ) 6, 49–51, 113, 118–119, 125, 129, 132, 135, 139, 144–146, 149, 155, 157, 201, 211; Rule IM-5101-2 **51**; SPAC listing change 66
national corporate law frameworks: SPACs and conflicts with 123–128
Netfin Acquisition Corp. 177
New AMEX 132, 135, 139, 144, 145, 149, 211
Newton, Sir Isaac 1–2
New York Stock Exchange (NYSE) 113, 119–120, 129, 132, 135, 139–140, 144–146, 149, 157, 201, 211
Niel, Xavier 122
Nikola Corporation 176
North America Securities Administrators Association 45–46, 46n9
NYSE AMEX: Company Guide 51–52, **52**; SPAC listing change 66
NYSE Group Inc. 6, 49–51

Odyssey Acquisition S.A. (Odyssey Acquisition) 123
ontology of risk 71–73
Onyx Enterprises Int'l Corp. 156, 171
open systems, financial markets as 189–190
Orsero S.p.A. 119

Osborne, Ian 34, 121
OTC derivatives 103

Pace Holdings Corp 53
Pegasus Europe 122–123
Penny Stock Market (PSM) 43–46
Perella Weinberg Partners 24
Pershing Square Tontine Holding Ltd xxix, 32, 59, 129
Pershing Square Tontine Holdings (PSTH) 129
Pershing Square Tontine Holdings SPAC 32
phenomenology of contemporary financial systems 192–198
Pigasse, Matthieu 122
Pilvino, Todd 27
PIPE investors 7, 35
place of incorporation 164–165
price stability 39n90
private debt 23; welfare price of under-priced 12–17
private equity: funds 14, 29–30, 32, 42, 107, 112, 118, 207; SPAC as alternative to 26–40
Private Investment in Public Equity (PIPE): engagement letter 158–160; investment 153–154, 157, 158–160, 178, 181
private risks 80
Private Securities Litigation Reform Act (PSLRA) 161
privatised Keynesianism 17, 20, 92, 209
promote 34; defined 58; SPAC 58–61
Prospectus Regulation (Regulation 2017/1129) 112
public equity commitment (PIPE) 66–67
"public shares" 59
"public warrants" 59

Qur'an 74–75, 77

'real capital market' 97
redemption right 38–39, 56, 65–66
regulation: financial (*see* financial regulation); SEC 44–47; of SPACs at international level 110–123
Regulation 419 110
regulators and SPAC 35–36
reverse merger 28, 31, 33
Revo S.p.A. 120
Rhodium Resources Pte Ltd 177
*risiko* 82

risk 17–18; credit 18; defined in finance 18; epistemology of 70–71; human-humanity of 91–92; human-inhumanity of 91–92; mitigating, in SPACs 36–40; ontology of 71–73; overview 68–70; sociological connotation of 70; *see also* financial risk
*Risk, Uncertainty and Profit* (Knight) 18, 83
risk assessment 78–79; of lender 87
risk-aversion 68, 87–90
risk management 69, 77–78
risk-sharing, of *Shari'a vs.* risk-taking activity 73–77
risk-takers 68, 73, 85, 87, 90
risk-taking activity *vs.* the risk-sharing of *Shari'a* 73–77
Rosewood Hotel Group 4
Rule 144 167–168

Sagansky, Jeff 7
second-generation SPACs 130–131
Securities Act of 1933 3, 55, 161, 169, 175
Securities and Exchange Board of India (SEBI) 5
Securities Commission Malaysia 140
Securities Enforcement Remedies and Penny Stock Reform Act (PSRA) (US) 29, 46
Securities Exchange Act of 1934 3, 46, 55, 161, 175, 177
securities litigation related to De-SPAC transaction 175–176
self-organisation and autopoiesis of systems 186–188
self-regulation: embedded 105; role of law in 104–106; solutions through market practices and 128
Shapiro, Mary L. 45
share capital 61–63
shareholders: call option right 61; and De-SPAC phase 53; and SPAC 35
shares: common 61; 'founder shares' 59; "public shares" 59
*Shari'a* law 74; risk-sharing of 73–77
short selling: litigation based on reports of 176–177
Smith, Adam 86, 99
soft law: defined 106; and SPACs 106–107
soft law regulation 27–28, 128, 140; of Bursa Malaysia 130–131; of SPACs 133–144; 'top-down' 107, 138

*Sopra la Scoperta dei dadi* (Galileo) 72
Sousa, Miguel 27
South Sea Bill 1
South Sea Company 1; shares prices of 2
SPAC IPO 8, 24, 35
SPACs 2.0 52, **53**
SPACs 3.0 52–53, **53**
SPACs 3.5 52–53, **53**
SPAC securities litigation 173–180; breach of fiduciary duty claims 177–178; D&O insurance 178–180; litigation based on reports of short selling 176–177; securities litigation related to De-SPAC transaction 175–176; in the US 173–180
Spactiv S.p.A. 125
Special Purpose Acquisition Companies (SPACs): as alternative to private equity 26–40; based on legal standardised regulation 131–132; based on market practices 131; and Borsa Italiana S.p.A. (Euronext Group) 119–121; in Brussels 5; 'by-law approach' 145–149; codification of uncodified market practices in 55–56, *56*; and conflicts with national corporate law frameworks 123–128; contemporary financial systems 192–198; and Covid-19 22–25; craze in the U.S. 4; defined 2; and Euronext N.V. 121–123; European regulation of 111–113; as financial innovations and observers of markets 196–198; financial markets as financial systems 183–192; first-generation 48, **48–49**, 130–131; in India 5; in Indonesia 5; international corporate features and listing standards of 56–67; international financial regulation of 110–150; *vs.* IPOs 6–7; and the law 93–107; law and globalisation 198–201; and London stock exchange 113–119; Malaysian regulation of 10–12; as market-driven instruments 200–201; and market spontaneity 202; as money creation vehicles 92–93; multilevel SPAC definition 128–133; multi-sector-focused 4; as a non-legal instance 201–203; origin of 43–47; overview 10–12; regulation at international level 110–123; as risk-free investments 25–26; SEC on 3; second-generation 130–131; and soft law 106–107; soft law regulation of 133–144; solutions through market practices and self-regulation 128; and systemic failure 93–107; and uncertainty 202–203; 'without law' 132–133

Special Purpose Acquisition Rights Company (SPARC) 207
species 29, 29n69; of private equity 147
sponsor(s): compensation 60; conflict of interests between investors and 170–171; conflict of interests between underwriters and 172–173; disclosure duties of 169–173; ownership of the target 156–158; proxy statement and redemptions 171–171; and SPAC 32–34, 58–59; in the US 169–173
Stakeholder Aligned Initial Listing (SAIL) 34
structuring: deal at De-SPACing 151–165; deal at De-SPACing in the US 165–169
Sun, Chengye 27
Sun Capital Partners 165
*Sunnah* 74–75
systemic failure: role of law in 104–106; and SPACs 93–107
systemic risk 17; described 98; and market failure 96–99; *see also* risk

tender offer procedure 66
TheSpac S.p.A. 120, 125, 126
Tikehau Capital 122–123
Tokopedia 4
Tontine 60n35
'top-down' soft law regulation 107, 138
Toronto Stock Exchange (TSX) 110, 142–144
*tout court* 26, 101, 109, 112, 135, 208–209
Trian Acquisition I Corp. 25
Triterras Inc. 177
trust **63**, 63–64
TSX Company Manual 143–144
TSX Venture Exchange 143
Turkish Stock Exchange 110
2MX Organic 122, 123
Tykvova, Tereza 27

uncertainity 17–18; and financial risk 82–84; and management competence 37; mitigating, in SPACs 36–40; in modern economies 90–91; and neo-classical economics 86; SPACs and 202–203

uncertainty-aversion 87–90
underwriters: conflict of interests between sponsor(s) and 172–173; disclosure duties of 169–173; and SPAC 34–35
UnitedHealth 176
United States: disclosure duties of sponsor and underwriters in 169–173; Securities and Exchange Commission 3, 6, 29, 45, 173; SPAC securities litigation in 173–180
Universal Music Group xxix, 59, 129
US House Committee on Financial Services 3
US Securities and Exchange Commission (SEC) 3, 6, 29, 45, 173; blank check companies 29, 40; regulation 44–47; Rule 419 44–47; Special Purpose Acquisition Companies 3

valuation, of acquisition target 161–163
Value for Italy S.p.A. 125
Varela, Francisco 187
VectoIQ Acquisition Corp. 176
*VectoIQ vs Nikola* 171
Voegelin, Eric 71
volatility and SPAC 8

warrants 61–62
winding up procedure 64–65
'world capital market' 97

Zouari, Moez-Alexandre 122

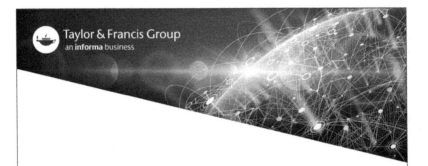